North Backroads & 4-Wheel Drive Trails

By **CHARLES A. WELLS**

Easy • Moderate • Difficult
Backcountry Driving Adventures

FunTreks, Inc.

Published by FunTreks, Inc.
P.O. Box 49187, Colorado Springs, CO 80949-9187
Phone: (719) 536-0722
Fax: (719) 277-7411
E-mail: books@funtreks.com
Web site: www.funtreks.com

Copyright © 2004 by FunTreks, Inc.

Edited by Shelley Mayer

Cover design, photography, maps, and production by Charles A. Wells

First Edition

All rights reserved. No part of this book may be reproduced or transmitted in any form by any means, electronic or mechanical, including photocopying, recording or by any information storage and retrieval system without the written permission from the author, except for inclusion of brief quotations in a review.

Library of Congress Control Number 2004102760
ISBN 0-9664976-5-1

Produced in the United States of America

To order additional books, see order form in back of this book or go to our Web site at www.funtreks.com.

DISCLAIMER

Travel in California's backcountry is, by its very nature, potentially dangerous and could result in property damage, injury, or even death. The scope of this book cannot predict every possible hazard you may encounter. If you drive any of the trails in this book, you acknowledge these risks and assume full responsibility. You are the final judge as to whether a trail is safe to drive on any given day, whether your vehicle is capable of the journey, and what supplies you should carry. The information contained herein cannot replace good judgment and proper preparation on your part. The publisher and author of this book disclaim any and all liability for bodily injury, death, or property damage that could occur to you or any of your passengers.

ACKNOWLEDGMENTS

My sincere thanks to the following individuals and organizations who helped with this book:

The U.S. Forest Service, Bureau of Land Management, California State Parks and Death Valley National Park. I worked with a long list of hard-working staffers who provided courteous and professional advice.

Sierra Trek leaders and officers of the California Association of 4-Wheel Drive Clubs including: Robert Reed, Dick Shannon, Carrol Bryant, Jim Harris, Jim Bramham, Don Klusman, Ron Kellogg & family, Jack Raudy, Kathy & Dave Avery, David Renschler and Warner Anderson.

Jon Aichele of the Bakersfield Trailblazers, who shared his knowledge of local trails then took me out on runs by himself and with the club, one of the most active and hard-working clubs in the state. Other members I'd like to thank include: Rod Brown, Russ Warshaw, "Crazy Joe" Mahafey, Ken Lollich, Randy Worley, Ron Scharp and Joe Stocker.

Mary Krupka and Darrell & Annie Cramphorn of 4x4 In Motion, who guided me on the Rubicon, Slickrock Trail and Deer Valley Trail. Mary also took me on Niagara Rim where she made the "Rock Pile" look easy. Additional thanks to other club members Richard Reed and Bob Dake.

Tom Grancey, owner of Foothill Offroad and member of the Grass Valley 4-Wheelers, who took me through Snake Lake, Gold Valley, Signal Peak and Hell Hole trails. From the same club, thanks to Martin Ward for his lead on Sierra Buttes, John Ketchersid and Walt Burres.

Dave Wheeler for his highly informative and enthusiastic tour of the Lost Coast. Dave also provided photographs of Usal Beach and Bear Harbor that he took on a clear day.

Pam Rocca, John Chilcote and Ed Leckey of the North Tahoe Trail Dusters; Jody Clarke and Robert Adams of the Westside 4-Wheelers; Steve Sampson, Joe Pontes and Rob Huebschmann of the Wine Country Rock Crawlers; Brian Hamilton and Kathy Watkins of the Mammoth Lakes 4-Wheelers; Brooks Gilbert and Jeff Godde of the Hi Desert 4-Wheelers; Doug Poppelreiter of the Pair-O-Dice 4-Wheelers; Dennis Porter and Aldon Bailey of the Rat Pack 4WD Club; and Don Kidd of Cal-Sierra 4x4. These folks guided me on local trails or provided helpful advice.

Individuals Roger and Andy Scovell who guided me on the Dusy; Mark Mooney, Greg Santos, Doug Peterson and Randy Klafehn for showing me Hollister Hills; John Mueller, John Ulfeldt, Dave Wong, Jack Downing, Peter Locoby, T.C. Smith, Eric Kaul and the Calson family. And thanks to all those who allowed me to take their pictures whose names I missed.

Shelley Mayer, for her thorough editing of this book, Joan Aaland, who keeps our office running smoothly, daughter, Marcia LeVault, for her many hours of hard work, and my wife, Beverly, for her encouragement.

Laurel Lakes, Trail #38, rated moderate.

Contents

Page	Topic
6	Trails Listed by Area (& Green-Sticker trails specified)
7	Trail Locator Map
8	Trails Listed by Difficulty, Ratings Defined
10	Trails Listed Alphabetically, Author's Favorites

11 INTRODUCTION
13	How to Use This Book
13	Selecting the Right Trail for Your Vehicle
14	California Laws, Licensing and Fees
15	ATVs and Dirt Bikes
15	OHV Areas and SVRAs
16	National Parks and Forests
16	Safety Tips
18	Backcountry Survival
20	Checklist
21	Your Responsibilities as a Backcountry Driver
22	Backcountry Driving Lessons
29	Final Comments
30	Map Legend

31 THE TRAILS *(Individual trails listed on next page)*
32	Area 1-	Mt. Shasta, Redding, Eureka, Santa Rosa
46	Area 2-	Red Bluff, Grass Valley, Downieville, Gold Lake
80	Area 3-	Auburn, Lake Tahoe
106	Area 4-	South Lake Tahoe, Arnold, Bear Valley, Sonora
124	Area 5-	Bridgeport, Lee Vining, Mammoth Lakes, Bishop
152	Area 6-	Big Pine, Lone Pine
166	Area 7-	San Jose, Coalinga, San Luis Obispo
190	Area 8-	Fresno, Shaver Lake
220	Area 9-	Bakersfield, Lake Isabella, Ridgecrest, Mojave

255 APPENDIX
256	GPS Basics
260	GPS Waypoint Coordinates
274	Glossary
275	References & Reading
277	Addresses & Phone Numbers
282	Index
286	The Author & His Vehicles

Trails Listed by Area

Green-sticker vehicles see footnote.

Pg. No./ Trail, Rating (Easy, Mod., Diff.)

32 **AREA 1**
   Mt. Shasta, Redding, Eureka, Santa Rosa
34   1. Mt. Shasta Loop (**E**)
36   2. Bowerman Ridge (**E**)*
38   3. Shasta Bally Peak (**E**)*
40   4. Lost Coast, Redwoods (**E**)*
44   5. Cow Mountain OHV Area (**D**)

46 **AREA 2**
   Red Bluff, Grass Valley, Downieville, Gold Lake
48   6. Peligreen Jeepway (**M**)
52   7. High Lakes (**D**)
56   8. Stag Point (**M**)
58   9. Cleghorn Bar (**D**)
60   10. Poker Flat (**M**)*
64   11. Gold Valley (**M**)
68   12. Snake Lake (**D**)*
70   13. Deer Lake (**M**)
72   14. Sierra Buttes (**E**)
76   15. Tyler-Foote Crossing (**E**)

80 **AREA 3**
   Auburn, Lake Tahoe
82   16. Bear Valley Loop (**M**)
84   17. Fordyce Creek (**D**)
88   18. Signal Peak (**D**)
90   19. Shirttail Canyon (**E**)
92   20. Mt. Watson (**E**)
94   21. Blackwood Cyn., Ellis Pk.(**M**)
96   22. Hell Hole (**D**)
98   23. Rubicon (**D**)
104 24. Barrett Lake (**D**)

106 **AREA 4**
   South Lake Tahoe, Arnold, Bear Valley, Sonora
108 25. Strawberry Pass (**D**)
110 26. Deer Valley (**D**)
112 27. Corral Hollow (**M**)
114 28. Slickrock Trail (**D**)*
116 29. Niagara Rim (**D**)
120 30. Eagle Peak (**M**)
122 31. Dodge Ridge (**E**)

124 **AREA 5**
   Bridgeport, Lee Vining, Mammoth Lakes, Bishop
126 32. Bodie Ghost Town (**E**)
128 33. Kavanaugh Ridge (**M**)
130 34. Copper Mountain (**E**)
132 35. Horse Meadows (**E**)
134 36. Deadman Pass (**E**)*

Pg. No./ Trail, Rating (Easy, Mod., Diff.)

136 37. Backway to Inyo Craters (**E**)
138 38. Laurel Lakes (**M**)
140 39. Sand Canyon (**M**)
142 40. Wheeler Ridge (**D**)
144 41. Buttermilk Country (**E**)
146 42. Coyote Flat (**M**)
150 43. Silver/Wyman Canyons (**E**)

152 **AREA 6**
   Big Pine, Lone Pine
154 44. Mazourka Canyon (**M**)
156 45. Armstrong Canyon (**M**)
158 46. Movie Rd./Alabama Hills (**E**)*
160 47. Swansea-Cerro Gordo Rd. (**M**)
162 48. Racetrack via Hunter Mtn. (**M**)*

166 **AREA 7**
   San Jose, Coalinga, San Luis Obispo
168 49. Hollister Hills SVRA (**D**)
172 50. Old Coast Road (**E**)*
174 51. Prewitt Ridge (**E**)
176 52. South Coast Ridge (**E**)
178 53. Pichacho Peak (**D**)
182 54. Oceano Dunes SVRA (**M**)
184 55. Pine Mountain (**D**)
186 56. Garcia Ridge (**M**)
188 57. Twin Rocks (**M**)

190 **AREA 8**
   Fresno, Shaver Lake
192 58. White Bark Vista (**E**)
194 59. Mirror/Strawberry Lakes (**D**)
198 60. Coyote Lake (**D**)
200 61. Brewer Lake (**M**)
202 62. Bald Mountain (**D**)
206 63. Swamp Lake (**D**)
210 64. Voyager Rock (**E**)
212 65. Dusy/Ershim Trail (**D**)
218 66. Spanish Route (**D**)

220 **AREA 9**
   Bakersfield, Lake Isabella, Ridgecrest, Mojave
222 67. Monache Meadows (**E**)
224 68. Sherman Pass 4x4 Trail (**D**)
228 69. Rancheria Road (**E**)
230 70. Freeway Ridge (**D**)
234 71. Jawbone to Lake Isabella (**E**)
238 72. Jawbone OHV Area (**M**)
242 73. Bonanza Gulch/EP15 (**M**)
246 74. Opal Cyn./Last Chance Cyn. (**M**)
250 75. Rand Mountain (**M**)

*Green-sticker vehicles not allowed or not recommended for these trails.

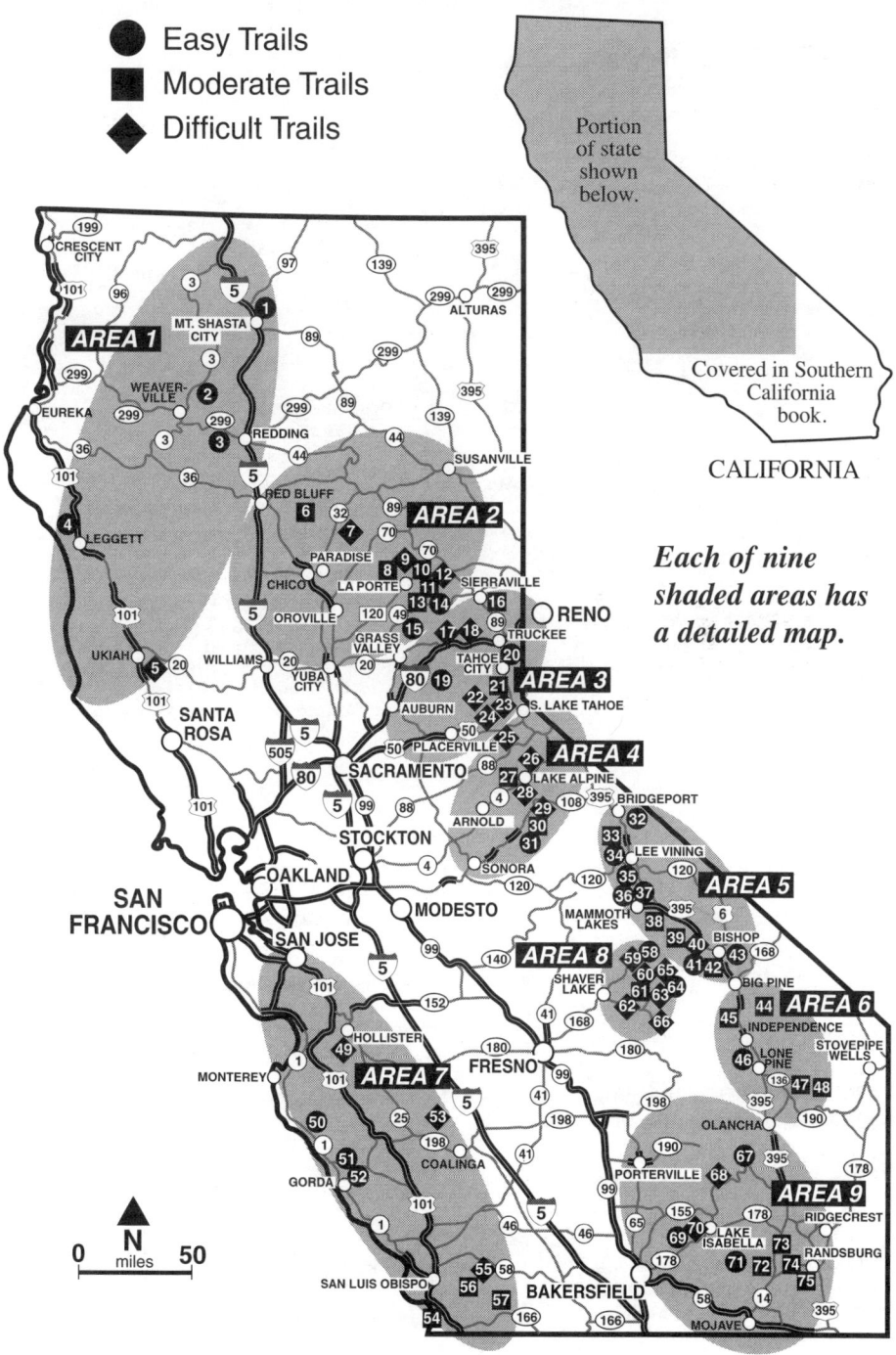

Trails Listed by Difficulty

● Easy

Trails are grouped into three major categories: easy, moderate and difficult. Within each group, trails at the top of the list are easier than at the bottom. If you drive a trail and find it too easy, try one lower on the list. Conversely, if you find a trail too difficult, try one higher on the list. You may have to skip several trails on the list to find a significant difference.

Easier → More Difficult

Pg.	No./Trail
228	69. Rancheria Road
90	19. Shirttail Canyon
34	1. Mt. Shasta Loop
172	50. Old Coast Road
122	31. Dodge Ridge
176	52. South Coast Ridge
192	58. White Bark Vista
158	46. Movie Road/Alabama Hills
76	15. Tyler-Foote Crossing
40	4. Lost Coast, Redwoods
134	36. Deadman Pass
222	67. Monache Meadows
126	32. Bodie Ghost Town
130	34. Copper Mountain
174	51. Prewitt Ridge
132	35. Horse Meadows
92	20. Mt. Watson
36	2. Bowerman Ridge
144	41. Buttermilk Country
38	3. Shasta Bally Peak
150	43. Silver/Wyman Canyons
136	37. Backway to Inyo Craters
234	71. Jawbone to Lake Isabella
210	64. Voyager Rock
72	14. Sierra Buttes

Trail Ratings Defined →

Trail ratings are very subjective. Conditions change for many reasons, including weather and time of year. An easy trail can quickly become difficult when washed out by a rainstorm or blocked by a fallen rock. You must be the final judge of a trail's condition on the day you drive it. If any part of a trail is difficult, the entire trail is rated difficult. You may be able to drive a significant portion of a trail before reaching the difficult spot. Read each trail description carefully for specific information.

Easy: Gravel, dirt, clay, sand, or mildly rocky road. Gentle grades. Water levels low except during periods of heavy runoff. Full-width single lane or wider with adequate room to pass most of the time. Where shelf conditions exist, road is wide and well-maintained with minor sideways tilt. Four-wheel drive recommended on most trails but some are suitable for two-wheel drive under dry conditions. Clay surface roads, when wet, can significantly increase difficulty.

Moderate   ◆ **Difficult**

Pg.	No./Trail	Pg.	No./Trail
120	30. Eagle Peak	58	9. Cleghorn Bar
242	73. Bonanza Gulch/EP15	218	66. Spanish Route
154	44. Mazourka Canyon	224	68. Sherman Pass 4x4 Trail
70	13. Deer Lake	44	5. Cow Mountain OHV Area
94	21. Blackwood Cyn.,Ellis Peak	202	62. Bald Mountain
200	61. Brewer Lake	108	25. Strawberry Pass
112	27. Corral Hollow	142	40. Wheeler Ridge
238	72. Jawbone OHV Area	230	70. Freeway Ridge
138	38. Laurel Lakes	114	28. Slickrock Trail
140	39. Sand Canyon	169	49. Hollister Hills SVRA
48	6. Peligreen Jeepway	184	55. Pine Mountain
246	74. Opal Cyn./Last Chance Cyn.	178	53. Pichacho Peak
60	10. Poker Flat	52	7. High Lakes
128	33. Kavanaugh Ridge	110	26. Deer Valley
156	45. Armstrong Canyon	96	22. Hell Hole
182	54. Oceano Dunes SVRA	88	18. Signal Peak
188	57. Twin Rocks	198	60. Coyote Lake
250	75. Rand Mountain	194	59. Mirror/Strawberry Lakes
56	8. Stag Point	68	12. Snake Lake
146	42. Coyote Flat	206	63. Swamp Lake
64	11. Gold Valley	116	29. Niagara Rim
82	16. Bear Valley Loop	104	24. Barrett Lake
162	48. Racetrack via Hunter Mtn.	212	65. Dusy/Ershim Trail
160	47. Swansea-Cerro Gordo Road	98	23. Rubicon
186	56. Garcia Ridge	84	17. Fordyce Creek

Moderate: Rutted dirt or rocky road suitable for most sport utility vehicles. Careful tire placement often necessary. Four-wheel drive, low range, and high ground clearance required. Standard factory skid plates and tow hooks recommended on many trails. Undercarriage may scrape occasionally. Some grades fairly steep but manageable if dry. Soft sand possible. Sideways tilt will require caution. Narrow shelf roads possible. Backing may be necessary to pass. Water depths passable for stock high-clearance vehicles except during periods of heavy runoff. Mud holes may be present especially in the spring. Rock-stacking may be necessary in some cases. Brush may touch vehicle.

Difficult: Some trails suitable for more aggressive stock vehicles but most trails require vehicle modification. Lifts, differential lockers, aggressive articulation, and/or winches recommended in many cases. Skid plates and tow hooks required. Body damage possible. Grades can be steep with severe ground undulation. Sideways tilt can be extreme. Sand hills very steep with soft downslopes. Deep water crossings possible. Shelf roads extremely narrow; use caution in full-size vehicle. Read trail description carefully. Passing may be difficult with backing required for long distances. Brush may scratch sides of vehicle.

Trails Listed Alphabetically

Pg.   No./Trail, Rating (Easy, Mod., Diff.)   **Pg.   No./Trail, Rating** (Easy, Mod., Diff.)

Pg.	Trail		Pg.	Trail
156	45. Armstrong Canyon (M)		158	46. Movie Rd./Alabama Hills (E)
136	37. Backway to Inyo Craters (E)		34	1. Mt. Shasta Loop (E)
202	62. Bald Mountain (D)		92	20. Mt. Watson (E)
104	**24. Barrett Lake (D)**		116	**29. Niagara Rim (D)**
82	16. Bear Valley Loop (M)		182	**54. Oceano Dunes SVRA (M)**
94	21. Blackwood Cyn., Ellis Peak (M)		172	50. Old Coast Road (E)
126	**32. Bodie Ghost Town (E)**		246	74. Opal Cyn./ Last Chance Cyn. (M)
242	**73. Bonanza Gulch/EP15 (M)**		48	6. Peligreen Jeepway (M)
36	2. Bowerman Ridge (E)		178	53. Pichacho Peak (D)
200	61. Brewer Lake (M)		184	55. Pine Mountain (D)
144	41. Buttermilk Country (E)		60	**10. Poker Flat (M)**
58	9. Cleghorn Bar (D)		174	**51. Prewitt Ridge (E)**
130	34. Copper Mountain (E)		162	**48. Racetrack via Hunter Mtn. (M)**
112	27. Corral Hollow (M)		228	69. Rancheria Road (E)
44	5. Cow Mountain OHV Area (D)		250	75. Rand Mountain (M)
146	**42. Coyote Flat (M)**		98	**23. Rubicon (D)**
198	**60. Coyote Lake (D)**		140	39. Sand Canyon (M)
134	**36. Deadman Pass (E)**		38	3. Shasta Bally Peak (E)
70	**13. Deer Lake (M)**		224	68. Sherman Pass 4x4 Trail (D)
110	26. Deer Valley (D)		90	19. Shirttail Canyon (E)
122	31. Dodge Ridge (E)		72	**14. Sierra Buttes (E)**
212	**65. Dusy/Ershim Trail (D)**		88	18. Signal Peak (D)
120	30. Eagle Peak (M)		150	43. Silver/Wyman Canyons (E)
84	**17. Fordyce Creek (D)**		114	**28. Slickrock Trail (D)**
230	70. Freeway Ridge (D)		68	12. Snake Lake (D)
186	56. Garcia Ridge (M)		176	52. South Coast Ridge (E)
64	11. Gold Valley (M)		218	66. Spanish Route (D)
96	22. Hell Hole (D)		56	8. Stag Point (M)
52	7. High Lakes (D)		108	25. Strawberry Pass (D)
169	49. Hollister Hills SVRA (D)		206	**63. Swamp Lake (D)**
132	35. Horse Meadows (E)		160	47. Swansea-Cerro Gordo Road (M)
238	72. Jawbone OHV Area (M)		188	57. Twin Rocks (M)
234	**71. Jawbone to Lake Isabella (E)**		76	15. Tyler-Foote Crossing (E)
128	33. Kavanaugh Ridge (M)		210	64. Voyager Rock (E)
138	**38. Laurel Lakes (M)**		142	**40. Wheeler Ridge (D)**
40	4. Lost Coast, Redwoods (E)		192	58. White Bark Vista (E)
154	44. Mazourka Canyon (M)			
194	59. Mirror/Strawberry Lakes (D)			
222	67. Monache Meadows (E)			

Author's favorite trails are shown in boldface type.

10

INTRODUCTION

Looking down on Mono Lake and Lee Vining from Copper Mountain, Trail #34, rated easy.

Introduction

As I complete this guidebook—my sixth—I look back and ponder how it came to be. It was only six years ago I published my first book, *Guide to Colorado Backroads and 4-Wheel Drive Trails*. Since I had never done anything like this before, I was quite surprised when the book sold well enough for me to quit my regular job and write books full time. I've been slowly working my way around the western United States cranking out about one book a year. I've completed two books on Colorado and one each for Arizona, Moab, UT, southern California and now this one on northern California. If my health and back hold up, I hope to write and publish many more books. Over the years, I've found some amazing places in the backcountry and some of the best are in this book. Hopefully, you'll have a chance to get to them in your four-wheel drive and see for yourself what I'm talking about.

  I don't think you can describe a place very well if you haven't seen it first hand, so I drive every trail myself and write the description from detailed notes. And, because I was once a graphic designer, I'm able to draw the maps and shoot what I hope are better-than-average photographs. For this book, I shot over 2,000 pictures and carefully selected over 400 to show you both the best and worst parts of each trail. Each map is tailored to a specific route and is designed to be simple and easy to follow. I find the best trails by seeking help from local residents and four-wheel-drive clubs. My customers tell me they love my books and I'm confident that once you've tried one, you'll join their ranks.

  Each book covers a wide range of difficulty levels. This book includes an equal number of easy, moderate and difficult trails guaranteed to satisfy and challenge drivers at all experience levels. Each trail description is very detailed to help you determine if the trail is right for you, your family and your vehicle.

  Every trail selected is unique and interesting in some way, even the very easy trails. Fortunately, northern California has many outstanding trails from which to choose. One thing you'll notice, as you look through the book, is that many trails lead to beautiful high-mountain lakes. So, remember to take a fishing pole (and fishing license). I've tried to provide a sampling of everything unique about northern California including a trip through redwood country, a beach experience, a tour of Mt. Shasta, several coastal routes, an unusual backway to famous Bodie Ghost Town and a wonderful drive from Alabama Hills to Mt. Whitney. A few northern desert trails are also covered, including a unique tour through northern Death Valley National Park. Most trails, however, fall along the eastern and western slopes of the great Sierra Nevada Mountains. Serious four-wheelers will be pleased to find detailed descriptions of many great hardcore trails including California's three most famous: the Rubicon, Fordyce Creek and the Dusy/Ershim.

Riders of ATVs and dirt bikes will be pleased to learn that most of the trails in this book allow green-sticker vehicles or have nearby OHV terrain. Six OHV areas are covered, including Cow Mountain, Clear Creek, Pozo/La Panza, Jawbone, Hollister Hills and Oceano Dunes. The last two are state vehicular recreation areas (SVRAs). Don't miss incredible Hollister Hills with separate parks for green-sticker and street vehicles.

My books promote responsible four-wheeling by showing people proper places to go and by encouraging low impact driving. I can't stress enough the importance of staying on designated roads and following the rules. We lose trails every year because of irresponsible drivers and riders who mindlessly abuse our public lands. This small group of violators overshadows an immense amount of good work done by the organized four-wheeling community. Many of the routes in this book have been adopted by four-wheel-drive clubs who work hard to protect and maintain their trails. Without their effort, far fewer trails would be open today. Please do your part by leaving no trace of your passage. If you see someone recklessly abusing the land, take their license number and report them to the nearest ranger station or appropriate authority (see appendix for addresses and phone numbers).

HOW TO USE THIS BOOK

Everything about this book is designed to be simple and easy to use. As you flip through the book, notice how trail headings always appear at the top of right-hand pages. Type is large and easy to read in a moving vehicle. Directions are written in plain narrative—no tables and few abbreviations. Numerous photos show actual trail conditions, not just beautiful scenery. Maps are easy to read, starting with a statewide locator on page 7. Area maps zoom in closer on nine specific areas. Finally, an individual map is provided for each of 75 trails. Although GPS is not required to find your way, waypoints are provided for those who use them. Coordinates are listed in the appendix. Mileages are accurate and rounded to the nearest tenth of a mile. Your mileage will likely vary because of different driving habits and road conditions. Historical information is included where applicable.

SELECTING THE RIGHT TRAIL FOR YOUR VEHICLE

It is important to select trails that are appropriate for your vehicle. Trails are divided into three general categories. A circle identifies easy trails, a square, moderate trails and a diamond, difficult trails. In addition, on pages 8 and 9, the trails are ranked from easiest to hardest within each of the three general categories explained below.

Easy: Suitable for all stock four-wheel-drive sport utility vehicles with high ground clearance and low range. Some trails can be driven in two-wheel drive without low range in dry weather. A few trails, under ideal conditions, are suitable for passenger cars.

Moderate: Suitable for most stock 4WD sport utility vehicles with high ground clearance and low range. For the toughest moderate trails, factory skid plates, tow points, and all-terrain tires are recommended. These options are available from your dealer or local four-wheel-drive shop.

Difficult: Suitable for some aggressive stock 4WD sport utility vehicles with very high ground clearance, excellent articulation, tow hooks, and a full skid plate package. All-terrain tires are a minimum, mud terrains preferred. A winch or differential lockers are recommended for the most difficult trails. Drivers who spend a great deal of time on the most difficult trails may find it necessary to modify their vehicles with higher ground clearance, oversized tires, and heavy duty accessories. A trail is rated difficult if any spot on the trail is difficult. You may be able to enjoy much of a trail before running into the difficult portion. Read the trail description carefully.

CALIFORNIA LAWS, LICENSING AND FEES

California has the greatest number of off-highway vehicle (OHV) enthusiasts in the nation and the number is growing rapidly. In the last twenty years OHV registrations have increased 83%. Unfortunately, since 1985, land available for OHV recreation has decreased 47%. Much of this land was lost in 1994 when Congress passed the California Desert Protection Act. Over 7 million acres of land were designated wilderness and closed to OHV recreation. To deal with this problem, California has enacted special licensing classifications, strict OHV laws and additional fees which are explained as follows:

Street-Legal Vehicles. This classification includes licensed SUVs, Jeeps and dual-purpose motorcycles. They are allowed on major highways, forest roads, state park roads and in most OHV areas. Fees are paid when license plates are purchased and vary with vehicle type. Normal highway laws apply.

Green-Sticker Vehicles. This category includes ATVs, dune buggies, sand rails and unlicensed dirt bikes. These vehicles are allowed in OHV areas and on certain BLM and forest lands. Green stickers are good for two years. (See OHV laws on next page.)

Red-Sticker Vehicles. ATVs and motorcycles made after January 1, 1997, must meet stricter emission standards. Those that don't get a red sticker, which is exactly the same as a green sticker except the riding period is limited. Cost is same as green sticker.

National Forest Adventure Pass. You'll need a special Adventure Pass if you camp or stop to recreate in Los Padres National Forest. If you are just passing through, a pass is not required. This situation applies to five trails in this book: #51 Prewitt Ridge, #52 South Coast Ridge, #55 Pine Mountain, #56 Garcia Ridge and #57 Twin Rocks. Cost is $5 per day or $30 per year. Fee does not apply to green-sticker vehicles. You can get passes at Forest Service offices and at many local vendors (see www.fsadventurepass.org).

ATVs & DIRT BIKES

This book is primarily a guide for street-legal, off-highway vehicles. It is not intended to be a comprehensive guide for green-sticker vehicles (specifically ATVs and dirt bikes). Most trails in this book allow green-sticker vehicles but not all. **Trails where green-sticker vehicles are not allowed or not recommended are identified with an asterisk on page 6.** Dual-purpose motorcycles (i.e. street-legal dirt bikes) can run on both primary roads and legal open land. The following is a simplified list of state OHV laws.

State OHV Laws:
- Riders must wear approved safety helmets.
- A safety course is required for riders under age 18.
- A safety certification is required along with parental supervision for riders under age 14.
- ATVs cannot carry passengers.
- No riding while under the influence of alcohol or drugs.
- Speed is limited to 15 mph near campsites and groups of people. You are the final judge of unsafe situations. Be extra careful.
- Vehicles must have muffler, spark arrester and brakes plus lights if used at night.

In addition to state laws, most OHV areas have additional rules. Some common ones include:
- Safety flags must be used.
- No glass containers are allowed.
- No open alcoholic beverage containers are allowed.
- Campers cannot dump sewage or gray water.
- In most areas, you must pack out your trash.

Irresponsible use of ATVs and dirt bikes is one of the biggest concerns of the Forest Service, BLM and other land management agencies and a major reason for trail closures. It is your responsibility to understand and obey laws wherever you ride. You must stay on designated routes when required.

OHV AREAS AND SVRAs

Despite many land closures, California still has nearly 100 off-highway vehicle (OHV) areas. These areas include upwards of 100,000 miles of unpaved roads and countless acres of open land. Many of them are located in southern California and the major ones are covered in *Guide to Southern*

California Backroads & 4-Wheel Drive Trails. This northern book covers four OHV areas and two State Vehicular Recreation Areas. OHV areas include: Cow Mountain, north of Santa Rosa, Clear Creek Management Area, between Hollister and Coalinga, Pozo/La Panza, northeast of San Luis Obispo and Jawbone/Dove Springs, east of Bakersfield. SVRA areas include Oceano Dunes, south of San Luis Obispo and Hollister Hills, southeast of San Jose. If you would like a detailed listing and a map of all OHV areas across the state, contact the Off-Highway Motor Vehicle Recreation (OHMVR) Division of the California State Parks (see appendix).

NATIONAL PARKS AND FORESTS

Death Valley National Park. *Guide to Southern California Backroads & 4-Wheel Drive Trails* covers the southern portion of Death Valley National Park. Just one route in this northern book is inside the park. This special route is a compilation of several main roads and takes you to some of the best features in the park like the Racetrack, Teakettle Junction, Lost Burro Mine, Lippincott Grade, Saline Valley and Hunter Mountain. The route, suggested here, bypasses many miles of brutal washboard road. Higher portions of route can be blocked by snow for brief periods in the winter. Only street-legal vehicles are allowed in the park.

Yosemite National Park. Several routes in this book are located near the eastern gateway to Yosemite National Park near Lee Vining. (Four-wheeling is not allowed inside the park.) Because there are so few roads crossing east to west through the Sierra Nevada Mountains, you will most likely, at some time, pass through the park just to get from one side of the state to the other. Don't miss an opportunity to drive through the park on Tioga Pass Road (Highway 120). It is an incredible drive.

National Forests. This book includes routes in 11 different national forests: Eldorado, Inyo, Lassen, Los Padres, Plumas, Sequoia, Shasta-Trinity, Sierra, Stanislaus, Tahoe and Toiyabe. Rules and regulations are generally the same, but there are differences. You are responsible to know and obey all rules, so read forest maps carefully. Whenever possible, visit the closest ranger station to learn as much as possible about where you are going. (See appendix for listing.) Los Padres is the only forest of those listed above that requires an Adventure Pass. Plumas National Forest, in addition to its regular forest map, has a separate map for OHV trails.

SAFETY TIPS

File a flight plan. Determine where you are going and when you plan to return. Be as specific as possible. Inform a friend or relative and call them when you return. If something goes wrong, you'll have the comfort of knowing that at least someone knows where you are.

Travel with another vehicle. Your chances of getting stuck in the backcountry are immensely reduced with two vehicles. If one vehicle breaks down, you have a back-up. If you can't find anyone to travel with you, contact a local four-wheel drive club near the trail. To locate a club, contact the California Association of 4-Wheel Drive Clubs. (See appendix for contact information.) If you don't already belong to a club, consider joining one. It's a great way to learn and make friends.

Know location of closest hospital. Before you leave on any trip, check the location of the closest hospital or emergency facility in the area.

Carry extra maps. The maps in this book will clearly direct you along the trail. However, if you get lost or decide to venture down a spur road, you'll need additional maps with topographic information. Carry a compass or a GPS unit to orient yourself. At the end of each trail description, I list additional maps applicable to that specific area.

Booklet-style maps, like the *DeLorme Atlas & Gazetteer,* are very handy because they are easy to flip through and they cover the entire state. (Two volumes are required for California.) Latitude and longitude are printed along the edge of each map. With the simplest GPS unit, you can quickly determine your location. The *California Road & Recreation Atlas* by Benchmark Maps is very similar to the Gazetteer. It has better graphics but doesn't show quite as much backroad detail. Either atlas will work just fine.

The greatest amount of detail is shown on 7.5-minute U.S. Geological Survey Maps; however, each map covers a small area and many maps are required. Since I carry a laptop computer, I buy 7.5-minute maps on CDs. They are extremely economical and easy to use in this format, but they would be useless if something happened to my computer. I use them because they provide maximum detail for GPS tracking. In addition, I always carry paper maps.

Changing conditions. California's backcountry is fragile and under constant assault by forces of nature and man. Rock slides can occur or an entire road can be washed away from a single heavy rainstorm. A road may be closed without notice. Directional signs may be removed or vandalized. Route numbers are sometimes changed. Maps seldom keep up with changes and sometimes have mistakes. Take these factors into consideration when faced with a confusing situation. Rely on your own common sense.

High water, flash floods. Many of California's backroads cross or follow dry washes, small streams, and narrow canyons. Heavy rains can turn these places into raging torrents of water in minutes. Check weather forecasts and keep an eye on the sky. Be conservative and don't take chances. Cut your trip short if necessary. Don't attempt to cross a fast-flowing stream unless you've done it before and know what your vehicle can do. Wait if necessary; water levels usually go down quickly after a single rain shower. If you're in a narrow canyon and water begins to rise, drive perpendicularly out of the canyon if possible. If this is not possible, get out of your vehicle and climb to higher ground. Most people who die in flash floods attempt to outrun the rising water in their vehicles.

Inspect your vehicle carefully. Before you start into the backcountry, make sure your vehicle is in top operating condition. If you have a mechanic do the work, make sure he is reliable and understands four-wheeling. Tell him where you plan to take your vehicle. Pay particular attention to fluids, hoses, belts, battery, brakes, steering linkage, suspension system, driveline, and anything exposed under the vehicle. Tighten anything that may be loose. Inspect your tires carefully for potential weak spots and tread wear.

Wear your seat belt. You might think that because you're driving slowly, it's not necessary to wear your seat belt or use child restraints. I've learned through experience that you are much safer with a seat belt than without. Buckle up at all times.

Keep heads, arms, and legs inside a moving vehicle. Many trails are narrow. Brush, tree limbs, and rock overhangs may come very close to your vehicle. The driver must make it clear to every passenger to stay inside the vehicle at all times. Children, in particular, must not be allowed to stick their heads, arms, or legs out the windows.

Cliff edges. Watch children and be extremely careful around cliff edges. Hand rails are rarely provided. Watch for loose rock and stay away from these areas when it's wet, icy, or getting dark. If you climb up a rock wall, remember it's harder to get down than to climb up.

Lightning. During a storm, stay away from lone trees, cliff edges, and high points. Stay low to the ground or in your vehicle. Lightning can strike from a distant storm even when it's clear overhead.

Mines, tunnels, and old structures. Be careful around old mine buildings. Stay out of mines and tunnels. Don't let children play in these areas.

BACKCOUNTRY SURVIVAL

Self-reliance. Most of us live in populated areas and are accustomed to having other people around when things go wrong. In California's remote backcountry, you must be self-reliant. Don't count on anyone else's help. Try to anticipate what can go wrong and prepare accordingly.

Water is extremely important. I can't stress enough the importance of carrying and drinking plenty of water. This is especially true in the desert. I leave an extra five-gallon container in my vehicle at all times. A canteen is handy if you have to walk out. Running out of water under certain circumstances can be a fatal mistake.

First Aid. Always carry a good first-aid kit. Take a first-aid course and learn the basics. Make sure the kit contains a good first-aid book.

What to do if you have mechanical problems or you get lost. Stay with your vehicle. There's always a chance that someone will come along if you stay near the road. Your vehicle is easier to see than you are. Your car can provide shelter from wind, rain, heat and cold.

If you're familiar with the area and know exactly how far it is to hike out and are absolutely sure you can make it, consider walking out as a last resort. In the desert, wear loose clothing, take plenty of water, food, and rain protection to stay dry. Travel at night when it's cooler if the terrain is not too treacherous. Make sure you can see where you're walking.

Try to draw attention to yourself. Make noise anyway you can—whistles, horns, whatever you have. Don't run down your car battery. Build a smoky fire. Three fires in a triangle 150 feet apart are an international distress signal. Use flares if you have them. Some are designed for day use, others for night. Use a reflective mirror if you see an airplane or anyone in the distance.

Take your cellphone but remember you're often out of a service area. Sometimes cellphones work if you can get to higher ground. If you have a CB radio, broadcast on channel 19 or emergency channel 9. Continue intermittently to call out even if no one responds. Make sure you give your location. HAM radios work well in the backcountry. Consider getting a license.

Altitude sickness. Some people experience nausea, dizziness, headaches, or weakness the first time at high altitude. This condition usually improves over time. To minimize symptoms, give yourself time to acclimate, drink plenty of fluids, decrease salt intake, reduce alcohol and caffeine, eat foods high in carbohydrates, and try not to exert yourself. If symptoms become severe, the only sure remedy is to return to a lower altitude. Consult your doctor before going to higher altitudes if you have health problems.

Hyperthermia. When your body overheats it's called hyperthermia. Symptoms include dry, flushed skin, inability to sweat, rapid heartbeat, and a rising body temperature. Hyperthermia is often preceded by cramps. They may not go away by drinking water alone. You may need food or salt. If hyperthermia is allowed to progress you could collapse from heatstroke, which is extremely serious and can be fatal if not treated quickly.

To prevent hyperthermia, stay in the shade, don't overexert yourself, wear loose-fitting clothing, and drink plenty of water. If work is required to find or make shade, conserve your energy as best as possible.

Dehydration. As your body sweats to cool itself, it dehydrates. You may be drinking water but not enough. Eating may make you nauseous. You won't want to eat or drink. As symptoms get worse, your mouth will become dry, you may become dizzy, develop a headache, and become short of breath. At some point, you may not be able to walk or care for yourself. You must prevent dehydration before it happens. Drink more than just to quench your thirst. If you must conserve water, rest as much as possible, try not to sweat, and don't eat a lot. Digestion requires body fluids. If you have plenty of water, drink it.

Hypothermia. High mountain trails can get very cold, especially after the sun goes down. Even the desert gets cold at night. If it rains and gets windy, you could find yourself shivering in no time, especially if you've worked up a sweat during the day. Your hands and feet will become stiff. You may not be able to hold a match and start a fire. Again, prevention is the key. Put on a jacket before you begin to get cold. Stay dry. Change clothes if necessary. If you get too cold, blankets may not be enough to warm you. Build a fire, drink hot liquids, or cuddle up with someone else. Your car is a great shelter—use it.

CHECKLIST. No single list can be all inclusive. You must be the final judge of what you need. Here's a list of basic items:

- ❏ Carry plenty of water. Allow enough water for drinking and extra for your vehicle. Carry water purification tablets or a filtering device for emergencies.
- ❏ Food for normal eating and high-energy foods for emergencies. Energy bars, dried fruit, and hard candy store well.
- ❏ Extra clothing, shoes, sock, coats and hats even in the summer. Wool clothing keeps you warm when you're wet.
- ❏ Sleeping bags in case you get stuck overnight even if you're not planning to camp.
- ❏ A good first-aid kit including a first-aid book. Other important items include: sunscreen, insect repellent, safety pins, needles and thread, tweezers, pocket knife or all-purpose tool.
- ❏ Candles, matches, fire starter, and a lighter.
- ❏ An extra set of keys and glasses.
- ❏ Toilet paper, paper towels, wet wipes, and trash bags.
- ❏ A large plastic sheet or tarp.
- ❏ Rain gear, small tent or tarp, nylon cords.
- ❏ Detailed maps, compass or GPS unit, watch, and a knife.
- ❏ If you plan to make a fire, carry your own firewood. Make sure fires are allowed.
- ❏ A heavy-duty tow strap. (The kind without metal hooks on the ends.)
- ❏ A fire extinguisher. Make sure you can reach it quickly.
- ❏ Jumper cables, extra fan belts, stop-leak for radiator.
- ❏ Replacement fuses and electrical tape.
- ❏ Flashlight and extra batteries.
- ❏ Flares, signal mirror, police whistle.
- ❏ Extra oil and other engine fluids.
- ❏ A full tank of gas. If you carry extra gas, make sure it's in an approved container and properly stored.
- ❏ A good set of tools, work gloves, and a complete service manual for your vehicle.

- ❑ Baling wire and duct tape.
- ❑ An assortment of hoses, clamps, nuts, bolts, and washers.
- ❑ A full-size spare tire.
- ❑ A tire pressure gauge, electric tire pump that will plug into your cigarette lighter, and a can of nonflammable tire sealant.
- ❑ A jack that will lift your vehicle fairly high off the ground. Take a small board to place under the jack. Carry a high-lift jack if you can, especially on more difficult trails. Test your jack before you leave home.
- ❑ Shovel and axe. Folding shovels work great.
- ❑ Tire chains for winter mountain travel. They can also help if you get stuck in the mud.
- ❑ CB radio and/or cellular phone.
- ❑ Portable toilet.
- ❑ If you have a winch, carry a tree strap, clevis, and snatch block.

Maintenance. Backroad travel puts your vehicle under greater stress than normal highway driving. Follow maintenance directions in your owner's manual for severe driving conditions. This usually calls for changing oil, oil filter, and air filter more frequently as well as more frequent fluid checks and lubrications. Inspect your tires carefully; they take a lot of extra abuse. After your trip, make sure you wash your vehicle. Use a high pressure spray to thoroughly clean the underside and wheel wells. Automatic car washes usually are not adequate. Do it yourself, if you want your vehicle in good shape for the next trip.

YOUR RESPONSIBILITIES AS A BACKCOUNTRY DRIVER

Make sure you know and follow backcountry *Tread Lightly* guidelines. Consider joining the national *Tread Lightly* organization (see appendix for contact information). Although most damage is done by deliberate violators, some is done by well-intentioned, ignorant drivers.

Stay on the trail. This is the single most important rule of backcountry driving. Leaving the trail causes unnecessary erosion, kills vegetation, and spoils the beauty of the land. Scars remain for years. Don't widen the trail by driving around rocks and muddy spots and don't short cut switchbacks. When you have to pass another vehicle, do so at designated pull-overs. Sometimes the edge of the trail is defined by a line of rocks. Don't move the rocks or cross over them. Drivers who leave existing trails risk fines and cause trails to be closed. Practice diligently to leave no trace of your passage.

The Desert Tortoise. The Desert Tortoise is a *threatened species* and their population is being monitored as part of the Desert Tortoise Recovery plan. If you see a Desert Tortoise anytime during your travels, stay clear. Do not pick it up unless it is in mortal danger. Tortoises store water in their bladders which they may empty if frightened which could be fatal. They like shade, so check under your vehicle before driving away.

Wilderness Areas. It is a serious offense to drive in a designated wilderness. These areas are usually well marked and clearly shown on maps.

Private Property. Pass through private land quietly and stay on the road at all times. Don't disturb livestock. Leave gates the way you find them unless posted otherwise.

Ruins and archaeological sites. It is a federal crime to disturb archaeological sites. Don't touch them or climb inside. Do not remove or touch historical artifacts. Don't camp or picnic near an archaeological site.

Trash disposal and litter. Carry plastic trash bags and pack out your own trash, including cigarette butts. Where waste receptacles are provided, use them. When possible, clean up after others. Keep a litter bag handy and pick up trash along the trail.

When nature calls. The disposal of solid human waste and toilet paper is becoming a big problem as more visitors head into the backcountry. Arid climates do not decompose these materials as fast as they are being left behind. It is generally advisable to carry a portable toilet. Otherwise, keep a small shovel handy and bury feces 4 to 6 inches deep, away from trails, campsites and at least 300 feet from any water source, which includes dry washes. Seal toilet paper and feminine hygiene products in a small plastic bag and discard with your trash.

Campfires. You must have a fire permit to build a fire anywhere on public lands in California. Permits are free and available at forest offices and many other places. Regulations vary across the state and restrictions may apply when fire danger is high. Always use fire rings when they are provided. Try to build fires in spots where others have had a fire. Bring your own firewood whenever possible and know local regulations for firewood gathering. Thoroughly douse all campfires. Carry out fire debris with your trash. Consider using a propane camping stove instead of building a fire. Stoves are very convenient for cooking and are environmentally preferred.

Washing, cleaning, and bathing. If you must use soap, use biodegradable soap but never around lakes or streams. Heat water without using soap to clean utensils whenever possible.

BACKCOUNTRY DRIVING LESSONS

Trail Etiquette. A little common courtesy goes a long way in making everyone's travel in the backcountry more enjoyable. After all, we're all out to have fun. Take your time and be considerate of others. If you see someone approaching from behind, look for a wide spot on the trail, pull over and let him pass. Conversely, if you get behind a slowpoke, back off or look for a scenic spot to pull over for a while. Stretch your legs and take a few pictures. When you're out of your vehicle, pick a wide spot where you can pull over so others can get by. A horn is rarely needed in the backcountry. Don't play your radio loudly. When you see bikers, pull over and let them pass. Ask if they have enough water. Don't let your pet bark or chase wildlife.

The basics. If you have never shifted into low range, grab your owner's manual now and start practicing. Read the rest of this book, then try some of the easy trails. Gradually you'll become more proficient and eventually you'll be ready to move up in difficulty.

Low and slow. Your vehicle was designed to go over rocky and bumpy terrain but only at slow speed. Get used to driving slowly in first gear low range. This will allow you to idle over obstacles without stalling. You don't need to shift back and forth constantly. Get into a low gear and stay there as much as possible so your engine can operate at high RPM and at maximum power. If you have a standard transmission, your goal should be to use your clutch as little as possible. As you encounter resistance on an obstacle or an uphill grade, just give it a little gas. As you start downhill, allow the engine's resistance to act as a brake. If the engine alone will not stop you from accelerating, then help a little with the brake. When you need more power but not more speed, press on the gas and feather the brake a little at the same time. This takes a little practice, but you will be amazed at the control you have. This technique works equally well with automatic transmissions.

Rocks and other high points. Never attempt to straddle a rock that is large enough to strike your differentials, transfer case or other low-hanging parts of your undercarriage. Instead, drive over the highest point with your tire, which is designed to take the abuse. This will lift your undercarriage over the obstacle. As you enter a rocky area, look ahead to determine where the high points are, then make every effort to cross them with your tires. Learn the low points of your undercarriage.

Using a spotter. Sometimes there are so many rocks you get confused. In this case, have someone get out and guide you. They should stand at a safe distance in front, watching your tires and undercarriage. With hand signals, they can direct you left or right. If you are alone, don't be embarrassed to spot for yourself by getting in and out of your vehicle several times.

Those clunking sounds. Having made every attempt to avoid dragging bottom, you'll find it's not always possible. It is inevitable that a rock will contact your undercarriage eventually. The sound can be quite unnerving the first time it happens. If you are driving slowly and have proper skid plates, damage is unlikely. Look for a different line, back up and try again. If unsuccessful, read on.

Crossing large rocks. Sometimes a rock is too large to drive over or at such a steep angle your bumper hits the rock before your tire. Stack rocks on each side to form a ramp. Once over the obstacle, make sure you put the rocks back where you found them. The next driver to come along may prefer the challenge of crossing the rock in its more difficult state.

Getting high centered. You may drive over a large rock or into a rut, causing you to get lodged on the object. If this happens, don't panic. First ask your passengers to get out to see if less weight helps. Try rocking the vehicle. If this doesn't work, jack up your vehicle and place a few rocks under the tires so that when you let the jack down, you take the weight off the high point. Determine whether driving forward or reverse is best and try again. You may have to repeat this procedure several times if you are seriously high centered. Eventually you will learn what you can and cannot drive over.

Look in all directions. Unlike highway driving in which your primary need for attention is straight ahead, backcountry driving requires you to look in all directions. Objects can block your path from above, below, and from the sides. Trees fall, branches droop, and rocks slide, making the trail an ever-changing obstacle course.

Scout ahead. If you are on an unfamiliar trail and are concerned that the trail is becoming too difficult, get out of your vehicle and walk the trail ahead of you. This gives you an opportunity to pick an easy place to turn around before you get into trouble. If you have to turn around, back up or pull ahead until you find a wide flat spot. Don't try to turn in a narrow confined area. This can damage the trail and perhaps tip over your vehicle.

Anticipate. Shift into four-wheel drive or low range before it is needed. If you wait until it is needed, conditions might be too difficult, e.g., halfway up a hillside.

Blind curves. When approaching blind curves, always assume that there is a speeding vehicle coming from the opposite direction. This will prepare you for the worst. Be aware that many people drive on the wrong side of the road to stay away from the outer edge of a trail. Whenever possible, keep your windows open and your radio off so that you can hear an approaching vehicle. You can usually hear motorcycles and ATVs. Quiet SUVs are the biggest problem. Collisions do occur, so be careful.

Driving uphill. The difficulty of hill climbing is often misjudged by the novice driver. You should have good tires, adequate power, and be shifted into four-wheel drive low. There are four factors that determine difficulty:

Length of the hill. If the hill is very long, it is less likely that momentum will carry you to the top. Short hills are easier.

Traction. Smooth rock is easier to climb than dirt.

Bumpiness. If the road surface undulates to the point where all four tires do not stay on the ground at the same time, you will have great difficulty climbing even a moderately steep hill.

Steepness. This can be difficult to judge, so examine a hill carefully before you attempt it. Walk up the hill if necessary to make sure it is not steeper at the top. If you are not absolutely sure you can climb a hill, don't attempt it. Practice on smaller hills first.

If you attempt a hill, approach it straight on and stay that way all the way to the top. Do not turn sideways or try to drive across the hill. Do not use excessive speed but keep moving at a steady pace. Make sure no one is coming up from the other side. Position a spotter at the top of the hill if necessary. Do not spin your tires because this can turn you sideways to the hill. If you feel you are coming to a stop due to lack of traction, turn your steering wheel back and forth quickly. This will give you additional grip. If you stall, use your brake and restart your engine. You may also have to use your emergency brake. If you start to slide backwards even with your brake on, you may have to ease up on the brake enough to regain steering control. Don't allow your wheels to lock up. If you don't make it to the top of the hill, shift into reverse and back down slowly in a straight line. Try the hill again but only if you think you learned enough to make a difference. As you approach the top of the hill, ease off the gas so you are in control before starting down the other side.

Driving downhill. Make sure you are in four-wheel drive. Examine the hill carefully and determine the best route that will allow you to go straight down the hill. Do not turn sideways. Use the lowest gears possible, allowing the engine's compression to hold you back. Do not ride the clutch. Feather the brakes slightly if additional slowing is needed. Do not allow the wheels to lock up. This will cause loss of steering and possibly cause you to slide sideways. The natural reaction when you begin to slide is to press harder on the brakes. Try to stay off the brakes. If you continue to slide despite these efforts, turn in the direction of the slide as you would on ice or snow and accelerate slightly. This will help maintain steering control.

Parking on a steep hill. Put your vehicle in reverse gear if pointing downhill and in forward gear if pointing uphill. For automatic transmissions, shift to park. Set your emergency brake hard and block your tires.

Tippy situations. No one can tell you how far your vehicle can safely lean. You must learn the limitations through practice. Remember that sport utility vehicles have a higher center of gravity and are less stable than a passenger car. However, don't get paranoid. Your vehicle will likely lean a lot more than you think. Drive slowly to avoid bouncing over. A good way to learn is to watch an experienced driver with a vehicle similar to yours. This is an advantage to traveling with a group. Once you see how far other vehicles can lean, you will become more comfortable in these situations. Remember, too, that you're likely to slide sideways before you tip over. This can be just as dangerous in certain situations. Use extreme caution if the road surface is slippery from loose gravel, mud, or wet clay. Turn around if necessary.

Crossing streams and water holes. You must know the high water point of your vehicle before entering any body of water. Several factors can determine this point, including the height of the air intake and the location of the computer module (newer vehicles). Water sucked into the air intake is a very serious matter. If you don't know where these items are located, check with your dealer or a good four-wheel drive shop. A low fan can throw water on the engine and cause it to stall. You may have to disconnect your fan belt. Water can be sucked into your differentials so check them regularly after crossing deep streams.

After you understand your vehicle's capabilities, you must assess the stream conditions. First determine the depth of the water. If you are with a group, let the most experienced driver cross first. Follow his line if he is successful. If you are alone, you might wait for someone else to come along. Sometimes you can use a long stick to check the depth of small streams or water holes. Check for deep holes, large obstacles, and muddy sections. If you can't determine the water depth, don't cross. A winch line or long tow strap can be used as a safety line to pull someone back if he gets into trouble, but attach it before entering the water. It must also be long enough for him to reach shallow water on the other side. Once in the water, drive slowly but steadily. This creates a small wake which helps form an air pocket around the engine. I've seen people put a piece of cardboard or canvas over the front of their vehicle to enhance the wake affect. This only works if you keep moving. After exiting a stream, test your brakes. You may have to ride them lightly for a short distance until they dry out. Always cross streams at designated water crossings. Don't drive in the direction of the stream. Try to minimize disruption of the water habitat.

Mud. Don't make new mud holes or enlarge existing ones. Stay home if you have reason to believe the trail will be too wet. Some trails, however, have permanent mud holes that you must cross. Mud can build up suction around your tires and be very difficult to get through. Always check a mud hole carefully to see how deep it is. Take a stick and poke around. Check the other side. If there are no tracks coming out, don't go in. If you decide to cross, keep moving at a steady pace and, if necessary, turn the steering wheel back and forth quickly for additional traction. If you get stuck, dig around the tires to break the suction and place anything hard under the tires for traction. It may be necessary to back out. If you are with a friend, and you are doubtful if you can get through without help, attach a tow strap before you enter so that you can be pulled back. But beware, sometimes the mud can be so bad, even a friend can't pull you out. Your only protection against this happening is to use your head and not go in the mud in the first place. When I've seen people stuck this badly, it is usually due to a total disregard for the obvious. If you can't get through the mud, search for an alternate route but don't widen the trail.

Ruts. If you get stuck in a rut and have no one to pull you out, dig a small trench from the rut to the right or left at a 45-degree angle. The dirt you remove from this trench should be used to fill the rut ahead of the turning point. If both tires are in parallel ruts, make sure the trenches are parallel. Drive out following the new rut. Repair any damage after you get out.

Gullies or washouts. If you are running parallel to a washed-out section of the trail, straddle it. If it becomes too large to straddle, drive down the middle. The goal is to center your vehicle so you remain as level as possible. This may require that you drive on the outer edges of your tires, so drive slowly and watch for any sharp objects. If you begin to tilt too far in one direction, turn in the direction of the tilt until you level out again. Sometimes it helps to have a spotter. To cross a gully from one side to the other, approach at a 45-degree angle and let each tire walk over independently.

Ravines. Crossing a ravine is similar to crossing a gully. Approach on an angle and let each tire go through independently. If the ravine is large with steep sides, you may not be able to cross at an angle because it could cause a rollover. If you don't cross at an angle, two things can happen. You will drag the front or rear of your vehicle, or you will high center on the edge of the ravine. If this is the case, ask yourself if you really need to cross the ravine. If you must cross, your only solution is to stack rocks to lift the vehicle at critical points.

Sand. Dry sand is more difficult than wet sand (unless it's quicksand). In either case, keep moving so that your momentum helps carry you through. Stay in a higher gear and use a little extra power but don't use excessive power and spin your tires. If necessary, turn your steering wheel back and forth quickly to give your tires a fresh grip. Airing down your tires is often necessary. Experiment with different tire pressures. Make sure you have a way to air up after you get through the sand. If you do get stuck, wet the sand in front of your tires. Try rocking the vehicle. If necessary, use your floor mats under the tires.

Sand Dunes. Limit yourself to smaller dunes. Stay off the soft side of the dune where the wind is depositing the sand. Soft sand will not support your vehicle. Worse than getting stuck, you could roll over. To avoid digging in, don't accelerate quickly or slam on your brakes. When helping someone else get unstuck, be careful not to spin your wheels or you'll get stuck. Use a winch if you have one.

Washboard roads. Washboard roads are a natural part of backcountry travel. Vibration from these roads can be annoying. It is a problem for everybody so don't think there is something wrong with your vehicle. Experiment with different speeds to find the smoothest ride. Slowing down is usually best, but some conditions may be improved by speeding up a little. Be careful around curves where you could lose traction and slide. Check your tires to make sure they are not overinflated.

Airing down. There may be times when you need to let air out of your tires to get more traction or improve your ride, e.g., when driving through sand, going up a steep hill, or driving on washboard roads. It is usually safe to let air out of your tires until they bulge slightly, provided you are not traveling at high speed. If you let out too much air, your tires may come off the rims, or the sidewalls may become vulnerable to damage by sharp objects. Consider how or where you will reinflate. A small air pump that plugs into your cigarette lighter is handy for this purpose. Airing down on hard-core trails is essential. I've seen some wheelers with larger tires air down to as little as 3-5 lbs. A typical SUV can usually be aired down to 18 to 20 lbs. without noticeable handling difficulties at low speeds.

Winching. Next to tow points and skid plates, a winch is one of the best investments you can make. If you drive more difficult trails and you don't have a winch, travel with someone who does. I've known some hard-core wheelers who have gone for years without owning a winch but they always travel with a group. If you never intend to buy a winch, carry a high-lift jack or come-along. Although these tools are slow and inconvenient when used in place of a winch, they can get you out of difficulty when there is no other way.

If you own a winch, make sure you also have these five basic winch accessories:

1. Heavy-duty work gloves.

2. A tree strap—looks like a tow strap but is shorter. It has a loop on each end.

3. A snatch block—a pulley that opens on the side so you can slip it over your winch cable.

4. A clevis—a heavy U-shaped device with a pin that screws across one end. This enables you to connect straps together and to your vehicle. It has many other uses.

5. A heavy-duty chain with grab hooks to wrap around rocks. It's also handy when trying to pull another vehicle that does not have tow points.

Winching tips:

• Your winch cable should be lined up straight with the pulling vehicle. If you can't pull straight, attach a snatch block to a large tree or rock to form an angle. This technique also works for pulling a fallen tree off the trail.

• If your winch cable bunches up at one end of the spool but there's still room for the cable, let it go and rewind the cable later.

• When winching from trees, attach to the largest tree possible using your tree strap and clevis. If no tree is large enough, wrap several smaller trees. The strap should be put as low as possible on the tree. Finding a decent size tree in the desert may be impossible.

• Keep your engine running while winching to provide maximum electrical power to the battery.

• Help the winch by driving the stuck vehicle slowly. Be in the lowest gear possible and go as slowly as possible without spinning your tires. Don't allow slack in the winch cable. This can start a jerking motion that could break the cable.

• If there is not enough power to pull the stuck vehicle, attach a snatch block to the stuck vehicle and double the winch cable back to the starting point. This block-and-tackle technique will double your pulling power.

• Set the emergency brake on the anchor vehicle and block the wheels if necessary. In some cases, you may have to connect the anchor vehicle to another vehicle or tree.

• Throw a blanket or heavy coat over the winch cable while pulling. This will slow the end of the winch cable if it breaks and snaps back.

• Make sure there are at least 5 wraps of the winch cable left on the spool.

• Never hook the winch cable to itself. Use a tree strap and clevis. Never allow the winch cable to kink. This creates a weak spot in the cable.

• If tow points are not available on the stuck vehicle, attach to the vehicle's frame, not the bumper. Use your large chain to wrap around the frame. If you are helping a stranger, make sure he understands that you are not responsible for damage to his vehicle.

• Never straddle or stand close to the winch cable while it is under stress.

• When finished winching, don't let the end of the cable wind into the spool. It can become jammed and damage your winch. Attach the hook to some other part of your vehicle like a tow point.

FINAL COMMENTS

I've made every effort to make this book as accurate and as easy to use as possible. If you have ideas for improvements or find any significant errors, please write to me at FunTreks, Inc., P.O. Box 49187, Colorado Springs, CO 80949-9187. Or, send e-mail to: *books@funtreks.com*. Whether you're a novice or expert, I hope this book makes your backcountry experience safer, easier, and more fun.

Map Legend

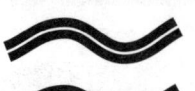

- Interstate
- Paved Road*
- Easy Trail*
- Moderate Trail*
- Difficult Trail*
- Other Road*
- Described in text
- Hiking Trail
- Boundaries & Divides
- Cliff, Canyon
- Railroad
- Mountain Peak (MT. SHASTA)
- Lake, Sand Dune
- Map Orientation (N)
- Interstate (5)
- U.S. Highway (50)
- State & County Road (58)
- Forest Service Road (586)
- BLM Road (EP26)
- Starting point of trail (Start here)

- Toilet
- Gas
- Parking
- Picnic Area
- Camping
- Mine
- Hiking
- Cabin
- Water Crossing
- Fishing
- ATVs, Dirt bikes
- Scenic Point
- Windmill
- Ghost town
- Major Obstacle
- GPS Waypoint (05)

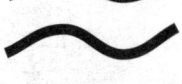

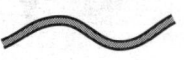

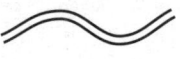

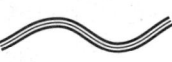

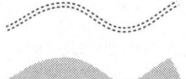

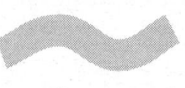

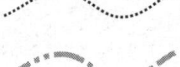

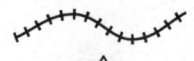

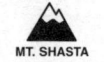

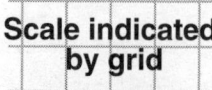

Scale indicated by grid

Scale is different for each map; check grid size at bottom of map.

** These items repeated on each map for your convenience. See Mini Key.*

THE TRAILS

Descending towards Buck Island Lake on the Rubicon, Trail #23, rated difficult.

AREA 1

Mt. Shasta, Redding,
Eureka, Santa Rosa

1. Mt. Shasta Loop
2. Bowerman Ridge
3. Shasta Bally Peak
4. Lost Coast, Redwoods
5. Cow Mountain OHV Area

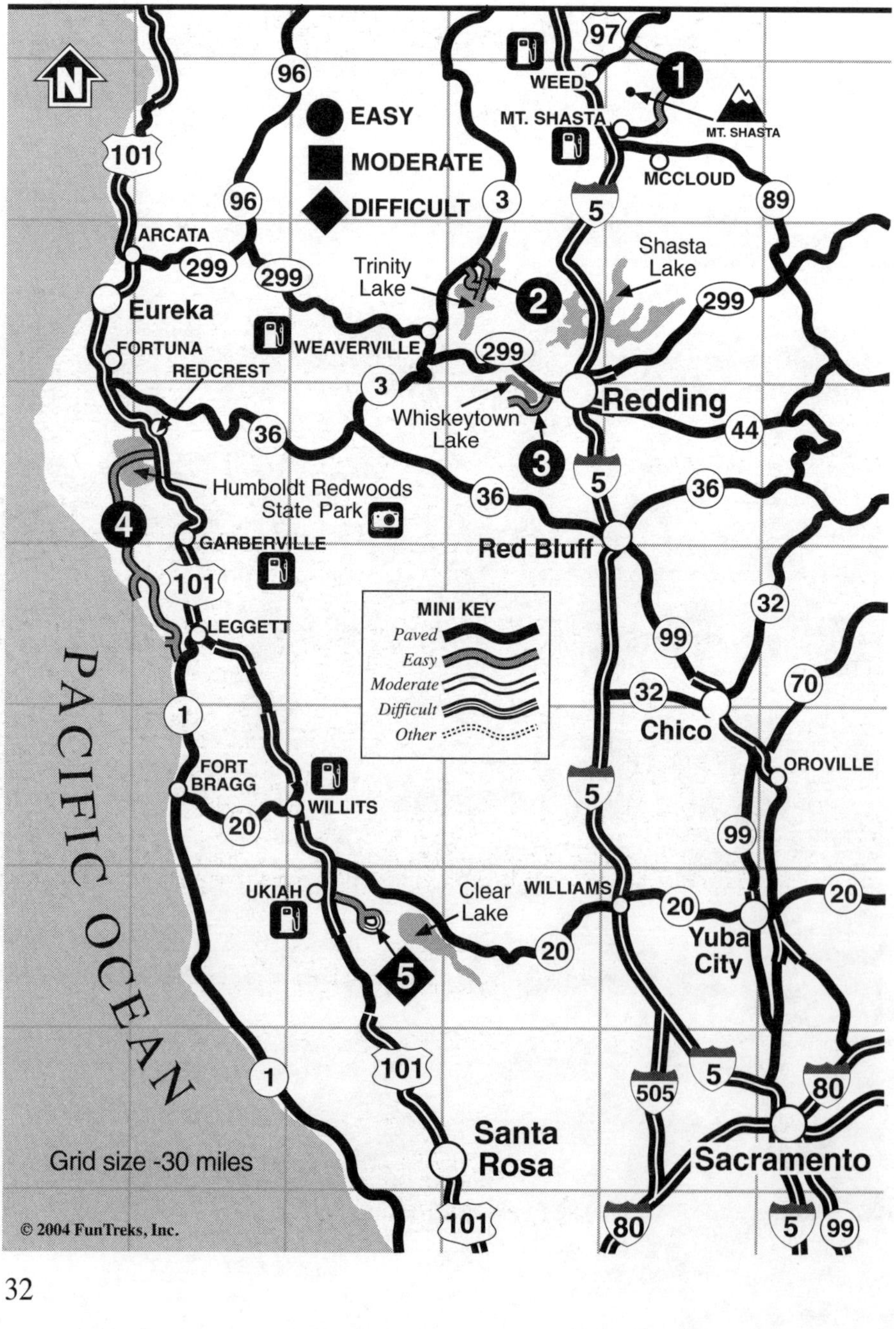

AREA 1
Mt. Shasta, Redding, Eureka, Santa Rosa

No backroad guidebook on northern California would be complete without showing you California's giant redwoods. *Lost Coast Trail*, after taking you through a remote coastal area featuring short side trips to historic Bear Harbor and forgotten Usal Beach, exits through Humboldt Redwoods State Park and connects to "Avenue of the Giants." This area features some of the largest redwoods in California including "Founders Tree" (Ht. 346 ft., dia. 12.7 ft., circum. 40 ft.). Farther north, *Mt. Shasta Loop* circles around Mt. Shasta on easy forest roads and exits via Military Pass. West of Redding, you'll climb a very steep road to *Shasta Bally Peak* above beautiful Whiskeytown Lake, a National Recreation Area. Travel along narrow *Bowerman Ridge* to a remote picnic spot on a peninsula in the middle of Trinity Lake north of Weaverville. All of these trails are rated easy so everyone can enjoy them. Those looking for hardcore challenges can find them at Cow Mountain OHV Area, featuring many steep, narrow trails and rocky ravines. It's located just an hour north of Santa Rosa.

Lost Coast (Trail #4) exits through Humboldt Redwoods State Park just south of Redcrest.

33

View of Mt. Shasta from south side in late summer.

Water damage possible.

Below Military Pass.

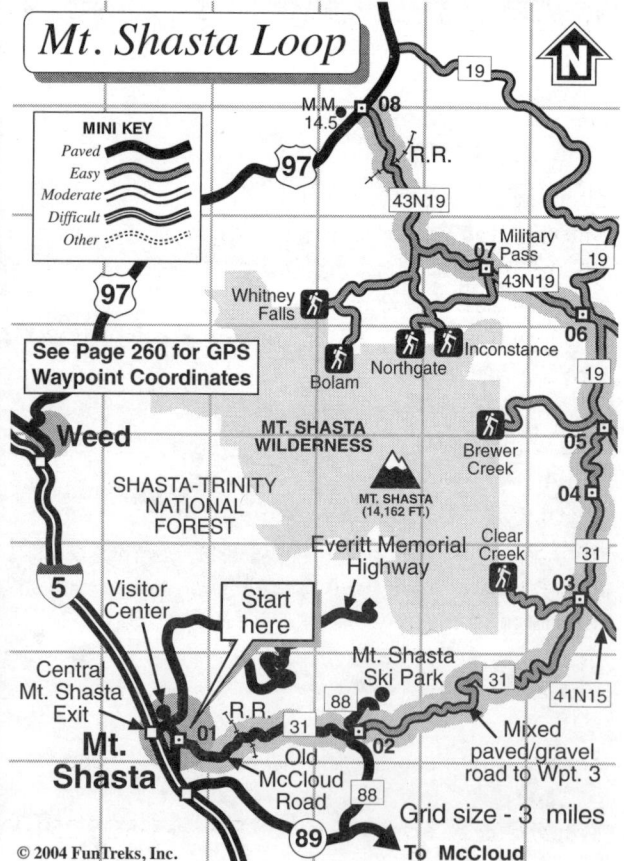

© 2004 FunTreks, Inc.

34

Mt. Shasta Loop ①

Location: North of Redding. Northeast of Mt. Shasta City.

Difficulty: Easy. Well graded, but don't drive when wet or snowy.

Features: Forest roads circle base of volcanic Mt. Shasta and connect to hiking trails at lower elevations. Permit required to hike above 10,000 ft. Best views descending from Military Pass. Drive on a clear day.

Time & Distance: 38.2 miles from I-5 to Hwy. 97. Allow about 3 hours.

To Get There: Turn right off I-5 at Central Mt. Shasta exit. Follow Lake Street past visitor center to Mt. Shasta Boulevard and turn right. The road swings right and heads south. Stay on S. Mt. Shasta Blvd. for 0.6 miles and turn left on Old McCloud Road (not McCloud Avenue).

Trail Description: Reset odometer at start of Old McCloud Rd (01). Head east on McCloud as it becomes F.S. 31. After about 6 miles of winding pavement, turn left at a major T intersection at Hwy. 88 just after the nordic ski center. Hwy. 88 curves left immediately at 6.2 miles (02). You go straight on unmarked, roughly paved F.S. 31. *Reset your odometer.* The road will alternate between gravel and rough pavement and is fairly well marked. Stay right at 3.4 and 6.4 miles. Road damage possible at Mud Creek Dam at 8.8 miles. Bear left at 9.2 then go straight at 11.7 (03) when you reach a major 4-way intersection (41N15 joins on right). Good view of Mt. Shasta at 13.4 miles. Bear right at 13.9. Stay left at 15.2 miles (04) on lesser road. Cross a rocky spot at 15.5. Bear right at 15.7 as equal roads diverge.

Reset your odometer and turn left at 17.9 miles (05) when you intersect with wider F.S. 19. A good road immediately goes left to Brewer Creek Trailhead. You go straight. Stay on this wide graded road 3.8 miles, then bear left at a diagonal intersection (06) onto a smooth 2-track road. Bear right on F.S. 43N19 at 4.2. Go straight at Military Pass at 7.0 miles (07) then right at 9.4. Great views from here as you stay on well marked but rougher 43N19 all the way to Hwy. 97, reached at 14.1 miles (08) near mile post 14.5.

Return Trip: Left on Hwy. 97 takes you back to I-5 in about 15 miles.

Services: Full services in Mt. Shasta and Weed.

Maps: Shasta-Trinity National Forest, USGS 250,000 scale map, Weed, CA

Remote camping and picnic spot is also used by boaters. You'll think you're on an island.

End of road is steep and narrow in places.

Part of Trinity Lake below Bowerman Ridge.

Bowerman Ridge

Start here

See Page 260 for GPS Waypoint Coordinates

WHISKEYTOWN-SHASTA-TRINITY NATIONAL RECREATION AREA

Guy Covington Drive

Covington Mill (Residential Area)

BILLYS PEAK

TO WEAVERVILLE

Bowerman Barn

BOWERMAN PEAK

Seasonal Gate

Alpine View

Hayward Flat

35N31Y

36N35

TRINITY LAKE

TRINITY LAKE

Steep & narrow (Avoid when wet)

TRINITY LAKE

MINI KEY
Paved
Easy
Moderate
Difficult
Other

Grid size - 1 mile
© 2004 FunTreks, Inc.

36

Bowerman Ridge ❷

Location: Northwest of Redding, northeast of Weaverville.

Difficulty: Easy. Mostly a wide, graded road except for one steep, narrow section. Tight trees in a few places. Avoid when wet. Closed in winter.

Features: Dramatic high views of massive Trinity Lake. See Mt. Shasta on a clear day. Secluded camping or picnicking. Alpine View F.S. campground.

Time & Distance: Allow 3 hours for this 22-mile loop. The drive from Redding through Weaverville is long but very scenic.

To Get There: Take Hwy. 299 west from Redding to Weaverville. Then follow Hwy. 3 north 25.5 miles to well marked Bowerman Ridge on right.

Trail Description: Reset your odometer as you turn off Hwy. 3 [01]. Head east following signs for 36N35. Bear right at 0.7 miles. Look over your left shoulder to see Mt. Shasta at 3.3 miles. A road joins on the right and one branches off to the left at 4.4 miles. Bear left at 5.3. Go straight at 6.1 where 35N24 goes right. Stay right at 6.2. Continue straight at 6.4 miles (02). (You'll come back to this point later.) Soon you'll see the lake on both sides of the road as it becomes apparent you're on a ridge. Stay right at 8.0 as the road gradually descends through tightening trees. Several steep roller-coaster hills remain before reaching a secluded picnic spot at 10.5 miles (03).

Retrace route 4.1 miles to gated road on left (02) (closed in winter). *Reset your odometer.* Continue downhill on mostly good road before reaching a paved road at 4.7 miles (04). Alpine View Forest Service Campground is to the left. Right takes you past historic Bowerman Barn on the way back to Highway 3, reached at 7.9 miles (05).

Return Trip: Turn left on Hwy. 3 to return to Weaverville.

Services: Weaverville. Vault toilets at many campgrounds along Hwy 3.

Historical Highlights: Handcrafted Bowerman Barn, built in 1878, is all that remains of the Bowerman Ranch, which once served as a stage stop.

Maps: Shasta-Trinity National Forest, USGS 100,000-scale map, Redding, CA, Trinity Unit map of the Whiskeytown-Shasta-Trinity National Recreation Area, DeLorme Atlas & Gazetteer.

Whiskeytown Lake covers 3,200 acres and has 36 miles of shoreline.

This section of road was sandy and steep.

Excellent tent camping at Sheep Camp.

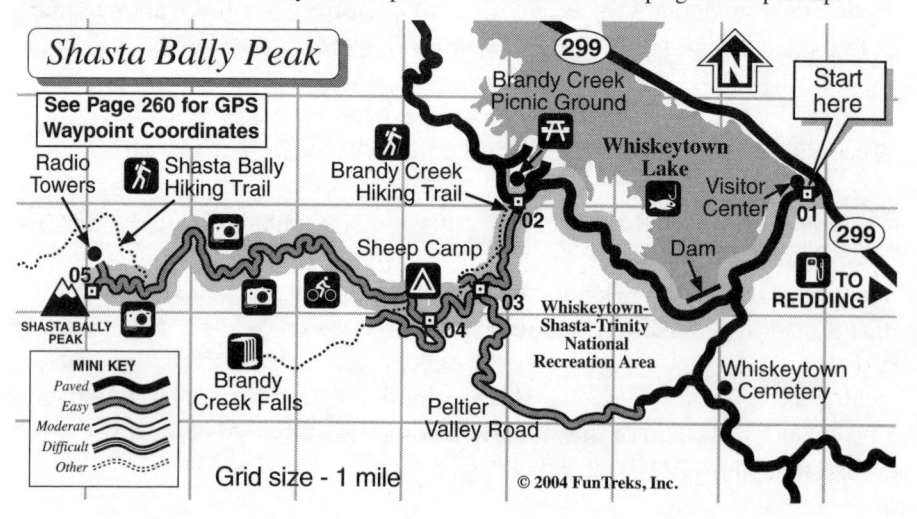

Shasta Bally Peak

See Page 260 for GPS Waypoint Coordinates

Radio Towers
Shasta Bally Hiking Trail
Brandy Creek Hiking Trail
Brandy Creek Picnic Ground
Whiskeytown Lake
Start here
Visitor Center
299
Sheep Camp
Dam
TO REDDING
SHASTA BALLY PEAK
Whiskeytown-Shasta-Trinity National Recreation Area
Brandy Creek Falls
Peltier Valley Road
Whiskeytown Cemetery

MINI KEY
Paved
Easy
Moderate
Difficult
Other

Grid size - 1 mile

© 2004 FunTreks, Inc.

38

Shasta Bally Peak ③

Location: West of Redding.

Difficulty: Easy but rutted in places and very steep. Four-wheel drive and low range recommended. Road closed if it gets too wet. Check at visitor center for road status. Street-legal vehicles only.

Features: An exhilarating drive with several miles of sustained steep climbing to an elevation above 6,100 feet. Outstanding views of Whiskeytown Lake and Mt. Shasta. A short drive from Redding. Fee required.

Time & Distance: Takes about an hour to drive 14 miles one way to top.

To Get There: Take Highway 299 west from Redding about 7 miles and turn left at road to well-marked visitor center. Pay fee inside visitor center.

Trail Description: Reset your odometer at visitor center (01). Follow paved road south around lake. Turn right and cross dam at 1.5 miles. Brandy Creek Picnic Area goes right at 4.5 miles. You continue straight. Ignore the next road to the left. Turn left at 4.6 miles (02) following signs to Shasta Bally. Pavement ends. Bear left uphill at 4.8. Continue down the middle at a 3-way fork at 6.0 miles (03). Turn right following a sign to Sheep Camp at 7.0 miles (04). Just after a small bridge, you'll see Sheep Camp on the right.

The real fun starts after Sheep Camp. The road narrows in places and gets very steep. Views are great as you climb above the trees. You'll want low range if you stop on a steep section and start again. After passing gated radio towers, the trail ends in tight manzanita brush at 12.9 miles (05). On a clear day you can easily see Mt. Shasta to the north.

Return Trip: Return the way you came. When you reach the main paved road, left will take you on a pleasant trip around Whiskeytown Lake.

Services: Full services in Redding. Sheep Camp is nicely set up with barbecue grills, bear-proof waste containers, picnic tables, flat tent sites and a modern vault toilet (but make sure you have bug repellent).

Maps: The best map for this area is the one you get when you pay your entry fee at the visitor center. Other helpful maps include Shasta-Trinity National Forest, USGS 100,000 scale map, Redding, CA, and the DeLorme Atlas and Gazetteer.

Wildflowers and sunshine above Usal Beach.
Photo by Dave Wheeler

Trail can get muddy. 
Returning from Bear Harbor.
Photo by Dave Wheeler

346 ft. Founders Tree.
Turn left for Usal Beach immediately after this bridge.

Lost Coast, Redwoods ④

Location: Along the Pacific Coast between Fort Bragg and Eureka.

Difficulty: Easy but remote. Usal Road is subject to deterioration and can be rutted and muddy so avoid when wet. It is also narrow and steep in places. Be careful in the soft sand at Usal Beach. The drive improves north of Four Corners where you'll encounter some local traffic. The last part of trip is paved. Best weather is in April and May.

Features: Explore remote coastal terrain. Enjoy beautiful ocean views and and camp at historic Usal Beach. Pass through Humboldt Redwoods State Park where you'll see some of the largest redwood trees in California. Take a side trip through Sinkyone Wilderness State Park to remote Bear Harbor. Consider side trips on Saddle Mountain Road and Smith Etter Road. Both roads have outstanding high-elevation ocean views. The trip ends at popular "Avenue of the Giants," a major tourist area for viewing redwoods.

Time & Distance: 88.1 miles from Hwy. 1 to Avenue of the Giants counting side trips to Usal Beach and Bear Harbor. Allow a full day.

To Get There: Take Hwy. 101 north past the tiny town of Leggett where Hwy. 1 intersects. Turn left on Hwy. 1. Go southwest 14.7 miles to Mendocino County Road 431 on the right near mile marker 90.88.

Trail Description: Reset your odometer at the start of County Road 431 (01). Ocean views start within first half mile (weather permitting). Stay left at 2.6 miles. Read information board for Usal Beach at 5.7 miles and continue straight. At 6.0 miles (02) cross a long wooden bridge and turn left for Usal Beach (fee area). Stay right on narrow road as camp spots branch off to left. Road ends at a sandy parking area at 6.4 miles. Primitive toilets available. Driving on beach is not allowed.

Return to the wooden bridge (02) *and reset your odometer.* Turn left and proceed 0.1 miles to a 4-way intersection then go straight. Road is not maintained from this point. New logging roads may cut across the main road at any time so be careful to stay on the original road. Bear right at 4.5 miles then left at 9.4 and 12.0. Four Corners is reached at 19.3 miles (03). Turn left to reach Sinkyone Wilderness State Park (fee area) in 3.5 miles. The road continues another 2.5 miles to Bear Harbor Hiking Trail. This last section is a narrow, scenic road and is the best part of trip. During bad weather or times of heavy use, a gate may block entry to this area.

Return to Four Corners, reset your odometer and turn left. At 1.0 miles continue straight past tiny Whale Gulch School. Bear left at 1.7 miles. Watch for mailboxes that mark many private roads that branch off. The road becomes paved at 4.2 miles before passing two developed campgrounds. Turn left when you reach paved Briceland Shelter Cove Road at 6.6 miles. Turn right onto Kings Peak Road at 7.0 miles (04).

Reset your odometer and head north. Bear right uphill at 2.1 miles where West Rancho Lane goes left. Continue straight at 3.6 miles. Continue straight again at 6.3 where Saddle Mountain Road goes left, then bear left at Horse Mountain Recreation Site at 6.4 miles. Stay right downhill at 9.4 where King Range Road joins on left. Drop into a valley and cross a bridge. Stay left at 12.4 and join paved Wilder Ridge Road. Pass Smith Etter Road at 18.7 miles and Honeydew Creek Recreation Site at 19.2 miles. At 20.2 miles, stay right over a steel bridge past the little burg of Honeydew. Follow this paved road through Humboldt Redwoods State Park to Avenue of the Giants reached at 42.7 miles (05).

Return Trip: Take Avenue of the Giants north to an exit just south of Redcrest where you can get on Hwy. 101 going either direction. Or head south on Avenue of the Giants and rejoin Hwy. 101 at various points.

Services: Gas up at the Peg House about 2 miles north of the intersection of Highways 1 and 101. Gas also available at Garberville, Redcrest, Honeydew and Shelter Cove. Full services in Eureka, Fortuna and Garberville. Most developed campgrounds along route have primitive toilets.

Historical Highlights: Usal Beach was once a bustling mill town and logging port. When the tide is low, wharf pilings of an 1890s pier can still be seen extending from the beach. Harvesting of giant redwoods was a major business in those days but ended after World War II when the largest redwoods were finally gone. U.S.A.L. is an acronym for USA Lumber, a company that logged the area for many years. As you drive along the road, watch for larger redwood stumps left from virgin timber cuttings. The stumps dwarf third generation redwoods that are still being logged today. Before Highway 101 was built in the 1920s, Usal Road served as a major stage route between Eureka and San Francisco. Plans originally called for Highway 1 to continue along the coast, but rugged terrain forced the Highway to turn east and connect with Highway 101. For this reason, the area became known as the Lost Coast. Only the southern, most remote portion of the Lost Coast is described here.

Maps: King Range National Conservation Area map, USGS 250,000-scale map, Ukiah and Eureka, CA, DeLorme Atlas & Gazetteer, Benchmark Road and Recreation Atlas.

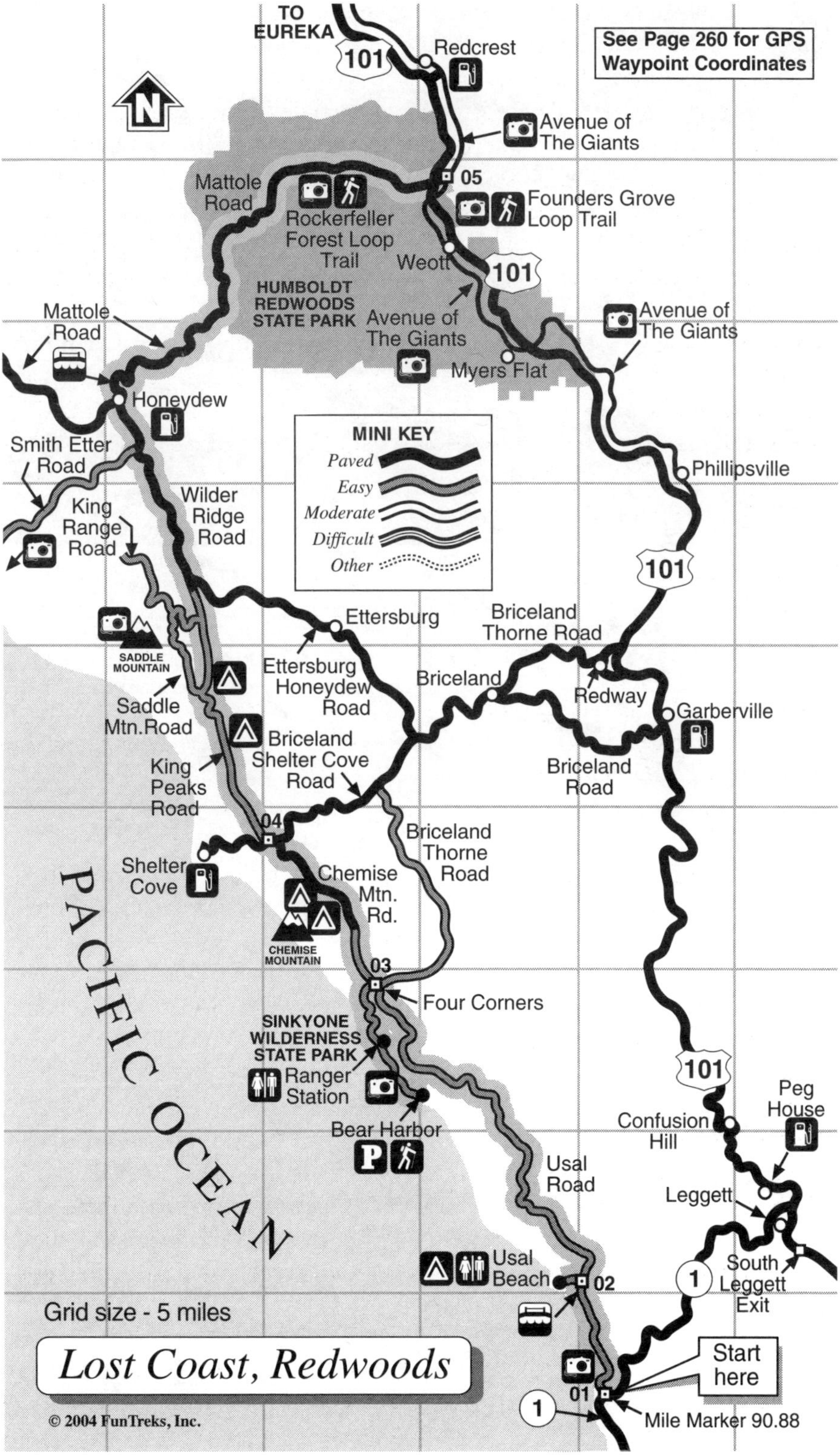

Lost Coast, Redwoods

Hills are steep and loose.　　Scenic high point. Clear Lake can be seen in distance.

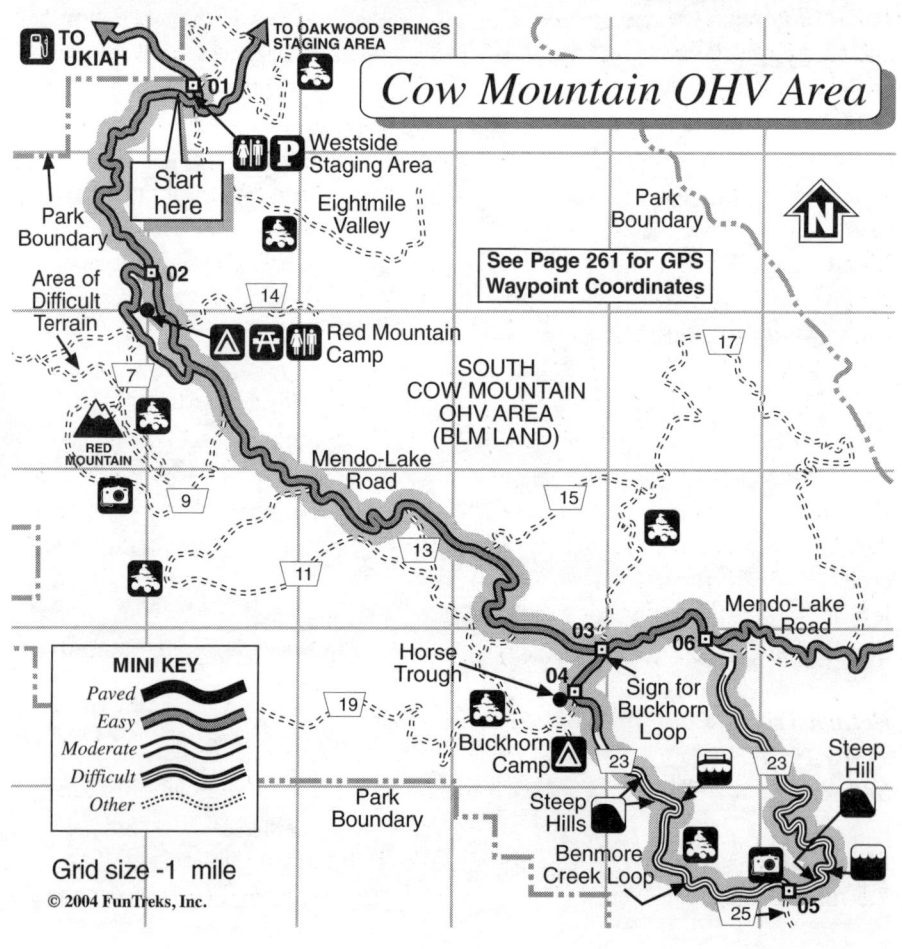

Cow Mountain OHV Area

TO UKIAH

TO OAKWOOD SPRINGS STAGING AREA

Westside Staging Area

Start here

Eightmile Valley

Park Boundary

Park Boundary

See Page 261 for GPS Waypoint Coordinates

Area of Difficult Terrain

Red Mountain Camp

SOUTH COW MOUNTAIN OHV AREA (BLM LAND)

RED MOUNTAIN

Mendo-Lake Road

Mendo-Lake Road

Horse Trough

Sign for Buckhorn Loop

Buckhorn Camp

Steep Hills

Steep Hill

Park Boundary

Benmore Creek Loop

MINI KEY
Paved
Easy
Moderate
Difficult
Other

Grid size -1 mile

© 2004 FunTreks, Inc.

44

Cow Mountain OHV Area ◆5

Location: North of Santa Rosa, east of Ukiah and west of Clear Lake.

Difficulty: Difficult. Steep, narrow climbs and descents through tight brush. Rutted and washed out in places with occasional rock obstacles.

Features: South portion of the park allows 4WD and green sticker vehicles. This area covers 52,000 scenic acres with elevations between 800 and 4,000 feet. Only Benmore Creek Loop Trail is described here. Camp at Red Mtn. CG inside park. Open all year except during rainy periods. No fees.

Time & Distance: Benmore Loop measures 5.5 miles and is 8.0 miles from the Westside Staging Area. Allow about 3 hours. Explore many other trails.

To Get There: At Ukiah, get off Hwy. 101 at Talmage Rd. Go east 1.5 miles and turn right on East Side Road. Make a left on Mill Creek Road in another 0.3 miles. Follow signs to South Cow Mountain, reached in another 5.8 miles. As you enter park, turn right into the Westside Staging Area.

Trail Description: Reset your odometer at staging area (01). Bear right out of the staging area heading south. Turn right within 0.1 miles on wide Mendo-Lake Road. Continue straight at 2.3 miles (02). Right takes you to Red Mountain Campground with picnic tables and toilet. West, beyond the campground is a complex network of fun trails and challenging rock obstacles. Go straight again at 2.9 past the south entrance to Red Mtn. C.G. Stay left at 5.3 miles. At 7.6 miles (03) turn right at a sign for Buckhorn Loop. Turn left at 8.0 miles (04) on marked Trail #23 (Benmore Creek Loop).

Reset your odometer. Head southeast as the trail gets more difficult. Bear left at 1.1 and cross bridge. Climb a steep section at 1.4 and descend at 2.4. Bear left at 2.8 miles (05). Another steep spot at 3.0 bottoms out at a creek. Make a sharp left uphill at 4.1. Bear right at 4.2, 4.3 and 5.3. Bear left at 5.4 and 5.5 miles (06). You should now be back on Mendo-Lake Road. Stay left at 6.4 and you'll see sign for Buckhorn Loop where you started (03).

Return Trip: Return the way you came.

Services: Full services in Ukiah. Vault toilets at staging and camping areas.

Maps: BLM Map of Cow Mountain available free at staging area, USGS 7.5 minute map, Purdys Gardens, CA, DeLorme Atlas and Gazetteer.

AREA 2

Red Bluff, Grass Valley, Downieville, Gold Lake

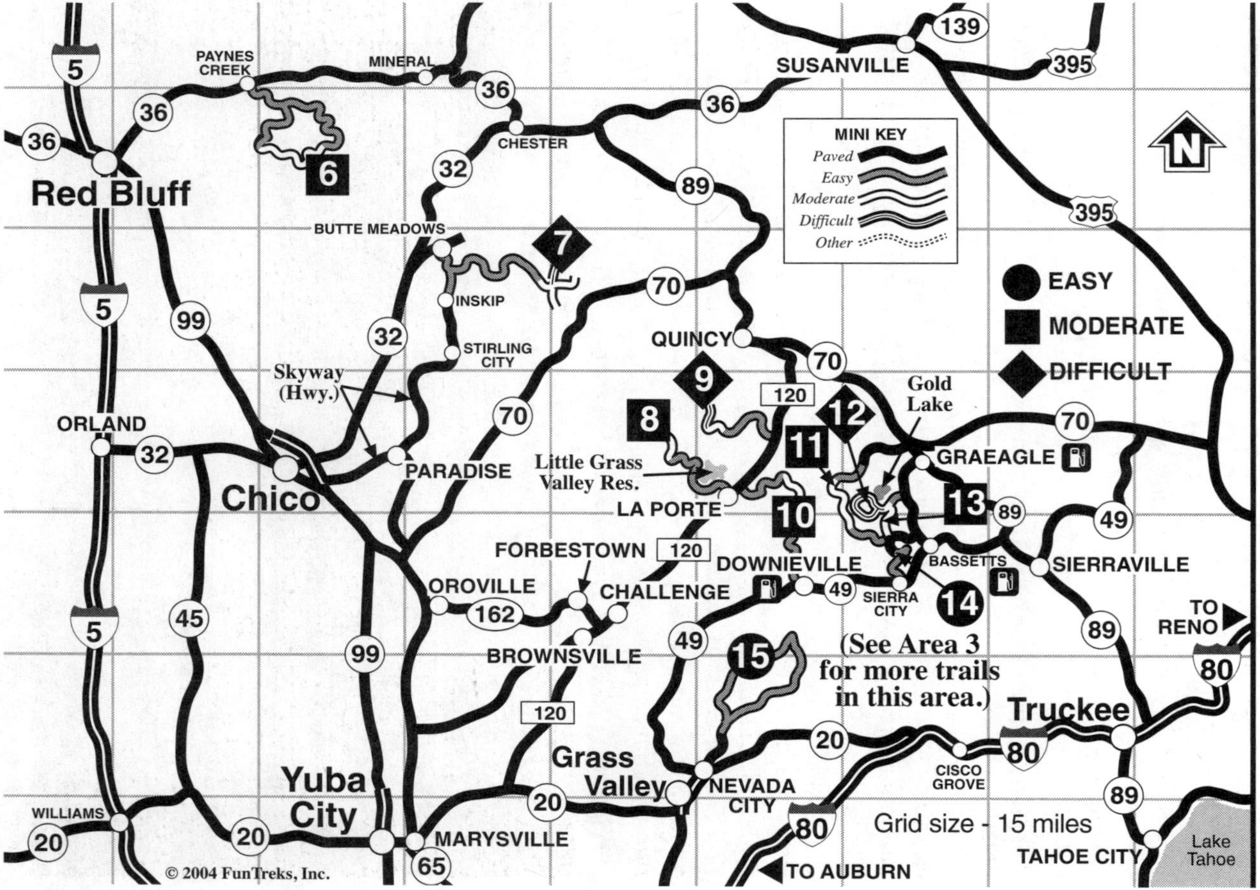

6. Peligreen Jeepway
7. High Lakes
8. Stag Point
9. Cleghorn Bar
10. Poker Flat
11. Gold Valley
12. Snake Lake
13. Deer Lake
14. Sierra Buttes
15. Tyler-Foote Crossing

AREA 2
Red Bluff, Grass Valley Downieville, Gold Lake

The best trails in Area 2 are near Gold Lake, located inside the Lakes Basin Recreation Area. Nowhere in California is this kind of beauty combined with such exhilarating drives. The best way to Gold Lake departs north from Sierra City via the *Sierra Buttes Trail*. Outstanding views unfold below as you climb this narrow, winding (but easy) road to a most unusual lookout tower. From there, hook up with *Deer Lake Trail* to Gold Lake or connect to the longer and more challenging *Gold Valley Trail,* which eventually passes through Plumas-Eureka State Park featuring an outstanding museum and ghost town site. Hardcore enthusiasts will love a rocky, clifflike descent on *Snake Lake Trail* directly southwest of Gold Lake.

North of Downieville, descend to remote and historic *Poker Flat*. Here, you'll find an OHV campground, remains of old buildings and curious mining shacks sometimes occupied by modern-day prospectors. The *Poker Flat Trail* also serves as a shortcut to La Porte and popular Little Grass Valley Reservoir. Outstanding trails nearby include *Stag Point* and *Cleghorn Bar,* which features twisting descents to remote fishing points along the "designated wild and scenic" Feather River.

Author checks conditions before descending to *Deer Lake (Trail #13)*.

Moderate terrain begins after this sign.  Manuever around fallen trees.

Much of the trail follows ridges along the Ishi Wilderness northern boundary.

Turn right here.  Reinforced crossing at Antelope Creek.

Peligreen Jeepway 6

Location: East of Red Bluff, southeast of Paynes Creek.

Difficulty: Moderate. After a well-graded forest road, the trail narrows to a rough, one-lane path over hilly, remote terrain. Portions of the route are rocky and bone jarring. Other portions can be slick and muddy if wet. Steep in places with loose rock, but there are no difficult obstacles. The first part of Jeepway passes through a burned out area where fallen trees have blocked the route in several places. Bypasses have formed but they are faint and route finding can be challenging at times. Tight brush in places may scratch vehicle. Suitable for any seasoned, high-clearance 4-wheel-drive SUV. The trail sees little use, so don't count on help from passersby. Best driven in spring and fall. Dangerously hot in summer. Closed in winter.

Features: A long winding drive over a series of rugged volcanic ridges. Some drivers will find the area starkly beautiful; others, harsh and desolate. The route passes through the Tehama State Wildlife Area which is closed December through March. It is also closed the last week in October for hunting season when a permit is required. For exact closure dates, see appendix for phone number of wildlife area. Green-sticker vehicles must stay on established roads inside the wildlife area.

Time & Distance: The entire unpaved loop measures 36 miles, of which 24 miles are easy forest roads. Allow a full day.

To Get There: From Highways 99 and 36 east of Red Bluff, take Highway 36 east in the direction of Lassen Volcanic National Park. After 20 miles, turn right on Paynes Creek Loop at mile marker 64. Go 0.4 miles and turn right on Plum Creek Road just after Paynes Creek Store. Follow paved road 8.3 miles to Ponderosa Way (F.S. Road 28N29, also County Road 707B).

Trail Description: Reset your odometer and turn right on Ponderosa Way (01). Stay on this wide gravel road as it winds south through scenic forest. Cross a wooden bridge at 9.6 miles. Stay on the main road as it curves slightly to the right at 11.7 miles where F.S. 28N29F crosses. Turn right at 12.6 miles (02) at a sign for Peligreen Jeep Trail marked as F.S. 28N57.

Reset you odometer as you turn right. Bear left at 0.7 miles then at 1.4 miles (03), turn right at another sign for the Peligreen Jeep Trail (top photo opposite page). This route drops downhill into a fire-damaged canyon where many dead trees have fallen across the trail. (If you wish to avoid this part of the route, you can continue straight on a longer but easier loop around the canyon. See map.) The first blockage of the trail is at 1.8 miles. Detour around on the left side and rejoin the trail within 0.1 miles, then bear left downhill. Weave your way around other smaller blockages as the trail gradually swings right downhill. You reach bottom at 2.2 and begin to climb as the trail becomes more defined. A road goes right at 2.8 miles but don't turn yet. Continue just a bit farther to 2.9 miles (04) where you'll see a large sign for Rancheria Hiking Trail straight ahead.

Reset your odometer and turn right at above sign (04). Weave around some big trees as the trail follows along a fence bordering the Ishi Wilderness. Stay left around a large log blocking the trail at 0.4 miles (05). This is the site of Peligreen Place but nothing remains. The road weaves uphill within sight of the wilderness boundary. Turn left at 1.3 miles where a faint trail goes right uphill along Indian Ridge. Pass through a fence opening at 1.5 miles. More fence openings will follow. Make a steep, rocky climb at 2.8 miles. Weave uphill through Black Oak Grove Campground at 3.2 miles. Not much here except a few fire rings and shade. There's a sign here for Kingsley Cove and Table Mountain Hiking Trails that go south into the wilderness. An important fork is reached at 4.7 miles (06). Turn right following a sign to Grapevine Jeepway. There's a wild horse corral just down the hill but it's hard to see.

Reset your odometer as you turn right (06). The road gets a little rougher with tighter brush. A cattle guard marks the boundary to the Tehama State Wildlife Area (closed in winter) at 2.9 miles. The 4-wheel-drive road ends at 4.4 miles (07), where you'll make a sharp right turn onto Ishi Road. This wide gravel road drops downhill and crosses Antelope Creek at a reinforced crossing. It soon passes Fischer Campground and climbs out of the canyon. Ishi Road ends at a gated parking area with information board at 11.2 miles (08). Turn right on Hogsback Road, 28N24. Turn left at 13.1 miles (09) on a shortcut route (High Trestle Road) back to paved Plum Creek Road at 15.8 miles (10). Left on Plum Creek takes you back to Highway 36.

Return Trip: Left on Hwy. 36 takes you back to Red Bluff. If you are heading to Lassen Volcanic National Park, don't take the shortcut at High Trestle Road. Follow Hogsback Rd. east to Plum Creek then turn right for Hwy. 36.

Services: Pit toilets at Fischer Campground. Full services in Red Bluff.

Historical Highlights: There is no longer a Ranger Station at Panther Spring. The burn area you pass through was part of the Campbell Fire that occurred in 1990. It destroyed 90 percent of the Ishi Wilderness.

Maps: Lassen National Forest, USGS 100,000 scale map, Lake Almanor, CA, Tehama Wildlife Area Map, DeLorme Atlas and Gazetteer.

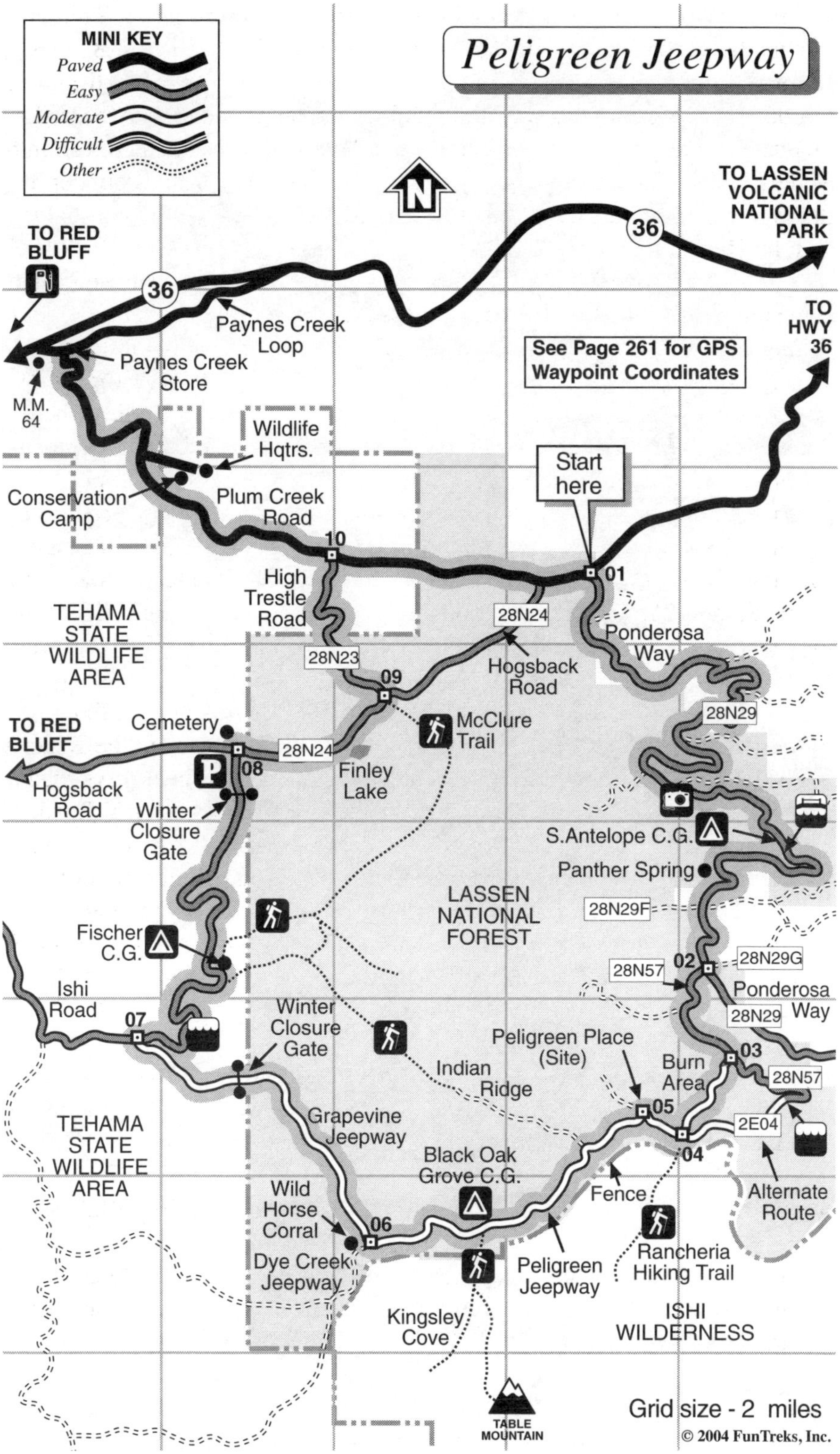
MINI KEY
Paved
Easy
Moderate
Difficult
Other
Peligreen Jeepway
TO LASSEN VOLCANIC NATIONAL PARK
36
TO RED BLUFF
36
Paynes Creek Loop
Paynes Creek Store
M.M. 64
TO HWY 36
See Page 261 for GPS Waypoint Coordinates
Wildlife Hqtrs.
Conservation Camp
Plum Creek Road
Start here
10
01
High Trestle Road
28N24
Ponderosa Way
TEHAMA STATE WILDLIFE AREA
28N23
09
Hogsback Road
28N29
TO RED BLUFF
Cemetery
McClure Trail
28N24
08
Finley Lake
Hogsback Road
Winter Closure Gate
S.Antelope C.G.
Panther Spring
LASSEN NATIONAL FOREST
28N29F
Fischer C.G.
28N57
02
28N29G
Ishi Road
Ponderosa Way
28N29
07
Winter Closure Gate
Peligreen Place (Site)
Burn Area
03
Indian Ridge
28N57
05
2E04
04
Grapevine Jeepway
TEHAMA STATE WILDLIFE AREA
Black Oak Grove C.G.
Fence
Alternate Route
Wild Horse Corral
06
Rancheria Hiking Trail
Dye Creek Jeepway
Peligreen Jeepway
ISHI WILDERNESS
Kingsley Cove
TABLE MOUNTAIN
Grid size - 2 miles
© 2004 FunTreks, Inc.

The very first obstacle has a bypass.    Campbell Lake and Long Lake.

Great camp spot near dam on south end of Long Lake.

Extreme obstacle at Morris Lake.    Tight trees on route to Ben Lomond Mountain.

High Lakes 7

Location: Northeast of Chico and Paradise.

Difficulty: Difficult. Trails are moderately rocky with interspersed difficult sections. A skilled driver can get a high-clearance, stock SUV through most of it but minor body damage should be a consideration. It also helps that several early obstacles have bypasses. Those looking for extreme rock challenges should head to Morris Lake. The last half mile of this route is very difficult. I elected to walk this section despite having ample body armor, 33-inch tires and air lockers.

Features: Spend a weekend exploring this gorgeous high plateau featuring numerous glacier-carved lakes. Camp, fish and relax in remote seclusion after a day of challenging rock crawling. Great routes for ATVs and dirt bikes but stay on existing trails and leave the area as you find it.

Time & Distance: The route, as described here, is about 30 miles, of which 17.3 miles are easy forest roads. Plan to spend at least a full day in the area.

To Get There: From Chico, take Hwy. 32 north about 27 miles from Hwy. 99. Turn right on paved Humboldt Road just before mile marker 37. Watch for a sign for the Outpost Restaurant at this intersection. Continue another 5.3 miles on Humboldt to Skyway (Road) at Butte Meadows. This intersection is about 0.4 miles after Butte Meadows Campground. Turn right on Skyway following signs to Stirling City.

Trail Description: Reset your odometer as you turn right on Skyway (01). The road is briefly paved before changing to dirt. Bear left uphill as roads branch off to the right. (Watch for fast-moving logging trucks. The crude route numbers you see painted on boards are used by the logging companies. These route numbers will not be used in this description.) Bear left at a major fork at 6.0 miles (02). (Right takes you to Inskip.) After turning left, the road quickly merges with Humbug Summit Road heading northeast. Bear left at 7.2 as a good road joins on the right. Bear right at 7.8 miles (03) on a paved road to Philbrook Lake. The pavement ends after a few miles. Turn left uphill at 10.9 miles on F.S. 25N05. Bear right at 12.8 miles where 25N15 goes left. You'll pass above Philbrook Lake. Stay right on the better road at 14.9 miles. Continue east until you reach a T intersection at 17.3 miles (04). An information board marks this spot.

Reset your odometer and turn right. Bear left within a few hundred feet. You'll cross private property for the next half mile so obey all signs. The road is marked as 6E11. Continue straight at 0.7 and stay right at 0.8. At 1.0 miles (05), make a hard right downhill away from Spring Valley Lake. The first rock challenge is just down the hill. (Stock vehicles can bypass this spot on the right.) The road goes around the south side of the lake. Bear right at 1.5 following a sign that says "Designated Route." Almost immediately, the road forks again. This time stay left. (Road 5E19 goes right here to Bear Lake.) The road gradually gets rockier with tougher spots at 3.2 and 3.3 miles. Stay left at 3.5 miles on 6E11 until reaching the next fork at 3.9 miles (06). From this point, there are three choices:

For Morris Lake, bear left then turn left again in about 200 feet on 6E08. *Reset your odometer.* After 0.3 miles, the road drops over a difficult granite outcropping to an extremely steep section of giant boulders. The lake is reached at 0.7 miles (07).

For Campbell Lake and Long Lake, *reset your odometer* and turn right. Follow the trail downhill as it winds along the western side of both lakes. There are a few moderately rocky spots going downhill, but nothing too tough. You'll find some great camping and fishing spots along the lakes. Bear right at 0.4 and 0.5, then left at 1.0 miles. (Trail 6E14 joins on the right. You can go out this way later.) At 1.1 miles, you can continue south or turn left on a short trail that leads to a nice camping spot by the Long Lake Dam.

For Saddle Lake and Grassy Lake, follow the above directions for Long Lake. *Reset your odometer* at 1.1 miles and continue south. You'll reach a fork at 0.3 miles (08). Saddle Lake is to the left and Grassy Lake to the right. The route to Saddle Lake has a steep set of difficult ledges to get over. Grassy Lake is overgrown but you can continue to explore several trails south of the lake.

Ben Lomond Mountain. I attempted to reach this easternmost point in the High Lakes Area, but the trail was blocked by fallen trees through a fire-damaged area. I did reach a beautiful overlook above Chips Lake after 2.5 miles (09).

Return Trip: Return the way you came, or you can take a more scenic route on the Skyway. Just head south at Waypoint (02) following signs to Inskip and Stirling City. The Skyway continues on to Paradise and Chico.

Services: You can top off your tank at the *Tank House Store*, located just 0.2 miles north of the starting point on Humboldt Road. Full services in Paradise and Chico.

Maps: Lassen National Forest, Off-Highway Vehicle Trails of the Almanor Ranger District, USGS 250,000-scale maps, Susanville and Chico, CA.

High Lakes

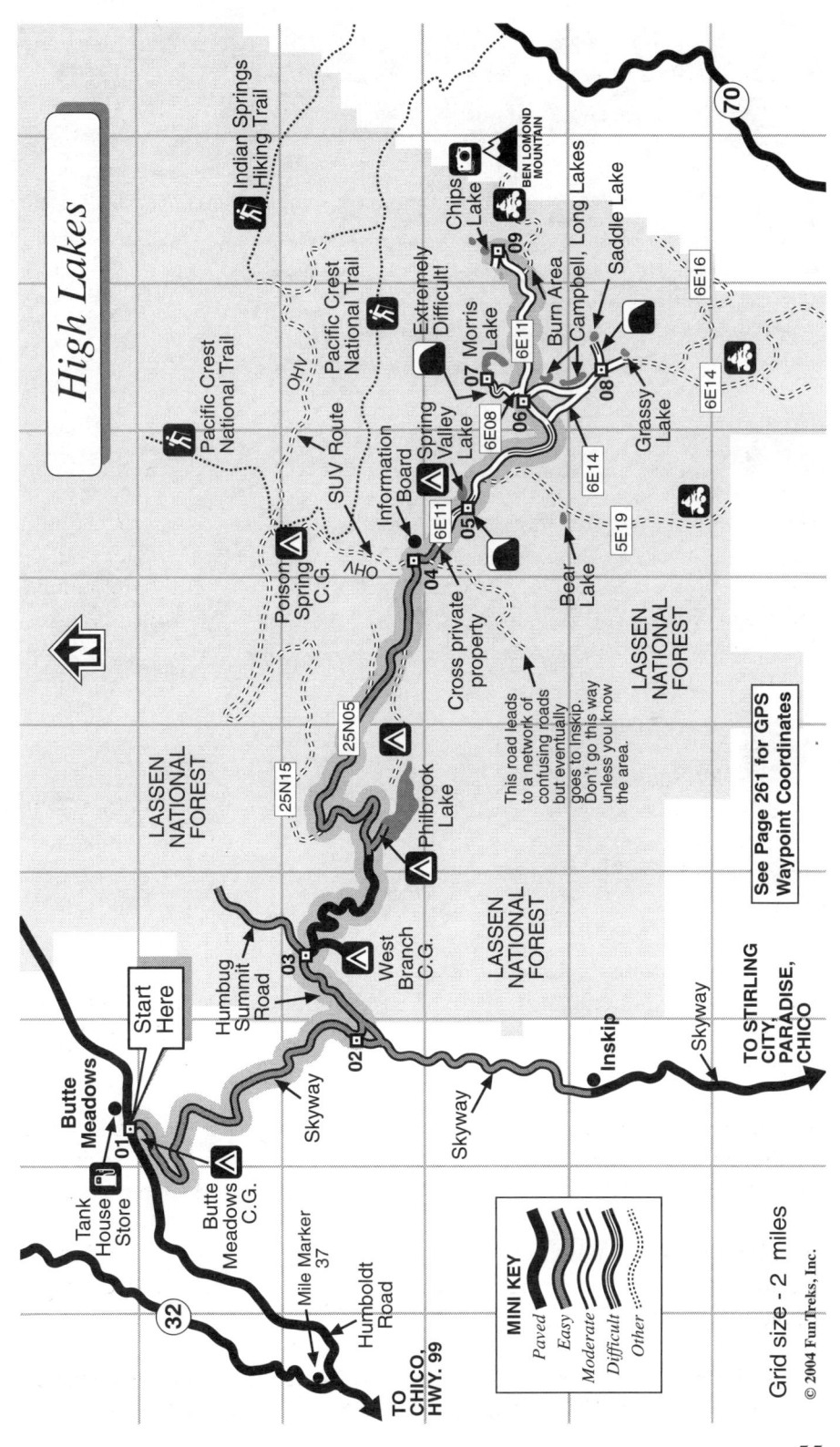

Not much room to pass.

Fishermen enjoy Stag Point OHV Campground.

Middle Fork of Feather River slightly upstream from campground.

Fishing near dam.

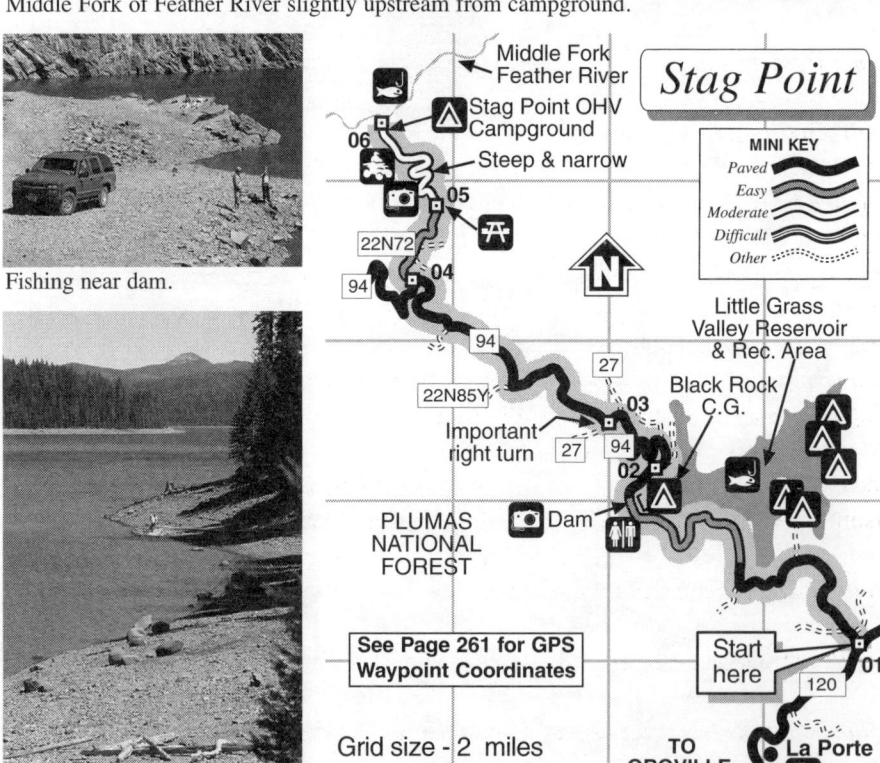

One small part of reservoir.

Stag Point

MINI KEY
- Paved
- Easy
- Moderate
- Difficult
- Other

Middle Fork Feather River
Stag Point OHV Campground
Steep & narrow
22N72
22N85Y
Important right turn
PLUMAS NATIONAL FOREST
Dam
Little Grass Valley Reservoir & Rec. Area
Black Rock C.G.
Start here
To Oroville, Yuba City
La Porte

See Page 261 for GPS Waypoint Coordinates

Grid size - 2 miles

© 2004 FunTreks, Inc.

56

Stag Point 8

Location: Northeast of Yuba City, north of La Porte.

Difficulty: Moderate. Steep, narrow switchbacks that drop 2800 feet in 2.7 miles. Minor ruts and tight brush in places. Could be difficult coming back up if trail is wet. Suitable for all 4-wheel-drive SUVs with low-range gearing when trail is dry. Best time to drive is late spring through fall.

Features: A heart-pumping descent to remote camping and fishing along the banks of the Feather River. One of a few points where river access is allowed in this designated "Wild and Scenic" river valley. Outstanding camping, hiking and boating at Little Grass Valley Recreation Area. (This trail is designated as OHV Route #34 on Plumas N.F. OHV map.)

Time & Distance: The trail itself measures only 2.7 miles; however, it is 15 miles to the trailhead from F.S. Highway 120. Allow 2 hours one-way.

To Get There: Drive 1.5 miles northeast of La Porte on paved F.S. Rd. 120.

Trail Description: Reset your odometer (01) and turn left following signs to Little Grass Valley Reservoir. Meander north, ignoring side roads, and cross dam. Go by the Black Rock C.G. and turn left at 6.1 miles (02) on F.S. 94. (Also note small posts with a number 34. This is the OHV marker for Stag Point.) After uphill switchbacks, turn left at 8.2 miles where F.S. 27 goes right. At 8.3 miles (03), turn right staying on F.S. 94. Stay on this paved road bearing right at 10.9 and 11.7 miles. At 13.5 miles (04), turn right uphill off the pavement onto easy gravel road 22N72. Stay left downhill at 14.3 miles. Stag Point Trailhead is reached at 15.1 miles (05). There's a camp spot with picnic table just before an information board. Proceed north on a narrow, single-lane road. It descends gradually at first, then quickly gets steeper. Watch for wide spots to pull over in case someone comes up the hill. Trail ends at OHV campground at 17.8 miles (06). River is short walk to left. Best fishing is in the fall when water level is lower. Take insect repellent.

Return Trip: Return the way you came.

Services: One gas pump at General Store in La Porte. Vault toilet at dam.

Maps: Plumas National Forest map, Plumas National Forest Summer-Use OHV map, USGS 250,000-scale map, Chico, CA.

Point where trail begins its steep descent.

This stock SUV made it.

One of several tight switchbacks. It gets worse.

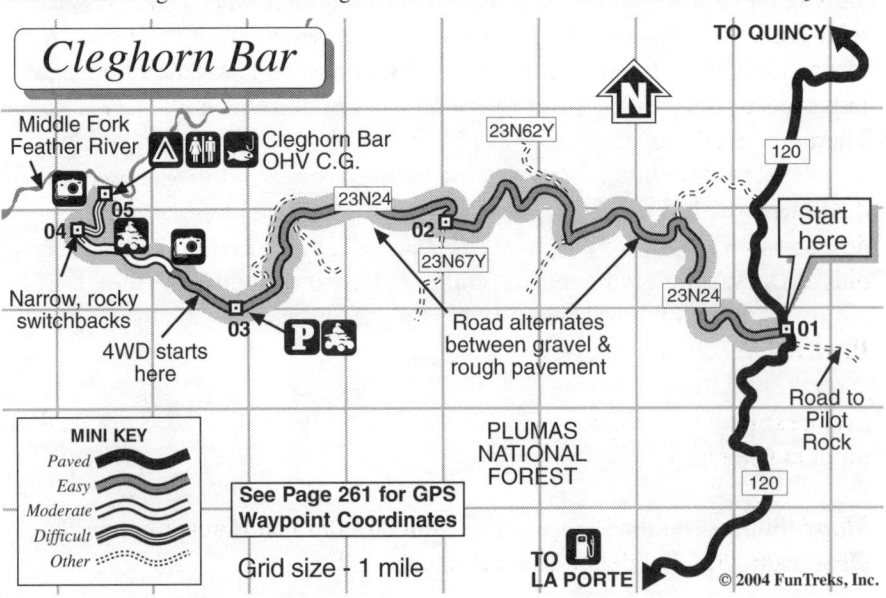

Feather River next to campsite.

Cleghorn Bar

TO QUINCY

Middle Fork Feather River
Cleghorn Bar OHV C.G.
23N62Y
120
23N24
02
23N67Y
Start here
Narrow, rocky switchbacks
04
05
03
4WD starts here
Road alternates between gravel & rough pavement
23N24
01
Road to Pilot Rock

PLUMAS NATIONAL FOREST

MINI KEY
Paved
Easy
Moderate
Difficult
Other

See Page 261 for GPS Waypoint Coordinates

Grid size - 1 mile

TO LA PORTE

120

© 2004 FunTreks, Inc.

Cleghorn Bar 9

Location: Northeast of Yuba City, northeast of La Porte.

Difficulty: Difficult in just one place. Similar to Stag Point Trail #8 except rougher, steeper and narrower towards the bottom. One tight switchback has been chewed up from uphill tire spinning. Stock 4WD SUVs with low-range gearing can make it when trail is dry. Not for novice drivers. Avoid when wet. Best time late spring through fall. Take insect repellent.

Features: A thrilling and scenic descent to the Middle Fork of the Feather River. Great camping and fishing especially in the fall. A designated "Wild & Scenic" area. (Identified as OHV Route #37 on Plumas N. F. OHV map.)

Time & Distance: The 4WD portion of the trail measures 3.3 miles. It is 8.6 miles to trailhead from Hwy. 120. Allow about 2 hours one way.

To Get There: Drive 12.3 miles northeast from La Porte on F.S. Hwy. 120 (La Porte/Quincy Road). Turn left on F.S. Road 23N24 at sign for Cleghorn Bar. This intersection is just after a sign for Pilot Rock.

Trail Description: Reset your odometer and head west on gravel road 23N24 (01). The road is partially paved in places. Bear left at 3.8 miles (note OHV marker #37). Turn right at 5.5 (02). Stay left at 6.4 and 6.6. Road gradually narrows to one lane in places. Bear right at 7.5 miles where lesser road goes left. Stay left at 8.3 as the road narrows. Start of 4WD trail is reached at 8.6 miles (03), identified with sign warning: "Road may be impassable to all vehicles one half mile from bottom due to loose rock." There's a small area to park if you are unloading ATVs or motorcycles.

Reset odometer and start downhill (03). An easy trail goes up and down for a while. There's a dramatic view at 1.3 miles where the trail descends in earnest. Very tight switchbacks at 3.0 miles (04) including the only difficult spot on the trail. Bottom is reached at 3.3 miles (05).

Return Trip: Return the way you came.

Services: One gas pump at General Store in La Porte. Primitive, roofless pit toilet at Cleghorn OHV Campground.

Maps: Plumas National Forest map, Plumas National Forest Summer-Use OHV map, USGS 250,000-scale map, Chico, CA.

Enjoy yourself in Downieville.

View from Saddleback Road on a foggy day.

Lookout is manned.

Crossing Canyon Creek at Poker Flat. Water can be deep.

Potosi Cemetery is an interesting place to look around.

1886 Scott home at Poker Flat.

North side climb is steep.

One of several remaining structures at Howland Flat.

Poker Flat 10

Location: Northeast of Grass Valley between Downieville and La Porte.

Difficulty: Moderate. Most of this route is easy; however, to reach Poker Flat, you must descend into a deep canyon and climb back out the other side. This stretch is steep, narrow and rough. One creek crossing can be deep during periods of heavy rain. Suitable for aggressive stock SUVs.

Features: A fun, challenging drive that passes through two historic 1850 gold mining towns: Poker Flat and Howland Flat. A few interesting structures still remain. If you have time, take the 0.8-mile side trip to manned Saddleback Fire Lookout. Camp at Poker Flat OHV Campground. This trail serves as a shortcut between Downieville and La Porte. Street-legal vehicles only allowed in Poker Flat area.

Time & Distance: It is 29 miles from Downieville to La Porte. Allow 5 to 6 hours. Add another 30 minutes for the side trip to Saddleback Lookout.

To Get There: Take Highway 49 to Downieville and gas up. Then head west 0.3 miles just past the Cannon Monument. Turn right on a graded dirt road. Although not marked at the start, this is Saddleback, County Rd. 509.

Trail Description: Reset your odometer as you turn off Hwy. 49 (01). The road climbs steadily with an occasional private drive branching away. Stay right at 2.0 miles and slightly right at 2.9. A major intersection is reached at 7.8 miles (02). Fir Cap OHV Trail goes hard right back down the mountain and reconnects with Saddleback Road. Left goes back to Hwy. 49 at Cal Ida on better Forest Road 25.

Reset your odometer (02) and follow the road north as it curves to the right. At 0.4 miles, the road to Saddleback Lookout goes right. (Side trip optional.) Continue straight for Poker Flat. At 1.3 miles (03) continue straight at a sign for Chimney Rock. At 2.4 miles, Chimney Rock is to the right. You continue straight until you reach a T intersection at 3.1 miles, where you turn right following a sign to Poker Flat OHV Trail. At 4.2 miles (04), this good road ends at a loop. Poker Flat OHV Trail continues north downhill on a narrow dirt road through the trees.

Reset your odometer and start downhill. Stay right uphill at 0.4 as the road gets more interesting. It undulates up and down then drops down the hill rather steeply. I drove this when it was wet and had no traction problems. Bear left at the bottom of the hill when the road forks at 1.8

miles. This is the roughest part of the trail. Right goes by a miner's shack then reconnects. You reach Canyon Creek at 2.0 miles. Before crossing the creek, walk a short distance left or right to see some interesting miner's shacks. These places are private property and are still being used intermittently, so be careful. Miners may not take kindly to intruders. Keep your distance and don't touch anything.

Check water depth and cross creek if it is safe. Turn right at road on other side and go by the Poker Flat OHV Campground. At 2.1 miles (05), you reach what remains of Poker Flat. A kiosk explains some history. The Scott Home is on its last legs. Don't go inside or touch anything. Take some time to look around the area. There is much to see along Canyon Creek.

Reset your odometer and turn left up the hill (05). The road is steep and rocky with banks on each side. After 2.0 miles the four-wheel-drive portion ends and the road crests over the hill. Bear left at 3.3 miles where a Jeep road goes right. Go by an old mine building, then turn left at a water tank at 3.5 miles (06). Potosi Cemetery is on the left. After that, you go through Howland Flat with several interesting old buildings. Bear right at a major fork at 8.4 miles (07) onto St. Louis Road. The road winds through a pretty area and crosses a new bridge next to historic St. Louis Bridge. Paved La Porte Road (F.S. 120) is reached at 13.7 miles (08).

Return Trip: The town of La Porte is about one mile to the left. Quincy is 34 miles to the right. If you stay on F.S. 120 to the left, it continues southwest and eventually connects to Highway 20. From there, right goes to Yuba City and left goes to Grass Valley.

Services: When I was in La Porte, a single gas pump was being installed at the General Store. La Porte also had a bar and a place to eat. Full services in Downieville, a great little tourist town.

Historic Highlights: Like so many mining towns, Poker Flat was born during the gold rush of the 1850s. Back then, $700,000 in gold was produced every month. At its peak, nearly 2,000 people occupied the town and surrounding area. Structures included several hotels and saloons, a masonic hall and a school. Hydraulic mining was the main method of gold extraction well into the 1880s. Some mining continued in the early 1900s. Recreational prospecting is still going on today. Poker Flat developed its notoriety largely from a fictional tale by Bret Harte entitled, "Outcasts of Poker Flat."

Howland Flat was part of an important placer mining district. The town's total output was estimated at $14 million.

Maps: Plumas or Tahoe National Forest map, Plumas National Forest Summer-Use OHV map, USGS 100,000-scale map, Portola, CA.

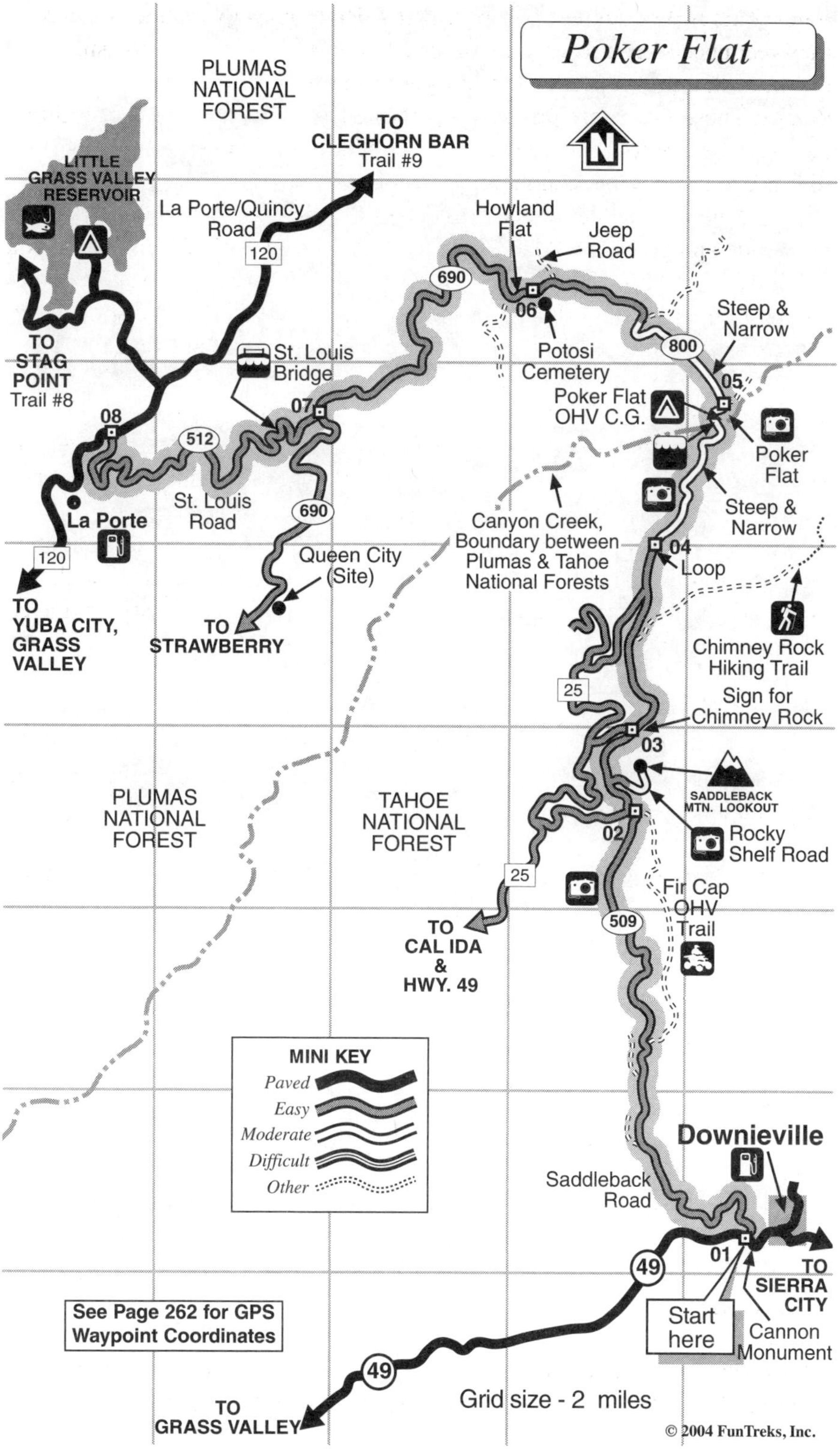

Poker Flat
N
PLUMAS
NATIONAL
FOREST
TO
CLEGHORN BAR
Trail #9
LITTLE
GRASS VALLEY
RESERVOIR
La Porte/Quincy
Road
120
Howland
Flat
Jeep
Road
690
06
TO
STAG
POINT
Trail #8
St. Louis
Bridge
Potosi
Cemetery
Steep &
Narrow
800
05
Poker Flat
OHV C.G.
07
08
512
Poker
Flat
Steep &
Narrow
St. Louis
Road
690
La Porte
Canyon Creek,
Boundary between
Plumas & Tahoe
National Forests
04
Loop
120
Queen City
(Site)
TO
YUBA CITY,
GRASS
VALLEY
TO
STRAWBERRY
Chimney Rock
Hiking Trail
25
Sign for
Chimney Rock
03
SADDLEBACK
MTN. LOOKOUT
PLUMAS
NATIONAL
FOREST
TAHOE
NATIONAL
FOREST
02
Rocky
Shelf Road
25
Fir Cap
OHV
Trail
509
TO
CAL IDA
&
HWY. 49
MINI KEY
Paved
Easy
Moderate
Difficult
Other
Downieville
Saddleback
Road
01
49
TO
SIERRA
CITY
See Page 262 for GPS
Waypoint Coordinates
Start
here
Cannon
Monument
49
TO
GRASS VALLEY
Grid size - 2 miles
© 2004 FunTreks, Inc.

This SUV was having no problems with the trail. One of several shallow creek crossings.

ATV rider pulls over to let larger vehicles pass.

Watch for mountain bikers.

Rusty boiler at Four Hills Mine.

Steep and rocky in places.

Here, road is also Pacific Crest Hiking Trail.

Gold Valley 11

Location: Northeast of Auburn and Grass Valley, northwest of Truckee, between Bassetts and Graeagle. In the Lakes Basin Recreation Area.

Difficulty: Moderate. Much of this route is easy but there are several miles of very rocky terrain. Stock SUVs can get through, but they'll need low-range gearing, high clearance and skid plates. Tight brush in places. Best driven late spring through fall.

Features: A long and challenging route passing through remote areas of the Lakes Basin Recreation Area. You'll begin in the heart of this recreational paradise where beautiful lakes, improved campgrounds and great hiking trails are everywhere. Go by massive Four Hills Mine with old rusty mining equipment and many open mine shafts. The trail then heads north along a scenic ridge that shares a route with the Pacific Crest National Scenic (Hiking) Trail. The last part of trip goes through Plumas-Eureka State Park with a terrific indoor/outdoor mining museum and ghost town site. (Small fee charged.)

Time & Distance: The non-paved portion of this route is 18.6 miles. About half of this is slow-going terrain. Add about 30 miles of paved road to complete the loop. Allow 4 to 5 hours driving time. The day will be gone before you know it, so start early.

To Get There: From Auburn and Grass Valley, take Hwy. 49 north and east past Downieville and on to tiny Bassetts. From Truckee, take Hwy. 89 north to 49 then go west to Bassetts. From Bassetts Station, take Gold Lake Highway west then north about a mile and a half. Turn left over a bridge following signs to Sardine Lake. After 0.2 miles turn right towards Packer Lake. Go another 2.7 miles and turn left. Climb uphill until you reach Packer Saddle at the top of a ridge in another 1.6 miles. You'll continue straight on a gravel road for Gold Valley Trail. Deer Lake Trail is to the right and Sierra Buttes Lookout is left on the paved road.

Trail Description: Reset your odometer at Packer Saddle (01). Continue straight (west) on a good gravel road. Ignore lesser side roads. Bear right downhill at 0.6 miles and left downhill at 1.3. Make a right turn at 1.5 miles (02) on wider gravel road 93-3. It goes west for a while then curves north. At 3.7 miles (03) turn left onto Rd. 93-3-7. This road drops downhill, crosses a small creek and gets rockier. Continue straight at 5.3 miles (04) where a trail

65

goes left to Smith Lake. A sign here indicates you are on Gold Valley OHV Trail. Continue north. Stay right at 5.5 miles. Continue straight at 6.1 and cross a small stream. The trail gets rockier. A few places will require careful tire placement to avoid body damage. Stay left at 7.6 miles (05). Right connects to difficult Snake Lake Trail #12. There's a small loop here where several roads converge. After you turn left, quickly turn left again.

The road remains rocky a bit farther. You'll go by an entrance to a youth camp near Hawley Lake at 8.4 miles. A surprisingly steep, rocky hill follows. Stay right at 9.3 then turn right again at 9.6. This takes you up and around the Four Hills Mine. As you climb the hill, look for mine shafts and a few pieces of mining equipment. You may want to stop and walk around the area. There is a lot to see if you take some time. Watch the kids carefully and stay out of mine shafts. Make a hard left at 9.8 miles and you'll leave the mine area.

The road improves as you begin to climb a broad open ridge. If you stop at 10.7 miles (06), and walk a short distance to the right, there's a great vista with several lakes below. Continuing on the trail from this point, you may share the road with hikers using the Pacific Crest National Scenic Trail. This ridge is also the dividing line between the Tahoe National Forest on the left and the Plumas National Forest on the right. Make sure you have a camera for this area. At 13.1 miles (07), you reach a T intersection called the A-Tree.

Reset your odometer and turn right on a good gravel road. Bear right at another T intersection at 2.1 miles following signs to Johnsville. Pass Ross Campground, then go straight at a 4-way intersection at 5.5 miles. The road is now paved. At 6.7 miles, you go by the Plumas-Eureka State Park Museum and Park Headquarters. It is definitely worth a stop. Bear right on a major paved road immediately after the museum. This road heads northeast past Mohawk then swings southeast towards Graeagle, reached at 12.9 miles (08).

Return Trip: Right on Hwy. 89 at Graeagle takes you back to Truckee. To get back to Bassetts, turn right off Hwy. 89 at Gold Lake Highway 1.7 miles southeast of Graeagle. This road takes you south to Bassetts in about 16 miles. Remember to turn right at the bridge 1.5 miles before Bassetts if you are camped in the Sardine Lake/Packer Lake area.

Services: Gas and a restaurant at Bassetts Station. Several gas stations and other services in Graeagle. Vault toilets at many F.S. Campgrounds at the beginning and end of this route.

Maps: Lakes Basin Recreation Area map, Tahoe or Plumas National Forest maps, Plumas-Eureka State Park map, USGS 100,000-scale map, Portola, CA.

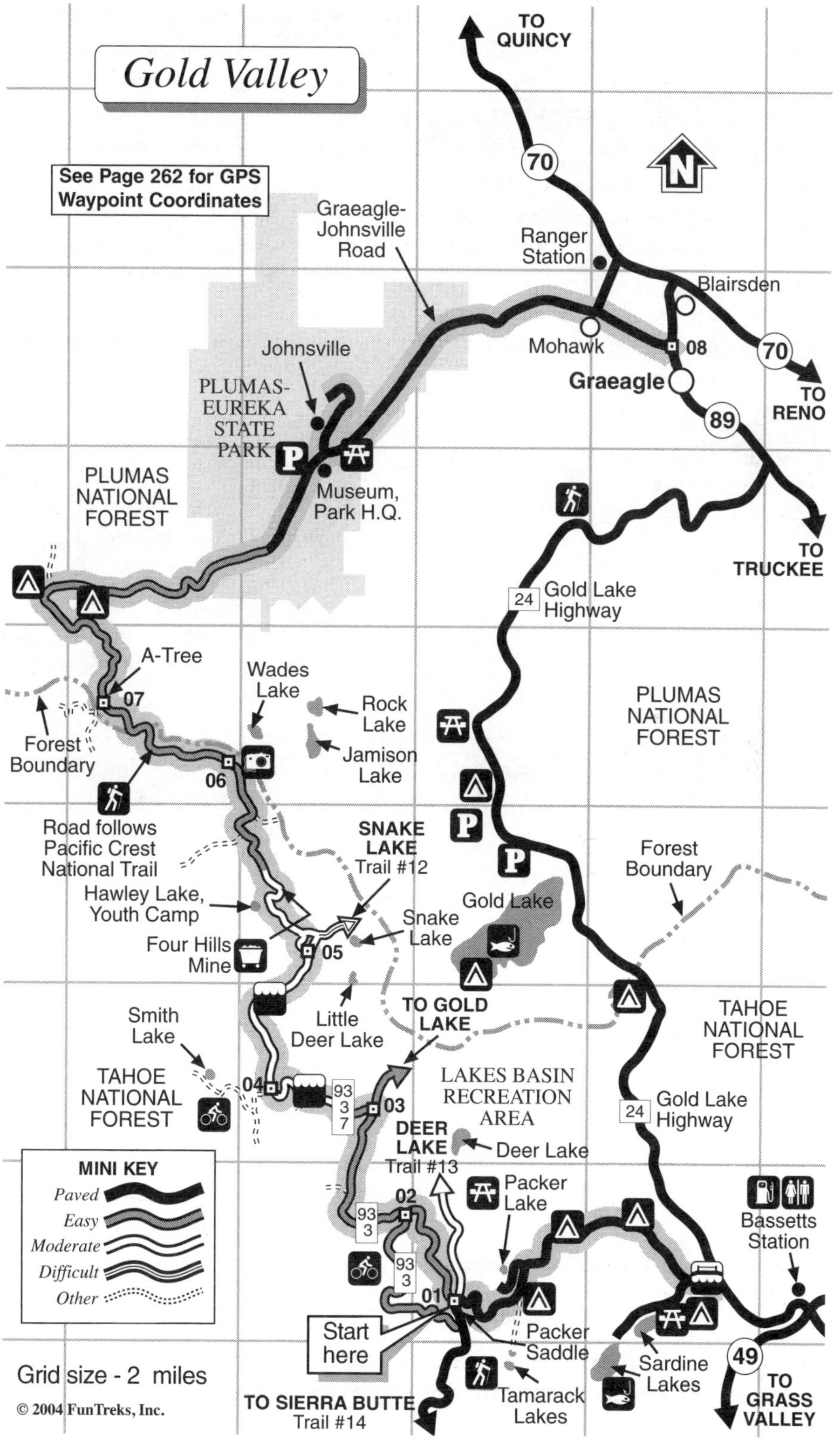
Gold Valley
See Page 262 for GPS Waypoint Coordinates
TO QUINCY
70
Graeagle-Johnsville Road
Ranger Station
Blairsden
Mohawk
08
70
Graeagle
89
TO RENO
Johnsville
PLUMAS-EUREKA STATE PARK
Museum, Park H.Q.
PLUMAS NATIONAL FOREST
TO TRUCKEE
24
Gold Lake Highway
A-Tree
07
Wades Lake
Rock Lake
Jamison Lake
Forest Boundary
06
PLUMAS NATIONAL FOREST
Road follows Pacific Crest National Trail
SNAKE LAKE Trail #12
Forest Boundary
Hawley Lake, Youth Camp
Gold Lake
Snake Lake
Four Hills Mine
05
Little Deer Lake
TO GOLD LAKE
TAHOE NATIONAL FOREST
Smith Lake
LAKES BASIN RECREATION AREA
TAHOE NATIONAL FOREST
04
93 3 7
03
DEER LAKE Trail #13
Deer Lake
24
Gold Lake Highway
MINI KEY
Paved
Easy
Moderate
Difficult
Other
Packer Lake
02
93 3
93 3
Bassetts Station
01
Start here
Packer Saddle
Sardine Lakes
49
TO GRASS VALLEY
Grid size - 2 miles
© 2004 FunTreks, Inc.
TO SIERRA BUTTE Trail #14
Tamarack Lakes

The trail climbs high above Gold Lake.

Responsible four wheelers in action!

Snake Lake where steep descent begins.

Taking a break near Little Deer Lake.

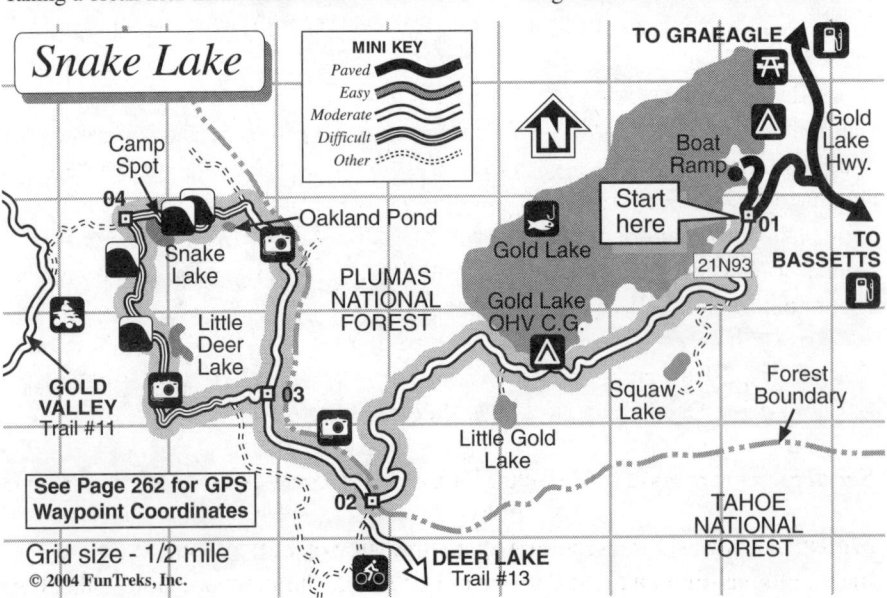

Tough section above Snake Lake.

Snake Lake

MINI KEY
- Paved
- Easy
- Moderate
- Difficult
- Other

TO GRAEAGLE

Camp Spot
04
Oakland Pond
Snake Lake
Little Deer Lake
GOLD VALLEY Trail #11
03
PLUMAS NATIONAL FOREST
Gold Lake
Gold Lake OHV C.G.
Boat Ramp
Start here
01
21N93
Gold Lake Hwy.
TO BASSETTS
Squaw Lake
Little Gold Lake
Forest Boundary
TAHOE NATIONAL FOREST
02
DEER LAKE Trail #13

See Page 262 for GPS Waypoint Coordinates

Grid size - 1/2 mile
© 2004 FunTreks, Inc.

68

Snake Lake 12

Location: Northeast of Auburn and Grass Valley, northwest of Truckee between Bassetts and Graeagle. In the Lakes Basin Recreation Area.

Difficulty: Difficult. Very rocky and extremely steep above Snake Lake. Driven uphill, this point requires lockers front and rear and very low gears. Trail is not suitable for stock SUVs.

Features: Relatively short but obstacles and views are memorable. ATVs and dirt bikes are not allowed between Summit Lake and Oakland Pond.

Time & Distance: An out-and-back trail with a loop at the end. As described here, the trail measures 9.6 miles. Allow 3 to 4 hours. This route also connects to Gold Valley Trail #11 and Deer Lake Trail #13 (see map).

To Get There: Use same directions as Gold Valley Trail #11, but instead of turning at the bridge to Sardine Lake (1.5 miles north of Bassetts), continue north on Gold Lake Highway another 5.0 miles to Gold Lake boat ramp entrance. Turn left and follow paved road 0.4 miles to start of trail on left.

Trail Description: Reset your odometer at start (01). Head south on a rocky road. Stay right at 0.4 miles at sign to Squaw Lake. Continue around the southern end of Gold Lake, passing OHV Campground. Go straight at 1.5 past Little Gold Lake. The trail turns south away from Gold Lake at 1.6. Stay left at 2.2 and right uphill at 2.6. Bear right at 2.8 miles (02) at OHV sign. (Walk right to great views of Gold Lake at 3.1 miles.) Go straight at 3.5 miles (03) where loop starts. Bear left at 4.0 and soon you will see Oakland Pond below. At 4.4 the trail heads downhill to Snake Lake over the toughest obstacle. Be very careful. You'll reach a nice camp spot on left when you reach bottom. Bear right and go around lake. Turn left at 5.1 miles (04). (Straight connects to Gold Valley Trail #11.) More rock challenges follow as you climb around Little Deer Lake. Bear left at 6.6 and reconnect to start of loop at 6.8 miles (03).

Return Trip: Turn right and go out the way you came in. An alternate way out is to drive Deer Lake Trail #13. (See map at left then turn page.)

Services: Gas & food at Bassetts. Pit toilet at Gold Lake C.G. & boat ramp.

Maps: Lakes Basin Recreation Area map, Tahoe or Plumas National Forest maps, Plumas-Eureka State Park map, USGS 7.5-minute map, Gold Lake, CA.

Above Deer Lake, Sierra Buttes in distance.

Hiker enjoys Pacific Crest Trail.

Southern portion of drive is fairly easy.

Sign at Packer Saddle.

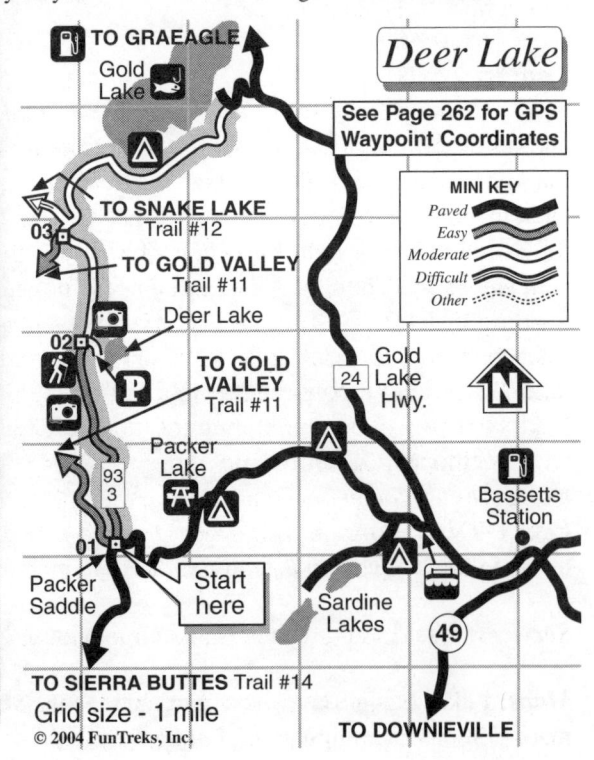

Steep and rocky in places.

Deer Lake

See Page 262 for GPS Waypoint Coordinates

MINI KEY
Paved
Easy
Moderate
Difficult
Other

TO GRAEAGLE
Gold Lake
TO SNAKE LAKE Trail #12
TO GOLD VALLEY Trail #11
Deer Lake
TO GOLD VALLEY Trail #11
Gold Lake Hwy.
Packer Lake
Bassetts Station
Packer Saddle
Start here
Sardine Lakes
TO SIERRA BUTTES Trail #14
TO DOWNIEVILLE

Grid size - 1 mile
© 2004 FunTreks, Inc.

70

Deer Lake 13

Location: Northeast of Auburn and Grass Valley, northwest of Truckee between Bassetts and Graeagle. In the Lakes Basin Recreation Area.

Difficulty: Moderate. A few steep, rough spots but mostly easy. Suitable for stock, high clearance 4-wheel-drive SUVs.

Features: Follows a high ridge across the center of the Lakes Basin Recreation Area. Stunning views of Deer Lake with Sierra Buttes as backdrop. Follows Pacific Crest National Scenic Trail. Fishing at two lakes.

Time & Distance: Only 6.8 miles from Packer Saddle to Gold Lakes Highway. Allow 1 to 2 hours. Add time for optional hike along scenic ridge.

To Get There:
   Starting at south end: Follow directions to Gold Valley Trail #11. When you reach Packer Saddle, turn right.
   Starting at north end. Follow directions to Snake Lake Trail #12. When you reach Waypoint 2 at 2.8 miles, turn left instead of right. Go another 0.1 miles and turn left.

Trail Description:
   Starting at south end. *Reset your odometer* (01) at Packer Saddle and head north on Road 93-3. Bear left at 0.8 miles. At 2.1 miles (02), a spur marked as Deer Lake Trail goes right down the hill. It drops steeply but ends in less than 0.2 miles at a parking area above the lake. Return to the top of hill and turn right following sign for Summit Lake OHV Trail. *Reset your odometer.* The trail winds through the trees over a few rough spots. Turn right at 1.2 miles (03). Follow this road northeast until it reaches Gold Lake at 2.4 miles. Turn right and follow the trail around the south end of lake. When you reach the paved road at 4.0 miles, turn right to reach Gold Lake Highway in another 0.4 miles.
   Starting at north end. After following "To Get There" directions above, *reset odometer* (03) and head up the hill following sign for Summit Lake OHV Trail. At 1.2 miles (02), Deer Lake Trail goes down the hill to the left. Right takes you to Packer Saddle in another 2.1 miles (01).

Services: Gas, food at Bassetts and Graeagle. Vault toilets at campgrounds.

Maps: Lakes Basin Recreation Area map, Tahoe or Plumas National Forest map, USGS 7.5-minute map, Gold Lake, CA.

Starting climb up mountain towards Sierra Buttes, seen on horizon.

Almost at the top of first crest after about 4 miles.

Steep stairs to lookout tower.

Road is closed to vehicles 0.7 miles from top. Note hikers leaving from base of tower.

Sierra Buttes 14

Location: Northeast of Auburn and Grass Valley, directly north of Sierra City. Northwest of Truckee.

Difficulty: Easy. A narrow shelf road that climbs steeply up the mountainside. Minor, loose rocks in a few places and quite steep towards the top. Anyone afraid of heights may be uncomfortable at times. Suitable for all stock, high-clearance 4-wheel-drive SUVs.

Features: Perhaps the most enjoyable easy trail in this book when driven, as described here, from Sierra City. The drive is fun, exhilarating and very beautiful. The view from Sierra Buttes Lookout is dizzying. A steep 3/4-mile hike is required to reach the lookout. Take plenty of water and don't forget your camera and binoculars.

Time & Distance: From Sierra City to the gate below the lookout tower is 6.4 miles. Allow about 1.5 hours to reach the top. From the lookout back down to Gold Lake Highway adds another 8.7 miles of mostly paved road.

To Get There: From Grass Valley, take Hwy. 49 past Downieville to Sierra City. From Truckee, take Hwy. 89 north then Hwy. 49 west to Sierra City. Once in Sierra City, turn north on Butte Street just east of the General Store.

Trail Description: Reset your odometer (01). Follow paved Butte Street uphill and bear left before 0.1 miles. Stay on paved road as it goes around a small bridge. Continue west until you reach gate to transfer station at 1.1 miles. Turn right off the pavement and climb. At 2.5 miles (02), turn right on a lesser road. After you make the turn, stay left. The road is not maintained from this point. The road traverses across the face of the mountain with great views below. If you stop, find a wide spot so you don't block the road. You reach a crest at 4.7 miles. Drop over the crest and follow road as it turns to the right. Bear right at 4.8 miles (03) at a sign for Sierra Buttes. The next stretch is a little rocky and washed out until you reach an intersection at 5.2 miles (04).

   Reset your odometer and continue slightly right uphill following sign for Sierra Buttes OHV Trail. The road is no longer rocky, but it is very steep with undulations. Traction might be a problem in rainy weather. Bear left at 0.4. Turn into a parking area on the left at 1.2 miles (05). The road is gated just around the corner so it's best to park here. A hiking trail leaves from the parking lot but I found it much easier to hike up the road. It is a bit longer but not nearly as steep. The stairs to the tower are well-built and open for public use. The tower is no longer manned.

After visiting the lookout, head back down the hill. Turn right and *reset your odometer* when you reach the intersection at the Sierra Buttes OHV sign (04). (Although this stretch was 1.2 miles going up, it measured less coming down.) Turn right and follow a much flatter road north. Go straight at 0.8 miles and ignore lesser roads that branch off. You reach the parking area for the Sierra Buttes Hiking Trail at 2.6 miles. Continue past this point until you reach paved Road 93 at 2.7 miles (06), then go right.

When you reach Packer Saddle at 3.1 miles (07), you have several choices: Left is the start of Gold Valley Trail #11; straight is Deer Lake Trail #13; right goes downhill to Gold Lake Highway in another 4.5 miles. This way takes you through a very popular area of lakes, campgrounds, picnic areas and hiking trails.

Return Trip: Right on Gold Lake Highway goes back down to Bassetts in about 1.5 miles.

Directions to Sierra Buttes Lookout from Bassetts: From Bassetts, take Gold Lake Highway west then north about a mile and a half. Turn left over a bridge following signs to Sardine Lake. After 0.2 miles turn right towards Packer Lake. Go another 2.7 miles and turn left. Climb uphill another 1.6 miles until you reach Packer Saddle at the top of a ridge (07).

Reset your odometer and follow paved Road 93 left around the corner. Bear left at 0.4 miles (06) onto a dirt road, then pass through parking area for Sierra Buttes Hiking Trail. Continue straight at 2.3 miles where 93-22 joins on right. This road is marked as a dead end but it is not. It goes by the Monarch Mine and eventually connects to the road that comes up from Sierra City. Bear left uphill at sign for Sierra Buttes OHV Trail at 3.1 miles (04). Bear left again at 3.5 miles before reaching a parking lot at 4.3 miles (05). Hike another 0.7 miles up the road to the Fire Lookout Tower.

Services: Gas and a restaurant at Bassetts Station. Restaurants, RV Park and a general store in Sierra City but no gas. (There was a station in town but it was out of business when I was there.)

Historical Highlights: Sierra City served as an important mining town starting in the 1850s. The quaint town consists of many turn-of-the-century buildings complete with boardwalks. Don't miss the Kentucky Mine Stampmill and Museum located just east of town on Hwy. 49.

Maps: Lakes Basin Recreation Area map, Tahoe National Forest map, USGS 7.5-minute map, Sierra City, CA.

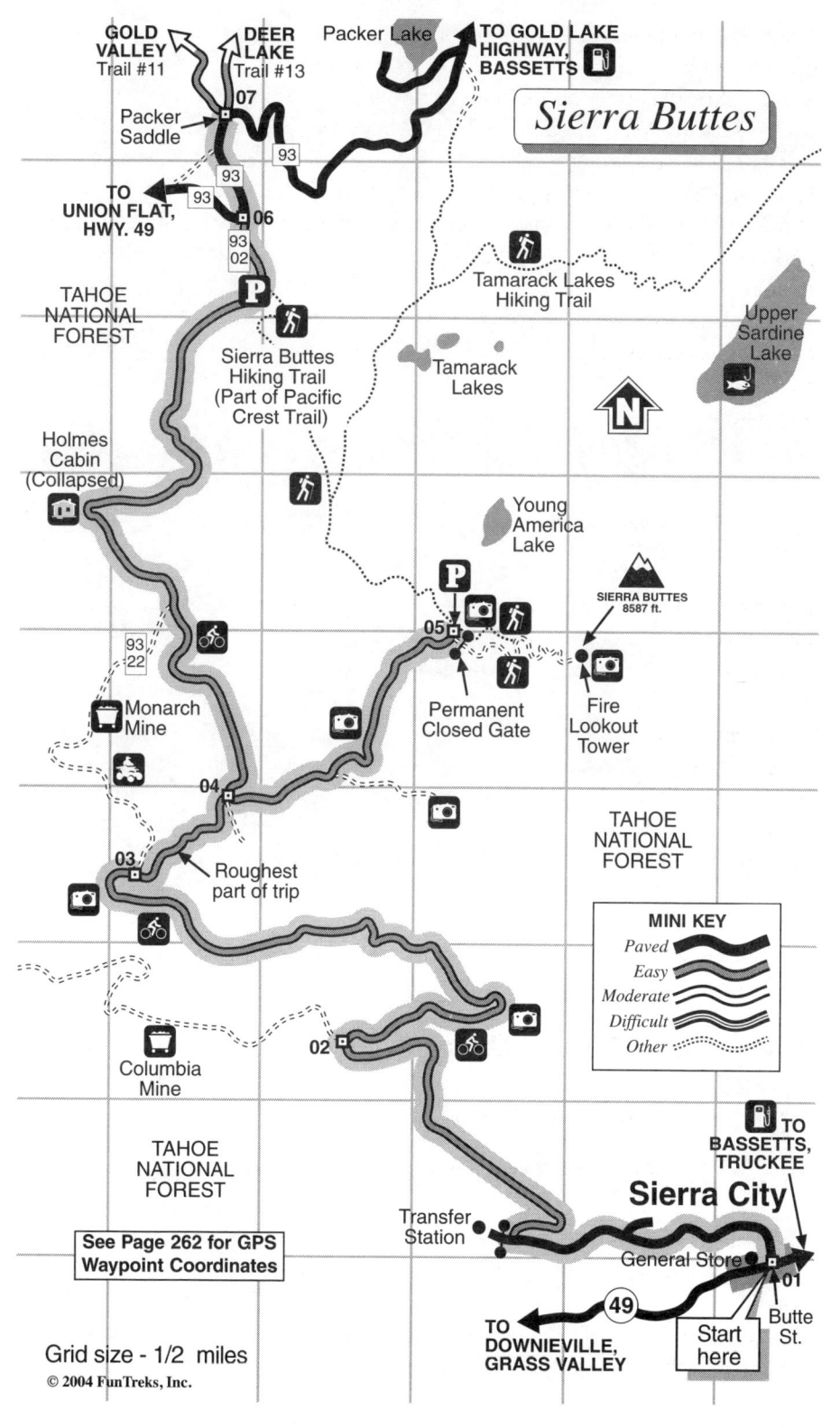

Sierra Buttes

GOLD VALLEY Trail #11
DEER LAKE Trail #13
Packer Lake
TO GOLD LAKE HIGHWAY, BASSETTS
07
Packer Saddle
93
93
TO UNION FLAT, HWY. 49
93
06
93 02
TAHOE NATIONAL FOREST
Tamarack Lakes Hiking Trail
Upper Sardine Lake
Sierra Buttes Hiking Trail (Part of Pacific Crest Trail)
Tamarack Lakes
N
Holmes Cabin (Collapsed)
Young America Lake
SIERRA BUTTES 8587 ft.
05
93 22
Permanent Closed Gate
Fire Lookout Tower
Monarch Mine
04
TAHOE NATIONAL FOREST
03
Roughest part of trip

MINI KEY
Paved
Easy
Moderate
Difficult
Other

02
Columbia Mine

TAHOE NATIONAL FOREST

TO BASSETTS, TRUCKEE

Sierra City

See Page 262 for GPS Waypoint Coordinates

Transfer Station
General Store
01
49
Butte St.
TO DOWNIEVILLE, GRASS VALLEY
Start here

Grid size - 1/2 miles
© 2004 FunTreks, Inc.

75

Rock walls along Tyler-Foote Road were built in 1913.    Hidden in brush next to road.

ATV on OHV portion of route.    Gold panning in wet suit at Tyler-Foote Crossing.

Swimming below bridge at Edwards Crossing.    Results of hydraulic mining.

76

Tyler-Foote Crossing ⑮

Location: Northeast of Grass Valley and Nevada City.

Difficulty: Easy. Most of the route is graded forest road; however, one portion follows a narrow shelf road down into a deep canyon. Another portion is steep and narrow with a few rocky places. Suitable for all 4-wheel-drive SUVs. Although route-finding is complex, roads are well marked most of the time. Light brush may touch vehicle in a few places.

Features: Follow an unusual, single-lane shelf road as it descends and crosses the Middle Yuba River. The former stagecoach route is constructed with near-vertical stone walls hand built by Italian stone masons over 90 years ago. Pass through Alleghany, an 1850s gold mining town that still has active mining today. On busy weekends, see modern-day prospectors panning for gold along the river. Fish and swim in cool, clear river eddies next to the road. Pass through Malakoff Diggins State Historic Park with roadside examples of hydraulic mining, a mining museum and the restored mining town of North Bloomfield.

Time & Distance: The 60-mile route, as described here, will take 6 to 8 hours. Consider an overnight campout to see everything along the way.

To Get There: Take Hwy. 49 north to Nevada City. Turn left on Hwy. 49 where the freeway ends, following signs to Downieville. Go only 0.3 miles before turning right on North Bloomfield Road.

Trail Description: Reset your odometer when you turn off Hwy. 49 (01). Head north, passing a ranger station, then turn right at 0.4 miles. (Make note of this turn because it's easy to miss on the return trip.) Follow this paved road more than six miles into the South Yuba Recreation Area. The road narrows significantly with tight turns then drops down and crosses a one-lane bridge over the Yuba River. This is a popular swimming spot.

At 8.9 miles, reset your odometer (02) and turn left on Grizzley Hill Road. (This begins a loop; you'll return to this point later.) Stay right at 0.1. Continue straight as several good roads join. It becomes paved at 2.9 miles. Turn right on Tyler-Foote Road at 3.1 miles. After the Columbia Hill Fire Station, turn left at 4.3 miles, staying on Tyler-Foote Road (now gravel). Stay left at 4.8 where a dead end road goes right.

Reset your odometer at 6.4 miles (03) where you reach a confusing intersection. Ignore the road that goes hard left and its immediate branch. Go a bit farther and turn left on a lesser road with a sign that says "Subject

77

to closure due to storm." This is F.S. 191 but it is not marked yet. The road gets rougher and soon begins to descend. Continue straight when a road joins at 0.9. At various points, you can see the Middle Yuba River far below as you wind down the side of a steep-walled canyon. The vertical stone walls which support the road are daunting. Pay close attention as you twist around many blind curves. At 2.4 miles you'll cross the river and start up the other side. (Look for gold prospectors panning in the river.)

The climb up the other side is a more typical shelf road and is now marked as F.S. 191. Continue straight at 5.4 and 6.0 following signs to Alleghany. The road gets narrow in places as it switchbacks along Kanaka Creek. The road turns sharply to the right as it goes by a gated, active mine at 10.0 miles. Bear left at a T after a small ravine at 11.3 miles.

Reset your odometer when you reach paved Miners Street at 13.2 miles (04). Continue straight as the road merges with Main Street going into Alleghany. Operating businesses include a general store and bar. You'll also go by a mining museum, but I didn't see any hours of operation. You may have to call to arrange a tour. Turn right downhill after the Post Office at 0.8 miles on Kanaka Creek Road. Turn right at 2.1 and drop down to a bridge. Stop before the bridge to see a hidden stamp press on the left and an old bridge on the right. Cross the main bridge and climb a steep hill. Bear right at 2.5 then left at 3.2 at an OHV sign. A road joins on right at 3.4 miles. Ignore a road to Minnesota Flats on right then immediately turn right at next road to German Bar (05) before 3.5 miles.

Reset your odometer at above turn (05). Bear right at 1.7 and 2.9 miles as you pass through Plumbago mining area (note red roofs). Bear right at 4.3 and cross bridge. Great spot to camp and swim on right at 4.4 miles (06). (Please respect many mining claims in the area.) Turn left uphill at 4.5 and climb steep, narrow road. Bear right at 5.8 then go straight at top of hill at 6.1. Bear left on unmarked road at 6.5 miles (07). Bear left at 7.1 before reaching Graniteville Rd. at 9.5 miles (08).

Reset odometer and turn right (08). Bear left at 1.9 miles staying on Graniteville/N. Bloomfield Road. The road swings south and reaches North Bloomfield at about 5.5 miles (09). Pay small fee at museum and pick up pamphlet that explains what to see in state park. Continue west as you wind through the park. Good view of Malakoff Diggins hydraulic mines at 7.0 miles. Stay left at 8.3 where Lake City and Backbone Roads join on right. Complete the loop when you reach Grizzley Hill Road at 10.8 miles (02).

Return Trip: Turn left and retrace route back to Hwy. 49 after 8.9 miles.

Services: Full services in Grass Valley and Nevada City. No gas along route.

Maps: Tahoe National Forest map, USGS 100,000-scale map, Truckee, CA, Malakoff Diggins State Park pamphlet, DeLorme Atlas & Gazetteer.

Historical Highlights: Tyler-Foote Road was built in 1913 to provide better access to the rich mining town of Alleghany. If you look at a USGS 7.5-minute map of Alleghany, CA, you'll see at least 10 mines within a half mile of the town. The most famous of these is the "Sixteen-to-One Mine," which started back in 1896 and is still in operation today. Modern-day production is a fraction of what it was in the beginning but, due to some creative mining techniques, the mine lives on. To learn more about the mine, go to www.origsix.com. Alleghany's early history dates back to the late 1850s. Original structures have long ago been destroyed by fire.

The 3,000-acre Malakoff Diggins State Park includes the largest and richest hydraulic gold mines in the world. The mining process was devastating to the environment, clogging rivers and poisoning farmland. The 1884 Sawyer Decision essentially ended the process and North Bloomfield slowly began to die. Much more information is available at the museum.

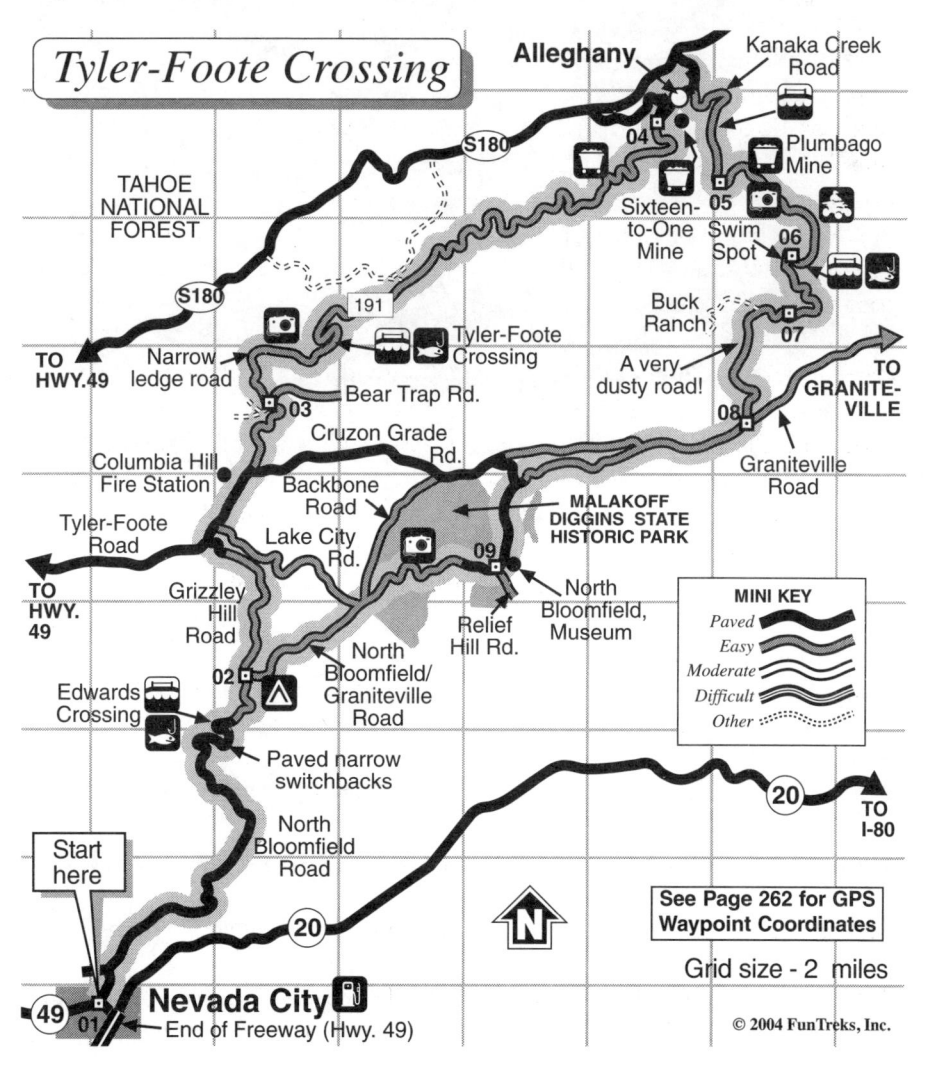

79

AREA 3

Auburn,
Lake Tahoe

16. Bear Valley Loop
17. Fordyce Creek
18. Signal Peak
19. Shirttail Canyon
20. Mt. Watson
21. Blackwood Cyn., Ellis Peak
22. Hell Hole
23. Rubicon
24. Barrett Lake

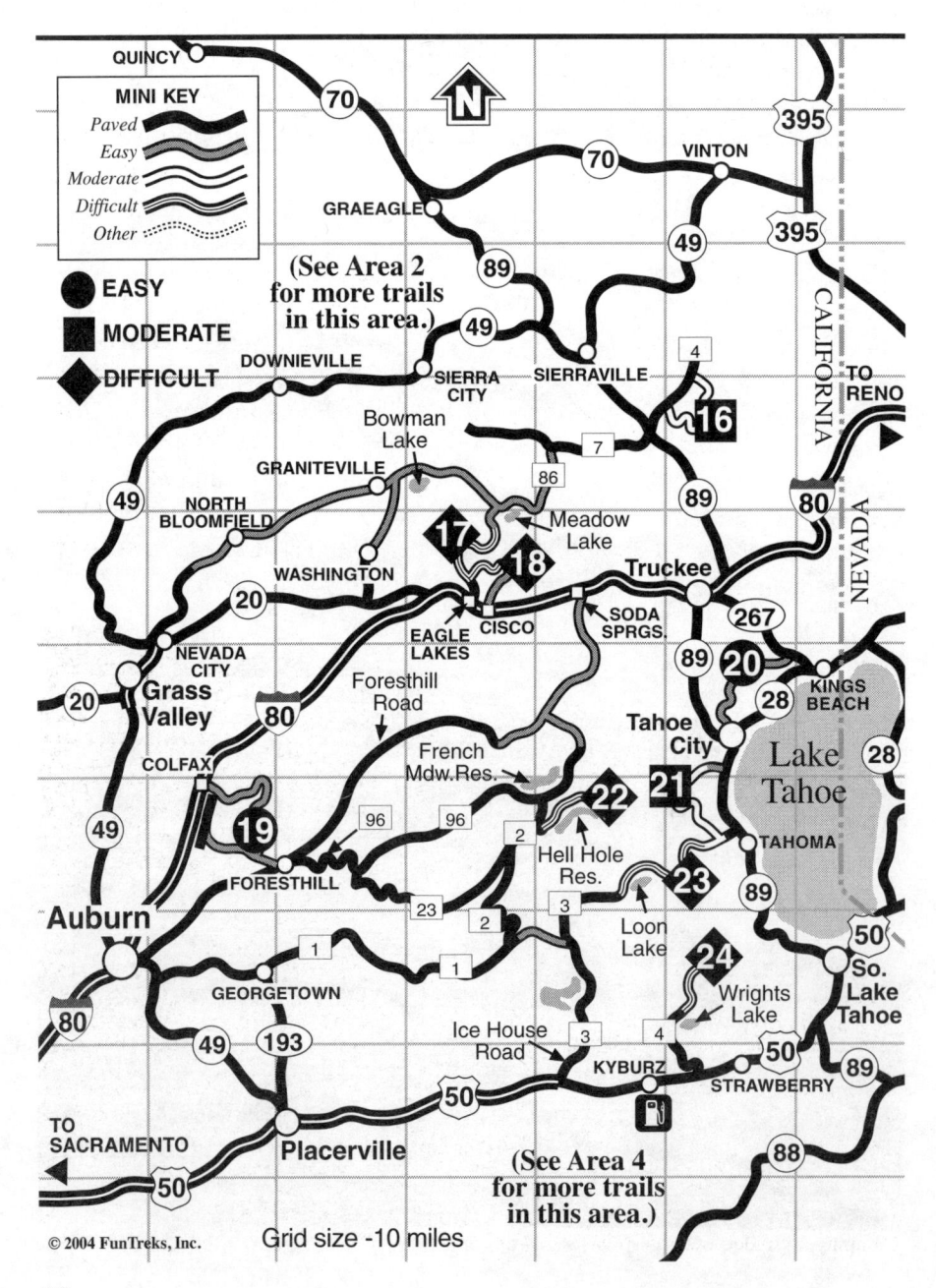

MINI KEY
Paved
Easy
Moderate
Difficult
Other

● EASY
■ MODERATE
♦ DIFFICULT

© 2004 FunTreks, Inc.   Grid size -10 miles

AREA 3
Auburn, Lake Tahoe

Scattered across the heart of the high Sierras, between Auburn and Lake Tahoe, are some of the finest four-wheel-drive trails in the world. At the top of the list is the mighty *Rubicon*, perhaps the most publicized trail of its time. The trail's reputation has been enhanced, in part, by Jeep Corporation, who frequently use and write about the trail. They even named a Jeep after it. If you think the stories are mostly hype, let me set the record straight—they're not. This trail is a perfect blend of beauty and challenge. Don't hesitate to experience it if you have the chance. A debatable second to the *Rubicon* is *Fordyce Creek,* selected by the California Association of 4WD Clubs 37 consecutive times for their very popular Sierra Trek event. The only shortcoming of *Fordyce Creek* is the limited time water levels are low enough to safely cross. While in the area, don't overlook *Barrett Lake, Hell Hole* and *Signal Peak* trails. Although much shorter than the aforementioned, they offer outstanding challenge without the heavy traffic. For stock SUV owners, *Mt. Watson* and *Blackwood Canyon/Ellis Peak* trails combine fun with incredible views of Lake Tahoe, while *Shirttail Canyon* has one of the best swimming holes in the California backcountry.

Camping at Spider Lake on *Rubicon Trail #23* (1996 photo).

First part of trip is relatively easy.

Difficult *Ball Peen Hill* is optional.

Group stops for lunch and enjoys the sun.

Last part of trail is rough and rocky.

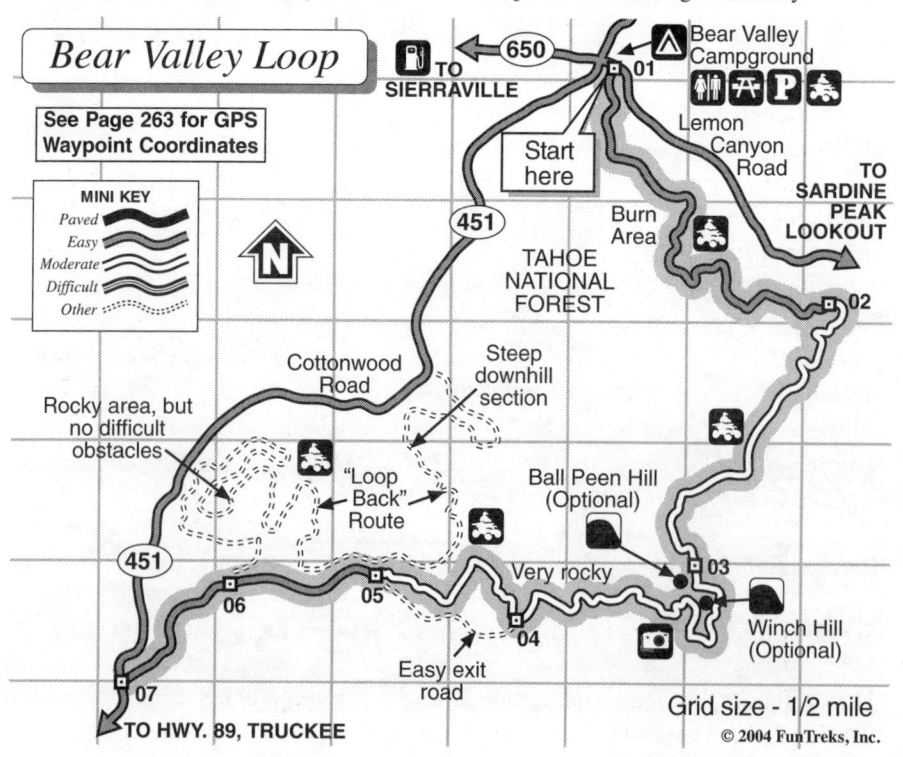

Bear Valley Loop

See Page 263 for GPS Waypoint Coordinates

MINI KEY
- Paved
- Easy
- Moderate
- Difficult
- Other

650 TO SIERRAVILLE

Bear Valley Campground

Start here

01

Lemon Canyon Road

451

Burn Area

TAHOE NATIONAL FOREST

TO SARDINE PEAK LOOKOUT

02

Cottonwood Road

Steep downhill section

Rocky area, but no difficult obstacles

"Loop Back" Route

Ball Peen Hill (Optional)

451

Very rocky

03

Winch Hill (Optional)

06   05   04

Easy exit road

07

TO HWY. 89, TRUCKEE

Grid size - 1/2 mile

© 2004 FunTreks, Inc.

Bear Valley Loop   16

Location: North of Truckee, southeast of Sierraville.

Difficulty: Moderate. Mix of easy dirt roads and rocky climbs. Difficult side obstacles are optional. Suitable for aggressive stock 4WD SUVs with skid plates. Trail is well marked with brown posts the entire way.

Features: Trail meanders up and down a series of steep rolling hills. First part of trip passes through fire damaged area. Contact Diablo 4-Wheelers Club regarding annual "Run-a-Muck" event held here in mid-July.

Time & Distance: "Straight-through" route, as described here, is 8.0 miles. Allow about 3 hours. "Loop-back" route adds another 6.2 miles and 2 hours.

To Get There: From Interstate 80 east of Truckee, take the Sierraville exit north on Hwy 89 about 15 miles to Little Truckee Summit. Turn right on Cottonwood Road (Sierra County Road 451) and go 5.4 miles to Lemon Canyon Road (County Road 650). Turn right and go another 0.1 miles past the Bear Valley Campground to OHV trail marker on right.

Trail Description: Reset your odometer at start (01). Bear slightly right at 0.5 miles where a road crosses. Turn right at 1.8. Driver's choice at 2.1 miles (02); left is loose and challenging. Stay right over a steep descent then climb again. Bear left at 2.6 then go straight at 3.3. Bear left at an exit sign at 3.7 then go right at 3.9. Driver's choice at 4.0 miles (03); difficult *Ball Peen Hill* is to the right. Another driver's choice at 4.2; left bypasses *Winch Hill*. After that, the marked trail gets rockier. You reach the top of a hill at 4.7 miles. Bear left at 4.8 then go straight at 5.1. Stay right at 5.2.

Straight at 5.6 miles (04) is the quickest way out. I went right on the marked trail which was much rockier. Work your way through a very rocky stretch at 5.8 miles then bear right on a better road at 6.6 miles (05). At 7.3 miles (06), right continues on the "loop back" route another 6.2 miles. This way has many bone-jarring rocks and one long, steep descent. Straight reaches Cottonwood Road at 8.0 miles (07).

Return Trip: Left on Cottonwood Road takes you back to Hwy. 89.

Services: Full services in Truckee, gas and food in Sierraville.

Maps: Tahoe National Forest map, USGS 7.5-minute maps, Sierraville and Sardine Lake, CA.

Spotters at work on Winch Hill #1.

Many miles of terrain like this.

Water crossing #1 during low-flow period.

Campsite next to Meadow Lake.

Crowd gathers for Sierra Trek raffle.

Grave of Summit City founder.

Fordyce Creek 17

Location: Northeast of Sacramento and Auburn, west of Truckee, between Cisco Grove and Meadow Lake.

Difficulty: Difficult. Tight maneuvering over miles of large, steep and awkwardly positioned boulders. Deep water crossings at low water flows; impassable during high water flows. Mechanical or body damage a frequent occurrence for all but the most aggressive modified vehicles. Rollovers are not uncommon. Minimum 33-inch tire size and one locker almost a necessity. Two lockers with very low gears recommended. Travel in a group with at least one winch-equipped vehicle.

Features: A premier hardcore trail. First-time users should consider driving this trail during the annual *Sierra Trek* event sponsored by the California Association of 4WD Clubs in early August. At that time, CA4WDC arranges with Pacific Gas & Electric to restrict water flow in Fordyce Creek to passable levels. Expert spotters and winches are provided at five critical points and no vehicle is ever left behind. Other than during this special period, water levels can drastically rise without warning, leaving vehicles stranded between stream crossings. Your best chance of a low flow rate, other than during the Sierra Trek, is in late September until the first snow fall. (See page 281 of appendix for **Fordyce Creek Stream Flow Rates**) The hardest part of the trail, on the north end, can be driven without crossing Fordyce Creek, but you must turn around and drive back out.

Time & Distance: Start early and allow one long day to go 12.3 miles to Meadow Lake. Be prepared to camp overnight in case problems occur.

To Get There: Exit Interstate 80 at Eagle Lakes Road 24 miles west of Truckee. Head north 0.9 miles and turn right at sign for Indian Springs Trailhead across from Indian Springs Forest Service Campground. Continue straight another 0.2 miles to staging area.

Trail Description: Reset your odometer at staging area (01) and continue left under power lines. (Right uphill goes to Signal Peak Trail #18.) Stay right at 0.6 miles following sign to Fordyce Creek. Stay right at 1.0 then go straight at 1.5. Stay right at 1.6 as the trail becomes more difficult. Go right at 1.9 miles (02). At this point, you turn away from Eagle Lakes onto the official Fordyce Creek OHV Trail. Stay right at 2.7 and left at 2.9. I drove this trail while participating in the *Sierra Trek* event described above. At 3.5

miles (03), our group was delayed due to a rollover at a point called Sunrise Hill. The right side of Sunrise Hill looked harder but the rollover occurred on the left. I went right. The first water crossing, at 3.8 miles (04), is followed by a scenic stretch along the creek. An area called *The Pools* is a popular place to camp at 4.2. A small boiler at 6.1 miles is an indicator you are nearing the Carlisle Mine just ahead on the left. Turn right downhill at 6.2 miles. *Winch Hill #1* is reached at 7.0 miles (05). Another water crossing at 7.5 is followed by Winch Hill #2 at 8.0 miles (06). Continue straight at 8.1 where a road goes left to a camp spot. The last water crossing is at 8.3 miles (07).

An important intersection is reached at 8.9 miles (08). It is marked by a large boiler and a giant steel gear (pelton wheel). The road to the right is called the *Committee Trail* or *Shortcut Route,* used as an early exit point for disabled vehicles during the Sierra Trek. It connects to the exit route for Signal Peak, Trail #18.

To continue on Fordyce Creek Trail, bear left (08). Pass through a narrow spot called the *Squeeze* then bear left at 9.0. Continue straight up very difficult *Launna's Hill* at 9.5 miles (09). It gets even harder as you reach *Winch Hill #3* at 10.0 miles (10) and *Winch Hill #4* at 10.5 miles (11). You'll go by a large water tank on the right before reaching *Winch Hill #5* at 10.9 miles (12). At the top of Winch Hill #5, continue north on a better road going past the Excelsior Mine. After another mile or so, with roads joining and branching off, the road swings right into an open area around Meadow Lake at 12.3 miles (13). This is base camp during the *Sierra Trek* event. It is also the historic site of Summit City (see below).

Return Trip: Go north bearing right past signs for Summit City, following Meadow Lake Road as it runs along the west and north shore of Meadow Lake. The rough but well defined road meanders for a distance then connects with smoother F.S 86 after 4.3 miles. Stay left another 6.6 miles until intersecting with paved F.S. Road 07. Go right at 9.5 miles to Hwy. 89. From there, right goes to Truckee, left to Sierraville.

Services: Gas at Cisco one exit east of Eagle Lakes Road. Vault toilets at start and Meadow Lake C.G. Full services in Truckee. Food, portable toilets, and showers are provided during *Sierra Trek*.

Historical Highlights: In 1864, Summit City had 4,000 residents, over 500 buildings, 80 saloons, 10,000 mining claims and 8 stamp mills. Separating the gold ore from its quartz host proved too costly, and by 1869 only 80 people remained. The town's founder, H.W. Hartley, is buried in a marked cemetery 0.5 miles northwest of the townsite (see map, photo).

Maps: Tahoe National Forest map, USGS 7.5-minute maps, Cisco Grove and English Mountain, CA, DeLorme Atlas & Gazetteer.

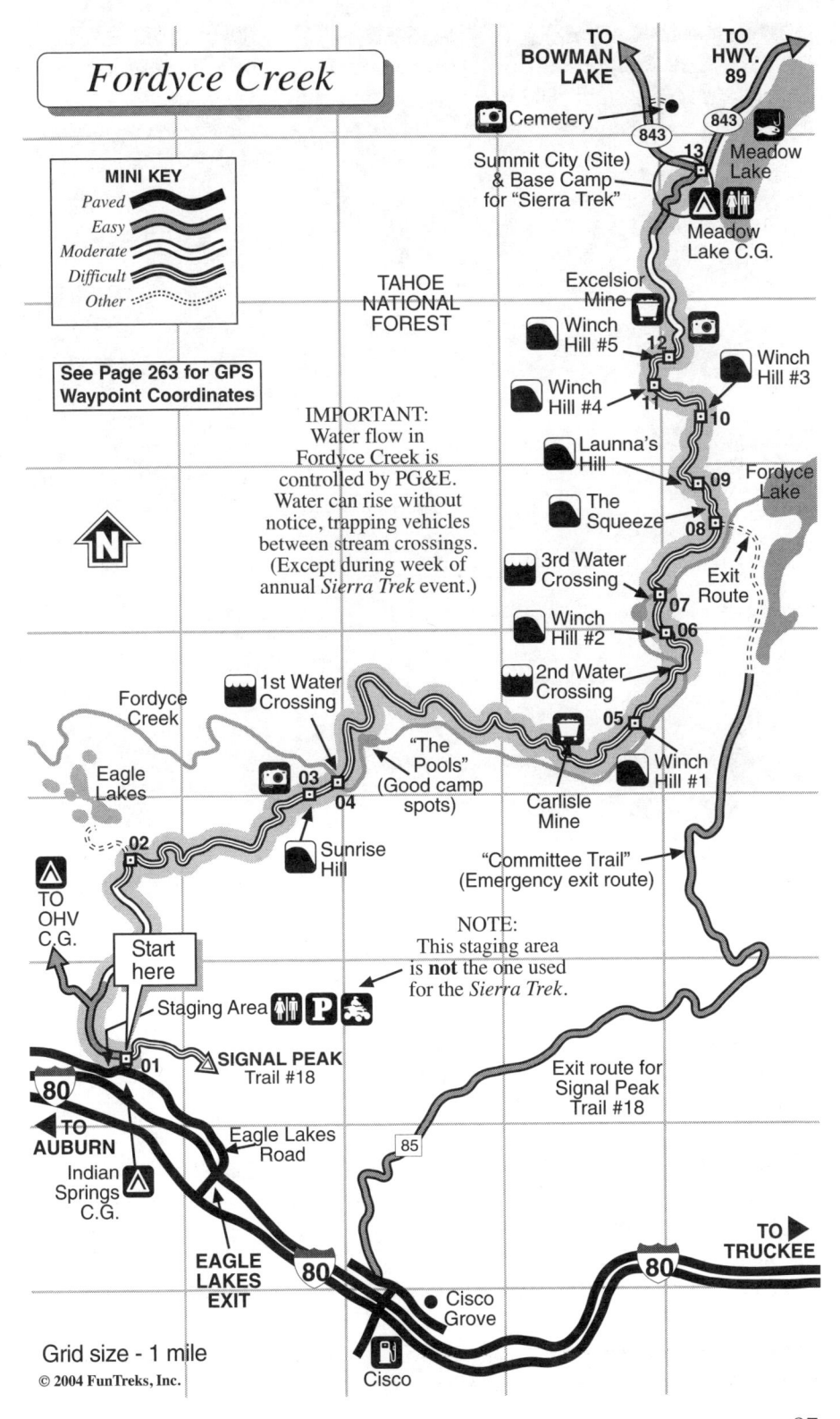

Fordyce Creek

MINI KEY
- Paved
- Easy
- Moderate
- Difficult
- Other

See Page 263 for GPS Waypoint Coordinates

TO BOWMAN LAKE
TO HWY. 89
Cemetery
843
Summit City (Site) & Base Camp for "Sierra Trek"
13
Meadow Lake
Meadow Lake C.G.
Excelsior Mine
Winch Hill #5
12
Winch Hill #3
Winch Hill #4
11
10
Launna's Hill
09
Fordyce Lake
The Squeeze
08
Exit Route
3rd Water Crossing
07
Winch Hill #2
06
2nd Water Crossing
05
Winch Hill #1
1st Water Crossing
Fordyce Creek
"The Pools" (Good camp spots)
Eagle Lakes
03
04
Carlisle Mine
Sunrise Hill
02
"Committee Trail" (Emergency exit route)

TAHOE NATIONAL FOREST

IMPORTANT:
Water flow in Fordyce Creek is controlled by PG&E. Water can rise without notice, trapping vehicles between stream crossings. (Except during week of annual *Sierra Trek* event.)

NOTE: This staging area is **not** the one used for the *Sierra Trek*.

TO OHV C.G.
Start here
Staging Area
01
SIGNAL PEAK Trail #18
80
TO AUBURN
Eagle Lakes Road
Indian Springs C.G.
85
Exit route for Signal Peak Trail #18
EAGLE LAKES EXIT
80
Cisco Grove
Cisco
TO TRUCKEE

Grid size - 1 mile
© 2004 FunTreks, Inc.

87

Easy on the gas pedal at this point.

Rocky and loose in places.

Trail gets easier as you near the top.

Abandoned lookout.

Signal Peak

TO FORDYCE CREEK
Trail #17
Fordyce Summit
SIGNAL PEAK EL. 7841 ft.

FORDYCE CREEK
Trail #17

Start here

Lookout

4H Camp

TO AUBURN

Staging Area

Eagle Lakes Road

Private C.G.

TAHOE NATIONAL FOREST

Cisco Grove

Cisco

TO TRUCKEE

MINI KEY
Paved
Easy
Moderate
Difficult
Other

See Page 263 for GPS Waypoint Coordinates

Grid size - 1/2 mile
© 2004 FunTreks, Inc.

88

Signal Peak 18

Location: Northeast of Auburn, west of Truckee and north of Cisco Grove.

Difficulty: Difficult. Narrow, steep road with tight brush and a couple of tippy rock challenges. Subject to washouts. Not for stock SUVs.

Features: Little used backroad to Signal Peak. Great views once you get above the trees. Short walk to abandoned, historic lookout station once used to spot fires in snowsheds along railroad that can be seen below.

Time & Distance: It is 4.2 miles to the top on difficult terrain and another 7.0 miles back down on easy road. Allow 3 to 4 hours.

To Get There: Exit Interstate 80 at Eagle Lakes Road 24 miles west of Truckee. Head north 0.9 miles and turn right at sign for Indian Springs Trailhead across from Indian Springs Forest Service Campground. Continue straight another 0.2 miles to staging area.

Trail Description: Reset your odometer at staging area (01). Bear right away from power lines up steep, rough road. Maneuver through narrow spot, site of a previous washout, at 0.6 miles. Bear right away from meadow at 1.5 miles (02) and climb through toughest part of trail. Rollovers have occurred here. Continue straight at 2.6 and 3.1. Roads to right are illegal switchback cuts. Stay on best traveled road as it switchbacks to top. Continue straight at 4.0. Stop at 4.2 miles (03) and hike to visible lookout station along ridge to right. From here, a reverse left turn takes you to top of Signal Peak with views to the north of Fordyce Creek Trail #17.

Reset odometer and head east down good road (03). Bear left at 1.5 and 1.7 miles. Within 100 feet you reach Fordyce Summit. Bear right at T (04). (Left goes to Fordyce Creek Trail #17 via the *Committee Trail*.) Bear right at 1.8 and 2.5 as road improves. Go by Woodchuck Flat 4H Camp on left at 3.7 miles. Road is paved at 6.5. Turn left at 7.0 miles (05) to reach Cisco Grove freeway entrance.

Return Trip: East on I-80 goes to Truckee and Reno, west goes to Auburn.

Services: Gas at Cisco. Vault toilet at start. Full services in Truckee.

Maps: Tahoe National Forest map, USGS 7.5-minute maps, Cisco Grove, CA, DeLorme Atlas & Gazetteer.

Remaining building at Iowa Hill.

Shirttail Canyon Road is easy.

Colfax-Foresthill Bridge was built in 1930.

Great swimming below the bridge.

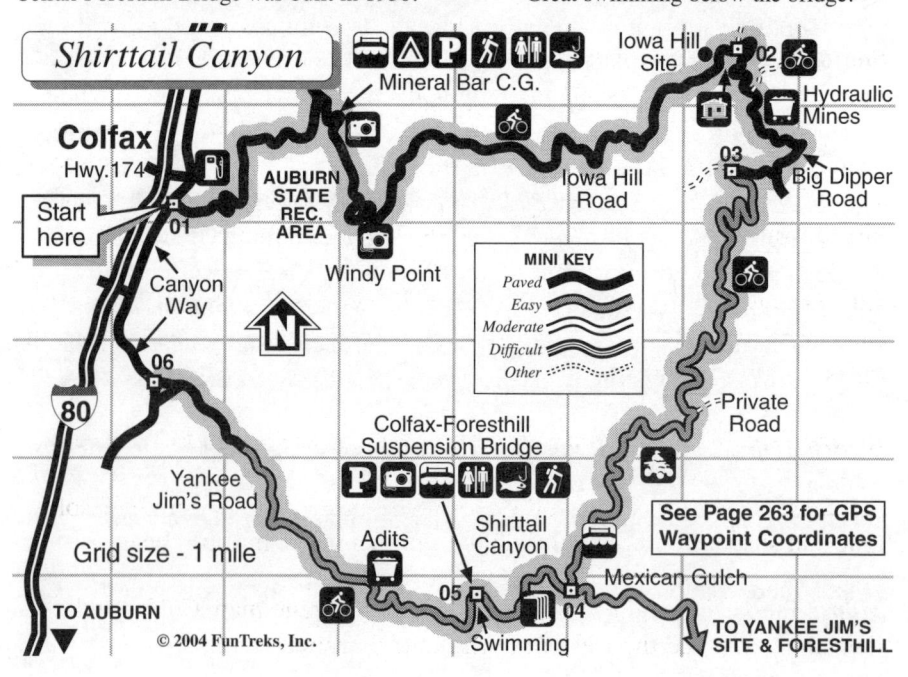

Shirttail Canyon

Colfax
Hwy. 174

Start here

Mineral Bar C.G.

Auburn State Rec. Area

Windy Point

Canyon Way

06

Yankee Jim's Road

Grid size - 1 mile

TO AUBURN

© 2004 FunTreks, Inc.

Iowa Hill Site

Hydraulic Mines

Iowa Hill Road

03

Big Dipper Road

MINI KEY
Paved
Easy
Moderate
Difficult
Other

Private Road

Colfax-Foresthill Suspension Bridge

Adits

Shirttail Canyon

05

Swimming

04

Mexican Gulch

See Page 263 for GPS Waypoint Coordinates

TO YANKEE JIM'S SITE & FORESTHILL

90

Shirttail Canyon 19

Location: Northeast of Auburn, east of Colfax and northwest of Foresthill.

Difficulty: Easy. Graded forest road. Four-wheel drive not needed when dry.

Features: See historic Iowa Hill and the Colfax-Foresthill Suspension Bridge. Get a close-up look at numerous hydraulic mines. Hike below bridge to large, crystal-clear swimming area. If you just want to swim, go directly to bridge from east end of Yankee Jim's Road.

Time & Distance: 26.0 miles as described here. Allow 2-3 hours.

To Get There: Take Interstate 80 to Colfax exit Hwy. 174. Follow Canyon Way south along east side of freeway 0.3 miles to Iowa Hill Road on left.

Trail Description: Reset your odometer when you turn left on Iowa Hill Road (01). Follow a narrow, winding paved road through Auburn State Recreation Area. At 8.9 miles, you'll cross a narrow, elevated strip of road through an area of hydraulic mines. If you stop to look, don't let the kids out of the car. There are sheer drop offs on each side of the road. The site of historic Iowa Hill is reached at 9.0. Turn right on paved Big Dipper Road at 9.4 miles (02) after the Iowa Hill Store. Stay right at 9.5. At 11.5, turn right on marked Shirttail Canyon Road. Turn left at 11.9 miles (03) at signs for Shirttail Canyon and Foresthill. The road changes to wide dirt and descends into Shirttail Canyon. Bear right uphill past a private road at 15.3 then cross a wooden bridge at 17.4. Bear right at 18.0 miles (04) after a short section of pavement. (Left goes to site of Yankee Jim's and Foresthill.) Cross suspension bridge at 19.4 miles (05) and park on other side. Grab a swimsuit and hike down to river on left. (The hike is steep but footing is good.)

Reset odometer and continue west on Yankee Jim's Road. Note mine adits on right at 1.6. Road soon becomes paved. Bear right at 4.7 to reach Canyon Way (06). Turn right and return to start of Iowa Hill Road at 6.6 miles (01). (For Auburn, turn left at I-80 exit before Iowa Hill Road.)

Return Trip: West/south on I-80 goes to Auburn, east/north to Truckee.

Services: Most services in Colfax. Iowa Hill has a general store. Portable toilets at suspension bridge during the summer when traffic is heavy.

Maps: Tahoe National Forest map, USGS 7.5-minute map, Colfax and Foresthill, CA, and the DeLorme Atlas and Gazetteer.

Looking south towards Lake Tahoe from the top of Mt. Watson.

Watson Lake can be reached entirely by paved road from Highway 267.

Fairly steep near the top.

92

Mt. Watson ⓴

Location: Southeast of Truckee, north of Tahoe City.

Difficulty: Easy. A mix of paved and gravel roads with one short rocky section near the top. The last part is an easy, short walk for those without skid plates. Suitable for any stock SUV.

Features: An absolutely stunning view of Lake Tahoe from the top of Mt. Watson. You can see a half dozen ski areas and other prominent features. Take binoculars and a camera. Camping, fishing and hiking at Watson Lake.

Time & Distance: It's 7.5 miles to the top of Mt. Watson and another 8.2 miles back down to Hwy. 267. Add about 1.4 miles for side trip to Watson Lake. Allow 2 to 3 hours for the whole trip.

To Get There: From the intersection of Highways 89 and 28 in Tahoe City, take Highway 89 towards Truckee. After only 0.1 miles, turn right on the very first side street, called *Fairway*. Follow road uphill 0.4 miles and turn left on Bunker. Turn left again in another 0.2 miles on an unmarked forest road that is paved a short distance before it leaves a residential area.

Trail Description: Reset your odometer at start of forest road (01). The mixed-surface road winds uphill. Stay left at 1.2 miles and the road is soon marked as F.S.16N73. Continue straight at 1.8 miles and join a paved road which continues to climb. At 6.0 miles (02), turn sharply to the right almost reversing direction on a rougher dirt road. There are a few steep places where you'll want 4-wheel drive. Turn right at 7.4 miles. This point is a bit rocky and some may prefer to walk the rest of the way. The road ends at 7.5 miles (03). Park here and climb to the rock outcropping pictured top left.

Return to paved road, *reset your odometer* and turn right. At 0.7 miles, Watson Lake is 0.7 miles to the right or you can continue straight 6.0 miles to Hwy. 267 (04).

Return Trip: Right on Hwy. 267 goes to Kings Beach, left goes to Truckee. A half mile north on Hwy. 267, a 4-mile paved road goes right to Martis Peak where you'll find a manned lookout tower with more great views.

Services: Full services in Tahoe City, Kings Beach and Truckee.

Maps: Tahoe National Forest map, USGS 100,000-scale map, Truckee, CA, and the DeLorme Atlas and Gazetteer.

Steep and narrow in places with tight brush.

This stock 1942 Willys breezed through.

View from the top of Ellis Peak. Lake Tahoe to left.

Ellis Lake, a great lunch spot.

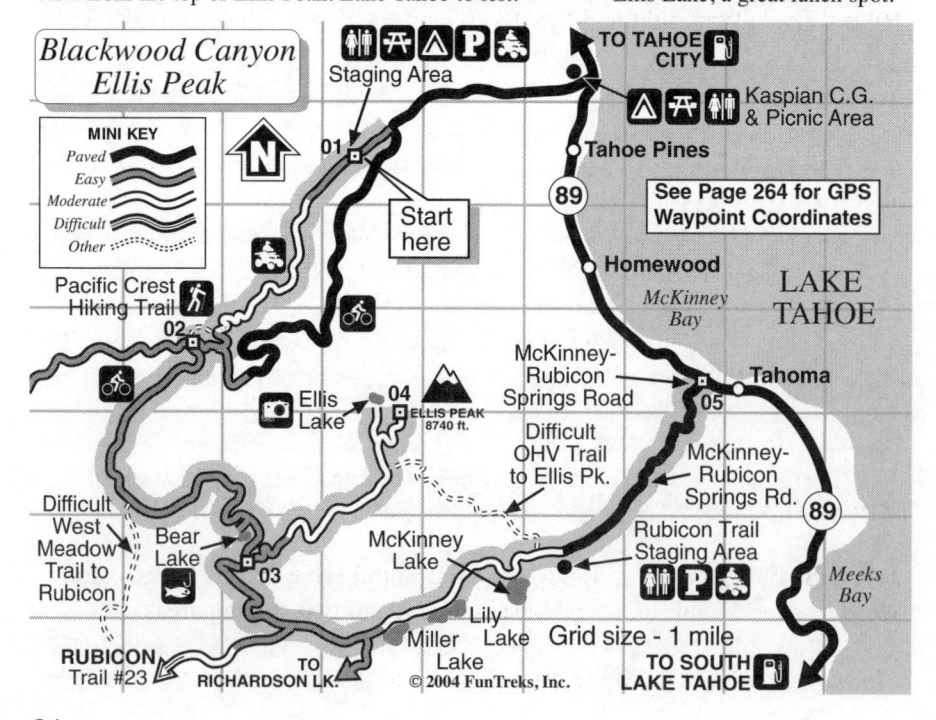

Blackwood Cyn., Ellis Peak 21

Location: West of Lake Tahoe, south of Truckee.

Difficulty: Moderate. Narrow, steep and rough in a few places but suitable for stock, high clearance SUVs. Some tight brush. Be careful when wet.

Features: Explores a beautiful, high area west of Lake Tahoe. Many lakes and viewpoints. Trail may not open until early July due to deer migration.

Time & Distance: 18.4 miles as described here; allow 3 to 4 hours.

To Get There: Head south from Tahoe City on Hwy. 89 approximately 4.3 miles to Kaspian Campground. Turn right on paved road signed to Barker Pass. (Campground is above road on right after you turn off Hwy. 89.) Head west and continue straight when paved road goes left at 2.2 miles. After another half mile, staging area is hidden in trees on right near vault toilet.

Trail Description: Reset your odometer at staging area (01). Head west on a road that narrows and climbs steeply in places. A wide circular area at 3.1 miles marks Barker Pass. Turn hard left, drop down to a gravel road and turn right. At 3.3 miles (02) turn left downhill near sign for Pacific Crest Hiking Trail. Turn right at 3.5 miles at sign for Barker Meadow OHV Trail. Turn left on a better road at 5.1. Stay left past difficult West Meadow Trail at 5.4. Continue straight at 7.5. (Bear Lake is right a short distance.) At 8.1 (03), turn left for Ellis Peak. Stay right at 8.8 and left at 9.2 and 10.3. At 10.6 miles, turn right for Ellis Peak. (Gorgeous Ellis Lake is to the left.) Park at 11.1 miles (04) and climb short distance to rocky Ellis Peak.

Return to main road and reset odometer (03). Continue straight downhill on good road. Stay left at 1.3 miles as you join McKinney-Rubicon Springs Road. It is rough in places. Rubicon Trail Staging Area is on right at 4.8 miles and then road becomes paved. Go straight at stop sign at 6.5. (See detail map on page 103.) Make a right on Springs Court at 6.6, a left on Bellview Ave. at 6.8 and a right on McKinney-Rubicon Springs Road at 7.0 until you reach Hwy. 89 at 7.3 miles (05).

Return Trip: Left on Hwy. 89 takes you back to start and Tahoe City.

Services: Full services in Tahoe City and South Lake Tahoe. No gas along western shore. Vault toilets at Kaspian C.G. and two staging areas.

Maps: Tahoe N. F., USGS 7.5-min. map, Homewood, CA, DeLorme Atlas.

Hell Hole Reservoir.

About two miles into the trail.

Steep and rough near the bottom.

Typical terrain around the reservoir.

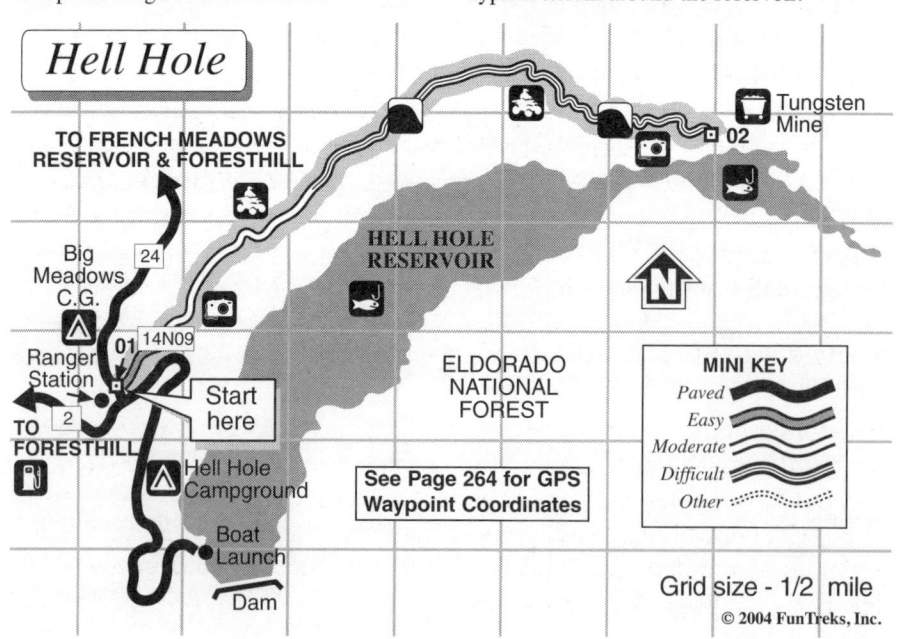

Hell Hole

TO FRENCH MEADOWS RESERVOIR & FORESTHILL

Big Meadows C.G. 24

Ranger Station
01 14N09

TO FORESTHILL 2

Start here

Hell Hole Campground

Boat Launch

Dam

HELL HOLE RESERVOIR

ELDORADO NATIONAL FOREST

Tungsten Mine 02

See Page 264 for GPS Waypoint Coordinates

MINI KEY
Paved
Easy
Moderate
Difficult
Other

Grid size - 1/2 mile

© 2004 FunTreks, Inc.

Hell Hole 22

Location: Northeast of Auburn and Foresthill, west of Lake Tahoe.

Difficulty: Difficult. Narrow and steep with challenging rock ledges. Not for stock vehicles. High ground clearance, large tires and at least one locker recommended. Help is a long way off. Don't go alone.

Features: A long drive to a short, but terrific hardcore trail. Ends at a very secluded spot along the shores of little-used, but very impressive, Hell Hole Reservoir. Makes a great weekend trip if you camp overnight and fish. Take bug repellent in the summer.

Time & Distance: Trail is only 4.0 miles long. Allow 1 to 2 hours each way depending upon vehicle capability.

To Get There:
From Foresthill: Follow paved Forest Roads 96, 23 and 2 east from Foresthill about 50 miles. Hell Hole Reservoir is well marked when you get on F.S. 2. Turn left just after the ranger station on F.S. 24. The trail is immediately to the right and was marked as 14N09.
From Lake Tahoe: Follow directions to Rubicon Trail #23 but turn west away from Ice House Road when you reach F.S. Rd. 1. This connects to F.S. Rd. 2 on a long, twisting drive north to Hell Hole Reservoir.

Trail Description: Reset your odometer as you leave the pavement onto 14N09 (01). The road starts unimpressively under power lines. Stay right at 0.4 miles where a lesser road goes left. At 0.5 a monument credits the Capital City Mountain Goats for adopting this trail. You also get your first look at the reservoir far below. The trail gets rougher after 1.5 miles with the first real challenge at 2.0 miles. A series of dramatic and difficult ledges begins at 3.4 miles and continues until you reach the lake at 4.0 miles (02). The shoreline changes radically depending upon the water level in the reservoir. Driving along the rocky shore is difficult rock crawling.

Return Trip: Return the way you came.

Services: Gas at Foresthill, full services in Auburn. Hell Hole Forest Service Campground has a vault toilet but there's nothing on the OHV trail.

Maps: Eldorado or Tahoe National Forest maps, USGS 7.5-minute maps, Bunker Hill, CA.

Loon Lake Staging Area.

The *Gatekeeper*.

Drop down into the *Granite Bowl* and bear right.

Pass this tree after Granite Bowl.

Author starts through *Big Sluice*.

Analyzing the situation at *Little Sluice Box* (1996).

Cairns sometimes mark the trail.

Camping below dam at Buck Island Lake.

Rubicon Trail 23

Location: Northeast of Placerville and west of Lake Tahoe.

Difficulty: Difficult. A mix of granite slabs, soft dirt, sharp rocks and large boulders that require precise maneuvering to avoid body damage. Several extreme sections can be bypassed but many very rough sections cannot. *Cadillac Hill* is very steep, tippy and potentially dangerous. During wet periods, one water crossing can be very deep and muddy. Extremely dusty with tight brush in places. With an expert spotter, you might get a stock, high clearance, short-wheel based 4WD vehicle through without body damage, but the average driver should not try it. Best done in a modified vehicle with ample body protection and lockers. Route-finding is difficult across the *Granite Bowl*, but after that the trail is well defined.

Features: Perhaps the best known and most popular 4x4 trail in the world. A rare combination of difficulty, beauty, length and pure rock-crawling pleasure. Great camping next to crystal-clear lakes with stunning views. Most people drive the trail in the direction described here, but it can be driven the other way. You may also enter the trail via Wentworth Springs (see Eldorado N.F. map). History buffs wishing to see more of the original Rubicon Trail will want to start in Georgetown. This adds about 50 miles to the trip but has several interesting historic features. The trail reaches elevations above 7,000 feet and is partially snow covered in the winter. However, only the *Granite Bowl* is officially closed to vehicular travel at that time. From a practical standpoint, however, the trail is for summer use. Check with U.S. Forest Service for special event closure dates.

   Important Note: *This trail receives extremely heavy use and is under constant scrutiny by environmental groups. Make sure you stay on designated routes at all times, follow "Tread-Lightly" guidelines, pack out your trash and use low-impact camping techniques. Presently, the trail has inadequate toilet facilities. Disposal of solid human waste and toilet paper is a major concern. Please bring plastic bags to clean up after yourself just like you would for your dog in a public park. If possible, bring a porta-potty. Make sure you have a fire permit and applicable licenses for fishing and hunting. A permit is also required to hike or camp in the Desolation Wilderness. (Day-use permit is free.)*

Time & Distance: The trail is 18.6 miles as described here. About 10 of that is very difficult. It can be driven in one day, but two days is the norm. Many people take three days to allow more time for camping and fishing.

99

Big ledges to climb north of Buck Island Lake.    Historic Rubicon Bridge.

One of many tight spots through the *Big Sluice*.

Water can be very deep.    Cadillac Hill is extremely steep, narrow and tippy.

To Get There: From U.S. Hwy. 50, at a point approximately 24 miles east of Placerville and 40 miles southwest of South Lake Tahoe, head north on paved, well-marked Ice House Road (F.S. 3). Turn right after 24 miles following sign to Loon Lake. (Straight takes you to the Wentworth Springs entrance with toilets.) Go about 6 more miles and cross a large concrete spillway. Last chance for toilet on right after spillway; none at staging area. Soon the pavement ends and you cross a long dam. Note staging area below on the left. Turn left just after the dam and follow a rough road around to staging area located on a large, flattop granite outcrop. Bear right (northeast) across staging area, not northwest towards the green building.

Trail Description: *Reset your odometer before descending northeast side of staging area* (01). There is no clear start to the trail. Drop down the granite slope about 300 feet and turn right (east) on a better defined path. The first tough obstacle, called the *Gatekeeper*, is reached at 0.3 miles (02). If you have significant problems here, do not go any farther; it only gets worse.

Reset your odometer at the "Gatekeeper." After squeezing through this obstacle, swing left (north) and climb to the top of a granite dome. Drop to the bottom on the other side and bear slightly right uphill over a series of ledges, doing your best to follow existing tire marks. Continue heading north; do not go east. A large boulder with a painted red arrow at about 0.6 miles (03) points to the right. Do not turn right; continue north around the boulder. (Loon Lake should be on your right, not in front.) If you turn east too soon, you'll drop into forbidden Pleasant Meadow. The correct point to leave the *Granite Bowl* is marked with a sign on a large tree at about 0.7 miles (04). After this point, the trail is clearly defined.

Reset your odometer at the marked tree (04) (see photo). Continue weaving north. Wentworth Springs Trail (an alternate entrance) joins on the left at 0.5 miles (05). Ellis Creek crossing at 0.8 miles marks the point where the trail turns east (right). A tough spot at 0.9 miles has a bypass to the left. Negotiate *Walker Hill* at 1.7 miles, followed by a tough test of articulation at 1.8. Left at 2.8 miles (06) is the bypass for the *Little Sluice Box*. This is an extreme obstacle where damage is likely even for the most aggressive vehicles. *Little Sluice* rejoins on the right at 3.0 miles (07). The main trail continues left down a tricky ledge called *Thousand Dollar Hill*. At 3.3 miles bear left. (Right goes to fantastic Spider Lake.)

Stay right at 3.8 miles as you descend towards Buck Island Lake. Stay left at 4.3 miles (08). This is the exit point for the *True Big Sluice*, another extreme rock crawling challenge. At 4.7 miles (09), you reach a point below the dam for Buck Island Lake. A great camp spot on the right is very popular. Cross a creek and follow the trail up along the left side of the dam. The trail winds along the north side of the lake with some of the toughest terrain yet. More camp spots can be found along the shore. Stay left at 5.3 miles and drop down a steep hill. A sharp switchback to the left at 5.6 miles

(10) marks the beginning of what is now called the *Big Sluice*. It is 0.2 miles of tight, giant boulders. Your articulation and ground clearance will be tested. There are no bypasses.

Below *Big Sluice* is a nasty water hole that can be deep in places during wet periods. Watch someone go through first to figure out the correct line. Cross *Rubicon Bridge* and enter Rubicon Springs, a popular place to camp. During special events, hundreds camp here along the Rubicon River. It is private property and a small fee is charged. It is also extremely dusty when dry. Bear left, then right at 6.5 miles. At 6.6 miles (11), prudent drivers will go left to avoid a difficult obstacle straight ahead. The road winds through Rubicon Springs and passes a helicopter pad at 6.8 miles (12).

Reset your odometer at the helipad. Go either way at 0.1. Follow the road along the river without crossing it (unless you want to camp on the other side). Stay right at 0.9 following a small sign to Tahoe, then pick a line through a stretch called the *V-Notch*. *Cadillac Hill* starts at 1.1 miles (13) where a tight switchback goes uphill to the right. This section is narrow, tippy and extremely steep. Use caution. Turn right at the top of *Cadillac Hill* at 1.9 miles. Stay left at 2.6 then go straight at 2.7 where a sign points left to Barker Meadows OHV Trail. One last tough spot remains at 3.7 miles.

Blackwood Canyon/Ellis Peak Trail #21 joins on the left at 4.8 miles (14). The road widens as you go by the first of several lakes. Stay left at 5.8 where a road goes right to Richardson Lake. Continue east past three more lakes. A difficult OHV trail goes left to Ellis Peak at 8.1 miles just before reaching the Rubicon Staging Area at 8.3 miles (15).

Continue east on a welcomed paved road after the staging area. (Do not park on streets.) Go straight at a stop sign at 10.0. Make a right on Springs Court at 10.1, a left on Bellview Avenue at 10.3 and a right on McKinney-Rubicon Road at 10.5. Hwy. 89 is reached at 10.8 miles (16).

Return Trip: Left on Highway 89 goes to Tahoe City and Truckee. Right goes to South Lake Tahoe.

Services: Full services in Placerville, Tahoe City and South Lake Tahoe. Last chance for gas eastbound on 50 is at Pollock Pines. Westbound travelers along Hwy. 50 can top off their tanks just west of Kyburz about 9 miles east of Ice House Road. Telephones and supplies are available at Icehouse Resort General Store 9 miles north on Ice House Road. Modern vault toilets at North Shore Campground before Loon Lake Staging Area and at final Rubicon Staging Area. Spider Lake, Buck Island Lake and Rubicon Springs have primitive outhouses.

Maps: Eldorado or Tahoe N.F., USGS 7.5-minute maps, Wentworth Springs and Homewood, CA, DeLorme Atlas. Also helpful: Sidekick Off Road map of Rubicon and the *4-Wheelers Guide to the Rubicon Trail* by William C. Teie.

103

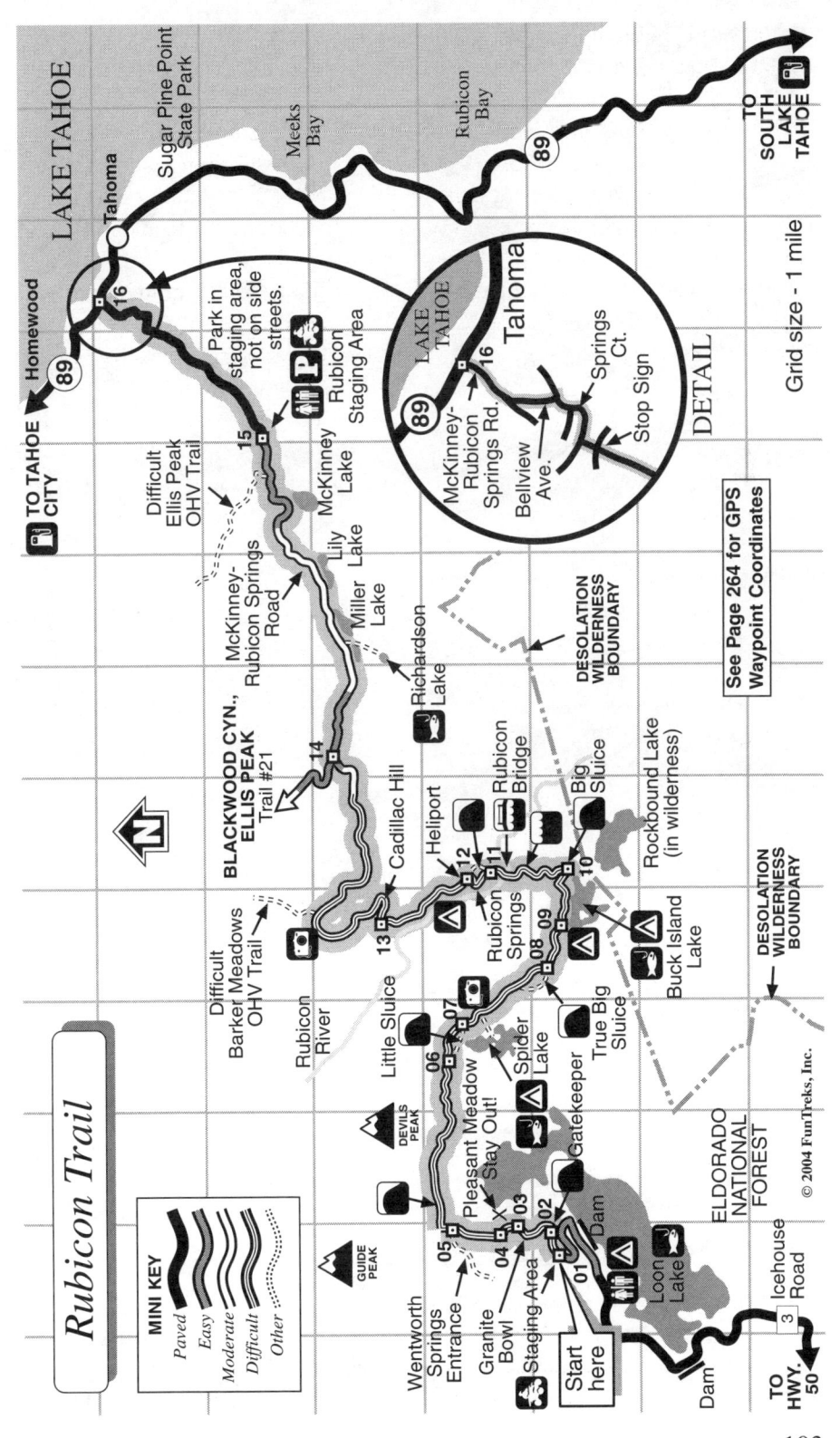

Phone number on sign is now (530) 644-6048.

Why it takes three hours to go four miles.

Trail is fun in a properly equipped vehicle.

Bring your canoe or inflatable boat.

ATV enthusiast camps near Barrett Lake.

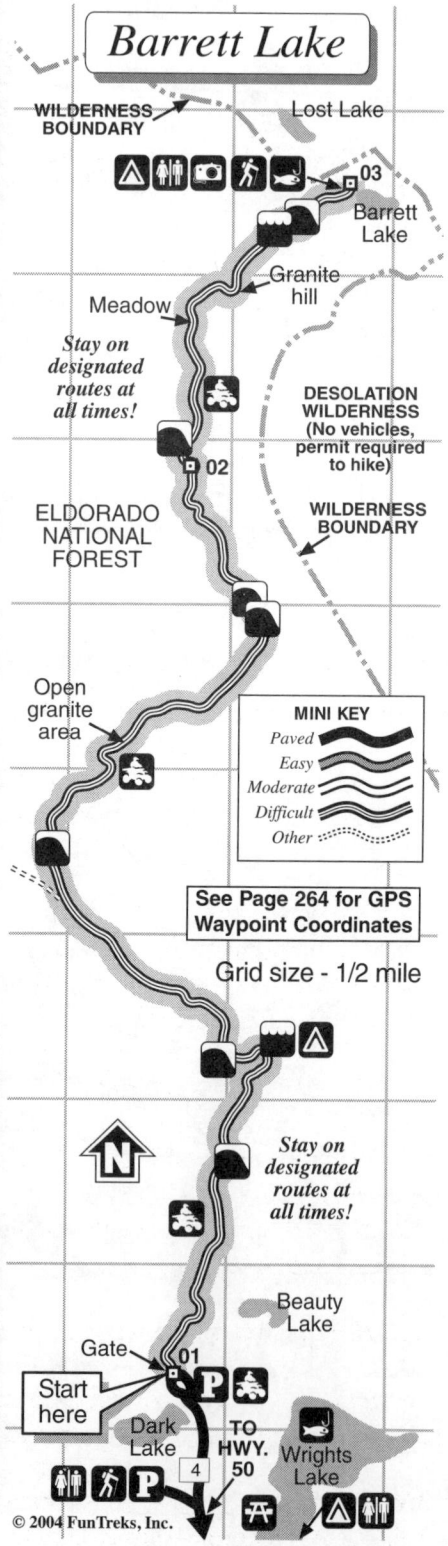

Barrett Lake

WILDERNESS BOUNDARY
Lost Lake
Barrett Lake
Granite hill
Meadow

Stay on designated routes at all times!

DESOLATION WILDERNESS
(No vehicles, permit required to hike)

ELDORADO NATIONAL FOREST

WILDERNESS BOUNDARY

Open granite area

MINI KEY
Paved
Easy
Moderate
Difficult
Other

See Page 264 for GPS Waypoint Coordinates

Grid size - 1/2 mile

Stay on designated routes at all times!

Beauty Lake

Gate
Start here
Dark Lake
TO HWY. 50
Wrights Lake

© 2004 FunTreks, Inc.

104

Barrett Lake 24

Location: East of Placerville and southwest of Lake Tahoe.

Difficulty: Difficult. Relatively short but a very difficult trail. Large boulders shift sometimes, increasing possibility of body damage. Very high ground clearance and lockers required. Narrow 6 ft.-wide gate at start of trail keeps out extra-wide vehicles. Not for stock SUVs. ATVs allowed.

Features: Camp, hike and fish at idyllic Barrett Lake at end of trail. Makes a great weekend trip. Forest Service closes trail without notice when it gets too wet. Call ahead for status (see top photo opposite page). A wilderness permit is needed to hike beyond Barrett Lake.

Time & Distance: Allow at least 3 to 4 hours one way for this 4.3-mile trip.

To Get There: Take Highway 50 about 35 miles east of Placerville to Wrights Lake Road (F.S. Rd. 4). This paved road is located between Kyburz and Strawberry. Turn north and follow a narrow, winding road uphill about 8 miles past visitor center and Wrights Lake Campground. Go another mile north past Dark Lake, following signs to Barrett Lake Jeep Trail. Road ends at a loop where Jeep Trail is well marked. Limited parking around loop.

Trail Description: Reset your odometer at gate (01). Head north through a rocky section. This part is mild compared to what follows, so if you have problems here, consider hiking. (Hiking is actually faster than driving.) The first challenging boulder field at 0.5 miles has a bypass on the right. The trail goes by a camp spot and turns left across Silver Creek at 0.9 miles. The creek is often dry by late summer. Several more boulder fields follow before you cross an open granite area at 2.1. More boulder fields follow with the worst part coming at 2.8 miles. Stay right at 3.3 miles (02) (bypass left) and drop down to a meadow. Bear left up granite hill at 3.8 and cross stream at 4.0. Negotiate challenging granite mounds before arriving at Barrett Lake at 4.3 miles (03).

Return Trip: Return the way you came.

Services: Gas at Kyburz. Store at Strawberry. Vault toilets at several points around Wrights Lake. Roofless pit toilet at Barrett Lake.

Maps: Eldorado National Forest map, USGS 7.5-minute map, Rockbound Valley, CA. DeLorme Atlas & Gazetteer.

105

AREA 4

South Lake Tahoe, Arnold, Bear Valley, Sonora

25. Strawberry Pass
26. Deer Valley
27. Corral Hollow
28. Slickrock Trail
29. Niagara Rim
30. Eagle Peak
31. Dodge Ridge

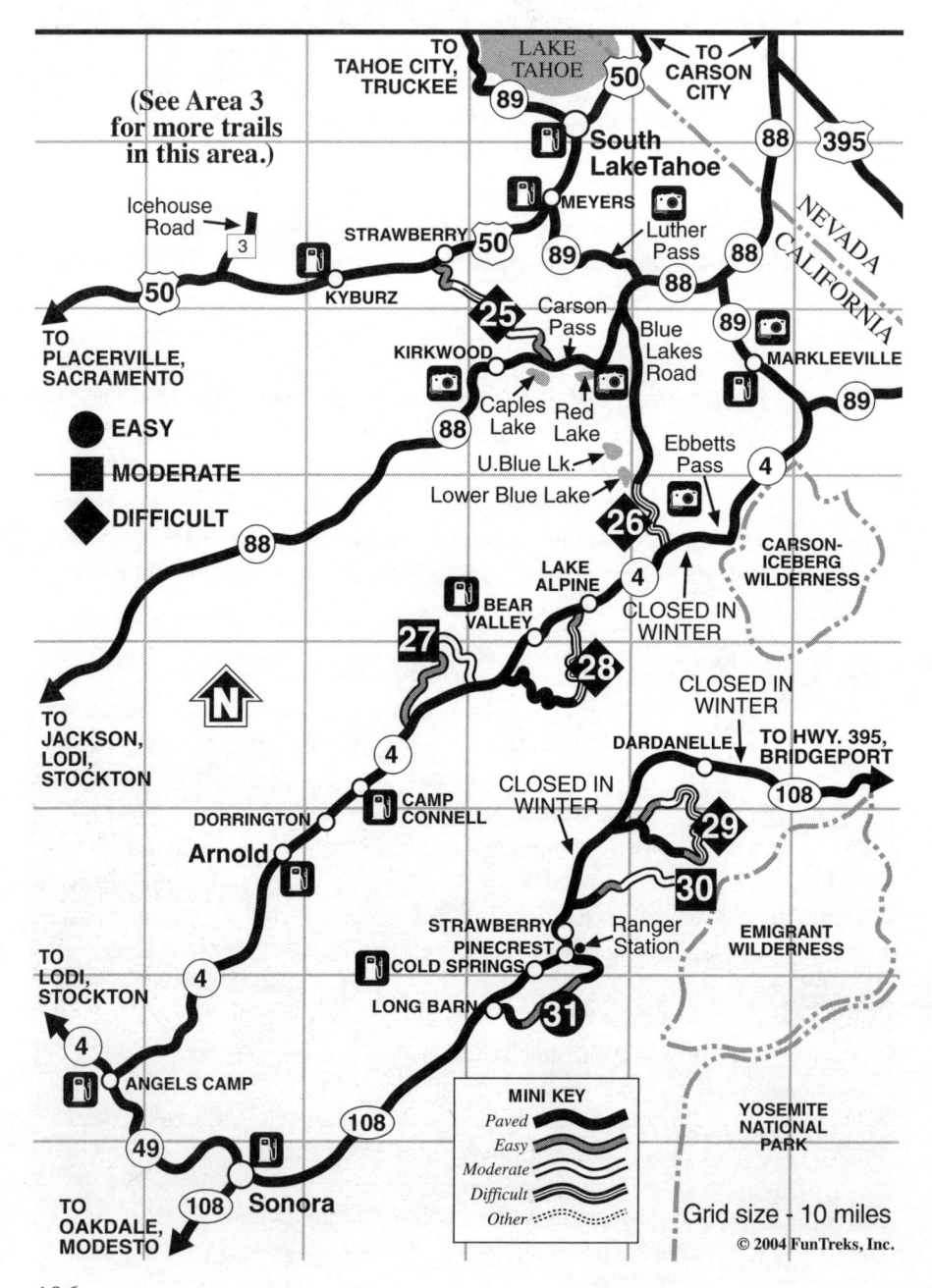

AREA 4

South Lake Tahoe, Arnold, Bear Valley, Sonora

It is no coincidence that good four-wheel-drive trails are often located near ski areas. Backroads that are scenic and fun to drive tend to be in steep, high places just like ski slopes. *Strawberry Pass* starts near Sierra-at-Tahoe Ski Area and ends near Kirkwood Ski Area. Moderate *Corral Hollow* climbs to a high point next to Bear Valley Ski Area. The trail literally passes within a few feet of the sign for "Tiggers" black diamond ski run. Easy *Dodge Ridge* is reached by following signs to the Dodge Ridge Ski Area near Pinecrest. Located just north of Pinecrest is moderate *Eagle Peak* and the very popular, but difficult, *Niagara Rim*. Memorable *Slickrock Trail* departs from Lake Alpine just east of Bear Valley, while difficult *Deer Valley* trail is just a few miles farther north. Needless to say, there is no wintertime wheeling in this area. In fact, main Highways 4 and 108 receive so much snow, the road's highest points are closed in the winter. But in the summer, this area is a recreational wonderland offering the best in motorized recreation, hiking, biking, camping, and fishing.

This great camp spot, across from the Bear Valley Ski Area, is accessed from Trail #27.

Be careful here or risk body damage.

Watch for range cattle.

Several camp spots along the south end of trail look down on Caples Lake.

A few muddy places.

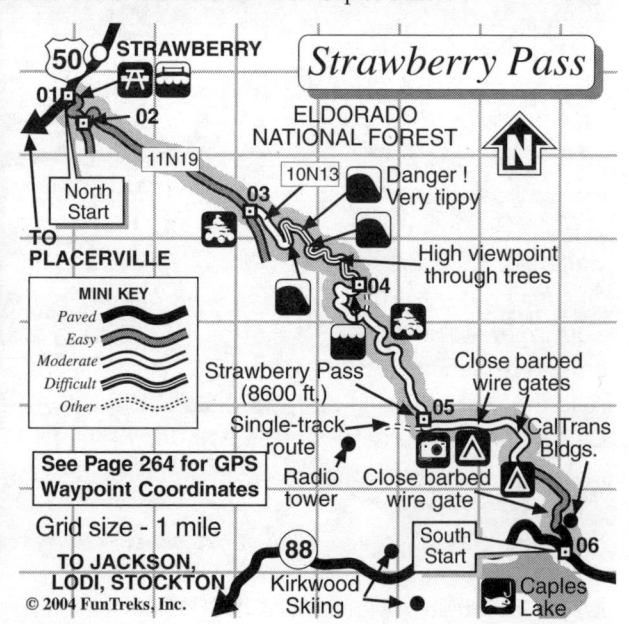

Strawberry Pass

STRAWBERRY

ELDORADO NATIONAL FOREST

11N19

10N13

Danger! Very tippy

North Start

TO PLACERVILLE

High viewpoint through trees

MINI KEY
- Paved
- Easy
- Moderate
- Difficult
- Other

Strawberry Pass (8600 ft.)

Close barbed wire gates

CalTrans Bldgs.

Single-track route

Radio tower

Close barbed wire gate

See Page 264 for GPS Waypoint Coordinates

Grid size - 1 mile

TO JACKSON, LODI, STOCKTON

© 2004 FunTreks, Inc.

88

Kirkwood Skiing

South Start

Caples Lake

108

Strawberry Pass 25

Location: East of Placerville and southwest of Lake Tahoe.

Difficulty: Difficult. North half is steep, narrow, and brushy with two rock challenges and one very tippy spot. The south half is easy to moderate, very scenic and suitable for stock SUVs. Three gates. ATV and dirt bike routes.

Features: An adventurous shortcut between Highways 50 and 88, but don't drive it to save time. Great views of Caples Lake from south side.

Time & Distance: Allow about 3 hours one way for this 12.5-mile trip.

To Get There: **From north:** Turn south off Hwy. 50 about a half mile southwest of Strawberry. This road is F.S. 7 but it's not well marked. A picnic area at this point is hard to see. You'll see a bridge after you turn. **From south:** From Hwy. 88, on northeast side of Caples Lake, head north on paved road to CalTrans Maintenance Station.

Trail Description: **From north:** *Reset your odometer as you turn off Hwy. 50* (01). Cross bridge and swing right. Turn left at 0.6 miles (02) on 11N19. Stay right at 0.8 then bear left on 10N13 at 3.2 miles (03). Road narrows and gets very steep with difficult spots starting at 4.1 miles. Several driver's choices. Be very careful at 4.5 miles where it is very tippy. (My tip gauge went to 32 degrees!) Tough rock squeeze at 4.8 then more climbing. Stay right at 5.3 and 6.2 miles (04). Make no turns until you reach scenic Strawberry Pass at 9.1 miles (05). Bear left here downhill on better road. Make no turns as you pass several camp spots with great views. Open and close wire gates at 9.5, 10.3 and 12.0 miles. Bear left on paved road at maintenance station at 12.1 before reaching Hwy. 88 at 12.5 miles (06).

From south: *Reset odometer at Hwy. 88* (06) and head north. Bear right uphill when pavement ends. Climb, then head west along scenic ridge, closing 3 gates behind you. Turn right uphill at wide spot before 3.4 miles. Turn right at top of ridge at 3.4 miles (05). Stay left at 6.3 miles (04) before crossing small stream. Two driver's choices at 7.2. Rock obstacle at 7.7 as road drops steeply and narrows. Stay left downhill at 8.0 at very tippy spot. Bear right at 9.3 miles (03) on 11N19. Stay left at 11.7 then turn right at 11.9 miles (02). Turn left across bridge before reaching Hwy. 50 at 12.5 miles (01).

Services: Gas at Kyburz. General store in Strawberry.

Maps: Eldorado N.F. map, USGS 100,000-scale map, Placerville, CA.

Watch for waterfall on west side of trail.

High water crossing Blue Creek.

Climbing the Rock Garden.

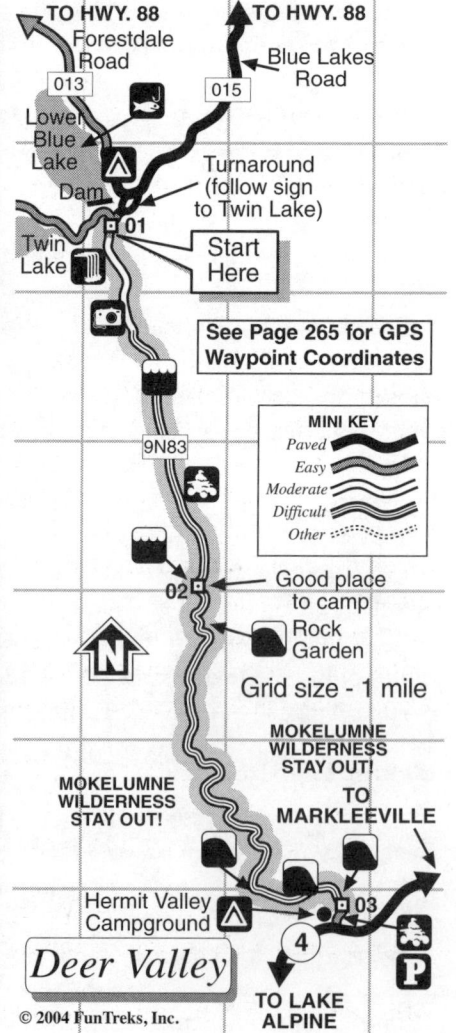

Southern half of trail is steep in places.

110

Deer Valley 26

Location: South of Lake Tahoe and east of Sacramento.

Difficulty: Difficult. Serious rock obstacles and potentially deep water crossings. Not for stock SUVs. High clearance and lockers recommended.

Features: Start of trail is a long drive from any direction but the scenery is superb. Hwys. 88 and 4 are National Scenic Byways. The Upper and Lower Blue Lakes area is a popular recreation destination offering many places to camp, hike, bike and fish. Deer Valley Trail passes through a non wilderness corridor of the Mokelumne Wilderness. Stay on designated route.

Time & Distance: Allow about 3 hours one way for this 6.6-mile trip.

To Get There: From Hwy. 88 north of Carson Pass, take Blue Lakes Road south through Hope Valley to Lower Blue Lake. Go straight (southwest) past kiosk at turnaround area following signs to Twin Lake. Turn right at building with green roof. You'll soon see Deer Valley Trail 19E01 on the left (also marked 9N83). If you drive the trail from the south end, start at Hermit Valley Campground located on Hwy. 4 north of Lake Alpine. This way is more difficult because it is uphill.

Trail Description: Reset your odometer at start of trail south of Lower Blue Lake Dam (01). Head south into the forest alongside Blue Creek. Note large waterfall on right. The trail soon gets rockier with a driver's choice at 0.9 miles. You'll reach a meadow and cross Blue Creek at 1.2 miles. The creek can be deep during wet periods, as it was when I drove the trail. Cross the creek again at 2.8 miles (02). This is a good area to camp. Pass through the difficult *Rock Garden* at 3.2 miles. The toughest part of trail follows as you descend more steeply over more rocky sections, especially at 5.7 and 6.2 miles. You'll descend one final rocky stretch as you drop into Hermit Valley Campground at 6.6 miles (03). Highway 4 is directly ahead.

Return Trip: Turn right on Hwy. 4 to reach Lake Alpine, Bear Valley and, eventually, Stockton. Left takes you over beautiful Ebbetts Pass to Markleeville, South Lake Tahoe and Carson City, NV.

Services: Gas at Meyers, Bear Valley and Markleeville. General store at Lake Alpine and Bear Valley. Full services in South Lake Tahoe and Arnold.

Maps: Eldorado N.F. map, USGS 100,000-scale map, Smith Valley, CA.

First part of trail is rocky.

Cross this meadow and climb a steep hill.

Bear Valley Ski Area.

Bear Trap Cabin is located in a scenic meadow.

ATV approaches cabin.

Second half of trail is easy.

© 2004 FunTreks, Inc.

Corral Hollow

MOKELUMNE WILDERNESS

Camp Spot
Bear Valley Ski Area
Cattle Gate
Bear Trap Cabin
Steep
TO BEAR VALLEY
7N11
Sign for Alpine County Line
Start here
Cabbage Patch Road
7N11
STANISLAUS NATIONAL FOREST
Grid size - 1 mile
TO ARNOLD

MINI KEY
Paved
Easy
Moderate
Difficult
Other

See Page 265 for GPS Waypoint Coordinates

112

Corral Hollow 27

Location: Northeast of Stockton and Modesto near Bear Valley Ski Area.

Difficulty: Moderate. First half is rocky and steep in places. Last half is easy. Can be muddy in spots when it rains. Suitable for any stock high clearance, 4-wheel-drive SUV with skid plates and low-range gearing.

Features: A mildly challenging drive to a high, scenic ridge. A good SUV adventure. Camp overlooking Bear Valley Ski Area or stay at Bear Trap "Cowboy" Cabin now owned by the Forest Service. Green Sticker vehicles are allowed except on Cabbage Patch Road.

Time & Distance: 13.9 miles as described here. Allow 3 to 4 hours.

To Get There: Head east on Hwy. 4 and turn north just after a sign for Alpine County Line about 0.6 miles before Bear Valley. The trail, marked 7A, is hidden in a clump of trees. There's a small area to park at start.

Trail Description: Reset your odometer at start (01). The trail winds through the trees over manageable embedded rocks before reaching a meadow of dense mule's ear at 1.6 miles. The trail climbs steeply over loose rock at 1.9 miles. After a driver's choice, you reach the top of ridge at 2.3 miles (02). To the right is a ski slope for Bear Valley Ski Area. Turn left and climb across the ridge. Pass through a barbed wire cattle gate at 2.9 and close it. After the gate, watch for a camp spot on the right with views of the ski area. The road winds downhill before reaching a fork at 6.3 miles (03). Right goes to Bear Trap Cabin. Check with the Forest Service in advance if you intend to stay in the cabin. Leave everything the way you find it.

Reset your odometer at the fork (03) and turn left (right if you visited the cabin). Continue straight at 2.0 miles where 7N11 joins on the right. Go straight again at 6.2 and 6.6 where two more roads join on right. Turn left when you reach a wide gravel road at 6.7 miles (04). This is Cabbage Patch Road. Continue straight at 7.2 miles before reaching Hwy. 4 at 7.6 miles (05).

Return Trip: Right on Hwy. 4 goes back to Stockton and Modesto. Left goes to Bear Valley and Lake Alpine.

Services: Gas in Arnold and Bear Valley. Outhouse at Bear Trap Cabin.

Maps: Stanislaus National Forest map, USGS 100,000-scale map, San Andreas, CA, Calaveras R.D. OHV map, DeLorme Atlas & Gazetteer.

Crystal-clear waters of Silver Creek.

The trail is fun to drive.

Final obstacle is the toughest.

Outflow stream from Utica Reservoir.

Steep section of slickrock.

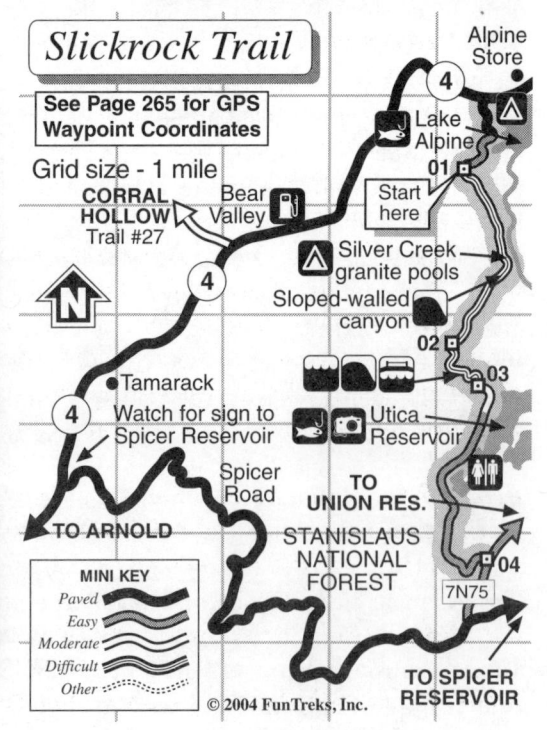

Slickrock Trail

See Page 265 for GPS Waypoint Coordinates

Grid size - 1 mile

CORRAL HOLLOW Trail #27

Bear Valley

Start here

Alpine Store

Lake Alpine

Silver Creek granite pools

Sloped-walled canyon

Tamarack

Watch for sign to Spicer Reservoir

Utica Reservoir

Spicer Road

TO UNION RES.

TO ARNOLD

STANISLAUS NATIONAL FOREST

7N75

TO SPICER RESERVOIR

MINI KEY
Paved
Easy
Moderate
Difficult
Other

© 2004 FunTreks, Inc.

114

Slickrock Trail 28

Location: Northeast of Modesto, immediately south of Lake Alpine.

Difficulty: Difficult. The first part of trail is moderate and suitable for aggressive stock SUVs. The last part has some challenging hardcore obstacles. A good driver in a seasoned SUV can probably get through okay.

Features: Much of trail traverses large rock slabs, giving you a little taste of Moab. Silver Creek flows over rocks beside the trail with wonderful clear pools in which to relax and play. Unique places to camp along the way. The south end of trail runs along beautiful Utica Reservoir, a scenic place to camp, mountain bike and flatwater kayak. Street-legal vehicles only.

Time & Distance: Allow about 3 hours for this 5.2-mile trip.

To Get There: Take Hwy. 4 to Lake Alpine north of Bear Valley. Turn right at west end of lake following signs to Lake Alpine C.G. Head south, staying to the right as roads branch left. When the bike trail goes right, you go left. Bear right at blue cabin then right again at private drive. Follow narrow road to well-marked trailhead 0.7 miles from Hwy. 4.

Trail Description: Reset your odometer at start (01). Head south through dense forest on a rough road. Soon, Silver Creek can be seen on the left cascading over granite slabs. The kids will enjoy this area and it's a great place to camp. The trail swings right away from the creek at 1.0 miles and drops into a dramatic sloped-walled canyon. The road alternates between woods and granite before reaching a steep granite descent at 2.1 miles (02). Stay right as you descend. A stream crossing follows with one last difficult obstacle at 2.6 miles. This ends the difficult part of trail. Stock SUVs can reach this point coming in from the south. Cross a high wooden bridge through a scenic area. The other end of trail is marked at 2.9 miles (03). After climbing one last slab, the road winds along the west end of beautiful Utica Reservoir. Forest Rd. 7N75, a wide gravel road, is reached at 5.2 miles (04)

Return Trip: Turn right on F.S. Road 7N75. Continue straight when you reach Spicer Reservoir Road in 0.7 miles. Follow this paved road another 7.8 miles to Hwy. 4 just south of Tamarack. From here, Arnold is left 22 miles.

Services: Gas at Bear Valley. General stores at Bear Valley and Lake Alpine.

Maps: Stanislaus N. F. map, USGS 7.5-minute map, Tamarack, CA.

Stay off your brakes on *Heartbreak Hill*.

Awesome scenery along the way.

Sidewall Suicide.

Climbing the worst part of the *Rock Pile*.

Starting through *Lion's Butt*.

Exiting canyon above the *Rock Pile*.

Niagara Rim 29

Location: Northeast of Modesto, Sonora and Pinecrest.

Difficulty: Difficult. Several dangerous tippy spots cannot be bypassed. Narrow and brushy in places with sharp lava rock that can cut sidewalls. Two popular obstacles, *Lion's Butt* and the *Rock Pile*, are optional. *Lion's Butt* has terrain similar to Moab but on a much smaller scale. Easy and difficult routes may be selected. The *Rock Pile* is strictly extreme hardcore 4-wheeling. Although modified vehicles are best suited for this trail, experienced drivers in high-clearance, well-equipped SUVs can get through if they avoid the extreme parts. Body damage is more likely for lesser-equipped vehicles. Excellent articulation or one locker is recommended.

Features: A popular, but not overused, hardcore trail offering difficult challenges and terrific scenery. A conveniently located OHV campground connects to several shortcut routes to key obstacles. These routes can also be used as early exits. This trail is adopted by the *4x4 In Motion* Club from Modesto. Contact them for information on Niagara Rim special events. (See state Web site *www.cal4wheel.com* for contact information.)

Time & Distance: The official trail measures only 6.4 miles. Allow about 3 hours not counting time spent on optional sections. By entering and exiting at different points, you can pick and choose your favorite parts of the trail. This trail makes a great weekend outing.

To Get There: Take Hwy. 108 northeast from Sonora to Pinecrest. Stay on 108 another 14.4 miles. Turn right on a paved road at signs for Eagle Meadows and Niagara OHV Campground. *Reset odometer.* Stay right at 0.3 miles and 0.9 miles. OHV Campground is on left at 2.8 miles (01). After the campground, stay right at 2.9. Start of trail is sharply left at 6.0 miles (02).

Trail Description: Reset your odometer at start (02). Head uphill past a small sign indicating this is an extreme trail. At 0.1 miles, *No-Way-Out Hill* is reached. Although it doesn't look that tough, rollovers have occurred here. Stay high and left against the manzanita bushes to avoid sliding and tipping to the right. Make sure your tires are adequately aired down. At 0.4 miles, swing left around unusual *P.H. Rock* (euphemistic acronym), then turn right down steep *Heartbreak Hill*. Shift into your lowest gear and avoid the temptation to slam on your brakes when your vehicle lurches over a rock ledge about half way down. Short wheel-based vehicles need to be especially careful to avoid flipping back over front.

Bear right at 1.0 miles where 5N09 joins on the left. Turn right at 1.5 miles (03) before a green gate. Straight through the gate is an early exit. At 1.7 the trail crosses an interesting lava flow and drops off a ledge called *Sidewall Suicide*. An incorrect line here can rip open a tire. Bear right downhill after this obstacle, away from the lava flow. Cross another lava flow at 1.9. Stay right at 2.1 miles where 5N12YA goes left. Be careful not to scrape your roof on the trees as you descend *Shale Hill* at 2.2 miles. You reach *Lion's Butt* at 2.3 miles (04). This area offers granite mounds in various sizes and angles. You can drive in different directions, selecting easy and difficult routes. Right takes you down into the mounds, straight is the bypass. After *Lion's Butt,* the trail turns west through a flatter, lightly treed area. This is a popular camping area because it provides access to *Lion's Butt* and the *Rock Pile*, which is just ahead. During special events, this area is called *Base Camp*. This point has a convenient access route from the OHV Campground.

Find the trail marker for 5N09A at approximately 3.0 miles (05) and *reset your odometer*. At this intersection, there is also an arrow pointing right to the *Rock Pile*. Follow the arrow until you reach a sign for the *Rock Pile* at 0.4 miles. This sign marks the exit point. Continue right past the sign another 100 feet to the entrance to the *Rock Pile* on the left (06). It's a nasty narrow canyon about 400 feet long and entirely optional. If you attempt it, and make it to the top of the canyon, turn right and circle back down over a series of granite ledges. Cross back over the canyon to come out at the exit point. Turn left and return to the entrance. To continue on the trail, bear right this time.

Reset your odometer as you leave the Rock Pile entrance point. Turn left at 0.1, followed by a hairpin right turn at 0.7 miles (07). (Left returns to the OHV Campground.) Pass a scenic viewpoint of Double Dome Rock at 1.7 then swing left. Negotiate a steep, loose hill at 2.0. Turn left at 2.6 miles (08) and 3.0 miles. Cross a paved creek bed at 5.0 and return to the paved entry road at 5.7 miles (09). Left takes you back to the OHV Campground. Right takes you out to Highway 108.

Return Trip: Turn left on Highway 108 to return to Pinecrest and Sonora. Right goes to Dardanelle and Bridgeport.

Services: Gas is available in Cold Springs a few miles west of Pinecrest. Strawberry has a general store and restaurant. Another general store is located by the marina at Pinecrest Lake. The OHV campground has a pit toilet and adequate room to park.

Maps: Stanislaus National Forest map, USGS 7.5-minute map, Dardanelle, CA, DeLorme Atlas & Gazetteer.

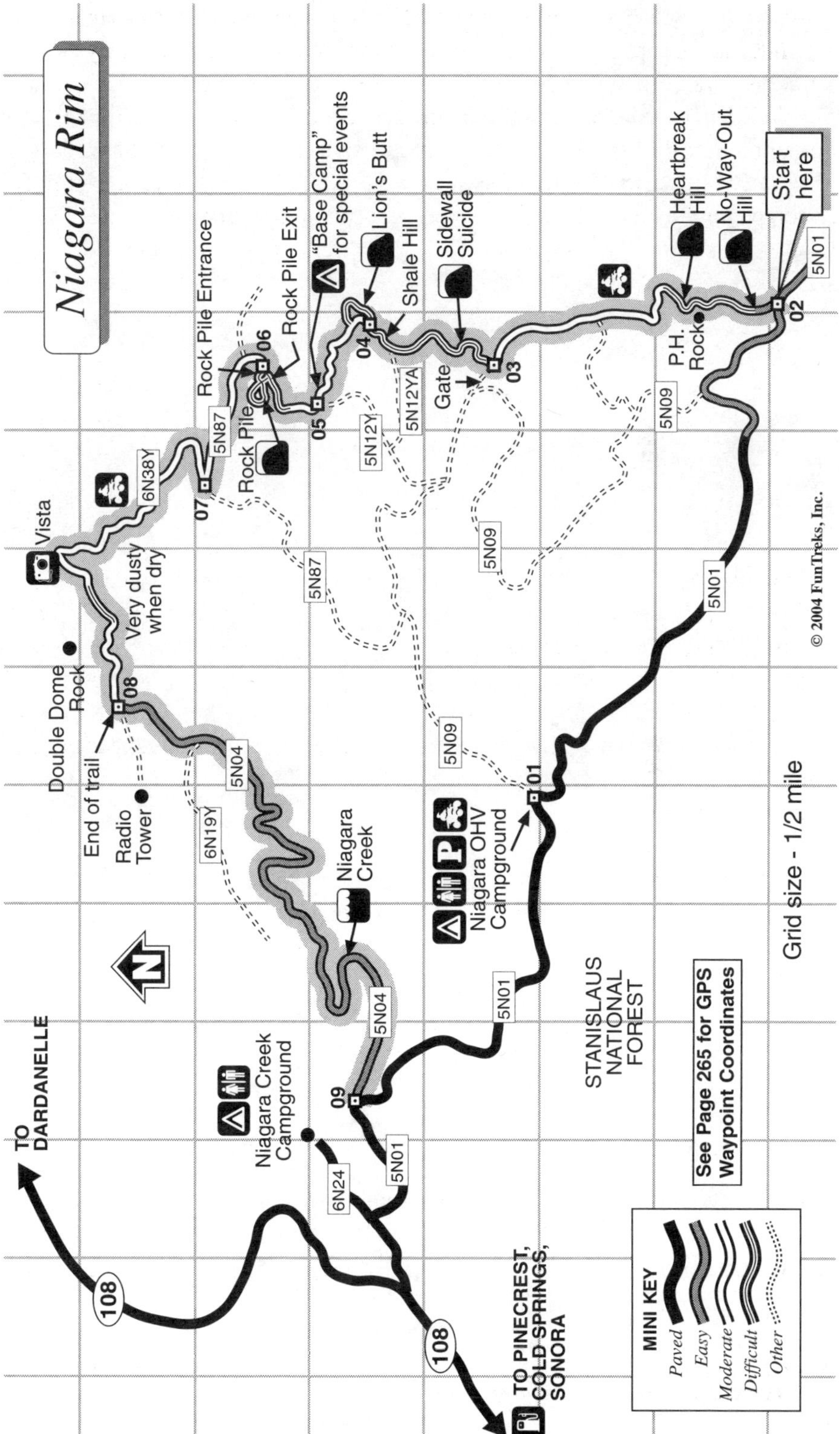

Niagara Rim
Start here
5N01
02
No-Way-Out Hill
Heartbreak Hill
P.H. Rock
5N09
03
Gate
Sidewall Suicide
5N12YA
Shale Hill
04
Lion's Butt
"Base Camp" for special events
05
5N12Y
Rock Pile Exit
06
Rock Pile Entrance
Rock Pile
5N87
07
6N38Y
Vista
Very dusty when dry
Double Dome Rock
08
End of trail
Radio Tower
6N19Y
5N04
5N09
01
Niagara OHV Campground
Niagara Creek
5N01
STANISLAUS NATIONAL FOREST
09
Niagara Creek Campground
6N24
TO DARDANELLE
108
TO PINECREST, COLD SPRINGS, SONORA
See Page 265 for GPS Waypoint Coordinates
Grid size - 1/2 mile
MINI KEY
Paved
Easy
Moderate
Difficult
Other
© 2004 FunTreks, Inc.

Striking volcanic terrain at start of trail.

Dramatic cliffs along the way.

Watch for fallen trees.

View from Eagle Peak at 9,386 feet.

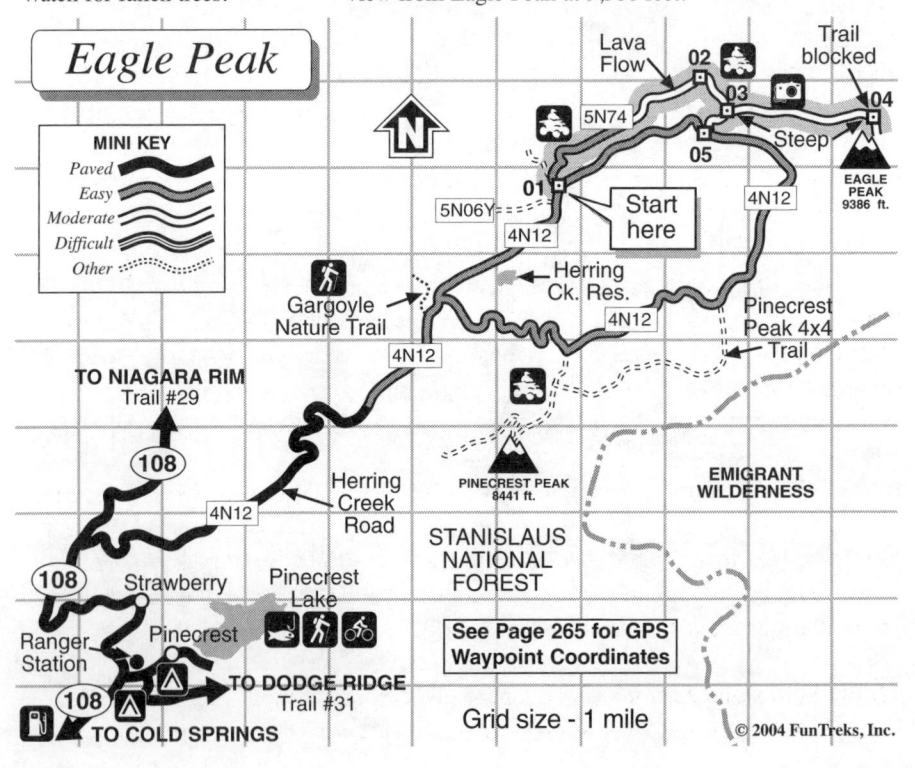

Eagle Peak

MINI KEY
Paved
Easy
Moderate
Difficult
Other

TO NIAGARA RIM
Trail #29

108

4N12

108

Strawberry

Ranger Station

Pinecrest
Pinecrest Lake

108

TO COLD SPRINGS

Herring Creek Road

TO DODGE RIDGE
Trail #31

Lava Flow

5N74

5N06Y

4N12

01

Start here

Herring Ck. Res.

4N12

4N12

PINECREST PEAK
8441 ft.

STANISLAUS NATIONAL FOREST

02

03

05

04

Trail blocked

Steep

EAGLE PEAK
9386 ft.

Pinecrest Peak 4x4 Trail

EMIGRANT WILDERNESS

Gargoyle Nature Trail

See Page 265 for GPS Waypoint Coordinates

Grid size - 1 mile

© 2004 FunTreks, Inc.

120

Eagle Peak 30

Location: Northeast of Sonora, Pinecrest and Strawberry.

Difficulty: Moderate. Most of the trail is easy but there are a few steep, rocky hills to climb. Suitable for all high-clearance SUVs with 4WD.

Features: A short and convenient outing to a remote, scenic mountain top. Enjoy hiking, biking and camping along trail and at nearby Pinecrest Lake, home to popular Meadowview and Pinecrest Forest Service Campgrounds.

Time & Distance: Complete loop measures 10.0 miles. Allow 2-3 hours.

To Get There: Head east on Hwy. 108. Bear left past the Ranger Station at the Pinecrest turnoff. Continue another 3.5 miles to Herring Creek Road and turn right. *Reset your odometer.* Continue on the road after the pavement ends at 5.4 miles. Just past the "Gargoyles" Nature Trail, turn left at 6.7 miles where a sign points right to Herring Creek Reservoir. The road climbs and gets a bit rougher. Bear right at 8.5 miles where 5N06Y goes left. Turn left at 8.7 miles on 5N74. This starts the 4-wheel-drive route.

Trail Description: Reset your odometer at start (01). Head northeast on 5N74, crossing mule-ear-covered meadows. Bear right at 0.4 miles. Go either way at 1.3. I went left at 1.8 to get around a fallen tree. At 2.3 miles the road vanishes as it crosses a wide lava flow. The road appears to go right but it does not. Head slightly left in a northeast direction. Gradually, the road reappears and swings to the right. The lava flow ends at 2.5 miles (02). The road leans a bit at 2.8. Bear left down a steep hill at 3.1 miles (03). The road climbs steeply through a scenic area and winds tightly through the trees. Deadfall blocked the road at 5.1 miles (04). I didn't have my chainsaw with me, so I hiked the last 0.2 miles. After seeing the peak, retrace your drive 2.0 miles back to the steep hill you came down (03), and turn left. When you reach 4N12 in another 0.4 miles (05), turn right.

Return Trip: Return to starting point on 4N12 and go out the way you came in.

Services: Gas is available in Cold Springs a few miles west of Pinecrest. Strawberry has a general store and restaurant. Another general store is located by the marina at Pinecrest Lake. Two F.S. campgrounds in Pinecrest.

Maps: Stanislaus National Forest map, USGS 7.5-minute map, Donnell Lake, CA, DeLorme Atlas & Gazetteer.

Get flyer that explains tour features.  Glacial *erratic* deposited at the *Cirque*.

Walk north a short distance for view of Pinecrest Lake.  The *Crooked Tree*.

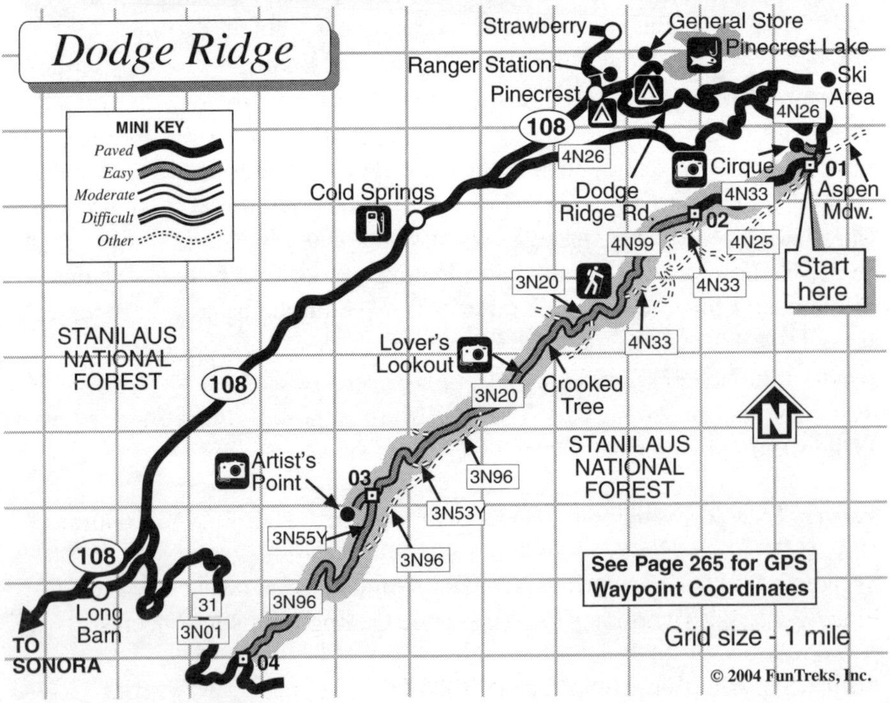

Dodge Ridge

MINI KEY
Paved
Easy
Moderate
Difficult
Other

Strawberry
General Store
Pinecrest Lake
Ranger Station
Pinecrest
Ski Area
108
4N26
4N26
Cirque
Cold Springs
Dodge Ridge Rd.
01 Aspen Mdw.
4N33
02
4N25
4N99
4N33
Start here
3N20
Lover's Lookout
4N33
3N20
Crooked Tree
STANISLAUS NATIONAL FOREST
Artist's Point
03
3N96
3N53Y
3N55Y
3N96
STANISLAUS NATIONAL FOREST
108
31
3N96
Long Barn
3N01
04
TO SONORA

See Page 265 for GPS Waypoint Coordinates

Grid size - 1 mile

© 2004 FunTreks, Inc.

122

Dodge Ridge 31

Location: Northeast of Sonora, southwest of Pinecrest.

Difficulty: Easy. High clearance needed but not 4-wheel drive when dry.

Features: Scenic, quiet backcountry SUV getaway close to popular Pinecrest Lake. Great camping, hiking, biking, fishing and boating in the area. Pick up a free flyer on the *Sierra Grandstand Tour* available at the Mi-Wok or Summit Ranger Stations. The flyer explains history, geology and numbered features along the route.

Time & Distance: From Pinecrest to Long Barn is 23.7 miles. Allow 3 hours.

To Get There: Take Hwy. 108 to Pinecrest. Turn right on Pinecrest Lake Road at Summit Ranger Station and *reset odometer*. Turn right at 0.3 miles on Dodge Ridge Road. Just before you reach Dodge Ridge Ski Area at 3.3 miles, turn right following sign to Aspen Meadow. At 3.7 miles, turn left on 4N26. A big sign for the *Sierra Grandstand Tour* is on the right at 5.4 miles. Go right to an interesting dead-end overlook called the *Cirque*. Turn around and come back to the sign. Then turn right and continue south another 0.3 miles to 4N33 on the right. The trail really starts here.

Trail Description: Reset your odometer at start of 4N33 (01). Bear right at 2.0 miles (02) on lesser 4N99. Go by *Pinecrest View* at 2.7 and *Bourland Overlook* at 3.2. Stay right at 3.9 as you rejoin 4N33. Go right then left at 4.5 on 3N20. Unusual *Crooked Tree* is on left at 5.4. Pass *Lover's Lookout* at 6.0. Continue straight at 6.7, 7.5 and 7.9 miles. Bear left at 8.0 miles when 3N49 goes right. Side trip to *Artist's Point* goes right at 8.9 miles (03) on 3N42. The road goes uphill to a nice view point with log benches at 9.0 and loops back. Continue right downhill when you return from *Artist's Point* following 3N55Y. Continue straight and merge with gravel road 3N96 at 10.1 miles. Turn right on paved F.S. 31 at 12.6 miles (04). As you proceed, watch for historic *Fahey Cabin* in a field off to the left. Long Barn is left at 17.9 miles. Turn right for Highway 108, reached at 18.0 miles.

Return Trip: Right on 108 goes back to Pinecrest. Left goes to Sonora.

Services: Gas at Cold Springs. General store and food near marina at Pinecrest Lake. Two major Forest Service Campgrounds in Pinecrest.

Maps: Stanislaus N.F. map, USGS 100,000-scale map, San Andreas, CA.

AREA 5

Bridgeport,
Lee Vining,
Mammoth Lakes,
Bishop

32. Bodie Ghost Town
33. Kavanaugh Ridge
34. Copper Mountain
35. Horse Meadows
36. Deadman Pass
37. Backway to Inyo Craters
38. Laurel Lakes
39. Sand Canyon
40. Wheeler Ridge
41. Buttermilk Country
42. Coyote Flat
43. Silver/Wyman Canyons

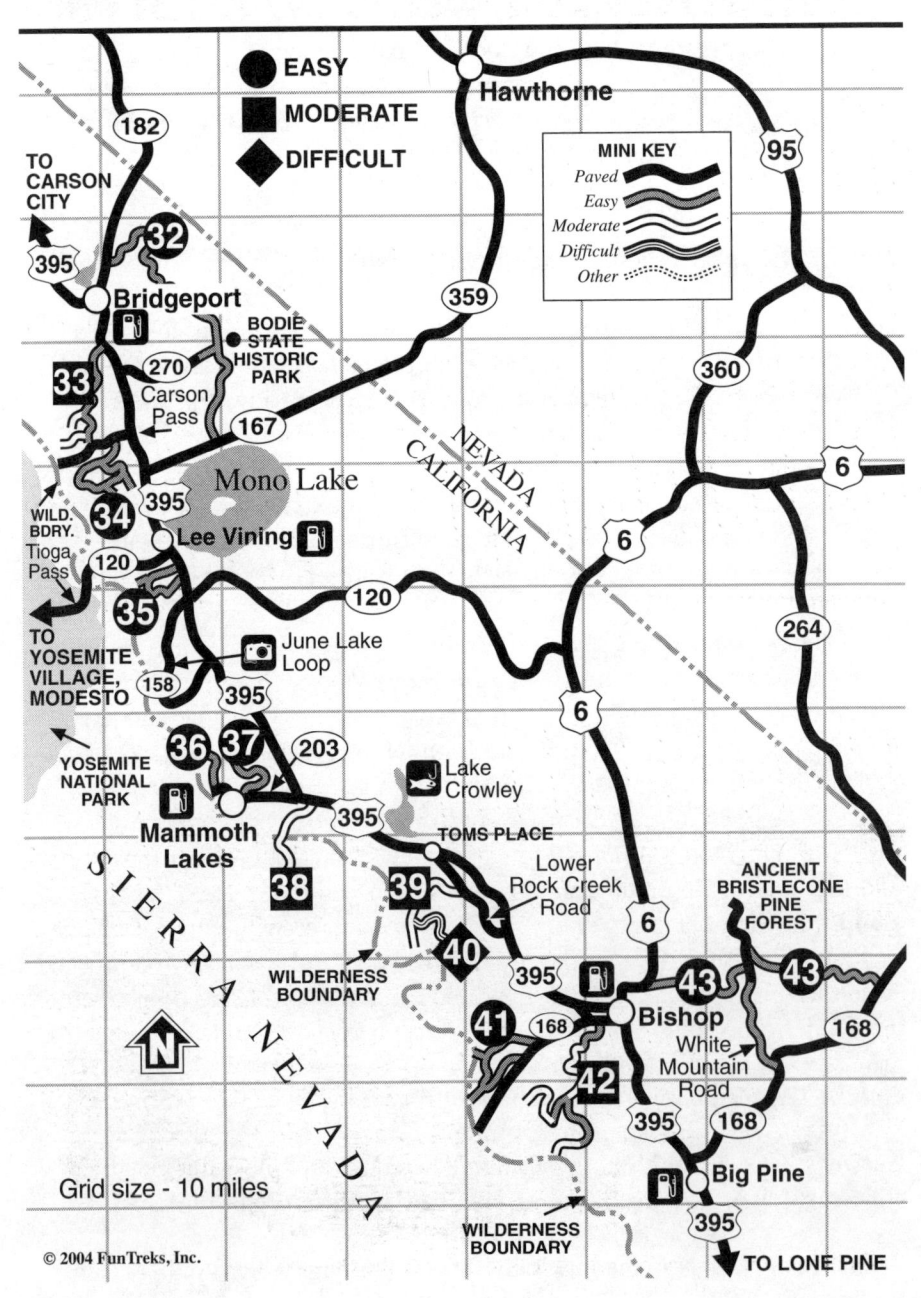

© 2004 FunTreks, Inc.

AREA 5

Bridgeport, Lee Vining, Mammoth Lakes, Bishop

What struck me about this part of California was how physically isolated it is from the western part of the state. The massive Sierra Nevada Mountain Range, with its wide band of national parks and wilderness areas, practically slices the state in half. At one point, there is a 140-mile stretch where no road crosses east to west. Despite this fact, throngs of outdoor enthusiasts visit and vacation in the area to enjoy its great weather and awesome natural beauty. SUV owners will be pleased to learn that, sandwiched between Highway 395 and wilderness areas to the west, are many beautiful backroads ideally suited for stock vehicles. Above Mammoth Lakes, easy but spectacular *Deadman Pass* looks down on the Mammoth Ski Area. A short distance east, enjoy a thrilling and photogenic shelf road to remote *Laurel Lakes*. Bishop has no less than five outstanding adventure roads within a few miles of town. Lee Vining, with several excellent backcountry routes, also serves as the eastern gateway to Yosemite National Park. And finally, you can travel via little-used backroads from Bridgeport to *Bodie,* perhaps the most authentic and best preserved ghost town in the world.

This old gas station is one of many things to see at Bodie Ghost Town, Trail #32.

125

Much to see at the Chemung Mine.

Begin tour of Bodie at west end of town.

Bridgeport as seen from Masonic Mtn.

Distant view of Bodie.

Remains of stone cabin at Masonic.

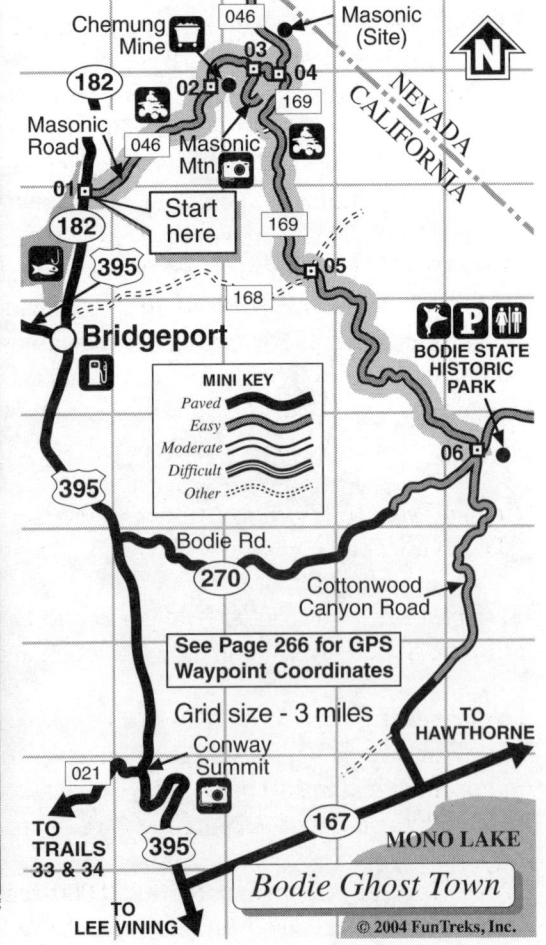

MINI KEY
Paved
Easy
Moderate
Difficult
Other

See Page 266 for GPS Waypoint Coordinates

Grid size - 3 miles

TO HAWTHORNE
TO TRAILS 33 & 34
TO LEE VINING
MONO LAKE

Bodie Ghost Town

© 2004 FunTreks, Inc.

126

Bodie Ghost Town 32

Location: East of Bridgeport, north of Mono Lake.

Difficulty: Easy. Any high clearance SUV can make it in dry weather.

Features: Most tourists reach Bodie Ghost Town (Bodie State Historic Park) via paved Hwy. 270. The trip described here is a more interesting backcountry route starting north of Bridgeport. On the way you'll see great views, structures at the Chemung Mine and the historic site of Masonic.

Time & Distance: Allow 3 hours for the 28-mile drive to Bodie. Add another 30 minutes to return via Hwy. 270 or a bit longer via Cottonwood Canyon.

To Get There: From Bridgeport, go 3.8 miles north on Highway 182 to Masonic Road (F.S. Road 046), on the right.

Trail Description: Reset your odometer as you turn off Hwy. 182 (01). Head east on wide graded road. At 5.0 miles (02), turn right on short side trip to Chemung Mine. Check out the buildings, then turn left back to main road at 5.3 miles. Continue to right. Nice camp spot on right at 6.3. A 1.2-mile side trip goes right at 7.3 miles (03) to 9,217 ft. Masonic Mountain with great views. Return to main road, *reset odometer* and continue right. Continue straight on 046 at 0.8 miles (04) for a short side trip to the old mining site of Masonic reached at 1.8 miles. Turn around and return to Rd. 169. *Reset odometer* and turn left. Continue straight at 6.7 miles (05) where 168 goes right. After several shallow creek crossings, you'll come over a rise at 14.0 miles and see Bodie in the distance. The parking lot is reached at 15.5 miles (06).

Return Trip: To return to Bridgeport, take Hwy. 270 west. For Lee Vining, take Cottonwood Canyon Road (good gravel) to Hwy. 167 and turn right.

Services: Most services in Bridgeport and Lee Vining. Modern vault toilets at Bodie State Historic Park. Pack a lunch and plenty to drink.

Historical Highlights: In 1879, Bodie had a population of 10,000. Only 5% of the town remains, but all the remaining structures are original with only minor modifications to help preserve what's left. A small fee is charged to help with the costs of keeping the park open.

Maps: Toiyabe N.F. map, USGS 250,000-scale map, Walker Lake, CA, DeLorme Atlas & Gazetteer and Bodie State Park 16-page brochure.

Dunderberg Peak behind unnamed lake.

Moderately rocky in places.

Thick wildflowers in every color along route.

One of several log cabins at end of trail.

Snow blocks trail in mid July.

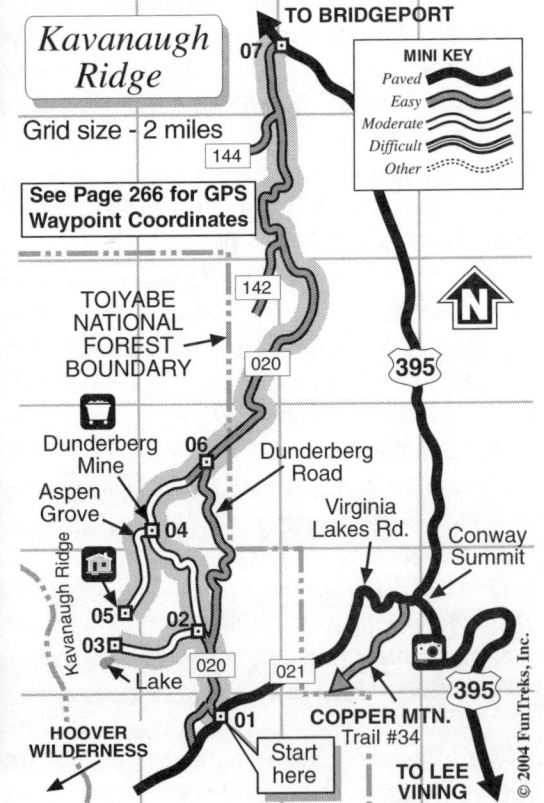

Hike past cabins to this mill site.

Kavanaugh Ridge

Grid size - 2 miles

See Page 266 for GPS Waypoint Coordinates

MINI KEY
Paved
Easy
Moderate
Difficult
Other

TO BRIDGEPORT

TOIYABE NATIONAL FOREST BOUNDARY

Dunderberg Mine
Aspen Grove
Kavanaugh Ridge
Dunderberg Road
Virginia Lakes Rd.
Conway Summit
Lake
COPPER MTN. Trail #34
HOOVER WILDERNESS
Start here
TO LEE VINING

395

© 2004 FunTreks, Inc.

128

Kavanaugh Ridge 33

Location: North of Lee Vining, south of Bridgeport.

Difficulty: Moderate. Steep and narrow in places with tight maneuvering through close trees and scratchy brush. Upper section may be blocked by snow well into July. Stock SUVs can make it but expect pinstripes in paint.

Features: Climbs above 10,000 feet near boundary to Hoover Wilderness. Travel restricted to existing roads. Dispersed camping at beautiful unnamed lake. Incredible early-summer wildflowers on way to forgotten log cabins.

Time & Distance: As described here, 18.7 miles. Allow 3-4 hours.

To Get There: Take Highway 395 to Conway Summit. Turn west on Virginia Lakes Road, F.S 021. After 4.5 miles, turn right on Dunderberg Creek Road, F.S. 020, following signs to Green Creek.

Trail Description: Reset your odometer at start of Dunderberg Road (01). Head north 1.3 miles and make a soft left turn on a road that almost parallels Dunderberg. Turn left uphill at 1.6 miles (02). This road winds steeply uphill over rocky terrain before reaching the lake at 3.1 miles (03). (Note: I had to hike part way because, in mid July, snow blocked the upper part of trail.) After visiting lake, go back down hill 1.5 miles (02), *reset odometer* and turn left. The road comes out of the trees, gets rockier and crosses a broad open area. A moderate rocky spot and small creek are crossed at 1.2 miles. Turn left at 1.4. Continue straight at 1.7 where lesser road goes left to a mine.

    Make an important left turn on a faint road that goes into a grove of aspen trees at 1.9 miles (04). Climb through tight trees and scratchy brush to a shelf road that opens up and heads south. (Great wildflowers in July.) At 3.6 miles, the road drops downhill to two log cabins at 3.7 miles (05). (You can hike downhill past the cabins to an old stamp mill.) Return 1.8 miles, *reset odometer* and turn left (04). Cross creek at 0.2 and turn right. Driver's choice at 0.4. Drop downhill to Dunderberg Road and turn left at 1.1 miles (06). Stay right at 5.1 and 5.8 before reaching Hwy. 395 at 8.6 miles (07).

Return Trip: Left on Hwy. 395 goes to Bridgeport, right to Lee Vining.

Services: Gas and other services available in Bridgeport and Lee Vining.

Maps: Toiyabe National Forest map, USGS 100,000-scale map, Bridgeport, CA, DeLorme Atlas & Gazetteer.

View from Conway Summit to Mono Lake, Lee Vining.

Looking southwest from Copper Mountain to Lundy Lake.

Easy, winding, two-track road.

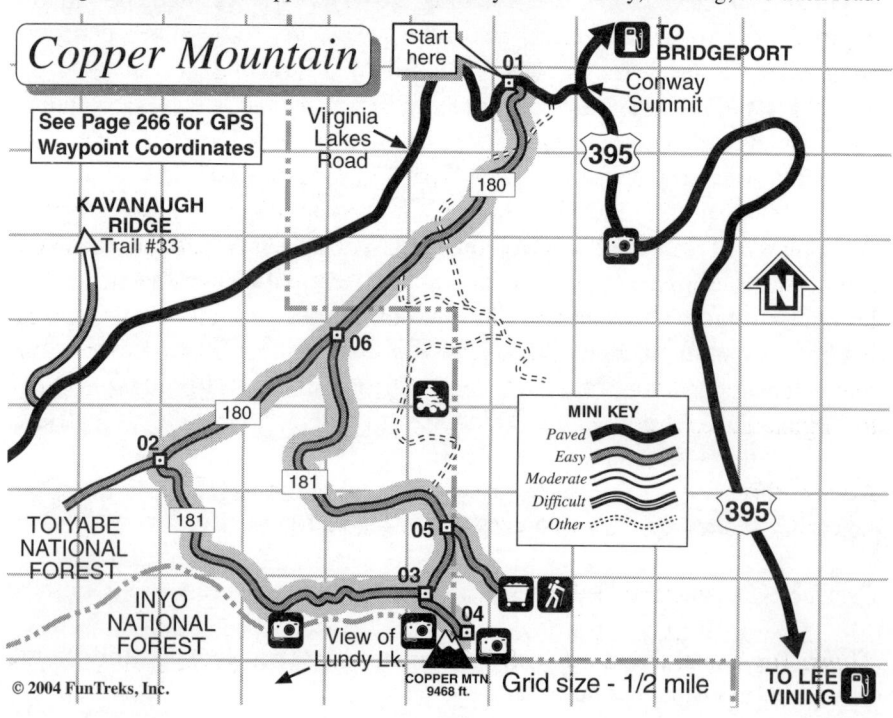

Copper Mountain

See Page 266 for GPS Waypoint Coordinates

KAVANAUGH RIDGE
Trail #33

TOIYABE NATIONAL FOREST

INYO NATIONAL FOREST

© 2004 FunTreks, Inc.

Start here

Virginia Lakes Road

Conway Summit

TO BRIDGEPORT

MINI KEY
Paved
Easy
Moderate
Difficult
Other

View of Lundy Lk.

COPPER MTN. 9468 ft.

Grid size - 1/2 mile

TO LEE VINING

130

Copper Mountain 34

Location: Northwest of Lee Vining, south of Bridgeport.

Difficulty: Easy. Brushy, bumpy two-track road traverses rolling foothills of the Sierras. Suitable for stock, high-clearance, 4-wheel-drive SUVs.

Features: High views of Mono Lake and Lundy Lake with towering Sierra Nevada Mountains as backdrop. See old mines and spring wildflowers.

Time & Distance: Allow 2 or 3 hours for this 12.2-mile loop with side trips.

To Get There: Take Hwy. 395 to Conway Summit and turn west on Virginia Lakes Road. Go 0.4 miles and turn left at sign for Jordan Basin.

Trail Description: Reset your odometer as you turn off Virginia Lakes Road (01). Continue straight at 0.5 miles when road crosses on a diagonal. Go straight again under power lines at 1.1. Continue straight at 2.0 miles (06). Later, you'll come back out the road on the left marked as F.S. 181. At 3.2 miles (02), turn left on the other end of 181. Straight dead ends. The road drops into a valley and climbs up the other side. It gets rockier in places but the views are outstanding. You reach a T intersection at 5.5 miles (03). Turn right for side trip to high point of Copper Mountain. Stay on the best traveled road until it ends about 6.0 miles (04). Great views of Mono Lake to the east but you can't see Lundy Lake to the southwest because the crown of the hill is blocking your view. Turn around and drive back about 0.1 miles and hike a few hundred feet to the left. A gorgeous view of Lundy Lake will soon appear.

Return to the T intersection (03) and *reset your odometer*. Go straight, continuing on 181. Pass through a range gate and close it behind you. An interesting road goes right at 0.4 miles (05). You can only go 0.6 miles before it becomes overgrown. You can hike farther downhill through an old mining area but be very careful of open mine shafts. Return to 181 and *reset your odometer*. Stay left at 0.2 and you'll return to F.S. 180 at 2.1 miles (06). Turn right to return to Virginia Lakes Road at 4.1 miles (01).

Return Trip: Right on Virginia Lakes Road goes back to Hwy. 395. Left takes you to moderate Kavanaugh Ridge, Trail #33.

Services: Gas and most services in Lee Vining and Bridgeport.

Maps: Toiyabe N.F. map, USGS 7.5-minute map, Lundy, CA, and DeLorme Atlas & Gazetteer.

Lower Horse Meadow; Mt. Gibbs in distance.

Hike into wilderness.

Steep, 3-mile hike to Gibbs Lake.

Rougher road going back down.

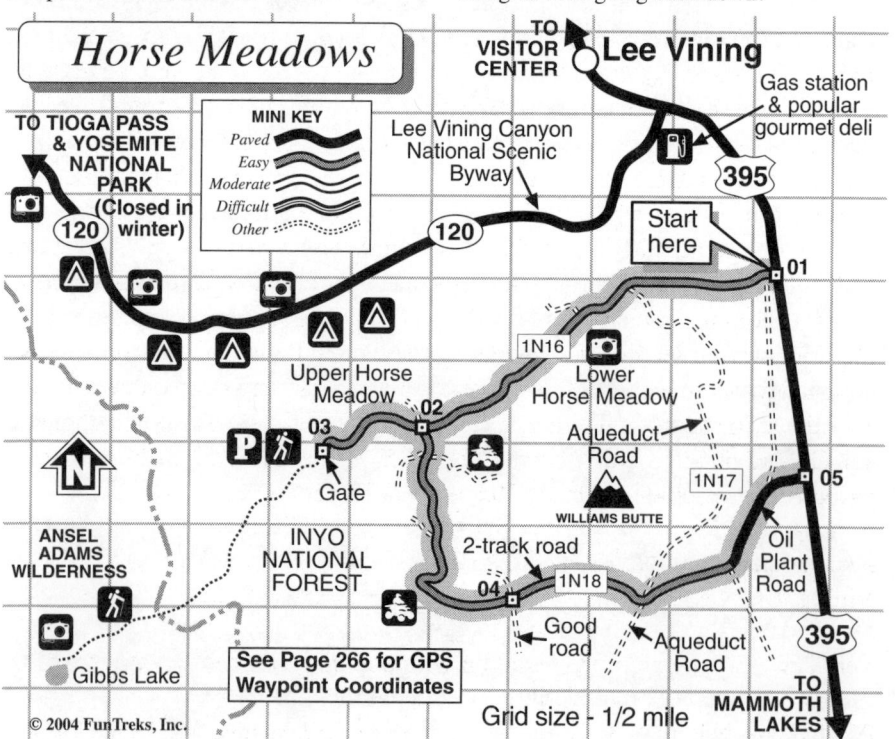

Horse Meadows

MINI KEY
- Paved
- Easy
- Moderate
- Difficult
- Other

TO TIOGA PASS & YOSEMITE NATIONAL PARK (Closed in winter)

TO VISITOR CENTER

Lee Vining

Gas station & popular gourmet deli

Lee Vining Canyon National Scenic Byway

395

Start here

01

1N16

Upper Horse Meadow

Lower Horse Meadow

02

Aqueduct Road

03

1N17

05

Gate

WILLIAMS BUTTE

ANSEL ADAMS WILDERNESS

INYO NATIONAL FOREST

2-track road

04

1N18

Oil Plant Road

Gibbs Lake

See Page 266 for GPS Waypoint Coordinates

Good road

Aqueduct Road

395

TO MAMMOTH LAKES

© 2004 FunTreks, Inc.

Grid size - 1/2 mile

132

Horse Meadows 35

Location: Immediately south of Lee Vining and Highway 120.

Difficulty: Easy. A bit steeper and bumpier coming out than going in but suitable for any stock, high-clearance SUV.

Features: Pass through two scenic meadows on the way to a great hiking trail into Ansel Adams Wilderness. This trail is close to the eastern entrance to Yosemite National Park. While in the area, make sure you drive Highway 120 to Tioga Pass and the loop around June Lake. Both of these paved drives offer incredible scenery and should not be missed by anyone. Stop at the Mono Basin Scenic Area Visitor Center just north of Lee Vining to learn about other things to do around Mono Lake.

Time & Distance: The 8.5-mile loop takes an hour. Add 3 hours for the hike.

To Get There: Take Hwy. 395 south 1.2 miles from Highway 120 and turn right (west) on an unmarked road. After you turn, several roads branch off in different directions. Stay on the main road heading west.

Trail Description: Reset your odometer as you turn off Highway 395 (01). The gravel road (F.S. 1N16) begins to climb gradually. Continue straight at 0.9 miles where Aqueduct Road goes left. Stay left at 1.3 where a lesser road goes right. You'll pass by Lower Horse Meadow before reaching a 4-way intersection in the trees at 2.2 miles (02). Continue straight. Wind through dense trees near Upper Horse Meadow. Bear left at 3.3 just before the road ends at a gate at 3.4 miles (03). I took the steep, 3-mile hike (each way) to Gibbs Lake into Ansel Adams Wilderness. It's well worth your time if you're in good shape.

From the gate, return 1.2 miles (02), *reset your odometer* and turn right. Continue straight (south) at a circular intersection at 0.1 miles. The road winds downhill through a ravine. Stay left at 0.7 before dropping steeply downhill at 1.1 miles. Go straight through a 4-way intersection on a lesser road at 1.6 miles (04). Go straight at 1.7 then bear left on a wide road at 2.6. The road becomes paved before reaching Highway 395 at 3.9 miles (05).

Return Trip: Left on Highway 395 goes back to Highway 120 and Lee Vining. Right goes to June Lake Loop and Mammoth Lakes.

Services: At Lee Vining. Gas station with popular gourmet deli at Hwy. 120.

Maps: Inyo N.F. map, USGS 7.5-minute maps Lee Vining, Mt. Dana, CA.

Watch for this sign.

Lingering snow on July 4th weekend.

View from top of trail back towards Mammoth Mountain.

Watch for hikers & bikers.

Trail is SUV friendly.

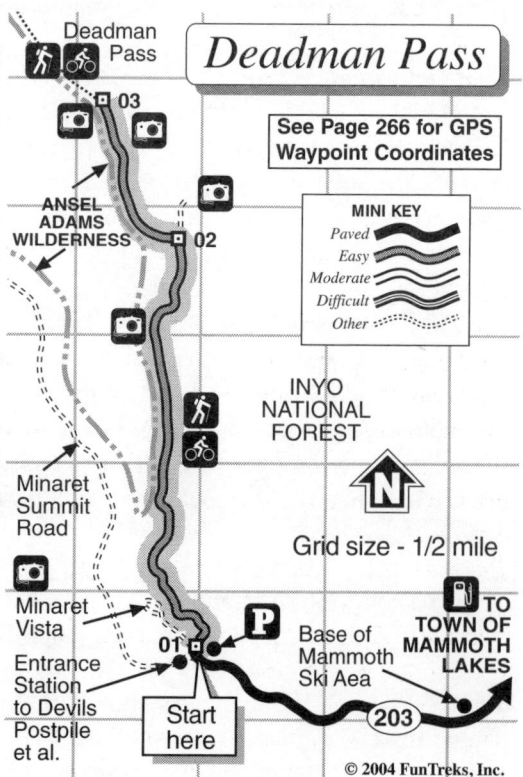

Deadman Pass

See Page 266 for GPS Waypoint Coordinates

MINI KEY
Paved
Easy
Moderate
Difficult
Other

Deadman Pass

ANSEL ADAMS WILDERNESS

INYO NATIONAL FOREST

Grid size - 1/2 mile

Minaret Summit Road

Minaret Vista

Entrance Station to Devils Postpile et al.

Start here

Base of Mammoth Ski Aea

TO TOWN OF MAMMOTH LAKES

© 2004 FunTreks, Inc.

134

Deadman Pass 36

Location: Northwest of Mammoth Lakes and Mammoth Mountain Ski Area.

Difficulty: Easy. Smooth road of compacted volcanic pumice with a few washed-out bumpy spots. Suitable for any high-clearance, 4-wheel-drive SUV. Snow may block trail well into July. Fine, white dust in summer.

Features: A short but stunningly beautiful trip that reaches an elevation over 10,000 feet directly across the valley from Mammoth Mountain. Watch for hikers and mountain bikers. Stay on designated roads. Volcanically created Mammoth Lakes Basin is a premier outdoor recreation area with incredible places to see and explore. Don't miss the drive up to Twin Lakes, Twin Falls and Lake Mary. To learn more, stop at the Mammoth Visitor Center on the right as you come into town on Highway 203.

Time & Distance: The trail is only 2.6 miles long. You can drive it both ways in less than an hour. Take a picnic lunch and enjoy the views.

To Get There: Take Hwy. 203 west into Mammoth Lakes from Hwy. 395. About 1.3 miles after the visitor center, follow 203 right uphill towards Mammoth Ski Area. Go another 5.4 miles on 203 and turn right towards Minaret Vista just before an entrance station for a major scenic recreation area that includes Devils Postpile and many popular campgrounds.

Trail Description: Reset your odometer as you turn right off Highway 203. (01). Go by a parking lot and follow a hard-packed road to the right. Then stay left and go by a sign for Deadman Pass marked as a bicycle and 4x4 vehicle route. Camping is allowed after 0.4 miles. Stay right at 0.5 miles where the bike path goes left. The road is chewed up for a short distance. You may need a little speed and momentum if your wheels lift off the ground. Stay left uphill at 1.6 then bear left at fork at 1.9 miles (02). Follow the road up a long ridge until the trail ends at 2.6 miles (03). Bikers and hikers can continue across Deadman Pass just ahead.

Return Trip: Return the way you came.

Services: Full services in Mammoth Lakes, a major resort and recreational community. Campgrounds fill up quickly on big holiday weekends.

Maps: Inyo N. F. map, Mammoth Lakes OHV and Biking Map, USGS 7.5-minute map Mammoth Mountain, CA, DeLorme Atlas & Gazetteer.

Short hike to Inyo Craters.

Narrow road in places but fun to drive. Looking southwest from overlook.

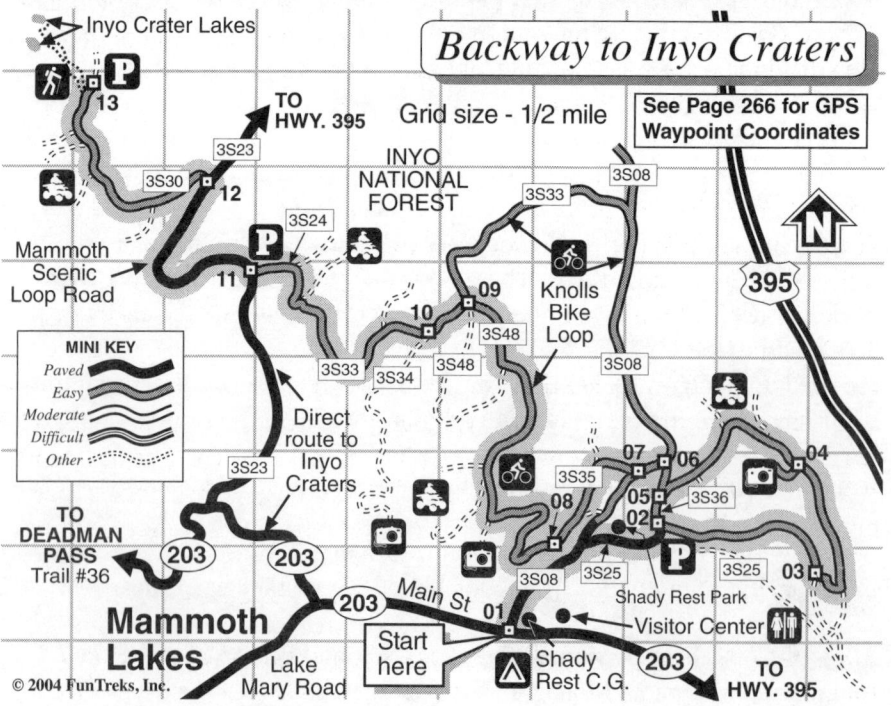

Backway to Inyo Craters

Grid size - 1/2 mile

See Page 266 for GPS Waypoint Coordinates

136

Backway to Inyo Craters ㊲

Location: Directly north of Mammoth Lakes.

Difficulty: Easy. Dirt roads, narrow and steep in places. Suitable for stock SUVs with 4WD. Easy to get lost, but it's part of fun. Good ATV area.

Features: Explore a fun maze of forest roads around Mammoth Lakes featuring overlooks of the area. Finish with a hike to interesting Inyo Craters.

Time & Distance: 12.2 miles as described here; allow 2 to 4 hours.

To Get There: Turn north off Hwy. 203 onto F.S. Road 3S08 just west of the Mammoth Visitor Center. Look for signs to Shady Rest Campground.

Trail Description: Reset your odometer at start (01). Drive north next to campground on 3S08. Turn right at 0.6 miles on paved 3S25. Pass through Shady Rest Park and swing left. At 1.1 miles (02), just after last parking area, turn right on narrow dirt road under power lines. Turn left at 2.2 miles (03) uphill away from power lines. Bear left at 2.3 when road joins on right. Driver's choice at 2.9; right is steeper. At 3.1 miles (04), bear left at T. Head uphill to overlook then return to T (04). Turn left and continue. Stay left at 3.7. At 3.9 miles, bear left then immediately right through X intersection. Go straight at 4.2 through 4-way intersection. Go straight, then immediately left at 4.4. Make hard right at 4.5 miles (05) on 3S36. You return to 3S08 at 4.7 miles (06); *reset your odometer* and turn left.

Turn right off 3S08 at 0.1 miles (07). Head west as roads crisscross. Turn left at 0.5 on 3S35. Go straight (southwest) at 0.7 and 0.9. Bear right away from power lines at 1.0 miles (08). Weave uphill on good road. Stay right at 1.8 miles. Both roads on left dead end. Stay right on Knolls Bike Loop at 2.1 and 2.8 miles. Follow 3S48 north. Bear left at 3.2 miles (09) on 3S33. Turn right at major fork at 3.4 miles (10), staying on 3S33. (Straight goes to a network of scenic overlooks.) Stay right at 3.9. At 4.4 miles, make a left then quick right on 3S24. Paved Mammoth Scenic Loop Road 3S23 is reached at 5.0 miles (11). *Reset odometer.* Go right 1.2 miles (12) to 3S30 on left. Follow well marked good road to Inyo Craters another 1.3 miles (13) to hiking trail and parking lot. Take shady hike uphill about 1/4 mile to craters.

Services: Full services and campgrounds in Mammoth Lakes.

Maps: Inyo National Forest map, Mammoth Lakes Off-Highway Vehicle and Biking Map, USGS 7.5-minute map Old Mammoth, CA.

Camping along Laurel Creek.

Looking up Laurel Canyon where road narrows.

Trail blocked near top on July 4th.

Bring your fishing pole.

Rocky but manageable for stock SUVs.

Land Rover group nears top.

Laurel Lakes

TO LEE VINING
TO MAMMOTH LAKES
Start here
TO BISHOP
Sherwin Ck. Road
Sherwin Creek Road
4S08
01
4S86

MINI KEY
Paved
Easy
Moderate
Difficult
Other

02

See Page 267 for GPS Waypoint Coordinates

INYO NATIONAL FOREST

Grid size - 1/2 mile

Laurel Lakes

LAUREL MTN.
11,812 ft.

03

JOHN MUIR WILDERNESS

© 2004 FunTreks, Inc.

138

Laurel Lakes 38

Location: Southeast of Mammoth Lakes.

Difficulty: Moderate. Narrow, steep and rocky shelf road. Good visibility of road ahead allows you to anticipate when passing will be necessary. Suitable for all stock, high-clearance 4-wheel-drive SUVs. Snow may block upper portion of trail well into July.

Features: The ultimate in SUV adventure roads. Challenging but not overwhelming with breathtaking scenery. Climb to secluded, crystal-clear mountain lakes near 10,000 feet and fish for brown and golden trout. Primitive, secluded camping along Laurel Creek in lower part of canyon. Great early-summer wildflowers and changing aspens in the fall. Trail is open to mountain bikers, hikers, ATVs and dirt bikes. A short and convenient drive from the town of Mammoth Lakes, a premier outdoor recreation destination.

Time & Distance: I measured 4.5 miles to the point where the trail was blocked by snow about a quarter mile before the lakes. It takes less than an hour to reach the lakes, but if you drive the trail on the 4th of July weekend, as I did, allow more time. Our group was blocked in by a large group of Land Rovers behind us. It took an hour just to get everyone turned around. The road is very narrow at the top.

To Get There: From Highway 395, turn south on Sherwin Creek Road about 1.3 miles east of the Highway 203 exit. Follow Sherwin Creek Road east briefly, then turn south. After 1.4 miles (01), turn left at sign for Laurel Lakes, F.S. Rd. 4S86. An alternate route from Mammoth Lakes is to take Sherwin Creek Road east from Old Mammoth Road about 4.3 miles.

Trail Description: *Reset your odometer at start* (01). Head south up the canyon. A lesser road goes right at 2.1 miles (02) to camp spots below. Continue straight uphill as the road narrows and gets steeper. You can see the lakes below as the road crests at 4.5 miles. The road ends at 4.8 miles (03).

Return Trip: Return the way you came.

Services: Full services in Mammoth Lakes. Make sure to stop at well-marked Mammoth Visitor Center on right as you come into town.

Maps: Inyo National Forest map, Mammoth Lakes Off-Highway Vehicle and Biking Map, USGS 7.5-minute map Bloody Mountain, CA.

Steep and rocky in places with outstanding scenery.

Sand Canyon Road.   Camp at end of trail next to this secluded lake.

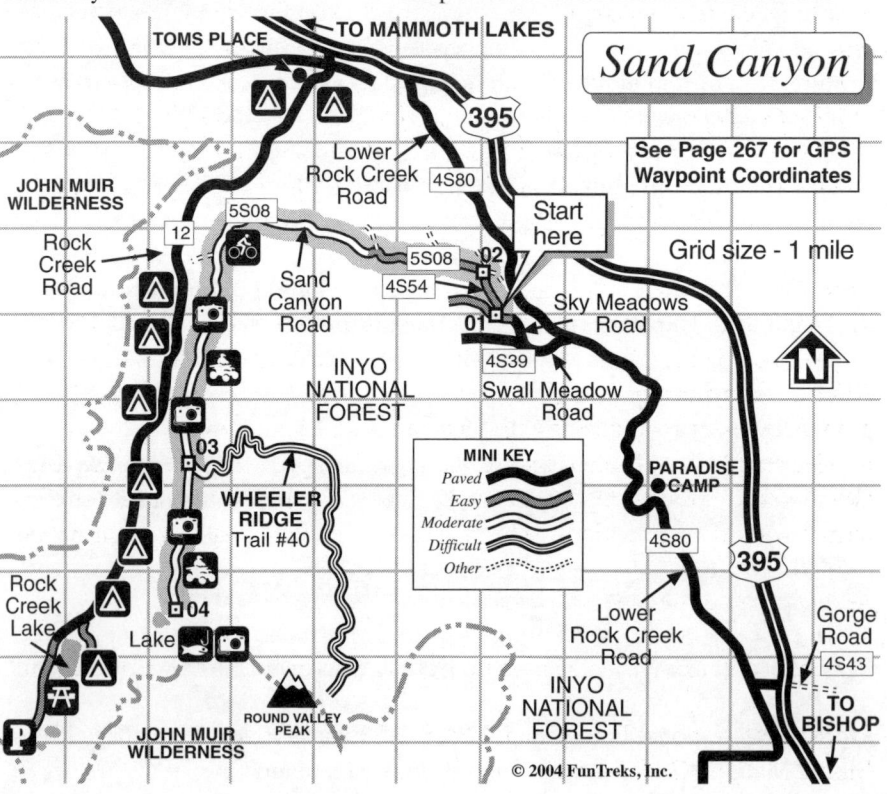

Sand Canyon

See Page 267 for GPS Waypoint Coordinates

Grid size - 1 mile

MINI KEY
Paved
Easy
Moderate
Difficult
Other

Sand Canyon 39

Location: Southeast of Mammoth Lakes, northwest of Bishop.

Difficulty: Moderate. Sandy in places, with brief rocky climbs and descents. Light brush in a couple of spots. Suitable for aggressive stock SUVs with high clearance and 4-wheel drive.

Features: Look down on popular Rock Creek Canyon from lesser-known high road along the eastern edge of canyon. Classic Sierra Nevada views of 13,000-ft. snow-capped peaks. Trail ends at secluded, picturesque lake at edge of John Muir Wilderness, where you can camp and fish. Thick wildflowers in late spring/early summer. Great downhill mountain biking.

Time & Distance: The trail measures 9.4 miles one way. Allow 3-4 hours for the round trip.

To Get There: From the north, get off Hwy. 395 at Lower Rock Creek Road about a mile east of Toms Place. Head south 4 or 5 miles and turn right following signs to Swall Meadow. From the south, get off Hwy. 395 about 2 miles north of the turnoff for Rovana. Watch for a sign to Paradise on left. Go west 0.1 miles and turn right on Lower Rock Creek Rd. Drive north 6.7 miles and turn left at sign to Swall Meadow. Head west on Swall Meadow Road (F.S. 4S39). After 0.6 miles, bear right on Sky Meadows Road. Go another 0.6 miles and turn right on unmarked, single-lane dirt road that passes through a small gravel pit.

Trail Description: Reset your odometer as you turn off Sky Meadows Road (01). Wind through gravel pit and head north across meadow. Turn left at 0.7 miles (02) on 5S08. Climb through short burned area. Bear left at 1.3 and 2.1. After a brushy section, the road begins to climb more steeply. Stay left at 4.7 where lesser road goes right. Nice camp spot with view at 4.8. Gets rockier at 6.0. Continue straight at 7.5 miles (03) where faint Wheeler Ridge (Mine Road), Trail #40, goes left. Sand Canyon Rd. descends over rockier terrain with incredible views. The trail ends at unnamed lake at 9.4 miles (04).

Return Trip: Return the way you came.

Services: Full services in Mammoth Lakes, Bishop. Food at Paradise Camp.

Maps: Inyo National Forest map, USGS 7.5-minute maps, Toms Place and Mount Morgan, CA, DeLorme Atlas & Gazetteer.

First part of trail is very rocky.

Great trail for ATVs and dirt bikes.

View of Round Valley from overlook.

Best to hike this dangerously narrow section.

Tough climb on way to wilderness.

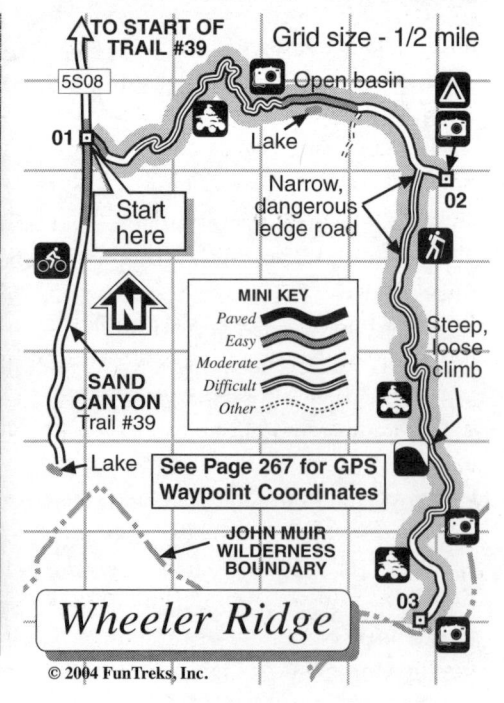

Wheeler Ridge

© 2004 FunTreks, Inc.

142

Wheeler Ridge 40

Location: Southeast of Mammoth Lakes, northwest of Bishop.

Difficulty: Difficult. The first part of trail weaves through the trees with difficult rocky climbs. It is not extreme, but probably too hard for most stock SUVs. Experienced drivers in vehicles with skid plates and decent ground clearance should be able to reach the overlook. Snow can block the trail well into July. Beyond the overlook is extremely dangerous and better suited for ATVs. The first half-mile is sandy, unstable and extremely narrow. Any small mistake could be disastrous. I would strongly urge you to hike or bike beyond the overlook. Once you start across that ledge you can't turn around, so inspect every inch on foot first if you decide to drive across. My vehicle was just barely narrow enough to drive the entire trail.

Features: You'll cross Wheeler Ridge at an elevation of about 11,000 feet to an overlook of awesome Round Valley. Great camp spot at overlook.

Time & Distance: It will take about an hour to go 7.5 miles through Sand Canyon to the start. Add another hour for the additional 3.1 miles to the overlook. This is an all-day adventure if you hike to wilderness boundary.

To Get There: Follow directions to Sand Canyon, Trail #39. Turn left at 7.5 miles following sign to Wheeler Ridge Mine Road.

Trail Description: Reset your odometer at start (01). A new, rerouted trail starts faintly curving east across a meadow. The trail climbs into the woods and gets rockier. You reach the top of the ridge at 1.9 miles and descend steeply to a broad basin with a small lake. Go around the lake and turn left at a T after a tiny creek at 2.4 miles. Follow a good ledge road downhill and turn left at 2.9 miles towards the overlook reached at 3.1 (02). After the overlook, go back 0.2 miles where the trail continues south (left) another 3.2 miles and stops at the boundary to John Muir Wilderness (03). To get there, you must cross the dangerous narrow shelf road described above, then negotiate a series of steep, loose hills. The last half-mile of trail is fairly easy as it climbs to a high point at the wilderness boundary.

Return Trip: Return the way you came.

Services: Full services in Mammoth Lakes, Bishop. Food at Paradise Camp.

Maps: Inyo N. F. map, USGS 7.5-minute maps, Mount Morgan, CA.

Classic views of Sierra Nevada Mountains.

A few rough spots but mostly wide and easy.

Park at wilderness boundary and hike.

Crossing McGee Creek.

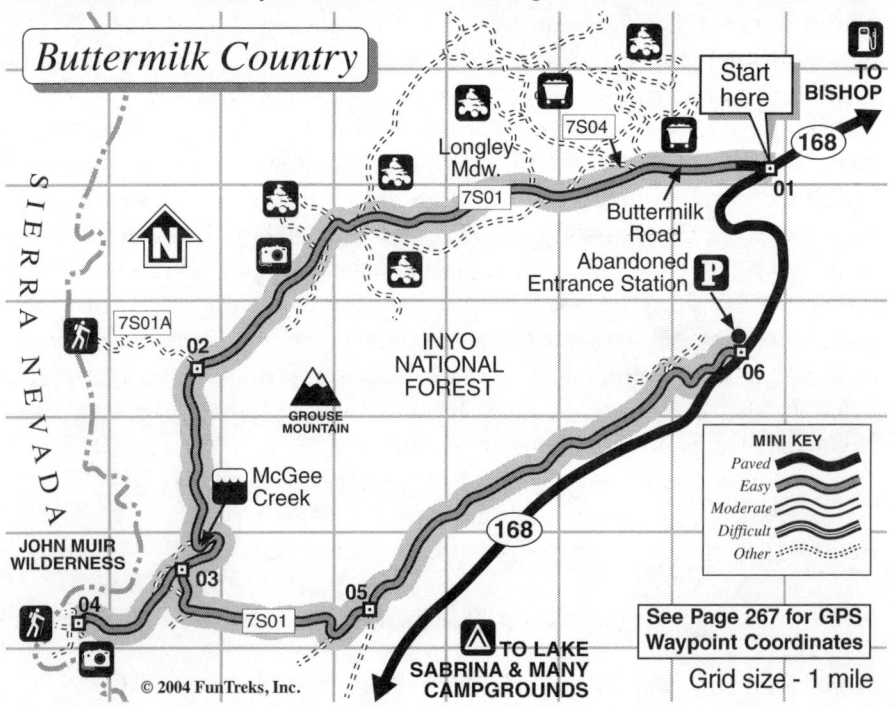

Buttermilk Country

MINI KEY
Paved
Easy
Moderate
Difficult
Other

See Page 267 for GPS Waypoint Coordinates

Grid size - 1 mile

© 2004 FunTreks, Inc.

144

Buttermilk Country 41

Location: Southwest of Bishop.

Difficulty: Easy. Variety of dirt roads ranging from smooth gravel to narrow, rocky two-tracks. Challenging, optional side trips on network of marked forest roads. Suitable for stock, 4WD, high-clearance SUVs.

Features: Tour scenic foothills below towering Sierra Nevada Mountains. Take side trips to wilderness hiking trails. Explore optional network of rougher roads around Longley Meadow. Many ATV and dirt bike trails.

Time & Distance: Allow about 3 hours for the 16.9 miles described here.

To Get There: From Hwy. 395 in Bishop, head west on West Line Street (Hwy. 168) 7.3 miles to Buttermilk Road (7S01) and turn right.

Trail Description: Reset your odometer at start (01). Head west on paved Buttermilk Road, which quickly changes to gravel. Continue straight at 1.1 miles where lesser 7S04 goes right. (This turnoff, and many others that follow, lead to a network of fun roads that eventually connect to Highway 395. You can spend many hours exploring the area.) Buttermilk Road narrows at 3.6 and gets rougher. Continue straight at 5.9 miles (02) where 7S01A goes right to Horton Lakes Hiking Trail. Stay left at 7.5 on what appears to be a lesser road and go past a nice camp spot. Cross McGee Creek at 7.6 miles and climb out of a wash. Turn right at 8.3 miles (03) on a pleasant side trip that climbs to the wilderness boundary. The road immediately splits but comes back together at 9.4. Go right at 9.9 and straight at 10.0. At 10.5 miles (04) the road splits in several directions. I spent time here exploring the area next to the wilderness, then returned to the main road (03) where I *reset my odometer* and turned right.

Continue straight at 0.2 then bear left downhill at 0.4 where a good road goes right uphill. Stay left at 1.8 then turn left on 7S15 at a T at 2.3 miles (05). (It seems like the wrong way, but it's not.) Follow ridge along a green aqueduct at 4.8, then turn right uphill at 5.8 miles. You reach Hwy. 168 at 6.4 miles (06) at an abandoned entrance station and parking lot.

Return Trip: Left on Hwy 168 goes back to Bishop.

Services: Full services in Bishop. Many campgrounds farther south on 168.

Maps: Inyo N. F. map, USGS 7.5-minute map, Tungsten Hills, CA.

Coyote Creek wildflowers.    Crossing Coyote Flat with views of the Palisade Group.

Shaded camp spots at Waypoint 7.

This stock SUV made it to Baker Creek.    Looking west from Schober Mine.

Rockiest part of trail leaving Baker Creek.    Stay on existing roads at all times.

Coyote Flat 42

Location: Southwest of Bishop.

Difficulty: Moderate. Much of the route is easy although narrow and steep in places. Skid plates are recommended for the last rocky mile nearing the hiking trail to Baker Lake into John Muir Wilderness. The final approach to Schober Mine is very steep and narrow but relatively smooth. Snow can block the trail well into July.

Features: Climb to a beautiful high plateau above Bishop. Most of the trail is near 10,000 feet with one route climbing over 11,000. Visit remote Schober Mine. Enjoy wildflowers in early summer along Coyote Creek which you will cross several times. Camp on the edge of John Muir Wilderness and hike to secluded lakes just inside the wilderness boundary. Enjoy dramatic views of the Palisade Group, the second highest cluster of glaciated peaks in the Sierra Nevada. Good fishing at Funnel Lake. ATVs and dirt bikes allowed but stay on existing roads at all times.

Time & Distance: Round trip is 57.6 miles as described here. Allow a full day if you drive the entire route. Makes a great weekend adventure.

To Get There: From Highway 395 in Bishop, go west on W. Line Street 1.5 miles to Barlow Lane. Turn left and go another mile to Underwood. Take Underwood west (right) another 0.8 miles to a gravel road on the left just before a curve. This is Coyote Valley Road (not marked).

Trail Description: Reset your odometer as you turn off Underwood (01) and head south. Bear right before substation at 0.1 miles and pass under power lines. Other roads branch off but the main road is obvious. Enter the Inyo National Forest at 3.3 miles. Note "Limited Use Area" signs, which means stay on existing roads. Bear left at kiosk at 3.9 miles (02) on 7S10 marked just ahead. As you climb higher, the road gets rougher with great views of Bishop, Owens Valley and the White Mountains. The long climb ends at 7.4 miles at the crest of a hill in a heavily forested area. You'll pass several good primitive camp spots. Continue straight at 7.7 miles where a road goes left. I shifted into low range at 8.8 miles to ascend the steepest part of trail. Stay on main road as lesser roads go left. Drop down into a small valley and cross Coyote Creek at 10.5 miles. Pass through the site of Peterson Mill at 10.9 miles. No buildings remain, so you'll have to look hard on the right side of road for remains. As you proceed, the road flattens out and becomes more dusty. An important fork is reached at 12.3 miles (03). Right goes to Schober Mine. Left continues on 7S10 to Baker Creek and John Muir Wilderness.

For Schober Mine, *reset your odometer* and turn right on 8S18. Near a cattle guard at 1.1 miles, Salty Peterson Tungsten Mine can be seen on the right. Cross creek again at 1.4 miles. In early summer, wildflowers grow abundantly along the creek. Stay right at 2.5 miles where a spur goes left to tiny, unimpressive Coyote Lake. Turn right on a faint two-track road at 3.0 miles (04). (Straight dead ends.) The faint road becomes better defined as it winds across Coyote Ridge above 11,000 feet. Great views unfold as you drop down the other side before reaching a corrugated metal cabin at 6.6 miles. Stay right through the trees after the cabin. When you come out of the trees, the narrow road drops steeply downhill to a T at 7.2 miles. Turn left at the T to Schober Mine, reached at 7.5 miles (05) on the left. Right at the T goes downhill another 1.6 miles to a boulder that blocks the narrow trail. Even if you could get around the boulder, the trail is gated at the bottom.

For Coyote Flat and Baker Creek, return 7.5 miles and turn right on 7S10 (03). *Reset your odometer.* Turn right again and cross creek at 0.2. The trail crosses broad Coyote Flat on an easy road. Stay left at 1.3 and 2.3 miles. At 3.0 miles (06), a road goes right to Funnel Lake, a popular fishing spot. You continue straight. Stay right past shaded camping in a cluster of trees at 6.7 miles (07). Head west uphill over increasingly rocky terrain. To your left you can see the impressive Palisade Group with peaks over 14,000 feet. Stay left at 7.5 and right at 7.8. After a few moderate challenges, the trail ends at a primitive camping area near the wilderness boundary at 9.0 miles (08). A hiking trail heads west to Baker Lake.

Return Trip: Return the way you came.

Services: Pit toilet at Baker Creek Hiking Trailhead. Full services in Bishop including Brown's Town Campground with full hookups on the south side of town. More RV parks north of town on Hwy. 395. Bishop is a popular tourist town with many great attractions. Don't miss the Laws Railroad Museum north of town on Highway 6.

Historical Highlights: Most of the mining in the area was done during World War II when tungsten was in demand. A. H. Peterson built the road to Coyote Flat in 1942 to access his mining claims and mill site. The Schober Mine was discovered by Harold Schober in 1940 and was profitable for several years. The mine was reached on the narrow road (now closed) that winds down the hill to the south fork of Bishop Creek.

Maps: Inyo National Forest map, USGS 100,000-scale map of Bishop, CA, DeLorme Atlas & Gazetteer.

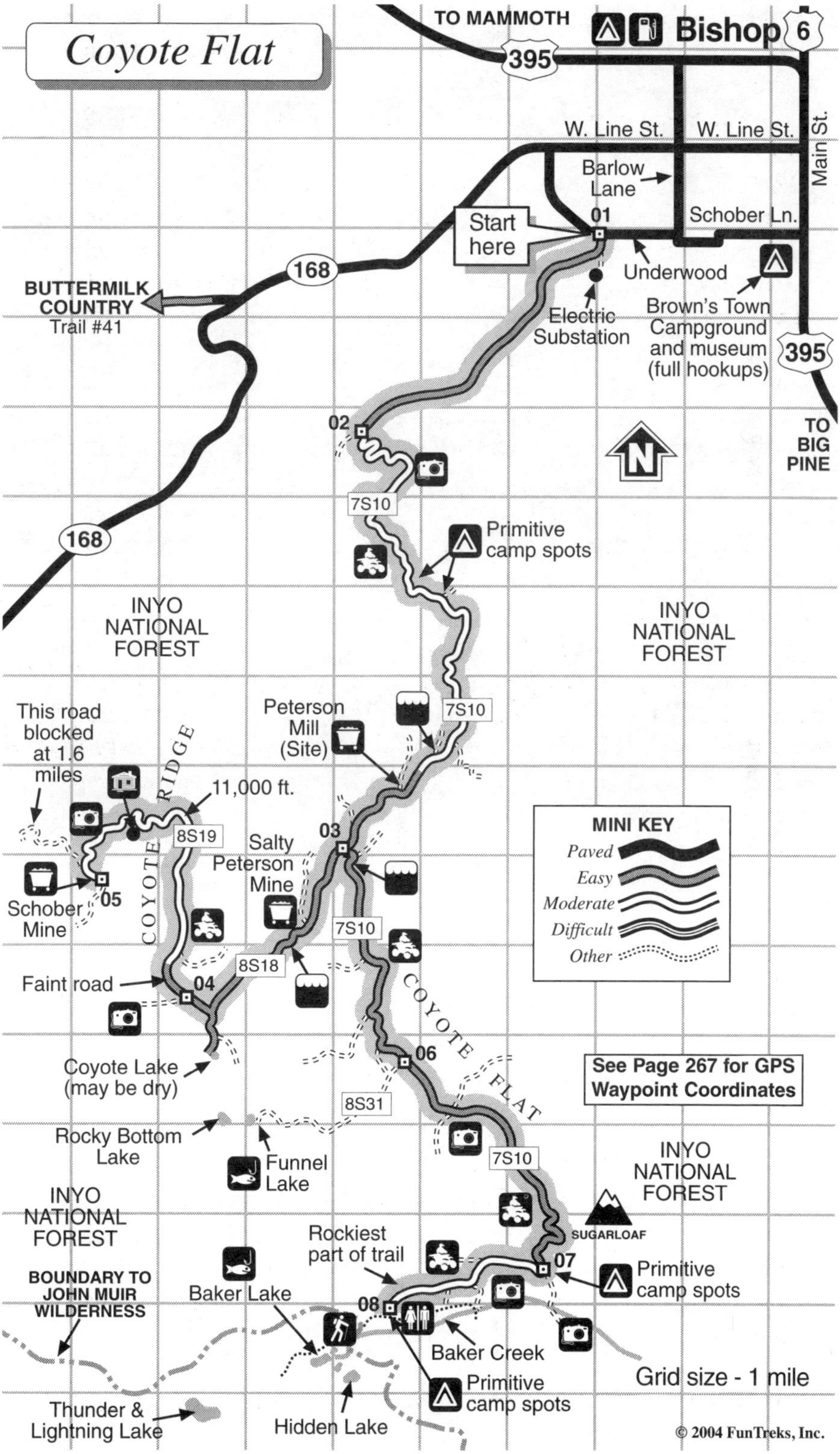

Coyote Flat
TO MAMMOTH
Bishop
395
6
W. Line St.
W. Line St.
Main St.
Barlow Lane
01
Start here
Schober Ln.
Underwood
168
BUTTERMILK COUNTRY Trail #41
Electric Substation
Brown's Town Campground and museum (full hookups)
395
TO BIG PINE
02
7S10
Primitive camp spots
168
INYO NATIONAL FOREST
INYO NATIONAL FOREST
This road blocked at 1.6 miles
Peterson Mill (Site)
7S10
COYOTE RIDGE
11,000 ft.
8S19
03
Salty Peterson Mine
05
Schober Mine
7S10
8S18
Faint road
04
COYOTE FLAT
06
Coyote Lake (may be dry)
8S31
MINI KEY
Paved
Easy
Moderate
Difficult
Other
See Page 267 for GPS Waypoint Coordinates
Rocky Bottom Lake
Funnel Lake
7S10
INYO NATIONAL FOREST
INYO NATIONAL FOREST
SUGARLOAF
Rockiest part of trail
07
Primitive camp spots
BOUNDARY TO JOHN MUIR WILDERNESS
Baker Lake
08
Baker Creek
Grid size - 1 mile
Primitive camp spots
Thunder & Lightning Lake
Hidden Lake
© 2004 FunTreks, Inc.

Very steep climb out of Silver Canyon.

Patriarch Tree is 36 feet in circumference.

One of several cabins at Roberts Ranch.

Intermittent water crossings not deep this day.

Small waterfall near trail in Wyman Canyon.

Eastern end of trail great for ATVs, dirt bikes.

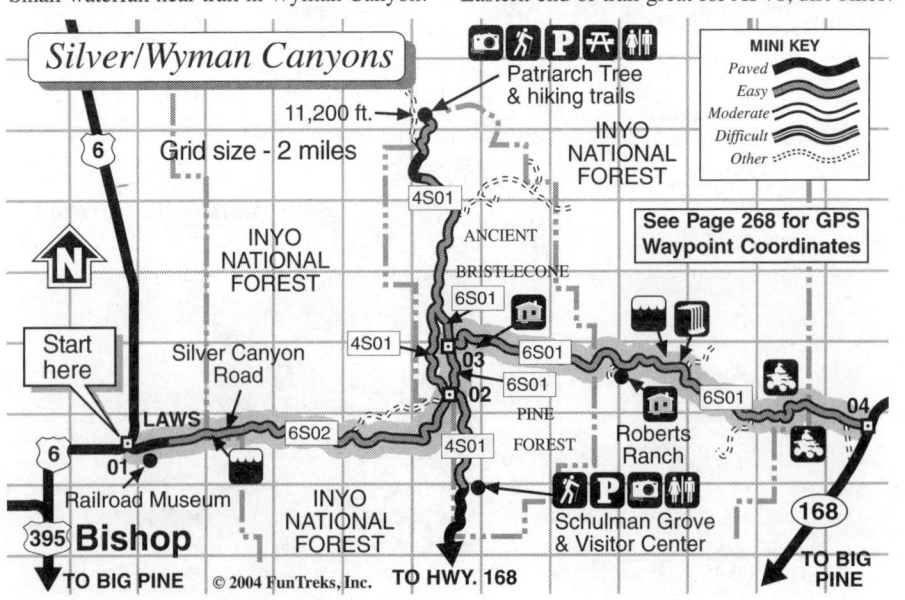

Silver/Wyman Canyons

Patriarch Tree & hiking trails

11,200 ft.

Grid size - 2 miles

INYO NATIONAL FOREST

MINI KEY
Paved
Easy
Moderate
Difficult
Other

See Page 268 for GPS Waypoint Coordinates

INYO NATIONAL FOREST

ANCIENT BRISTLECONE

4S01

6S01

Start here

Silver Canyon Road

4S01

6S01

03

6S01

02

LAWS

PINE FOREST

Roberts Ranch

6S02

4S01

04

01

Railroad Museum

INYO NATIONAL FOREST

Schulman Grove & Visitor Center

395 Bishop

168

TO BIG PINE

© 2004 FunTreks, Inc.

TO HWY. 168

TO BIG PINE

150

Silver/Wyman Canyons 43

Location: East of Bishop.

Difficulty: Easy. Mostly smooth gravel but very steep in places with several water crossings. Low-range gearing is advised. Summer only.

Features: Interesting west/east traverse of the White Mountains through the Ancient Bristlecone Pine Forest featuring 4,500-year-old trees.

Time & Distance: Allow 3 to 5 hours for the 27.6 miles described here.

To Get There: Follow signs to Laws north of Bishop on Hwy. 6. When 6 turns north at Laws, turn right on Silver Canyon Road.

Trail Description: Reset your odometer at start of Silver Canyon Road (01). Head east past the Railroad Museum. Pavement soon ends and road follows power lines into Silver Canyon. Cross creek and Inyo N.F. boundary at 2.4 miles where road becomes 6S02. Road turns sharply left at 7.8 miles and begins a steep climb up the mountainside. Stay right at 9.7 and left at 11.5 as roads branch right to radio towers. Main road 4S01, through Bristlecone Forest, is reached at 11.8 miles (02). Schulman Grove Visitor Center (and paved road to Hwy. 168) is downhill to right about 3 miles. Left, uphill goes to Patriarch Grove featuring world's largest bristlecone pine tree. Both side trips are worth the extra time. To reach Wyman Canyon, continue straight across 4S01 to 6S01 and go north. Or, if you are returning from Patriarch Grove, turn left on 6S01 and head south.
  Reset odometer at start of Wyman Canyon where 6S01 heads east downhill (03). Switchbacks drop into narrow canyon passing an old miner's cabin on right. Roberts Ranch is reached at 6.0 miles where several interesting cabins remain. Stay right at 8.4. The road is wet in places as underground water surfaces intermittently. Sometimes, it can be fairly deep. Pass through a small rocky canyon with waterfall at 8.6. In succession, turn as follows: right at 10.2 and 10.6, left at 11.7, right at 13.2, left at 13.6 and 14.3. Highway 168 is reached at 15.8 miles (04).

Return Trip: Big Pine is 29 miles to the right on Hwy. 168. From there, turn right on Hwy. 395 to return to Bishop in another 15 miles.

Services: Gas, food and lodging in Big Pine. Full services in Bishop.

Maps: Inyo National Forest map, USGS 250,000-scale map, Mariposa, CA.

AREA 6

Big Pine, Lone Pine

44. Mazourka Canyon
45. Armstrong Canyon
46. Movie Road/Alabama Hills
47. Swansea-Cerro Gordo Road
48. Racetrack via Hunter Mtn.

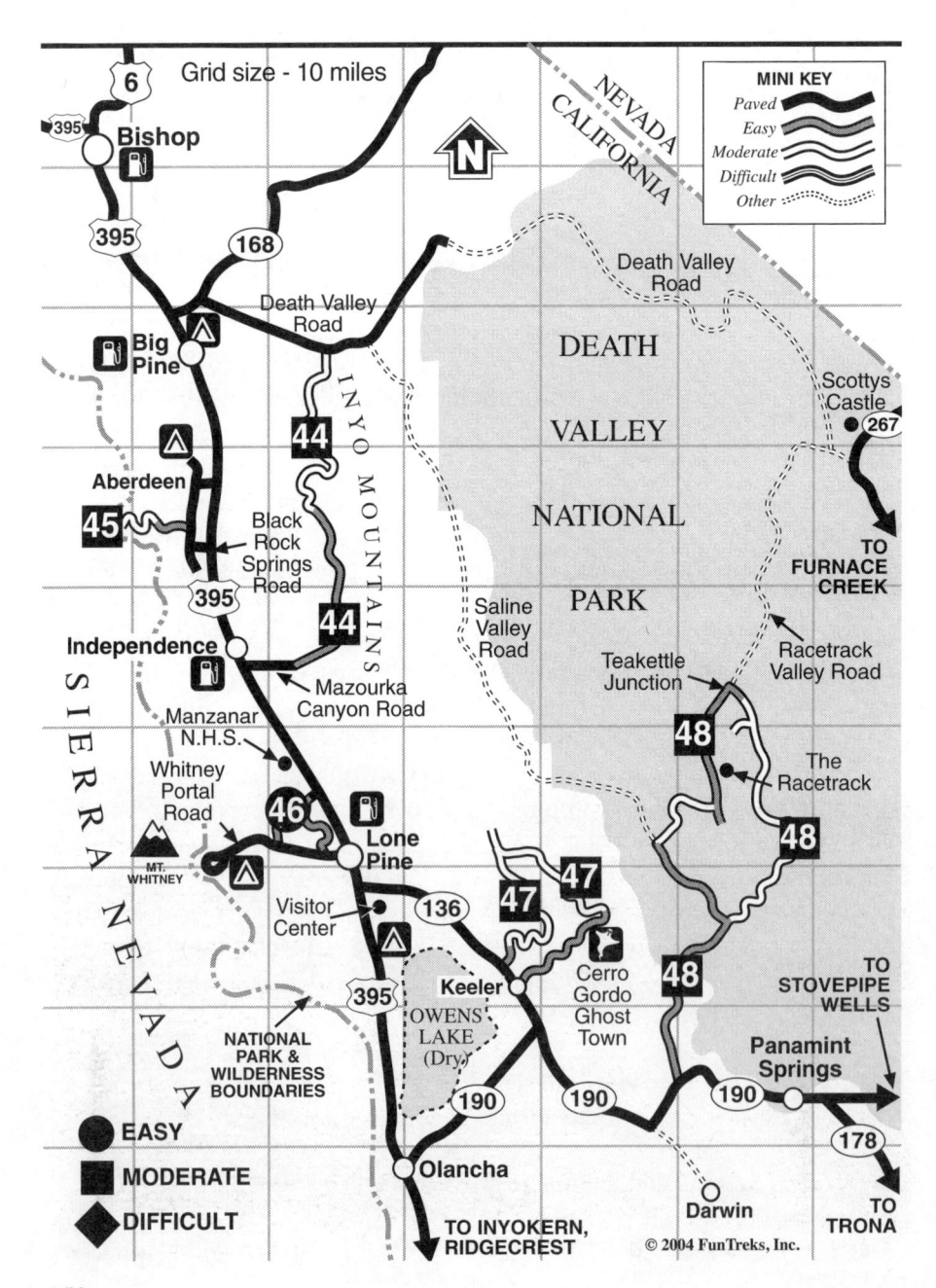

AREA 6
Big Pine, Lone Pine

Located in the shadow of Mt. Whitney along the western side of Death Valley National Park, Lone Pine serves as the unofficial gateway to the southern portion of the "Eastern Sierra," one of California's most popular recreation destinations. Summer traffic begins streaming up Highway 395 around Memorial Day and continues through mid-October. To learn more about the area, stop at the Eastern Sierra Visitor Center located at the junction of Highways 395 and 136. While there, pick up a map of the *Movie Road/Alabama Hills* Driving Tour. Although this trip doesn't require 4-wheel drive, it's a backroad adventure you won't want to miss. Four other trails in the area are all rated moderate. *Mazourka Canyon* starts in Independence and winds its way north through the Inyo Mountains to Big Pine. You'll cross challenging terrain with high views of the Sierras across beautiful Owens Valley. Climb a twisting, narrow shelf road to isolated and little-known *Armstrong Canyon*. Visit Cerro Gordo Ghost Town via challenging *Swansea-Cerro Gordo Road*. Finally, see mysterious moving rocks at the famous *Racetrack* playa in Death Valley National Park. We've chosen a lesser-used route that minimizes washboard roads and maximizes fun.

Mt. Whitney can be seen in distance (at right of picture) from Alabama Hills Arch.

153

Corral at Santa Rita Flat.

Looking south from Mazourka Peak.

Coming across Papoose Flat.

Narrow and rocky in places.

Rougher stretch after Badger Flat.

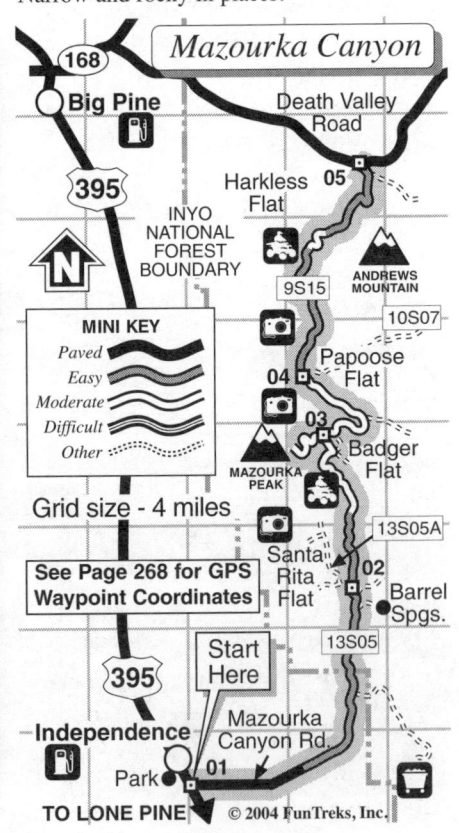

Mazourka Canyon

Big Pine
Death Valley Road
Harkless Flat — 05
INYO NATIONAL FOREST BOUNDARY
9S15
ANDREWS MOUNTAIN
10S07
Papoose Flat — 04
03
MAZOURKA PEAK
Badger Flat
13S05A
Santa Rita Flat — 02
Barrel Spgs.
Start Here
13S05
Independence
Mazourka Canyon Rd
Park — 01
TO LONE PINE

MINI KEY
Paved
Easy
Moderate
Difficult
Other

Grid size - 4 miles

See Page 268 for GPS Waypoint Coordinates

© 2004 FunTreks, Inc.

154

Mazourka Canyon 44

Location: Northeast of Independence, southeast of Big Pine.

Difficulty: Moderate. Very remote with one stretch that is steep, narrow and rocky. Suitable for aggressive, stock, high-clearance SUVs.

Features: High views of Owens Valley and the Sierra Nevada. Many secluded, scenic places to camp along this little-used trail. Interesting, remote mining spurs to explore. Climb 9,412-ft. Mazourka Peak.

Time & Distance: Allow 5 to 6 hours for 40 miles described here, counting side trip to Mazourka Peak. Allow extra hour for side trip to Santa Rita Flat.

To Get There: From Highway 395 just south of Independence, turn east on paved Mazourka Canyon Road across from city park.

Trail Description: Reset your odometer as you turn off Hwy. 395 (01). The pavement ends after 4.5 miles as the road swings north. At 8.4 miles, a rough, 7-mile side trip goes right to Betty Jumbo Mine. Continuing north, you soon enter Inyo National Forest on 13S05. At 12.4 miles (02), 13S05A goes left to Santa Rita Flat. This easy side trip has a network of scenic roads with vista points and places to camp.

Reset odometer and continue north on 13S05 as you gradually climb out of canyon. Stay left at sign for Badger Flat at 5.8 miles. Bear left again at 6.1. Turn left at 6.9 miles (03) for scenic side trip to Mazourka Peak reached at 8.8 miles. When you return, *reset your odometer* and continue.

Ignore lesser side roads until you reach sign for Papoose Flat at 0.5 miles. Turn left as road gets rougher. Drop down a steep ridge at 2.3 and bear left at grassy clearing at 2.8. Climb over another ridge bearing right at 5.3 and 6.1. Turn left at 6.4 miles (04) and start across Papoose Flat. Turn right at T on 9S15 at 7.8 miles. Bear right at 11.8 where Harkless Flat goes left. Drop downhill and bear right again at 12.8. Stay left at 16.8 just before reaching paved Death Valley Road at 16.9 miles (05).

Return Trip: Go left 11.3 miles on Death Valley Road (a.k.a. Saline Valley Road) to Highway 168. Left on 168 goes into Big Pine in another 2.3 miles.

Services: Gas, food and lodging in Independence and Big Pine.

Maps: Inyo National Forest map, USGS 250,000-scale maps, Fresno and Mariposa, CA, DeLorme Atlas & Gazetteer.

Wildflowers growing out of lava.

Unstable, boulder-strewn section near top.

Looking east over lava domes across Owens Valley to Inyo Mountains.

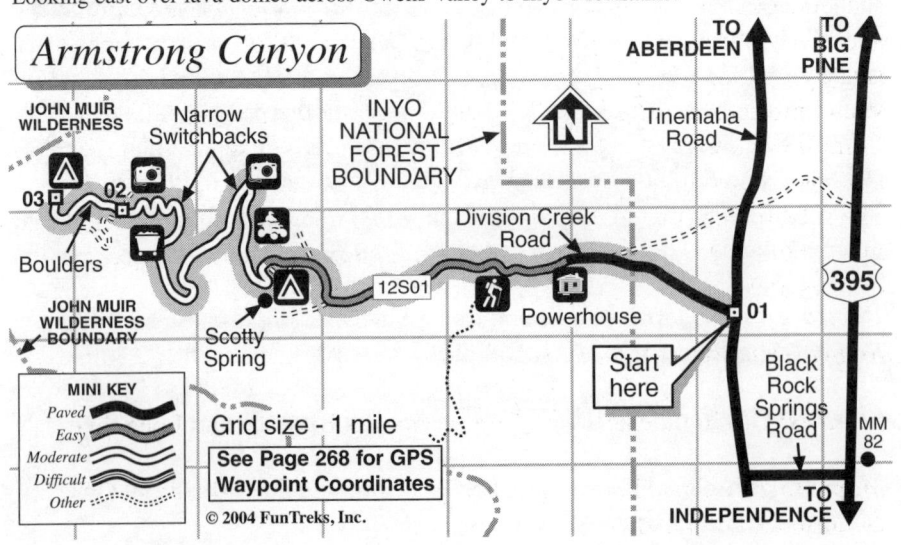

Armstrong Canyon

JOHN MUIR WILDERNESS
Narrow Switchbacks
INYO NATIONAL FOREST BOUNDARY
Tinemaha Road
03
02
Boulders
JOHN MUIR WILDERNESS BOUNDARY
Scotty Spring
12S01
Division Creek Road
Powerhouse
Start here
01
395
Black Rock Springs Road
MM 82

TO ABERDEEN
TO BIG PINE
TO INDEPENDENCE

MINI KEY
Paved
Easy
Moderate
Difficult
Other

Grid size - 1 mile

See Page 268 for GPS Waypoint Coordinates

© 2004 FunTreks, Inc.

156

Armstrong Canyon 45

Location: West of Highway 395 between Big Pine and Independence.

Difficulty: Moderate. Narrow, tippy shelf road with tight switchbacks. The last half-mile is rocky and susceptible to rock slides. Overgrown and brushy in places. Suitable for stock SUVs with low-range gearing.

Features: Pass mines on way to great camp spot in secluded wooded canyon. Wildflowers and dramatic views of lava domes from 8,300 feet.

Time & Distance: Trail measures 9.1 miles one way but only the last half is shelf road. Allow 3 to 4 hours for round trip.

To Get There: **From Independence**: Drive north about 9 miles on Hwy. 395 and turn left on Black Rock Springs Road near mile marker 82. Go west to Tinemaha Road and turn right. Go north 1.2 miles to Division Creek Road. **From Big Pine:** Drive south about 14 miles and turn right at sign for Aberdeen after mile marker 86.5. Go west 1 mile to Tinemaha Road and turn left. Go south 3.1 miles to Division Creek Road.

Trail Description: Reset your odometer as you turn off Tinemaha Road (01). Follow paved Division Creek Road west; you soon enter Inyo National Forest, and road becomes 12S01. Pavement ends at 1.5 miles. Continue west uphill past the Sawmill Creek Hiking Trailhead. Turn right at 3.5 miles staying on 12S01. Stay left on better road at 3.8. Stay right at 4.2 passing shaded camp spot in cluster of trees at Scotty Spring. The road swings left and climbs through a narrow brushy area beyond the trees, then turns sharply right uphill. The narrowest and tippiest part of the road follows as you climb across the face of the mountain to a wide spot of lava at 5.9. Complete more switchback turns passing mines and prospect holes. At 8.1 miles (02) bear right at a fork then make an immediate left within 30 feet. The road flattens out as you round an unstable boulder-strewn corner at 8.5 miles. Follow road through overgrown area to end of trail in shaded grove of trees at 9.1 miles (03). Picnic, hike or camp here in seclusion.

Return Trip: Return the way you came.

Services: Gas in Independence. Full services in Big Pine and Lone Pine.

Maps: Inyo National Forest map, USGS 7.5-minute map Aberdeen, CA, DeLorme Atlas & Gazetteer.

Paved drive to Mount Whitney.

Stay on existing roads at all times.

Some places are quite narrow.

Movie site #6-Gene Autry Rock. Note numbered post.

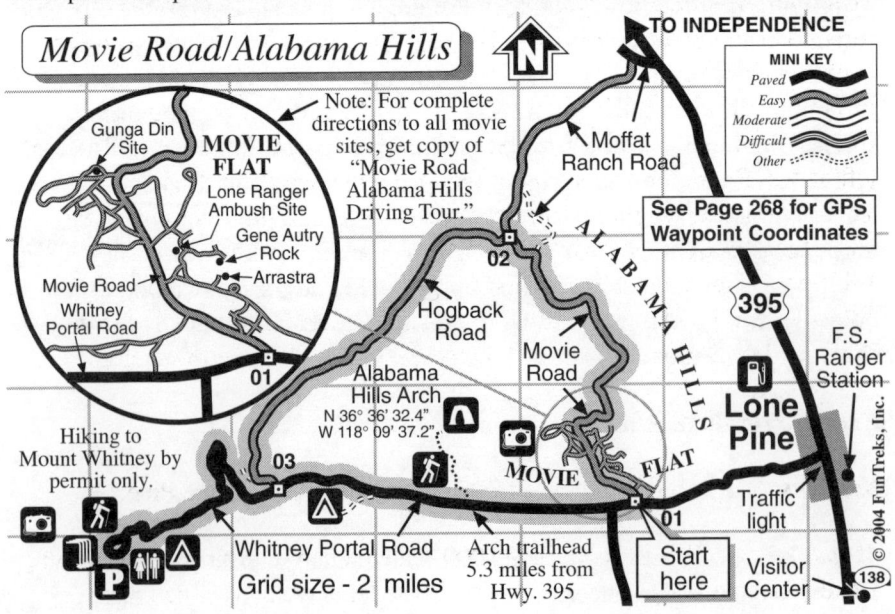

Movie Road/Alabama Hills

TO INDEPENDENCE

MINI KEY
Paved
Easy
Moderate
Difficult
Other

See Page 268 for GPS Waypoint Coordinates

Note: For complete directions to all movie sites, get copy of "Movie Road Alabama Hills Driving Tour."

MOVIE FLAT
- Gunga Din Site
- Lone Ranger Ambush Site
- Gene Autry Rock
- Arrastra
- Movie Road
- Whitney Portal Road

Moffat Ranch Road

Hogback Road

Movie Road

ALABAMA HILLS

395

Lone Pine

F.S. Ranger Station

Alabama Hills Arch
N 36° 36' 32.4"
W 118° 09' 37.2"

Hiking to Mount Whitney by permit only.

Whitney Portal Road
Grid size - 2 miles

Arch trailhead 5.3 miles from Hwy. 395

Start here

Traffic light

Visitor Center

138

© 2004 FunTreks, Inc.

158

Movie Road/Alabama Hills 46

Location: Directly west of Lone Pine.

Difficulty: Easy. Main roads are well graded. Spaghetti-like network of side roads is compacted sand, narrow in places and suitable for cars when dry.

Features: Spend an hour or all day exploring rock formations so unique they've been used in famous movie sets for over 70 years. Enjoy breathtaking scenery enroute to 14,495-ft. Mount Whitney. Only main roads are described here; for maximum fun, you'll want to explore dozens of side roads to movie sites in the Movie Flat Area. For detailed directions, pick up a free copy of the *Movie Road Alabama Hills Driving Tour* available at the Eastern Sierra Interagency Visitor Center south of Lone Pine. For a complete movie history, I highly recommend Dave Holland's pictoral guide, *On Location in Lone Pine*. To see Alabama Hills Arch, pictured on page 153, get directions at visitor center for one-hour, round-trip hike.

Time & Distance: The 25-mile trip on main roads, including Mt. Whitney, takes about 2 hours. Movie Flats can be done in an hour.

To Get There: Head west on Whitney Portal Road from Hwy. 395 at the light in the center of Lone Pine. Turn right after 2.7 miles on Movie Road.

Trail Description: Reset your odometer at historical marker at beginning of Movie Road and head north (01). The road starts as dirt then is paved for about a half mile. At 0.2 miles, a wide dirt road goes right and branches off in various directions. This is the start of the Movie Flat Driving Tour. Continuing north, turn right when you reach a major fork at 1.5 miles. Bear left at 5.2. *Reset your odometer* when you reach Hogback Road at 5.7 miles (02) and turn left. (Right takes you back to Hwy. 395 in 3.8 miles.) Head west, then south on Hogback Road. After 5.8 miles, turn left to reach Whitney Portal Road at 6.0 miles (03). Left takes you back to Movie Road in 5.4 miles (01). I highly recommend you first go right 3.9 miles to the end of Whitney Portal Road. This is a spectacular paved drive with much to see.

Return Trip: Take Whitney Portal Road east back to Lone Pine.

Services: Full services and campgrounds in and around Lone Pine.

Maps: Inyo N. F. map, USGS 100,000 scale map, Mt. Whitney, CA, Movie Road Alabama Hills Driving Tour, Alabama Hills Arch Walking Guide.

Trail begins through harsh terrain.

Salt Tramway crosses crest of Inyo Mountains.

Use caution crossing narrow shelf road.

Saline Valley Salt Tram at 8,720 ft.

Cerro Gordo Mines and Ghost Town.

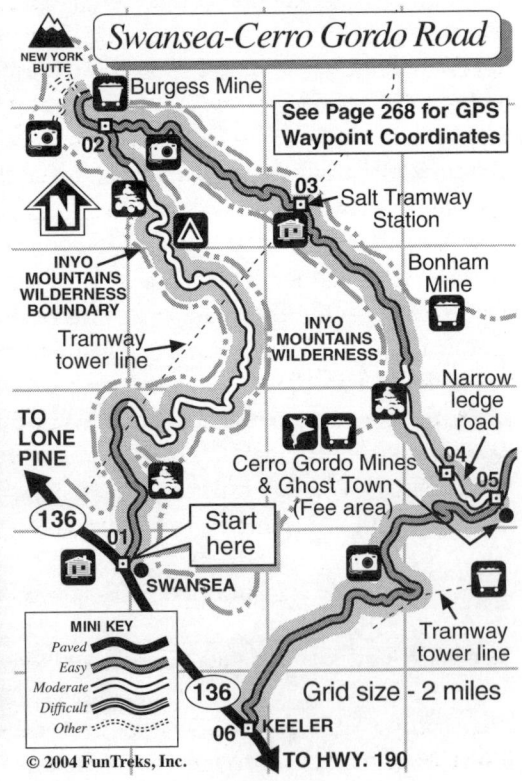

Swansea-Cerro Gordo Road

See Page 268 for GPS Waypoint Coordinates

NEW YORK BUTTE
Burgess Mine
Salt Tramway Station
Bonham Mine
INYO MOUNTAINS WILDERNESS BOUNDARY
Tramway tower line
INYO MOUNTAINS WILDERNESS
Narrow ledge road
TO LONE PINE
Cerro Gordo Mines & Ghost Town (Fee area)
Start here
SWANSEA
Tramway tower line
Grid size - 2 miles
KEELER
TO HWY. 190

MINI KEY
Paved
Easy
Moderate
Difficult
Other

© 2004 FunTreks, Inc.

Cerro Gordo Road below ghost town.

160

Swansea-Cerro Gordo Road 47

Location: Southeast of Lone Pine, north of Keeler.

Difficulty: Moderate. Steep, narrow and rocky in places. Last part of route is a narrow shelf road. Prone to washouts and rock slides. Suitable for aggressive stock SUVs with high clearance, low range and skid plates.

Features: Road climbs rapidly through wilderness to ridge atop Inyo Mountains. Great views, wildflowers and historical mining structures. Tougher, alternate route to privately owned Cerro Gordo Ghost Town.

Time & Distance: Allow 5 to 6 hours for the 33.3 miles described here.

To Get There: From Hwy. 395 in Lone Pine, take Hwy. 136 east 9.6 miles and turn left just before house with high fence. Small sign on mailbox says "Welcome to Swansea." Swansea is 3 miles northwest of Keeler.

Trail Description: Reset odometer at start (01). Head north into foothills as road gets steeper and rougher with worst section at 4.0 miles. Pass under line of tramway towers at 8.3 and climb through wooded area. Side roads dead end at wilderness boundary or at camp spots. Road flattens out after 12 miles and gets easier. At 12.9 miles (02), turn left for scenic side trip to Burgess Mine and New York Butte. For mine, go right at 13.1 and left at 13.6. Explore area, then return to main trail (02) and *reset odometer*.

Turn left and continue on trail. Road crosses narrow ridge with simultaneous views of Owens and Saline Valley. Salt Tram Station is reached at 4.2 miles (03). Elaborate signs explain history. At 6.9 miles, look downhill to left for Bonham Mine Complex. Begin steep descent at 8.2 down rough road to bottom of valley. (This section is difficult in opposite direction.) Turn right at 10.1 miles (04). Follow narrow, rocky shelf road to Cerro Gordo Mines & Ghost Town at 11.2 miles (05). (Guided tours 9 to 3, closed Wednesdays, reservations needed Nov. through April, $5/person.)

Reset odometer and head downhill on scenic, well-maintained Cerro Gordo Road. Highway 136 is reached at 7.8 miles (06) just south of Keeler.

Return Trip: At Hwy. 136, turn right for Lone Pine; left for Panamint Springs.

Services: Full services in Lone Pine. No gas in Keeler.

Maps: Trails Illustrated Map of Death Valley National Park, USGS 250,000-scale map, Death Valley, CA, DeLorme Atlas & Gazetteer.

Short side trip to this log cabin.  Terrain through Hunter Mountain area.

Lost Burro Mine.  Teakettle Junction.

"Moving Rocks" take a few minutes to find.  Lippincott Road is toughest part of trip.

Racetrack via Hunter Mtn. 48

Location: In Death Valley Nat. Park between Lone Pine and Stovepipe Wells.

Difficulty: Moderate. Although sandy, bumpy and rutted in places, most of this route is easy with the exception of Lippincott Road. This 7-mile shortcut from Racetrack Valley to Saline Valley Road is steep, narrow, rocky and often on the verge of being washed out. (Winter snow closures possible. Always check with Death Valley National Park on road conditions.) The side trip to Lost Burro Mine can also get rough. Still, the trail is suitable for experienced drivers in stock, high clearance SUVs with skid plates, 4-wheel drive and low-range gearing. Extremely remote. Go with another vehicle. Carry plenty of water and gas. Dangerously hot in summer.

Features: Seeing the "moving rocks" at The Racetrack is interesting and fun, but it would be a very long drive if that were the only thing to see. Fortunately, the route described here has other rewards. The drive itself is hilly in places with great views, including a spectacular view of Panamint Valley from Hunter Mountain. Teakettle Junction and the Lost Burro Mine are two other interesting features. Although you encounter a brutal washboard road through Racetrack Valley, this stretch is relatively short compared to the more commonly used route from Scottys Castle. Make sure you stay on designated roads at all times. Do not drive on The Racetrack playa or walk across if it is wet. It is theorized that the rocks are pushed by strong winds when the playa is wet, but no one knows for sure. A park fee may be collected by park rangers since there is no fee station along this route.

Time & Distance: The route described here is 87.4 miles counting two side trips. Allow a full day or camp overnight and make a weekend out of it.

To Get There: **From Lone Pine:** Take Highways 136 and 190 east about 35 miles and turn left on well marked Saline Valley Road. (Turn is 0.1 miles east of mile marker 41.50 on Hwy. 190.) **From Stovepipe Wells:** Take Highway 190 west to Panamint Springs. Continue west approximately 13 miles to Saline Valley Road on right.

Trail Description: Reset your odometer as you turn off Hwy. 190 (01). Head north on broken pavement of Saline Valley Road. Stay right at 4.8 miles where old Saline Valley Road joins on left. Go by a small cabin on left at 5.4 and continue straight at 6.0 where a road goes right to Lees Mines. You enter Death Valley National Park before reaching a road that goes left to

Cerro Gordo Peak at 8.3 miles (02). You go right. The road changes to washboard gravel but is very wide. Experiment with your speed. Sometimes going faster reduces washboard vibration but be careful not to slide. Also, watch for cattle on road. The road narrows and drops downhill after 14.3 miles with great views of Panamint Valley on the right.

A major fork is reached at 15.8 miles (03). Saline Valley Road goes left here. (You'll come back this way on return trip.) *Reset odometer* and turn right towards Hunter Mountain. Road narrows to one lane in places with tighter brush. The road can also be muddy when wet. There are several convenient places to pull over and camp through this area. When you reach a cattle guard at 5.5 miles (04), note opening in fence on right. Here, a single-lane road leads to a tiny log cabin at 0.7 miles.

Return to main road, *reset odometer* and continue to right. Stay right at 1.7 miles. (A 5-mile, one-way side trip goes left here to an overlook of Racetrack Valley and Hidden Valley.) At 2.7 miles, the road starts winding downhill and becomes narrow and rough in places. Turn left at 5.0 miles (05). Goldbelt Spring is to right. Stay left at 5.3 and 6.3 miles. Bear right at 10.7. Turn left at 16.2 miles (06) for the Lost Burro Mine. This rocky side trip adds 2.2 miles to your adventure. After visiting the mine, return to main road and continue left to Teakettle Junction, reached at 21.6 miles (07).

Reset odometer again and turn left on Racetrack Valley Road. (Right goes to Ubehebe Crater in about 22 miles. Beyond that is park entrance and Scottys Castle.) Stay left at 2.2 miles and you soon reach The Racetrack playa. To see the "moving rocks," go to last kiosk at 7.8 miles (08). Walk at least a half mile east towards the mountains on the other side of playa and begin search for the elusive rocks. Take plenty to drink. Distances are deceiving. Return to vehicle and continue driving south.

Reset odometer at 9.6 miles (09) and turn right to reach Lippincott Road. Left dead ends at primitive campground with toilet. The road quickly deteriorates after a miss-spelled warning sign at 0.2 miles. Pass the Lippincott Mine and descend through narrow valley. After approximately 3 miles, the road swings left and crosses a rocky alluvial fan before reaching Saline Valley Road at 7.1 miles (10). Turn left and climb through Grapevine Canyon to the road on which you entered at 17.7 miles (03). Right takes you back to Highway 190 in another 15.8 miles (01).

Return Trip: Right on Highway 190 goes to Lone Pine, left goes to Panamint Springs, Stovepipe Wells and Trona.

Services: Gas, food, lodging and camping in Lone Pine, Panamint Springs and Stovepipe Wells. Vault toilet at campground south of Racetrack.

Maps: Trails Illustrated Map of Death Valley National Park, USGS 250,000-scale map, Death Valley, CA, DeLorme Atlas & Gazetteer.

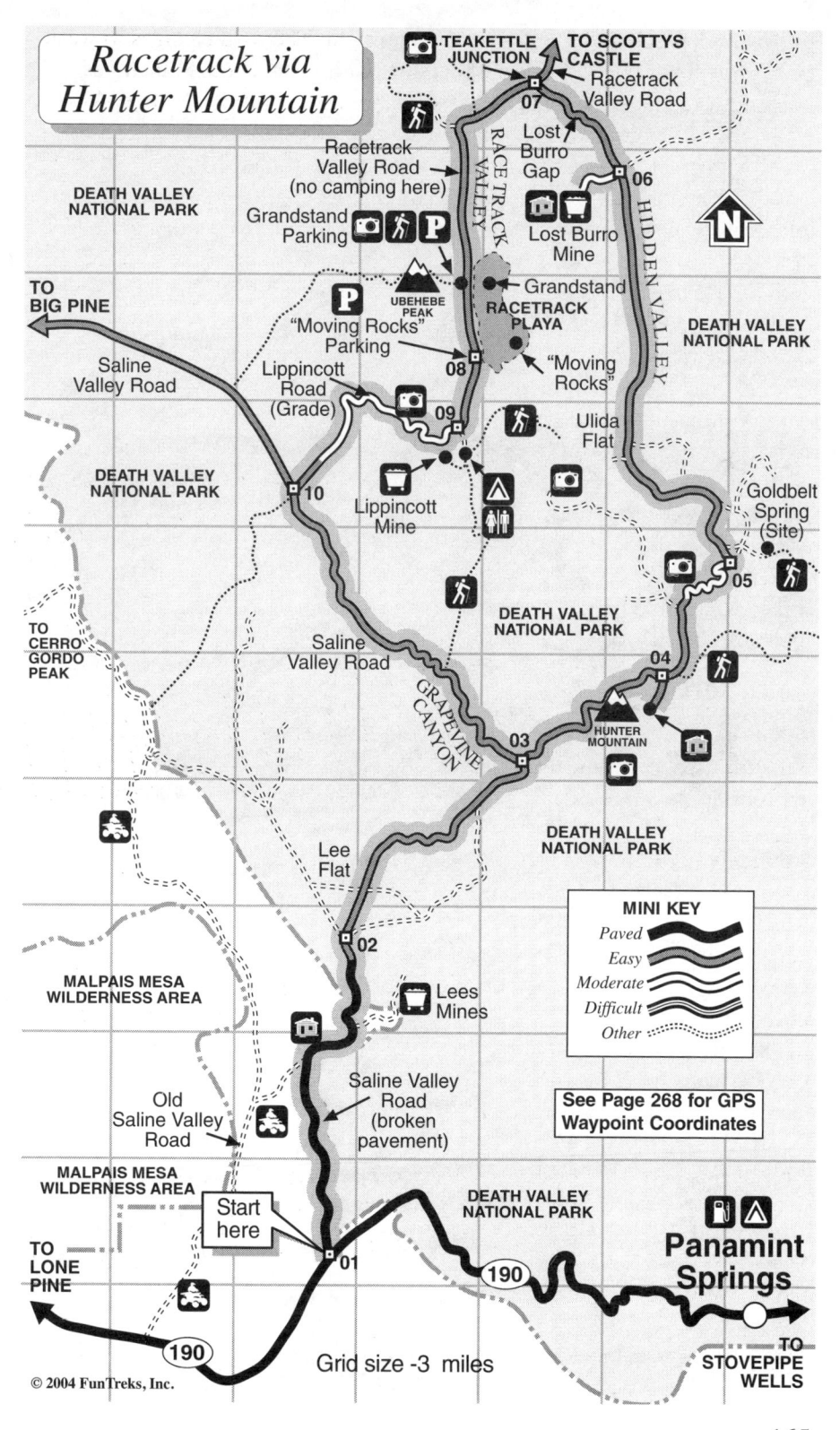

Racetrack via Hunter Mountain

AREA 7

San Jose,
Coalinga,
San Luis Obispo

49. Hollister Hills SVRA
50. Old Coast Road
51. Prewitt Ridge
52. South Coast Ridge
53. Pichacho Peak
54. Oceano Dunes SVRA
55. Pine Mountain
56. Garcia Ridge
57. Twin Rocks

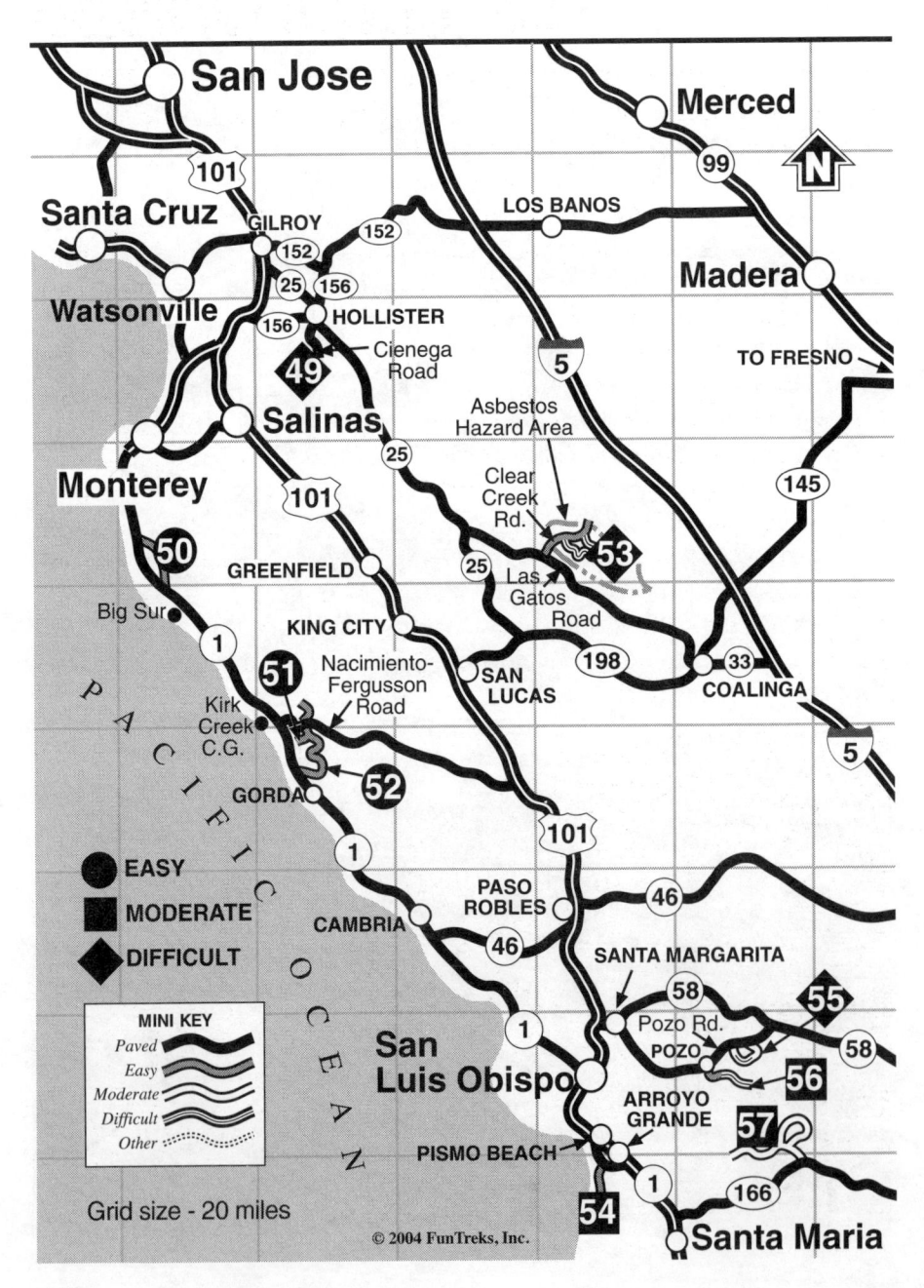

AREA 7
San Jose, Coalinga, San Luis Obispo

Not all four-wheeling in California requires a long drive to the Sierras. Several great four-wheeling areas can be found closer to the coast between San Jose and Santa Maria. One popular area is *Hollister Hills SVRA* (State Vehicular Recreation Area) about an hour south of San Jose. This park is unique because it has two separate areas. One is exclusively for ATVs and dirt bikes, the other for SUVs and Jeeps. Easy, moderate and difficult trails are offered, so everyone can find something of interest. *Oceano Dunes SVRA*, located south of San Luis Obispo is another great OHV park. It's one of the last beach areas in California where motorized recreation is allowed. You can play all day on dunes then camp along the beach. Farther north, where the Los Padres National Forest meets the ocean, easy forest roads like *Prewitt Ridge* and *South Coast Ridge* provide stunning coastal views. North of Big Sur, just off Highway 1, convenient *Old Coast Road* meanders through dense, moss-covered forest and high hills above the ocean. Farther inland, enjoy three lesser-known but challenging trails: *Pine Mountain, Garcia Ridge* and *Twin Rocks*. Finally, north of Coalinga, serious four-wheelers can test their skills on difficult *Pichacho Peak*, home of the popular "Molina Ghost Run."

Point at which *Old Coast Road* (Trail #50) departs from Highway 1.

Small section of the 4x4 Obstacle Course.

Difficult Fremontia Road.

Airborne at Lower Ranch.

SUV playtime.

Moderate McCray Road.

Partial view of Upper Ranch. Steep *Truck Hill* left center.

Hollister Hills SVRA 49

Location: Southeast of San Jose, northeast of Monterey and south of Hollister.

Difficulty: Difficult. A range of trails from easy to extremely difficult. Easy roads are well graded and gentle. Moderate roads are fairly smooth but steeper. Difficult trails vary significantly. Some are just steep; others are steep and rocky. You can also find trails with sand, mud, washed-out gullies and thick brush. The 4x4 obstacle course has some very difficult challenges. The *Tank Traps* are extremely difficult and not suitable for most vehicles. This trail consists of a series of deep, stair-stepped mud holes. Extreme events, like the *Top Truck Challenge,* use this trail.

Features: This is one of the most unique and exciting OHV parks in the state. Trails are provided for all vehicle types including stock SUVs, serious modified rigs, ATVs and dirt bikes. Entry fees are very reasonable. All vehicles must check in at the ranger station. Air stations are also located here. Those using the Upper Ranch will get a gate combination when they check in. A map of the park is also provided. All state regulations and licensing regulations apply. Stay on existing trails only. The park is open from 8 a.m. to sunset 365 days a year but is occasionally closed to the public for special events. Always call ahead to make sure park is open (see appendix).

The Lower Ranch is strictly for ATVs and dirt bikes. This section of park covers 2400 acres with 64 miles of riding trails. Most are one-way for safety reasons. Some trails are single-track for motorcycles only. The Lower Ranch has four campgrounds, a park store, two picnic areas, a practice motocross track, an ATV track, a TT track, a mini-bike trail, and a mini track. The park store and campgrounds are available to Upper Ranch customers as well. Red Sticker vehicles are allowed Oct. 1 through May 31.

The Upper Ranch is strictly for SUVs and Jeep-style vehicles (with a few exceptions for special events). This section of park covers 800 acres with 24 miles of trails. An area near the 4x4 obstacle course has flush toilets, ramadas and picnic tables. Overnight camping is allowed but space is limited. Sycamore Camp is a family campground and accommodates about 60 people. Water and flush toilets are available. Area 5 is used as a group camp and for special events a few times a year.

Time & Distance: No set time or distance. You can tour most of the Upper Ranch in a day. Makes a good weekend outing.

To Get There: Follow San Benito Street south through Hollister. Less than a mile south of town, turn right on Union Road. Cross a bridge and immediately turn left on Cienega Road. (Note: If you are approaching from the west side of Hollister on Union Road, turn right on Cienega Road before the bridge.) Once on Cienega Road, turn right at a T where Hospital Road goes left. The turn for the ranger station is another 4 or 5 miles south. Turn right at large signs for Hollister Hills and proceed to the ranger station. Pay entry fee and get the gate combination for the Upper Ranch. Return to Cienega Road and turn right. Head south to entry gate on right in about a mile. Relock the gate after passing through. Total driving time from San Jose is about an hour.

Trail Description: *Reset your odometer at the entry gate* (01). A good place to begin your adventure is at the 4x4 Obstacle Course. To reach the obstacle course, follow McCray Road east. Turn right on Garner Flat Road and follow it around to Foothill Road. It heads northwest into the day-use area next to the concrete restroom. Part of the obstacle course is in a gully just past the restroom. More of it is beyond the gully to the right (02). The obstacle course is much more difficult than most of the roads in the park except the Tank Traps.

Explore the park on your own, selecting routes suitable for your vehicle and skills. I highly recommend the moderate climb to *Hector Heights* on McCray Road. You can see most of the park from this high vantage point. Taking Fremontia Road part way makes this trip difficult. Another popular spot is *Truck Hill* located north of Bonanza Gulch Road. I also recommend taking Foothill Road where it loops around the *Tank Traps*. Hike up from the bottom of the *Tank Traps* to see this very nasty trail.

Return Trip: You must exit the park on McCray Road via the front gate through which you entered.

Services: Full services in Hollister and San Juan Bautista. Free air stations are located next to the ranger station. The park store in the Lower Ranch has general supplies, firewood and basic ATV/bike parts.

Maps: Hollister Hills State Vehicular Recreation Area map is provided with entry fee or go to California State Parks Web site (see appendix).

171

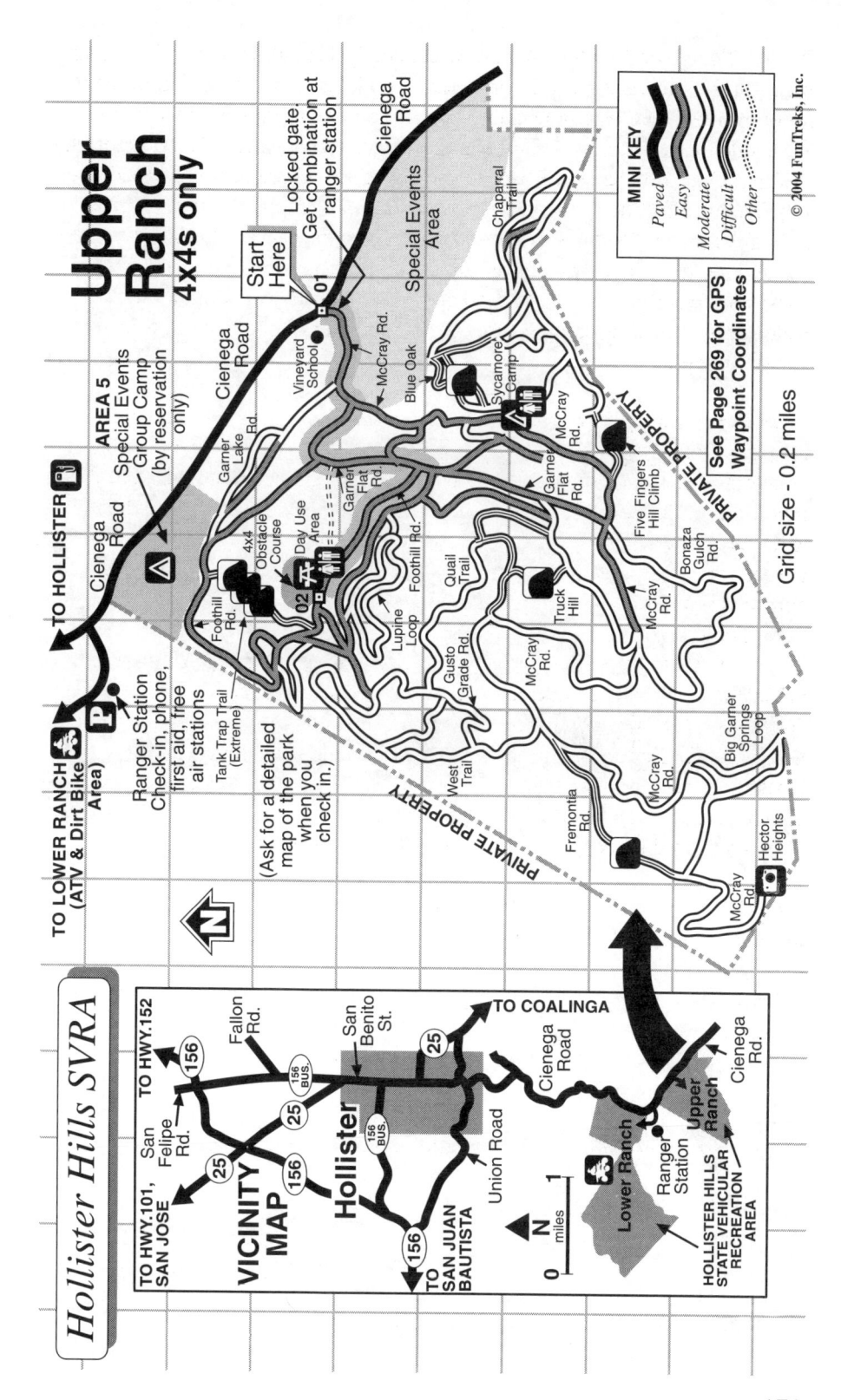

North end of road starts at Bixby Bridge.  Road is easy when dry. Stay off when wet.

South end near Highway 1. Watch for range cattle on road.

Large sycamores and redwoods.

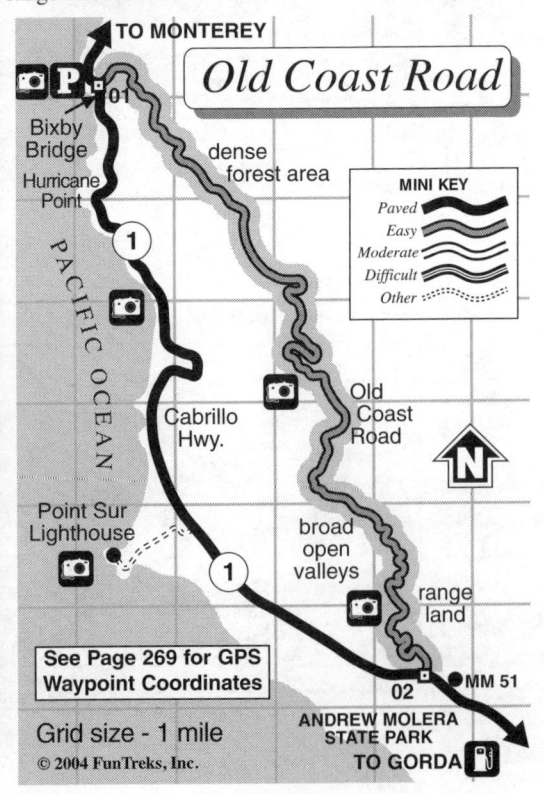

Old Coast Road

TO MONTEREY

Bixby Bridge
Hurricane Point
Cabrillo Hwy.
Point Sur Lighthouse
dense forest area
Old Coast Road
broad open valleys
range land
PACIFIC OCEAN

MINI KEY
Paved
Easy
Moderate
Difficult
Other

See Page 269 for GPS Waypoint Coordinates

Grid size - 1 mile

© 2004 FunTreks, Inc.

MM 51
ANDREW MOLERA STATE PARK
TO GORDA

172

Old Coast Road 50

Location: South of Monterey and north of Big Sur along the coast.

Difficulty: Easy. A wide, well-graded shelf road, steep in places with no guard rails. Do not drive when wet. Suitable for most passenger cars.

Features: A convenient, relaxing drive through moss-covered sycamore and redwood forest. Enjoy pastoral scenes and intermittent views of the Pacific Ocean from high hills above Hwy. 1. Close to Andrew Molera State Park.

Time & Distance: Allow 1 to 1 1/2 hours for this 10.4-mile trip. (Note: This route is only 2 miles longer than staying on Highway 1.)

To Get There:
Starting at north end: Turn east off Highway 1 onto Old Coast Road just north of Bixby Bridge. (Approximately 17 miles south of Monterey.)
Starting at south end: Turn east off Highway 1 onto Old Coast Road 0.2 miles north of mile marker 51.

Trail Description:
Starting at north end: *Reset odometer as you leave Highway 1* (01). Head east on shelf road that winds through Bixby Canyon. Road turns south and crosses Bixby Creek then runs along Sierra Creek through dense forest. Forest ends after 3.8 miles and road begins series of switchbacks through open valleys. Descend gradually through picturesque pastures with distant ocean views before returning to Highway 1 at 10.4 miles (02).
Starting at south end: *Reset odometer as you leave Highway 1* (02). Climb gradually through picturesque pastures and broad valleys. Distant ocean views emerge as you climb higher. Enter dense forest after 6.6 miles descending along Sierra Creek. Cross Bixby Creek and climb shelf road through Bixby Canyon back to Highway 1 at 10.4 miles (01).

Return Trip: Turn north on Highway 1 for Monterey and San Jose; south for Cambria and San Luis Obispo.

Services: Full services in Carmel and Monterey. If you are heading south on Highway 1, gas is available at Gorda (at premium prices). Hike one mile to primitive camping at Andrew Molera State Park. Park is largely undeveloped and popular with backpackers, cyclists and surfers.

Maps: USGS 100,000 scale map, Point Sur, CA, DeLorme Atlas & Gazetteer.

The end of Prewitt Ridge looks down on coastline and Highway 1.

Road drops steeply towards the end.

Prewitt Ridge Campsite.

Prewitt Ridge

See Page 269 for GPS Waypoint Coordinates

MINI KEY
Paved
Easy
Moderate
Difficult
Other

Start here

Grid size - 1 miles

N.Coast Ridge T.H.
CONE PEAK LOOKOUT 5155 ft.
Cone Peak T.H.

Nacimiento-Fergusson Road

TO MONTEREY

MM 19

Kirk Creek C.G.

PACIFIC OCEAN

TO GORDA

Alms Ridge Campsite

PRIVATE
PRIVATE
PRIVATE

Prewitt Ridge Campsite

FORT HUNTER LIGGETT MILITARY RES.

20S05

LOS PADRES NATIONAL FOREST

Apple Campsite

TRAIL #52

© 2004 FunTreks, Inc.

Road to Cone Peak narrow in spots.

174

Prewitt Ridge 51

Location: South of Monterey and north of Gorda.

Difficulty: Easy. Last part of trail is steep, narrow and rough. Cone Peak is rocky but easy. Suitable for stock 4WD SUVs. Avoid when wet.

Features: Pleasant forest drive returns to scenic viewpoint above Hwy. 1. Primitive, secluded camping along the way. Take optional side trip to Cone Peak Hiking Trailhead and Ventana Wilderness. Los Padres National Forest requires an Adventure Pass if you stop to recreate or camp.

Time & Distance: It is 14.4 miles to the end of Prewitt Ridge from Highway 1. This portion takes about 2 hours one way. Add another 2 hours for the 13.4-mile round trip to Cone Peak.

To Get There: Head east uphill on Nacimiento-Fergusson Road just south of Kirk Creek Campground near mile marker 19. Although Nacimiento-Fergusson Road is paved, it is narrow in places with many blind curves. Be careful. After 7.1 miles you reach a 4-way intersection. South Coast Ridge Road 20S05 goes right to Prewitt Ridge. Cone Peak is to the left.

Trail Description: Reset odometer at 4-way intersection (01).
For Cone Peak: Turn left uphill. Bear left at 0.6 miles. The road turns sharply right at 5.3 miles at Cone Peak Hiking Trail. The road ends at 6.7 miles (02) at North Coast Ridge Hiking Trailhead into Ventana Wilderness.
For Prewitt Ridge: Turn right on 20S05 and follow dirt road south. Stay right at 1.1 miles. Cross short section of pavement before reaching Apple Campsite on left next to small lake at 3.7. Private road on right at 4.0. Turn right at sign for Prewitt Ridge Camp and Alms Ridge at 4.5 miles (03). Stay on main road as lesser roads branch off. Turn right downhill at 5.1 miles (04) where small sign indicates rough road dead ends. (Left goes to Prewitt Ridge Campsite.) The road drops downhill steeply in places. Stay left at 5.6. Come out of trees with great coastal views then bear right at 6.9 miles. (Left is private.) Road ends at Alms Ridge Campsite at 7.3 miles (05).

Return Trip: Return the way you came or exit via South Coast Ridge Trail #52.

Services: Gas available at Gorda, a small tourist stop on Highway 1.

Maps: Los Padres National Forest, Monterey Ranger District, USGS 100,000-scale map Cambria CA, DeLorme Atlas & Gazetteer.

The day started cloudy at 3,000 feet.    Hill after hill of twisting road.

Final descent to Highway 1 on Willow Creek Road.

Mildly steep in places.

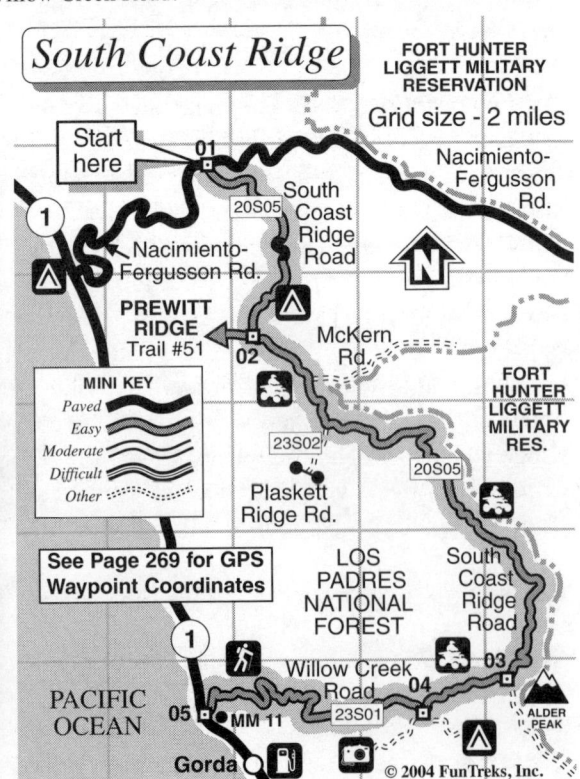

South Coast Ridge

FORT HUNTER LIGGETT MILITARY RESERVATION

Grid size - 2 miles

Start here

Nacimiento-Fergusson Rd.

South Coast Ridge Road

20S05

Nacimiento-Fergusson Rd.

PREWITT RIDGE Trail #51

McKern Rd.

FORT HUNTER LIGGETT MILITARY RES.

MINI KEY
- Paved
- Easy
- Moderate
- Difficult
- Other

23S02

20S05

Plaskett Ridge Rd.

See Page 269 for GPS Waypoint Coordinates

LOS PADRES NATIONAL FOREST

South Coast Ridge Road

PACIFIC OCEAN

Willow Creek Road

ALDER PEAK

MM 11

23S01

Gorda

© 2004 FunTreks, Inc.

176

South Coast Ridge 52

Location: South of Monterey, northeast of Gorda.

Difficulty: Easy. Suitable for all 4-wheel-drive SUVs with high ground clearance. Mildly steep in places and may be impassable when wet.

Features: Scenic drive reaching elevations above 3,000 feet. Los Padres National Forest requires an Adventure Pass if you stop to recreate or camp.

Time & Distance: 22.6 miles without side trips. Allow 3 to 4 hours.

To Get There: Head east uphill on paved Nacimiento-Fergusson Road just south of Kirk Creek Campground near mile marker 19. After 7.1 miles, turn right on well marked South Coast Ridge Road 20S05.

Trail Description: Reset odometer at start (01). Head south on dirt road staying right at 1.1 miles. Cross short section of pavement before reaching Apple Campsite on left next to small lake at 3.7. Prewitt Ridge goes right at 4.5 miles (02). *Reset odometer* and follow main road left uphill.

Bear right at 1.2 miles where McKern Road goes left. (Although McKern dead ends after 7 miles, it's a fun side trip.) Stay left at 2.3 miles where Plaskett Ridge Road 23S02 goes right. South Coast Ridge Road climbs above 3,000 feet with gorgeous views in all directions even though parts of the area are recovering from a 1996 fire. Watch for glimpses of the Pacific Ocean to the west. Continue straight at 8.2 miles where a closed road branches right. Continue straight at 10.4 miles (03) to return to Hwy. 1 via Willow Creek Road, a.k.a. Los Burros Road. (Left goes past Alder Peak and Three Peaks Lookout. The road eventually dead ends at a gate after 12 miles.) Stay right at 12.1 miles (04) on Willow Creek Road. (Two roads go left here. Hard left goes to Alder Creek Camp; easy left goes to viewpoint at San Martin Top.) Continue downhill on well-maintained road, enjoying closer ocean views along the way. Highway 1 is reached at 18.1 miles (05) near mile marker 11. A large sign identifies Willow Creek Road 23S01. Look for the sign if you drive the trail in the opposite direction.

Return Trip: Gorda is left one mile. Nacimiento-Fergusson Rd. is right 8 miles.

Services: Gas and food at Gorda. Primitive camping along the route.

Maps: Los Padres National Forest, Monterey Ranger District, USGS 250,000-scale map, San Luis Obispo, CA, DeLorme Atlas & Gazetteer.

Primitive camping and no water.

Start of trail marked as T103.

Many steep hills with tight, scratchy brush.

Toughest part of trail can be bypassed.

Cinnabar processing tumbler at mine site.

Some roads may be impassable when wet.

Trail is located in asbestos hazard area.

Major mine complex in Idria.

Pichacho Peak 53

Location: Southeast of Hollister, northwest of Coalinga.

Difficulty: Difficult. Narrow, steep and rocky with tight, scratchy brush. The worst sections are best done with lockers, but these sections can be bypassed. Hot and dusty in the summer. During wet periods, the park may be closed because roads become impassable. Best time to go is late fall and early spring when soil is moist but not wet. Route-finding is complex. Watch for rattlesnakes in the dry months. Stay on designated routes.

Features: This trail is located in the Clear Creek Management Area, a 50,000-acre OHV park managed by the Hollister Field Office of the BLM. The park includes fun roads for stock SUVs and has many excellent ATV and dirt bike trails. Many old cinnabar mines (an ore used to make mercury) are scattered around the park but most are off limits for safety reasons. The park is located inside an asbestos hazard area and warning signs are posted that the soil may be hazardous to your health. This stops some people from using the park, but others have been coming here for years. You must decide for yourself whether it is safe. A detailed map of the park is available at the Hollister Field Office. The map explains the asbestos situation in more detail. Call or write the BLM for a copy of the map or stop at the Hollister Field Office (see appendix). Pichacho Peak Trail is home of the *Molina Ghost Run*, a major event sponsored by the California Association of 4-Wheel Drive Clubs. Hundreds of vehicles show up for the event held annually in March.

Time & Distance: Allow about 4 hours for the 13.5-mile Pichacho Peak Trail. Add another 3 hours for the drive to Idria and back.

To Get There: **From Hollister:** Take Highway 25 south. Go 20 miles past Pinnacles National Monument and turn left on Coalinga-Los Gatos Road. In another 12 miles, turn left on Clear Creek Road at a brown BLM information board. Bear right after the paved water crossing and follow road less than 2 miles to Oak Flat Campground on left. **From Coalinga:** Head west on West Polk Avenue from McDonalds Restaurant on Highway 198. Just out of town, the road swings north and becomes Derrick Blvd. Go 4 miles north and turn left on Los Gatos Road. After more than 30 miles, turn right on Clear Creek Road at a brown BLM information board. Bear right after the paved water crossing and follow road less than 2 miles to Oak Flat Campground on left.

Trail Description: *Reset odometer at entrance to Oak Flat Campground* (01). Continue east on Clear Creek Road and immediately turn right towards a clearing with a stream at the bottom. Cross stream and turn right up a steep, narrow road marked T103. Stay left at 0.9 miles where T102 goes right. Stay right at 1.3 then right again at 1.4 miles (02) on T104. Continue straight on T104 at 1.8 where T109 goes left. The brush tightens as you climb relentlessly. Stay right uphill on T104 at 2.2. Bear left up a difficult spot at 2.3 miles then go straight crossing T122 at 2.4. Keep head and face well inside vehicle to avoid being poked in the eye with snapping branches.

Climb steeply to the top of Goat Mountain, reached at 3.0 miles (03). Stay left on T104 at 3.2 after a steep descent. Bear right at 3.6 where T122 goes left. Go straight at 4.2 on T104 and climb a steep hill. At 4.6 miles (04), before you reach top of hill, turn right off T104 and descend narrow, steep T139 (not marked). Next road on the left at 4.7 miles (05) is an optional loop.

Optional Red Rocks Hill Loop: *Reset odometer and turn left* (05). Turn left again at 0.1 and climb steep Red Rocks Hill (lockers required). At top of hill turn left. Turn right at 0.4 on T104. Drop down hill and turn left at 0.6 miles (04) until you reach start of loop again at 0.7 miles. *Reset odometer again,* only this time stay right.

Continuation of trail after loop: Bear right at 0.1 then make a hard left at 0.7 miles (06) on R007. Stay right at 0.8; then at 0.9, R007 curves right. Just before this point, however, you turn right on a lesser road that accesses the toughest part of the trail. (Hopefully, a few orange ribbons, from the Molina Ghost Run event, still mark trail.) Climb uphill through a difficult boulder field. Bear left at 2.8 past a mercury mine with large mining equipment still in place. At 2.9 miles (07) make a hard right on T141 as the road levels out. Turn right when you reach R005 at 3.7 miles (08). The road zigzags across an open area and passes a giant mud hole at 4.0. Make a hard left at "Four Corners" on R008 at 5.3 miles (09). Continue straight at 6.8 where T136 goes left. Bear left at 7.3 where T151 goes right. Return to Clear Creek Road R001 at 8.1 miles (10).

Return Trip: Left on R001 takes you back to Oak Flat Campground and Los Gatos Road. Before you leave the park, however, consider a visit to the historic mining town of Idria. To reach Idria, turn right and follow R001 north 6.8 miles. This easy drive is well marked. You'll see many other roads to explore along the way, including the interesting North Ridge route (R002).

Services: Oak Flat Campground and six staging areas along Clear Creek Road have vault toilets; however, no potable water is available anywhere in the CCMA. Full services in Hollister and Coalinga.

Maps: Clear Creek Management Area BLM map, USGS 100,000 scale map, Coalinga, CA, DeLorme Atlas & Gazetteer.

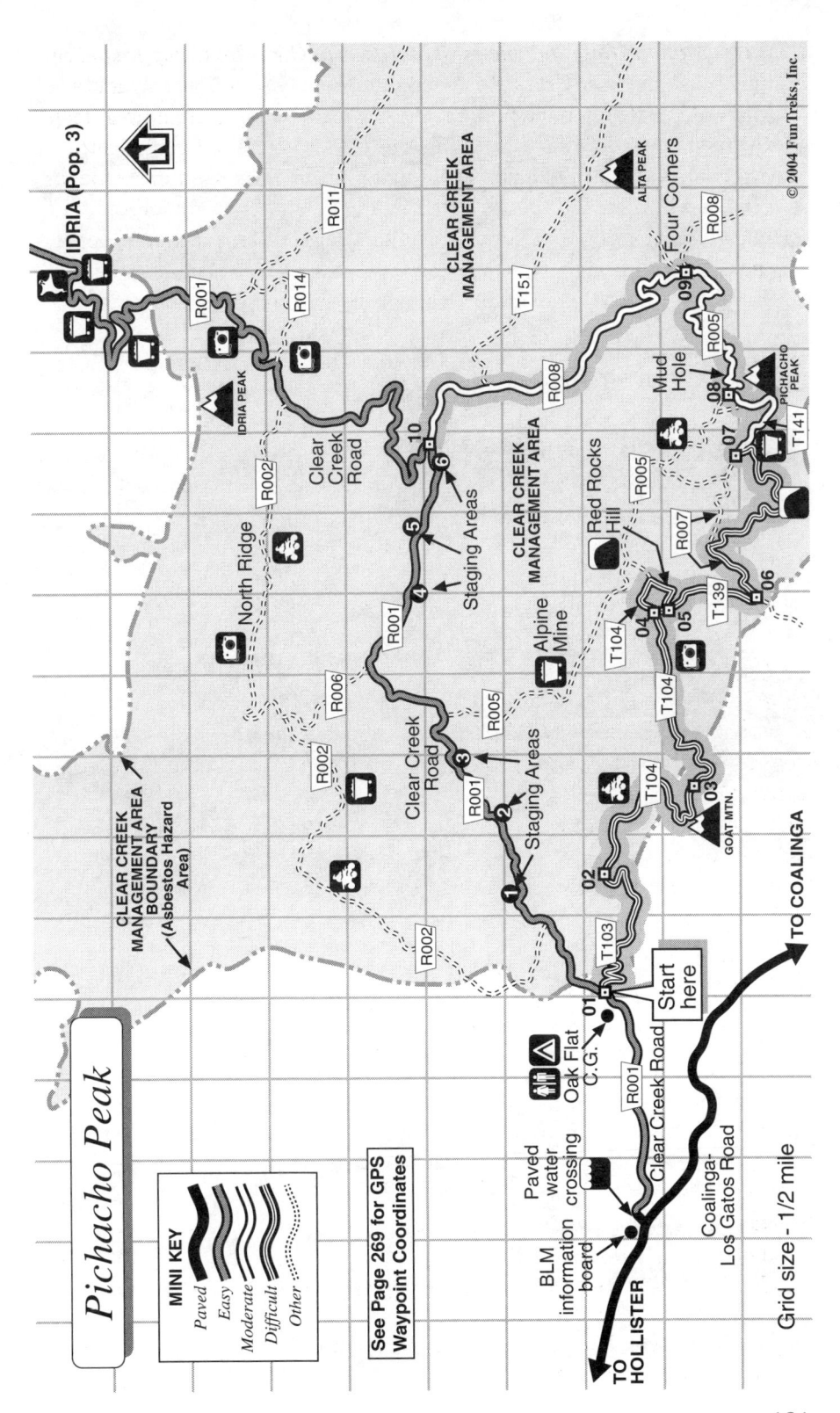

You can drive along beach but limit speed to 15 mph. Weather can be cool and overcast.

Campers set up in Worm Valley.

Big units camp on beach north of Sand Highway.

Obey all signs and stay out of fenced areas.

ATV with required flag.    Fees subject to change.

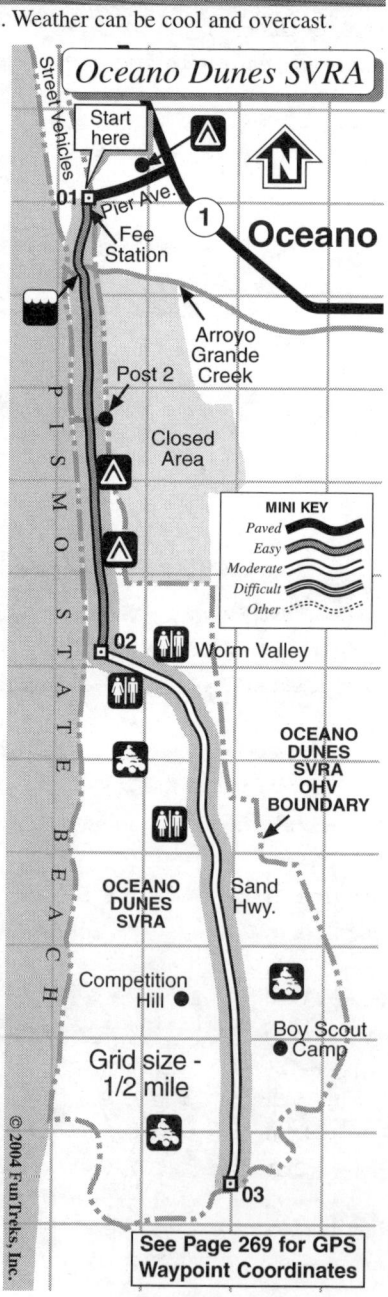

Oceano Dunes SVRA

Start here

01 — Pier Ave.
Fee Station

Oceano

Arroyo Grande Creek

Post 2

Closed Area

MINI KEY
Paved
Easy
Moderate
Difficult
Other

02 — Worm Valley

OCEANO DUNES SVRA OHV BOUNDARY

OCEANO DUNES SVRA

Sand Hwy.

Competition Hill

Boy Scout Camp

Grid size - 1/2 mile

03

See Page 269 for GPS Waypoint Coordinates

S.V.R.A. FEES
CAMPING
VEHICLE PER NIGHT $ 6.00
SR. CITIZEN (62 or OLDER) $ 4.00
NO REFUND AFTER 2 PM
DAY USE
(6 AM-11 PM)
VEHICLE PER DAY $ 4.00
SR. CITIZEN (62 or OLDER) $ 3.00
ANNUAL DAY USE
OCEANO DUNES ONLY $ 20.00
ALL OHV PARKS $ 40.00

© 2004 FunTreks, Inc.

182

Oceano Dunes SVRA 54

Location: South of San Luis Obispo, west of Oceano.

Difficulty: Moderate. This rating is for gentle grades only and not for the steeper dunes. Even in flat areas, you'll need to air down your tires and use common sense to avoid getting stuck in the soft sand. 4WD required.

Features: Oceano Dunes SVRA is an exciting 1500 acres of beach-front OHV terrain. Open to ATVs, dirt bikes, dune buggies and 4WD vehicles. Enjoy swimming, surfing, hiking and camping. Fee area. SUVs are exempt from rule requiring flags. Dogs must be on leash. Do not disturb birds.

Time & Distance: The OHV portion of the park is about 3-1/2 miles long by 1-1/2 miles wide (at the widest point). You can take a quick tour of the area in about an hour. Most people come for the weekend. Camping reservations recommended May 15-Nov. 20. (See appendix for contact information.)

To Get There: From Hwy. 101 at Arroyo Grande, take Grand Avenue west to Hwy. 1 and turn left. Go south more than a mile to Pier Avenue and turn right. Drive west a short distance to entry station. Get map when you pay.

Trail Description: Reset odometer at entry station (01). Head south along the beach. Cross Arroyo Grande Creek at 0.6 miles. This creek can be deep at times, especially at high tide. Use caution when crossing. The OHV area begins south of Post 2. To reach the Sand Highway, turn left at 2.1 miles (02) and go by an unmanned information center with toilet. Indistinct Sand Highway heads inland then turns south. Numbered posts help define the route, which ends at a fence at approximately 5.5 miles (03).

Return Trip: Return the way you came or work your way west across the dunes to the beach. You can drive along the beach as close to the water as you dare. Speed limit along the beach and near camping areas is limited to 15 mph. Obey all signs and stay out of fenced areas. Birds have right-of-way.

Services: Camping is allowed on beach and in the dune area south of Post 2. Bring your own water and pack out trash. Vault toilets provided. Full services in nearby towns. Commercial campgrounds near park. Free dump station located on Le Sage Drive, 1/10 mile north of Grand Avenue on Hwy. 1.

Maps: Oceano Dunes State Vehicular Recreation Area map, USGS 100,000-scale map, San Luis Obispo, CA, DeLorme Atlas & Gazetteer.

Steeper sections subject to washouts.

Watch for condors as you climb higher.

Road climbs across Pine Mountain.

Stairsteps are dangerously steep.

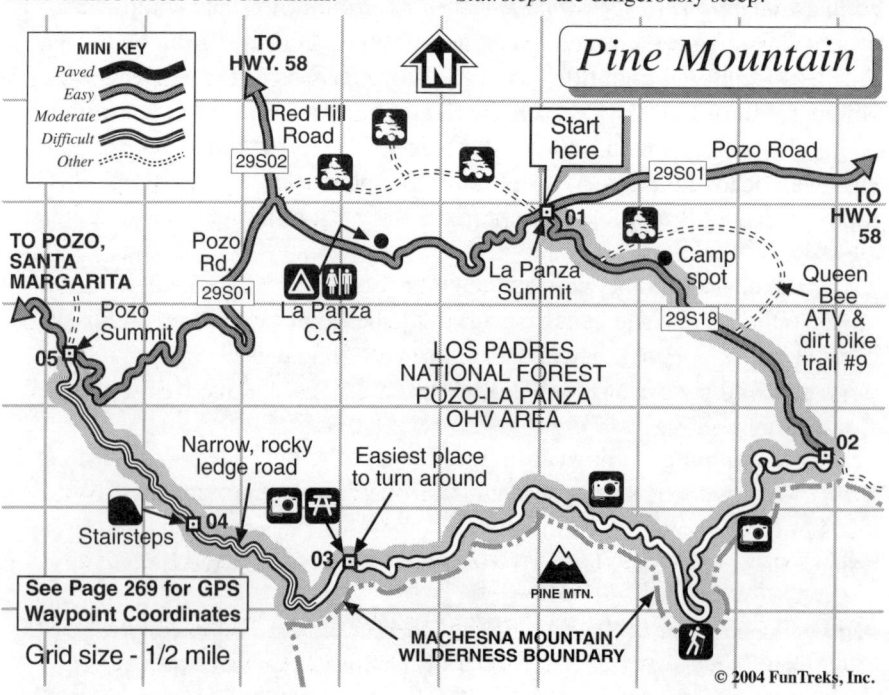

Pine Mountain

MINI KEY
- Paved
- Easy
- Moderate
- Difficult
- Other

TO HWY. 58

Red Hill Road
29S02

Start here

Pozo Road
29S01

TO HWY. 58

TO POZO, SANTA MARGARITA

Pozo Rd.
29S01

La Panza C.G.

La Panza Summit

01

Camp spot

29S18

Queen Bee ATV & dirt bike trail #9

Pozo Summit
05

LOS PADRES NATIONAL FOREST
POZO-LA PANZA OHV AREA

02

Narrow, rocky ledge road

Easiest place to turn around

Stairsteps
04

03

PINE MTN.

MACHESNA MOUNTAIN WILDERNESS BOUNDARY

See Page 269 for GPS Waypoint Coordinates

Grid size - 1/2 mile

© 2004 FunTreks, Inc.

184

Pine Mountain 55

Location: Northeast of San Luis Obispo, southeast of Santa Margarita in the Pozo-La Panza OHV Area.

Difficulty: Difficult. Most of the trail is easy to moderate and suitable for stock, high-clearance, 4WD SUVs. However, one spot, called the *Stairsteps*, near the end of trail, is extremely difficult and dangerous. Only experienced drivers in modified vehicles can get through. Stay off trail when wet.

Features: A fun drive to a high ridge along Machesna Mountain Wilderness. Very scenic with a chance to see soaring California condor. This is an excellent trail for SUVs despite having to turn around at the *Stairsteps*. Adventure Pass required if you stop to recreate or camp.

Time & Distance: Complete trail measures 9.2 miles. *Stairsteps* at 7.7 miles. Straight through takes 2-3 hours. SUVs allow 3 hours counting return trip.

To Get There: **From east side:** Turn off Highway 58 onto Pozo Road 0.3 miles west of mile marker 35. Travel west about 6 miles to La Panza Summit, which is 0.6 miles west of the "Adventure Pass" sign. Turn left on unmarked, single-lane road. **From west side:** Head east on Pozo Road from Pozo Ranger Station. (Don't miss right turn 1.4 miles east of Pozo where Park Hill Road goes straight.) Stay right at Red Hill Road and go past the La Panza Campground 1.3 miles to La Panza Summit. (Total distance from Ranger Station is 13.1 miles.) Turn right on single-lane road at summit.

Trail Description: Reset odometer at start (01). Head south on bumpy dirt road through popular ATV area. Bear right at 0.8. Bear right uphill at 2.3 miles (02) at SLO 4-Wheeler's sign. Trail gets steeper with washouts and turns west at top of ridge along wilderness boundary. Cross several rocky sections before arriving at high point marked by picnic table on right at 6.6 miles (03). This is easiest place to turn around. Trail gets very narrow and rocky as it drops down to the *Stairsteps* at 7.7 miles (04). After *Stairsteps*, a rough road continues to Pozo Road, reached at 9.2 miles (05).

Return Trip: Left goes to Pozo and Santa Margarita, right to start and Hwy. 58.

Services: In Santa Margarita. Two Forest Service campgrounds in area.

Maps: OHV Map, Santa Lucia Ranger District of Los Padres N.F., USGS 100,000 scale map, San Luis Obispo, CA, DeLorme Atlas & Gazetteer.

Difficult spots can be bypassed.

Steep and narrow with tight brush.

Ruts and minor washouts typical.

Seasonal wildflowers and high views.

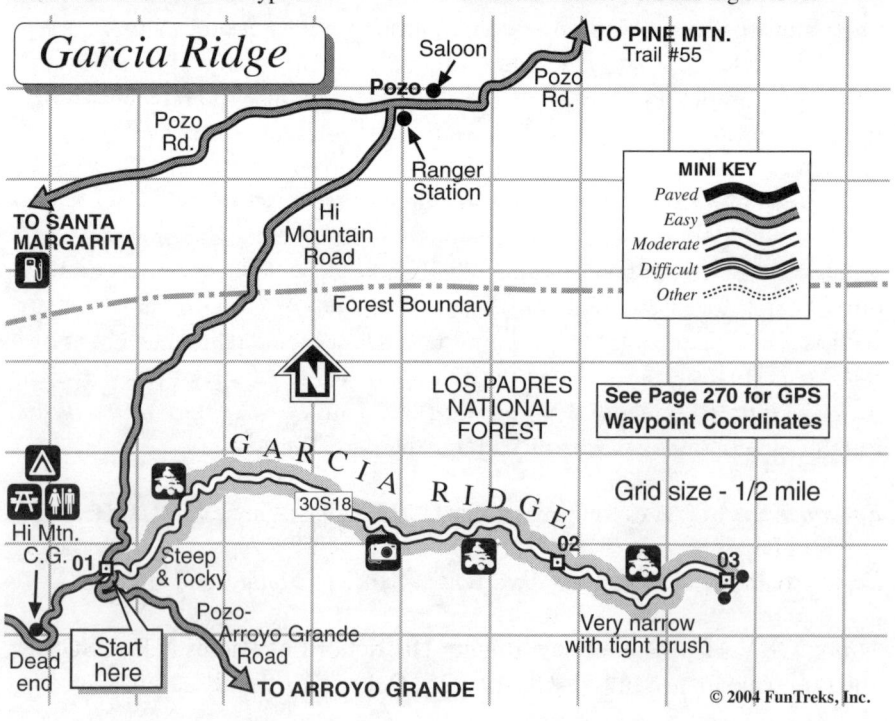

Garcia Ridge

MINI KEY
- Paved
- Easy
- Moderate
- Difficult
- Other

TO PINE MTN. Trail #55
Pozo Rd.
Saloon
Pozo
Ranger Station
Pozo Rd.
TO SANTA MARGARITA
Hi Mountain Road
Forest Boundary
LOS PADRES NATIONAL FOREST

See Page 270 for GPS Waypoint Coordinates

Grid size - 1/2 mile

Hi Mtn. C.G.
GARCIA RIDGE
30S18
Dead end
Start here
Steep & rocky
Pozo-Arroyo Grande Road
TO ARROYO GRANDE
Very narrow with tight brush

© 2004 FunTreks, Inc.

186

Garcia Ridge 56

Location: Northeast of San Luis Obispo, southeast of Santa Margarita in the Pozo-La Panza OHV Area.

Difficulty: Moderate. Series of steep climbs and descents along remote ridge. Extremely narrow in places with tight, scratchy brush. Difficult sections at start of trail can be bypassed. Tightest brush is at the end of trail. Suitable for aggressive SUVs with high clearance and 4WD.

Features: Scenic views from top of ridge. One way in and out. Spring and early summer wildflowers. Good trail for ATVs and dirt bikes. Adventure Pass required if you stop to recreate or camp.

Time & Distance: Trail measures 4.9 miles one way. Allow 2 hours to reach end of trail and return to start.

To Get There: Just east of Santa Margarita off Hwy. 58, take paved Pozo Road southeast. After more than 6 miles, bear right at major fork past general store (K.O.A. and county campground to left.). About 18 miles from Santa Margarita, turn right on Hi Mountain Road just before Pozo Ranger Station. Head south 3.6 miles to wide 3-way fork. Sign points right for Hi Mountain Road, straight to Arroyo Grande and left to Garcia Ridge.

Trail Description: Reset odometer and turn left to Garcia Ridge (01). The road quickly narrows and begins to climb. Driver's choice at 0.7 miles (left is a bit harder). Other small rock challenges follow. A wide spot with views is a good place for lunch at 2.4 miles. The trail splits at 3.5 miles (02). I went right downhill on the slightly wider route. The trail gets very narrow and seems to end, but soon widens again. The trail ends at 4.9 miles (03) where a pipe railing blocks the road.

Return Trip: Return to 3-way intersection at start (01). Consider exploring easy Hi Mountain Road that heads west. It goes past a forest service campground and a lookout tower and dead ends at hiking trail.

Services: Small gas station in Santa Margarita. Basic supplies at general store on Pozo Road 6 miles east of Santa Margarita. K.O.A north of general store. County campground north of K.O.A. at Santa Margarita Lake.

Maps: OHV Map, Santa Lucia Ranger District of Los Padres N.F., USGS 100,000 scale map, San Luis Obispo, CA, DeLorme Atlas & Gazetteer.

Start here and turn left after gate.

View of Big Rocks from Twin Rocks Trail.

Roller-coaster terrain fun to drive when dry.

Twin Rocks Trail adopted by local club.

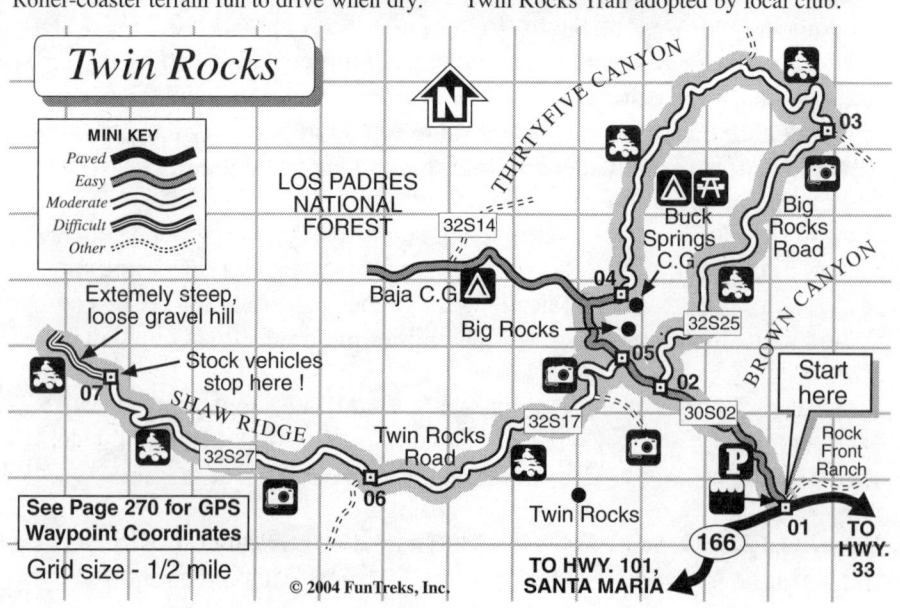

Twin Rocks

MINI KEY
- Paved
- Easy
- Moderate
- Difficult
- Other

Extremely steep, loose gravel hill

Stock vehicles stop here!

LOS PADRES NATIONAL FOREST

32S14
Baja C.G.
Big Rocks
THIRTYFIVE CANYON
Buck Springs C.G.
Big Rocks Road
BROWN CANYON
32S25
04
05
02
30S02
Start here
Rock Front Ranch
SHAW RIDGE
32S27
07
06
Twin Rocks Road
32S17
Twin Rocks
166
01
TO HWY. 101, SANTA MARIA
TO HWY. 33

See Page 270 for GPS Waypoint Coordinates

Grid size - 1/2 mile

© 2004 FunTreks, Inc.

188

Twin Rocks 57

Location: Northeast of Santa Maria, southeast of San Luis Obispo.

Difficulty: Moderate. Almost all of route is moderate, except for the last half mile. This difficult portion can be skipped. Otherwise, trail is suitable for stock 4WD SUVs with high ground clearance and low range gearing.

Features: Fun, roller-coaster terrain for 4WDs, ATVs and dirt bikes. Remote and scenic. Roads become impassable when wet, during which time the area may be closed. Adventure Pass required if you stop to recreate or camp. Primitive camping.

Time & Distance: Allow about 4 hours for the 17.1 miles described here. Add time to explore many other side roads.

To Get There: From Hwy. 166, turn north 0.2 miles east of mile marker 34 (about 26 miles east of Hwy. 101). Go through gate to Rock Front Ranch.

Trail Description: Reset odometer as you leave Highway 166 (01). Turn left immediately after ranch gate. Go past small staging area and climb paved hill. Bear right uphill at 1.5 miles (02) on Big Rocks Road. Soft dirt road is very steep in places. At 4.7 miles (03), bear left. Continue straight at 6.1 and 8.1. Bear right on better road at 8.3 miles then right again at Buck Spring Campground at 8.5 miles (04). At 8.8, stay left after cattle guard. At 9.5 miles (05), turn right on Twin Rocks Road (left goes back to start).

Reset odometer and begin steep climb up Twin Rocks Road (05). Bear right at 0.6 (left dead ends at scenic overlook). Stay right at 2.8 miles (06) at sign indicating steep hill ahead. Climb and descend along a high ridge with great views. At 5.7 miles (07), an ominous sign warns of extreme conditions ahead. Stock vehicles should turn around here. (What follows is a very steep hill with loose gravel, relatively smooth with no obstacles. The trail ends at the bottom of the hill where you must turn around at 6.2 miles.)

Return Trip: Return the way you came. When you reach the start of Twin Rocks Road (05), turn right, which takes you back to start at Highway 166.

Services: Full services in Santa Maria. Picnic tables and fire rings at Buck Springs Campground.

Maps: Los Padres National Forest, Monterey Ranger District, USGS 100,000-scale map, San Luis Obispo, CA, DeLorme Atlas & Gazetteer.

AREA 8

Fresno, Shaver Lake

58. White Bark Vista
59. Mirror/Strawberry Lakes
60. Coyote Lake
61. Brewer Lake
62. Bald Mountain
63. Swamp Lake
64. Voyager Rock
65. Dusy/Ershim Trail
66. Spanish Route

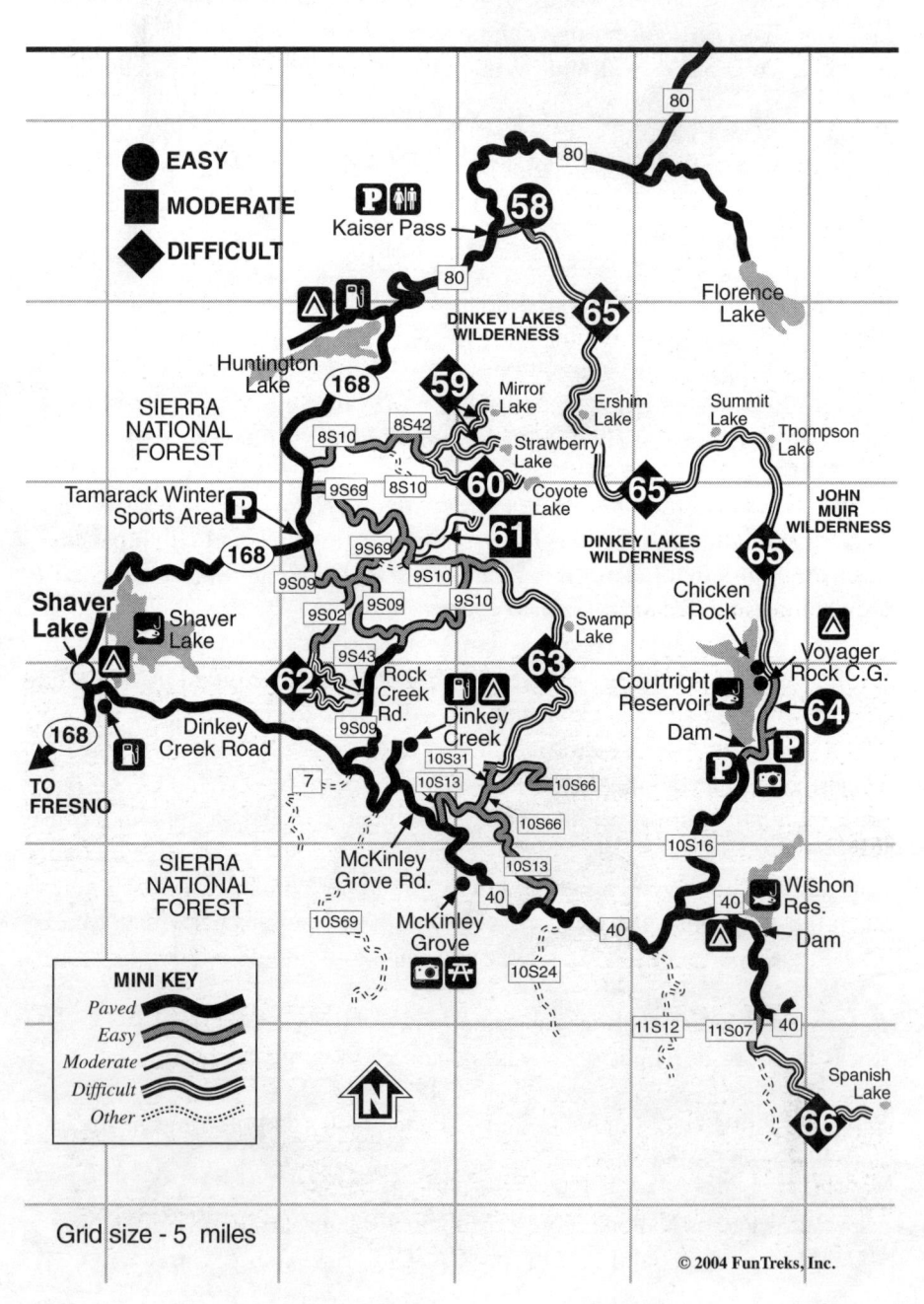

● EASY
■ MODERATE
◆ DIFFICULT

MINI KEY
Paved
Easy
Moderate
Difficult
Other

Grid size - 5 miles

© 2004 FunTreks, Inc.

AREA 8
Fresno, Shaver Lake

Nowhere in California are so many excellent four-wheel-drive trails clustered so conveniently. From the popular resort town of Shaver Lake, you can reach most of the trails within 15 to 45 minutes. In addition, all but two of the trails lead to great fishing lakes. The *Dusy/Ershim Trail* is perhaps the third most popular hardcore trail in the state. The trail is ranked just behind the Rubicon and Fordyce Creek. Of the "big three," the *Dusy* is, by far, the longest. Most people take two or three days to traverse its 31 miles. *Swamp Lake* is similar to the *Dusy* but can be driven in a day, although many people like to camp overnight along the route. *Coyote Lake* is the perfect 4-wheel-drive trail. Not too long, but very tough, it ends at a great camping and fishing lake. *Mirror Lake* has an extreme 100-foot rock climb that can't be bypassed. Because of this, most people opt for nearby *Strawberry Lake*. An experienced driver in an aggressive SUV will want to try popular *Bald Mountain*. Its Moab-like terrain is fun and very scenic. Most stock SUVs can get through moderate *Brewer Lake*. Finally, two easy trails deserve special mention—*White Bark Vista* and *Voyager Rock*. Both are exciting and beautiful with no chance of vehicle damage.

Two-Jeep family plus canoe—Mom, Dad and kids on way to *Coyote Lake, Trail #60*.

Observation point at White Bark Vista looks north to Lake Thomas A. Edison.

Sailing is popular on Huntington Lake.

One small rocky spot near top.

General store, restaurant and saloon at Lakeshore.

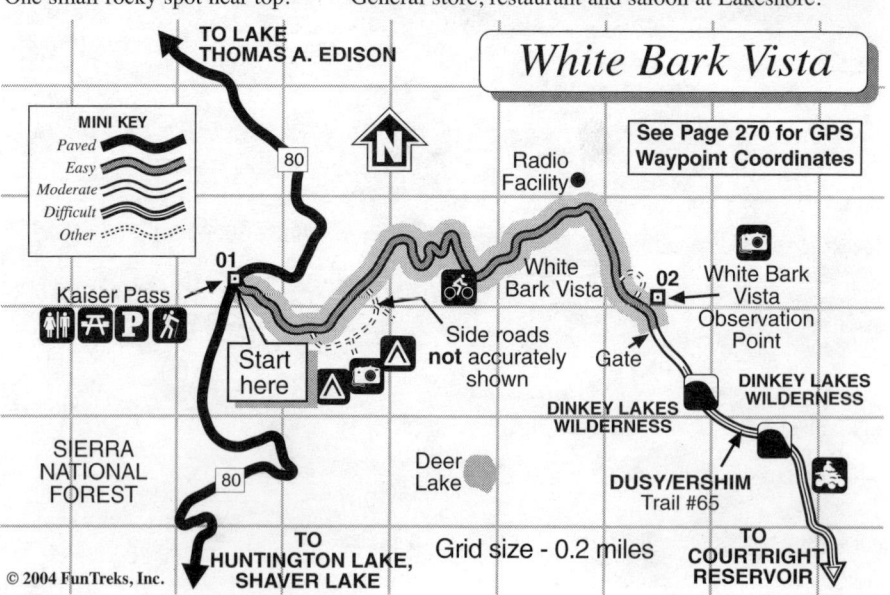

White Bark Vista

TO LAKE THOMAS A. EDISON

See Page 270 for GPS Waypoint Coordinates

MINI KEY
Paved
Easy
Moderate
Difficult
Other

80

Radio Facility

01

Kaiser Pass

White Bark Vista

02 White Bark Vista Observation Point

Side roads **not** accurately shown

Start here

Gate

DINKEY LAKES WILDERNESS

DINKEY LAKES WILDERNESS

SIERRA NATIONAL FOREST

Deer Lake

DUSY/ERSHIM Trail #65

80

© 2004 FunTreks, Inc.

TO HUNTINGTON LAKE, SHAVER LAKE

Grid size - 0.2 miles

TO COURTRIGHT RESERVOIR

192

White Bark Vista 58

Location: Northeast of Shaver Lake and Huntington Lake.

Difficulty: Easy. The short dirt portion is mostly graded with one small rocky spot near the top. This spot is easy to get around or you can park and walk the rest of the way. Suitable for any stock SUV.

Features: A beautiful paved drive to a short dirt road with incredible panoramic views from near 10,000 feet. On the way, you'll pass picturesque Huntington Lake as you climb to 9,184-ft. Kaiser Pass. Stop at the small resort town of Lakeshore for a relaxing restaurant lunch or picnic along the lake. People mistakenly overlook this trail because it's the northern entrance to the difficult *Dusy/Ershim Trail*. What a shame—this pretty, little drive couldn't be easier.

Time & Distance: The dirt road portion of the trail is only 1.2 miles but the start is 28 miles from Shaver Lake. With so many things to see, allow at least a half day to enjoy yourself.

To Get There: Take paved Highway 168 north from Shaver Lake. When you reach a T intersection at the east end of Huntington Lake after about 21 miles, turn right on paved F.S. Road 80. You'll see the Eastwood Visitor Center on the right. Left at the T goes to Lakeshore. Follow F.S. 80 as it winds dramatically uphill past campgrounds and parking areas for hiking and biking. After 5.6 miles, the paved road narrows to a single lane until it reaches Kaiser Pass at 7.4 miles. You'll see a sign for White Bark Vista on the right and modern vault toilets on the left.

Trail Description: Reset odometer as you turn off paved road at Kaiser Pass (01). Head uphill on wide gravel road. Lesser roads branch right to primitive camp spots, some with views. Stay right at 1.0 miles and maneuver through small rocky spot. The observation point at White Bark Vista is just beyond side road to left at 1.1 miles (02). A small plaque describes features in the valley below. A gate marks the start of *Dusy/Ershim* just ahead.

Return Trip: Return the way you came.

Services: Gas, food, marina, post office and general store in Lakeshore.

Maps: Sierra National Forest, USGS 7.5-min. map, Mount Givens, CA, DeLorme Atlas & Gazetteer.

All Red Mountain trails start at this sign cluster.

North end of Mirror Lake where trail ends.

Nasty hill returning from Mirror Lake.

Take your time on route to Strawberry Lake. Use a spotter if necessary.

Handy camp spot at Strawberry Lake. Take your fishing gear.

Mirror/Strawberry Lakes 59

Location: Northeast of Shaver Lake in the Red Mountain area.

Difficulty: Difficult. The trail to Mirror Lake has one section that will likely require winching. A 150-yard hill is very steep with large boulders that move around as you climb. Tight trees add to the likelihood of vehicle damage. Most people look at the hill and decide that nearby Strawberry Lake is a better alternative. Strawberry Lake has large boulders, too, but the trail is much flatter.

Features: These two trails are located in the Red Mountain Lakes Area which consists of five lakes: Mirror Lake, West Lake, Strawberry Lake, Red Lake and Coyote Lake. You'll pass West Lake on the way to Strawberry Lake and Red Lake on the way to Coyote Lake. All of the trails are difficult. A careful driver in a high-clearance SUV can probably make the short trip to West Lake but all other trails need a modified vehicle. If you park at the start and hike in, West Lake is the shortest hike followed by Mirror Lake. All lakes have camping spots, some with fire rings and crude picnic tables. Don't camp within 100 feet of lakes or in wet areas. Carry bug repellent or wait until after the first cold snap. This is a popular snowmobile and winter sports area in the winter.

The fish are fairly small in all the lakes except Coyote Lake. The smaller lakes freeze solid in the winter and have to be restocked every year. Apparently, Coyote Lake is deep enough that some fish survive the winter.

Time & Distance: Mirror Lake Trail is only 1.4 miles long. You can descend to the lake fairly quickly, but coming out is a different matter. Time spent on this trail depends entirely on driving skill and vehicle capability. Strawberry Lake Trail is 1.7 miles and takes about an hour each way.

To Get There: Take Highway 168 north from Shaver Lake. After approximately 10 miles, you'll cross the crest of Tamarack Ridge. Continue another 2.5 miles and turn right after Tamarack Creek Bridge. After you turn, you'll see a cluster of signs listing all the lakes with an indication of whether or not they are open.

Reset your odometer as you turn off Highway 168. Turn right after 1.9 miles, following sign to Red Mountain Trailhead. At 3.2 miles, turn left at an intersection by a corral. Continue straight as the road gets rougher at 4.7 miles then bear right at 4.8. The road climbs uphill and soon enters an area called Sand Flats before reaching a cluster of signs at 6.6 miles (01). All Red Mountain trails start here.

Trail Description: *Reset odometer* and turn left following sign to West Lake, Mirror Lake and Strawberry Lake (01). The road starts easy but soon gets rocky. Another fork is reached at 0.6 miles (02).

For Mirror Lake: *Reset odometer and turn left* (02). A forest service sign at 0.5 miles (03) warns of a difficult hill ahead and recommends you walk the trail before proceeding. The sign does not exaggerate. Do not go down this hill unless you know exactly what you are doing. After the hill, the trail remains difficult but not extreme. Cross over logs through a boggy spot before reaching the lake at about 1.1 miles. The road continues around the north side of Mirror Lake, passing three camping spots, each with a unique stovepipe fire ring. The trail ends at approximately 1.4 miles (04).

For Strawberry Lake: *Reset odometer and turn right* (02). The road forks again at 0.3 miles (05). (West Lake is to the right through the trees another 0.2 miles.) Stay left for Strawberry Lake. Several rocky ledges follow as you climb to the upper end of West Lake, which you can see on the right. Bear left at 0.4 miles and pass a frog pond. Another 1.3 miles of rough trail follows until you reach Strawberry Lake at 1.7 miles (06). You'll find several good camp spots near the lake.

Return Trip: Return the way you came.

Services: West Lake has a primitive pit toilet and crude log picnic tables. Gas, food and most services in Shaver Lake. There's an auto supply store just east of Highway 168 on Dinkey Creek Road. When coming from Fresno, the last place for gas at regular prices is in the town of Prather on Highway 168. There's also a gas station on Highway 168 south of Shaver Lake. A gas station at the corner of Dinkey Creek Road and Highway 168 in Shaver Lake is the most convenient but prices are higher.

Maps: Sierra National Forest map, USGS 7.5 minute maps, Huntington Lake and Dogtooth Peak, CA. The forest service also has individual information sheets on all the established OHV trails in the Shaver Lakes area. These sheets can be picked up at the Dinkey Creek Ranger Station in Dinkey Creek or the High Sierra Ranger District in Prather.

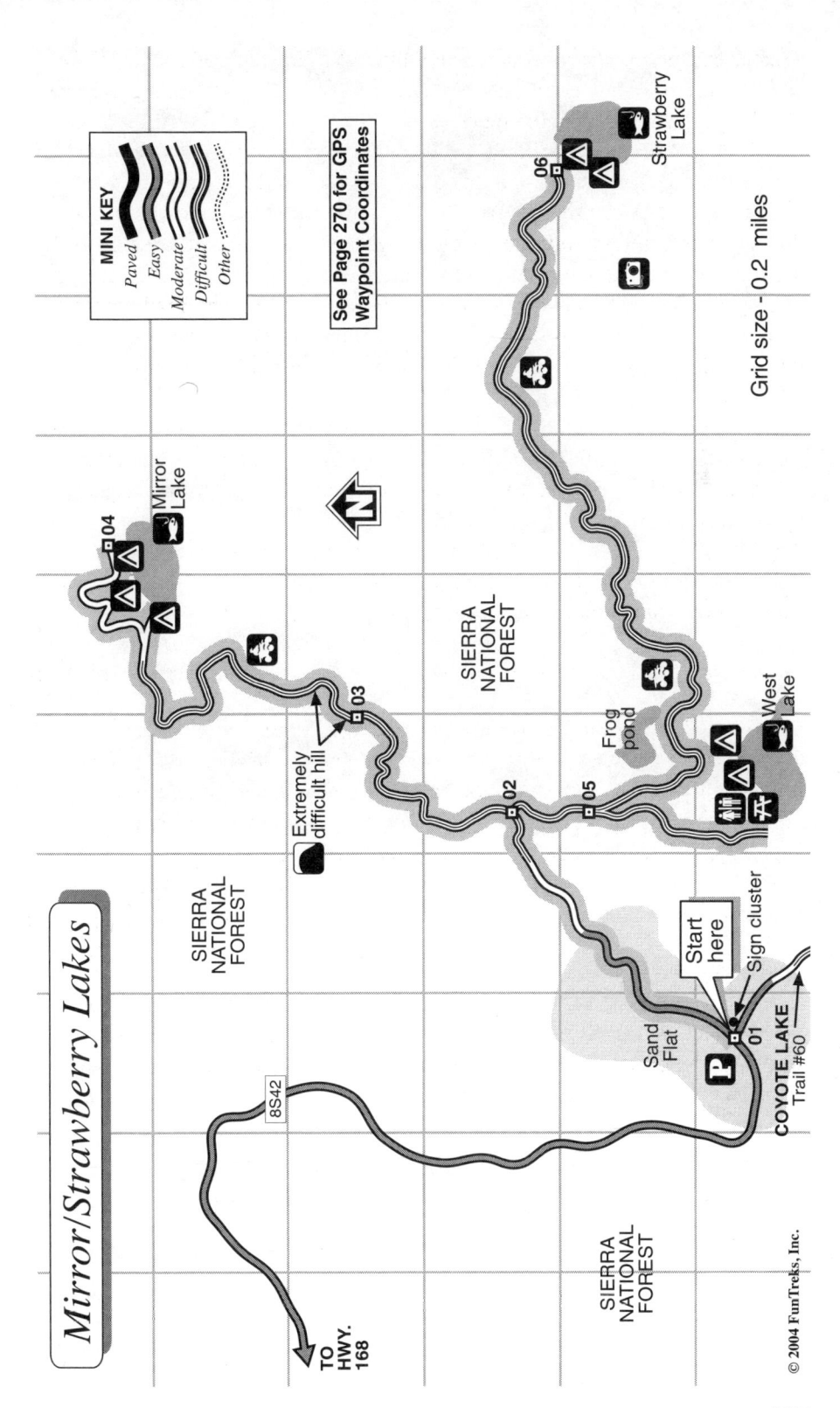

Mirror/Strawberry Lakes

MINI KEY
- Paved
- Easy
- Moderate
- Difficult
- Other

See Page 270 for GPS Waypoint Coordinates

Grid size - 0.2 miles

Strawberry Lake

Mirror Lake

SIERRA NATIONAL FOREST

Extremely difficult hill

Frog pond

West Lake

SIERRA NATIONAL FOREST

Sand Flat

Start here

Sign cluster

COYOTE LAKE
Trail #60

8S42

TO HWY. 168

SIERRA NATIONAL FOREST

© 2004 FunTreks, Inc.

197

Typical terrain. Lockers recommended.

Dad's Jeep.

Mom's Jeep.

Coyote Lake, largest in Red Mountain area.

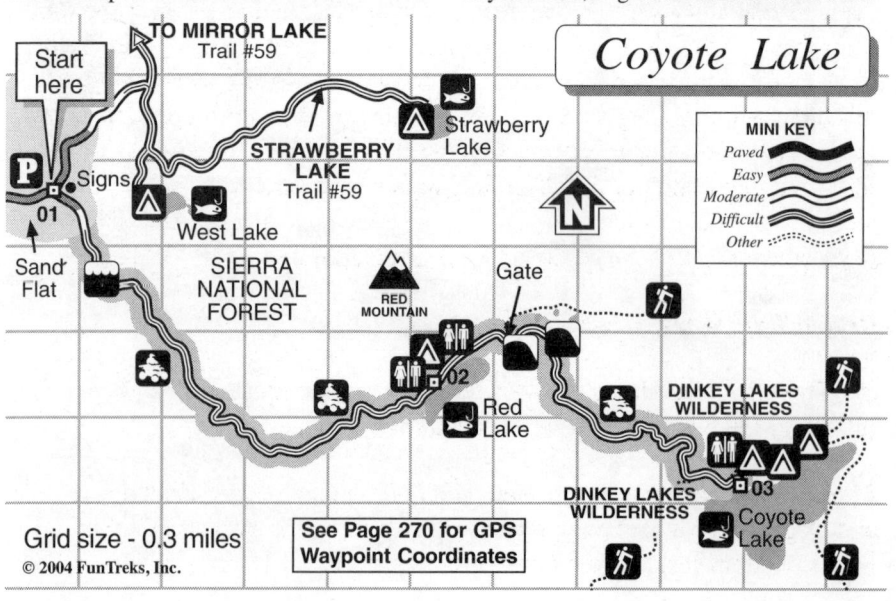

Coyote Lake

MINI KEY
Paved
Easy
Moderate
Difficult
Other

TO MIRROR LAKE
Trail #59

Start here

STRAWBERRY LAKE
Trail #59

Strawberry Lake

West Lake

Sand Flat

SIERRA NATIONAL FOREST

RED MOUNTAIN

Gate

Red Lake

DINKEY LAKES WILDERNESS

DINKEY LAKES WILDERNESS

Coyote Lake

Grid size - 0.3 miles
© 2004 FunTreks, Inc.

See Page 270 for GPS Waypoint Coordinates

198

Coyote Lake 60

Location: Northeast of Shaver Lake in the Red Mountain area.

Difficulty: Difficult. A series of challenging boulder fields, very narrow in places. One section, immediately after Red Lake, is borderline extreme with giant tree roots mixed with boulders. For modified vehicles only. Differential lockers recommended.

Features: The longest trail in the Red Mountain area with excellent camping and fishing. Coyote Lake, because it is the largest and deepest lake, has the best fishing. A great weekend trip. Popular winter sports area. Signs mounted high on trees are for snowmobiles. Don't camp within 100 feet of lakes or in wet areas. Pack out all trash. Trail enters wilderness at end.

Time & Distance: Properly equipped vehicles can expect to take 2 to 3 hours one way for the 3.8-mile trip to Coyote Lake.

To Get There: Follow same directions as specified in Mirror/Strawberry Lakes Trail #59.

Trail Description: Reset odometer at sign cluster where trail starts (01). Bear right following sign to Red Lake and Coyote Lake. The action starts within the first quarter mile with boulders and a small creek crossing. The trail then moderates until 1.1 miles where boulder fields start in earnest. Wide vehicles that can't squeeze between boulders will have to go over the top. A camp spot is reached at 2.0 miles as Red Lake comes into view. Go by the first of two pit toilets at 2.2 miles (02). You'll find prime camping through this area. After passing Red Lake, bear right and pass through a gate at 2.5 miles. The toughest part of trail follows as you maneuver between large tree roots and giant boulder fields. Other smaller lakes are scattered around the area. Coyote Lake is reached at about 3.8 miles (03). A ventilated toilet marks the largest of the camping areas around the lake.

Return Trip: Return the way you came.

Services: Both Red Lake and Coyote Lake have adequate toilets. The town of Shaver Lake has gas, restaurants and most services.

Maps: Sierra National Forest map, USGS 7.5 minute maps, Huntington Lake and Dogtooth Peak, CA. The forest service also has individual information sheets on all the established OHV trails in the Shaver Lakes area.

Moderate section.

Fun area for ATVs. Stay on existing roads.

Gets progressively more difficult near lake.

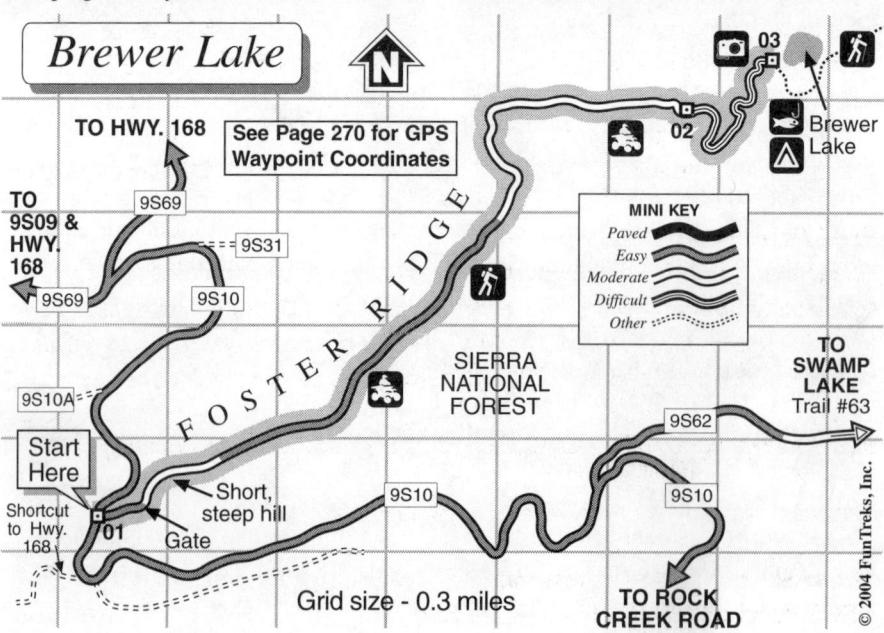

Brewer Lake.

Brewer Lake

TO HWY. 168

See Page 270 for GPS Waypoint Coordinates

TO 9S09 & HWY. 168

9S69

9S69

9S31

9S10

9S10A

Start Here

Shortcut to Hwy. 168

01

Short, steep hill

Gate

FOSTER RIDGE

SIERRA NATIONAL FOREST

9S10

02

03

Brewer Lake

MINI KEY
Paved
Easy
Moderate
Difficult
Other

9S62

9S10

TO SWAMP LAKE
Trail #63

TO ROCK CREEK ROAD

Grid size - 0.3 miles

© 2004 FunTreks, Inc.

200

Brewer Lake 61

Location: Northeast of Shaver Lake, north of Dinkey Creek.

Difficulty: Moderate. One moderate rocky challenge near the start requires high clearance and good articulation. Middle section of trail is mostly easy. Last half mile is difficult and hiking is required to reach lake. Suitable for aggressive stock SUVs except at the end. Finding start of trail is confusing because forest roads are not well marked. To avoid problems, follow these directions carefully. Make sure you refer to Area 8 map.

Features: Short, convenient, high ridge trail that ends at scenic lake. For owners of stock SUVs seeking more challenge than ordinary forest road. Good camping and fishing. Popular ATV trail.

Time & Distance: Takes less than an hour to go 2.4 miles to point where trail becomes difficult. Total length of trail to lake is 3.1 miles.

To Get There: **From south side:** Take Dinkey Creek Road 9.1 miles east from Hwy. 168 in Shaver Lake. Turn left on paved Rock Creek Road 9S09. *Reset odometer.* Head north 6.0 miles and turn right at T on F.S. Road 9S10. Follow broken pavement east then north. Continue straight where road goes right at 9.8. Continue straight again at 10.7 where 9S62 goes right to Swamp Lake Trail # 63. Head west on dirt/broken pavement to fork at 12.6 miles and bear right uphill on better road. Brewer Lake starts on right at 12.8 miles (01). **From west side:** (This way is shorter but more confusing.) Take Hwy. 168 north and turn right into Tamarack Snow Park. Follow 9S09 3.5 miles and turn left on 9S69. Go 1.9 miles and turn right on 9S10. Go 1.2 miles and turn left for Brewer Lake (01). Gate is left across sandy ridge.

Trail Description: *Reset odometer at start* (01). Climb through steep bumpy ravine at 0.2 miles. Vehicles with poor articulation may require a little speed and momentum to get up this short hill. Wind along easy scenic ridge until 2.4 miles (02) where trail begins difficult descent to lake. Go as far as you feel comfortable, then walk to lake reached at about 3.1 miles (03).

Return Trip: Return the way you came or alternate route described above.

Services: Nothing on trail. Return to Shaver Lake for basic services.

Maps: Sierra National Forest map, F.S. handout for Brewer OHV Route, USGS 7.5 minute map, Huntington Lake, CA.

Trail marker.

Cairn.

Steep hill requires low gear.

Water crossing.

Lookout tower.

View of Shaver Lake from Bald Mountain.

Turn right after ledges at this big tree with Jeep symbol.

Deep snow in trees in late May.

Last descent on South Loop.

Bald Mountain 62

Location: East of Shaver Lake.

Difficulty: Difficult. Rocky, steep and tippy in places. Best done in a modified vehicle. However, a good driver in an aggressive, high clearance stock SUV can get through with patience, a bit of rock stacking and an experienced spotter. For those willing to take some risk of minor damage, this is a very rewarding trail. Sometimes the snow doesn't melt in the shaded forested sections until mid-June. I found deep snow in late May and barely got through with the help of my winch. Route-finding is challenging because much of the trail crosses exposed granite where tire tracks are faint. The trail is marked with closely spaced Jeep symbols, but if you miss a turn, you can easily wander off in the wrong direction. Backtrack if necessary to last Jeep symbol. Best to drive the trail with someone who's done it before.

Features: Just a short drive from the town of Shaver Lake. High views of Shaver Lake from Bald Mountain Lookout. The trail is fun to drive and is reminiscent of slickrock trails in Moab, UT. Loop back to starting point or continue north on 9S02 and reconnect to F.S. Road 9S09, which goes west to Highway 168.

Time & Distance: The loop route measures 9.2 miles and takes 3 to 5 hours depending upon vehicle capability and driving skills. The straight-through route measures 7.4 miles and takes 2 to 3 hours. Allow extra time in case you get off course.

To Get There: From Highway 168 in Shaver Lake, take paved Dinkey Creek Road east 9.1 miles. Turn left on paved Rock Creek Road at sign for Swamp Lake. Go north 3.4 miles and turn left on F.S. Road 9S43.

Note: You can reach the Bald Mountain Lookout Tower on mostly easy roads if you come in from the north side via forest roads 9S09 and 9S02. Start on Hwy. 168 at Tamarack Winter Sports Area parking lot located on right side of road at top of Tamarack Ridge.

Trail Description: Reset odometer as you turn off Rock Creek Road. (01). Continue west uphill on wide road of broken pavement, and you'll see sign for Bald Mountain marked as F.S. Trail 25E09. A sign cluster at 0.2 miles is good place to pull over and air down your tires. An important fork at 0.3 miles (02) marks connecting point of north and south loop. Turn right on north loop. The broken pavement ends at 0.5 miles where the trail turns left.

203

A difficult spot follows at 0.6. (This is the first test for those in a stock SUV. If you find this spot too difficult, do not go farther.) At 0.7 miles, a steep, rocky climb begins. The hill is intimidating but not as hard as it looks, provided you are properly aired down and in first gear, low range. The trail splits briefly but immediately comes back together.

At 0.9 miles (03), the trail forks at cairn. Don't go left. This way shortcuts over to South Loop. Turn right and cross a large expanse of smooth granite following cairns and Jeep symbols. Descend other side to small stream crossing. Climb another short hill; then a series of rock ledges next to a big tree with a Jeep symbol at 1.1 miles (04) (see photo).

Reset odometer at this tree (04). Turn right downhill and weave between two large trees lying on the ground. Watch for Jeep symbol ahead. Another large tree blocks view of the trail so pay close attention as you head northeast. Climb another series of tough rock ledges then cross a large granite monolith. Watch for cairns as tire marks are hard to find. At 0.4 miles, bear left slightly over a tippy spot. At 0.5 miles (05), turn left and carefully climb over some tall rounded ledges. This may be toughest spot on trail. Above the ledges, stay left as the trail weaves through the trees. Watch for cairns and faded Jeep symbols. The trail begins to flatten out by 0.9 miles. At 1.7 miles (06), the trail swings south and passes through a forested area before it heads north again. (Snow might be encountered here in early summer.) At 3.3 miles (07), a road joins on the left. Turn left here to reach Bald Mountain Lookout on the south loop. Straight goes north and reconnects to 9S09 at 6.3 miles (08). Once on 9S09, turn left to reach Hwy. 168.

Reset odometer if you turn left for lookout tower (07). Head southwest and climb across open granite area. Tower is reached at 1.1 miles (09).

To return via south loop, *reset odometer* again at lookout tower and retrace your route a short distance until you can turn right downhill. The trail is not well marked here. Descend the mountain, looking for Jeep symbols. The trail zigzags downhill then heads directly south after about 1.1 miles (10). At approximately 1.7 miles (11), the trail turns east. Stay right at 2.1 miles (12) where trail splits left back to north loop. Stay left downhill at 2.5 miles as trail drops through tricky washed-out, rutted area. Trail turns north, and at 3.4 miles (02), reconnects to original trail. Turn right to return to Rock Creek Road reached at 3.7 miles (01).

Return Trip: Return the way you came.

Services: Gas and supplies in Dinkey Creek, which is left when you reach Dinkey Creek Road. Otherwise, return to Shaver Lake.

Maps: Sierra National Forest map, F.S. handout for Bald Mountain OHV Route, USGS 7.5 minute map, Dinkey Creek, CA.

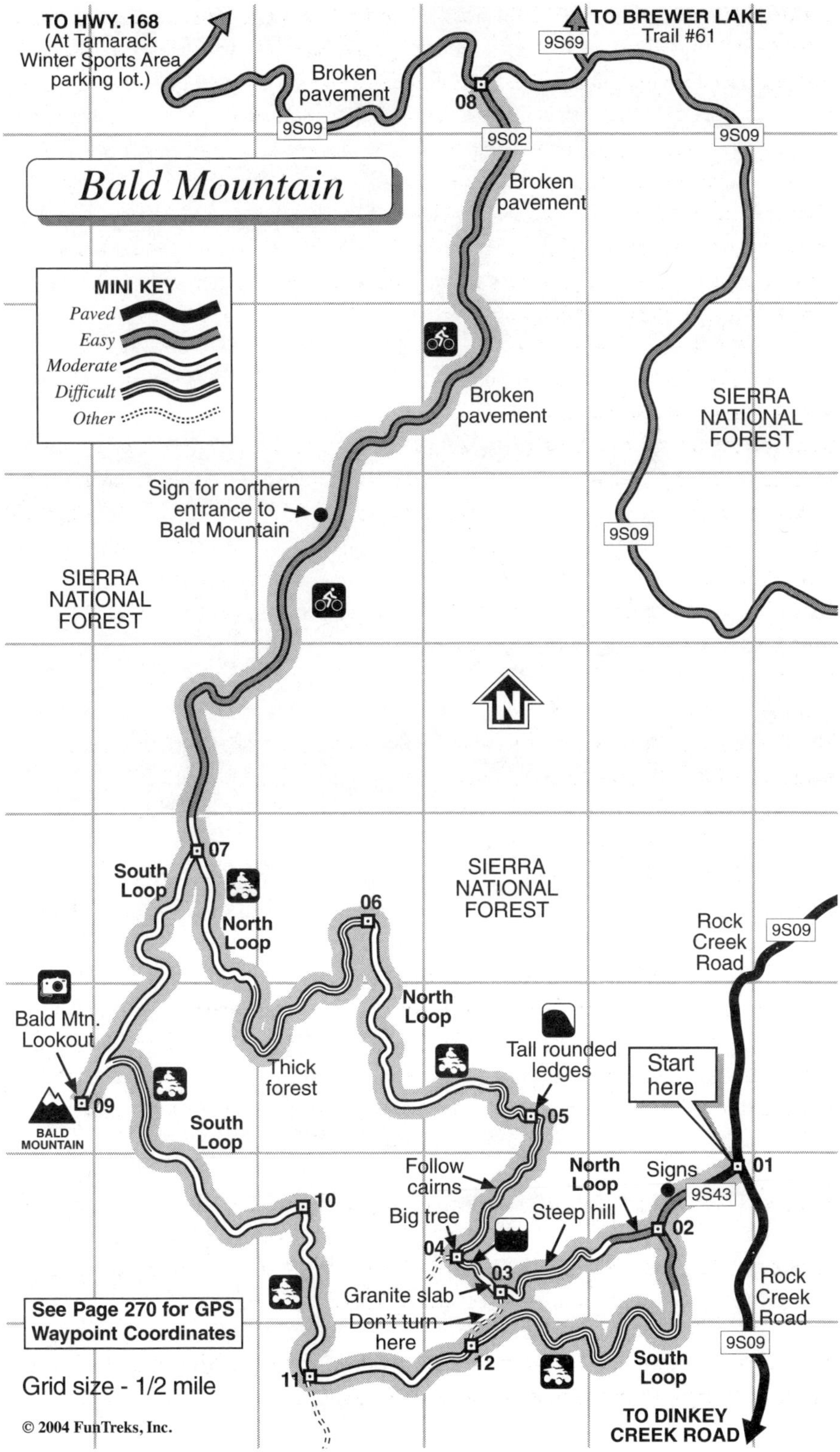
TO HWY. 168
(At Tamarack
Winter Sports Area
parking lot.)
Broken
pavement
9S09
08
9S69
TO BREWER LAKE
Trail #61
9S02
9S09
Bald Mountain
Broken
pavement
MINI KEY
Paved
Easy
Moderate
Difficult
Other
Broken
pavement
SIERRA
NATIONAL
FOREST
Sign for northern
entrance to
Bald Mountain
9S09
SIERRA
NATIONAL
FOREST
N
07
South
Loop
North
Loop
06
SIERRA
NATIONAL
FOREST
Rock
Creek
Road
9S09
Bald Mtn.
Lookout
North
Loop
Tall rounded
ledges
Start
here
Thick
forest
BALD
MOUNTAIN
09
South
Loop
05
Follow
cairns
North
Loop
Signs
01
9S43
10
Big tree
Steep hill
02
04
03
Granite slab
Rock
Creek
Road
See Page 270 for GPS
Waypoint Coordinates
Don't turn
here
12
9S09
South
Loop
11
Grid size - 1/2 mile
© 2004 FunTreks, Inc.
TO DINKEY
CREEK ROAD

Dinkey Creek store is close to start of trail.

Great views from high points along the route.

Places to camp and picnic along the route.

First of many very difficult obstacles.

Spots like this require very high clearance.

Trail passes close to Grouse Lake.

Swamp Lake 63

Location: East of Shaver Lake and Dinkey Creek.

Difficulty: Difficult. Large, challenging boulders and steep, hair-raising climbs. Muddy in places. Snow possible in early summer. Modified vehicles need very high ground clearance. Recommend at least one differential locker. For experienced drivers only. Don't go alone. Damage is possible even for the most capable vehicle. Definitely not for stock SUVs.

Features: Contrary to what its name implies, Swamp Lake Trail is a high-elevation mountain route climbing to 9,600 feet at one point. Although much of the trail is heavily forested, the scenery is very impressive from high vistas along the route. You pass several excellent fishing lakes, although some require short hikes. The trail can be driven in a day but most people stop and camp along the way. Makes a perfect weekend outing.

Time & Distance: With no delays and proper equipment, this 13.4-mile trail can be driven in 6 or 7 hours. However, it is best to allow at least one full day. Plan to spend even more time if you are traveling with a large group of vehicles.

To Get There: From Highway 168 in Shaver Lake, head east about 12 miles to Dinkey Creek. Turn right on McKinley Grove Road just before Dinkey Creek and go another 2.4 miles. *Reset odometer* and turn left on Big Fir Road 10S13 at sign for Swamp Lake and Hatch Lake. At 3.0 miles, turn left at wide intersection on 10S66. Bear left again at 4.2 on 10S31. You'll see gate for "Swamp Route" on right at 5.1 miles (01). Swamp Lake Trail can also be driven from north to south.

Trail Description: *Reset odometer at start* (01). The road starts easy but soon begins to climb. A high point with views is reached at 1.9 miles, followed by a rocky shelf road that requires some rock crawling. A hiking trail to Hatch Lake departs on the right at approximately 3.8 miles. Those willing to hike 20 minutes to Hatch Lake will be rewarded with good fishing. A log picnic table at 4.2 miles (02) marks the top of a 9,300-ft. ridge. Bear right and follow switchbacks down the mountain. When you reach the bottom at 5.6 miles (03), bear left after crossing the tiny south fork of Dinkey Creek. Right goes to Upper and Lower Mud Lake, an old mining area that is private property. Just after a small lake on the right at 5.8 miles, a nasty downhill obstacle is encountered. Be careful here; one misplaced tire could result in a rollover.

207

After this obstacle, the trail weaves along rocky Dinkey Creek, heading west, then north. After crossing an open expanse of rough granite, you approach a small lake. The trail is very obscure here. Stay to the right of the lake. On the east side of the lake at 6.5 miles (04), turn right up a steep rocky mound. After you get around the lake, bear left at a faint fork at 6.6 miles. At 6.8 miles (05), climb an extremely steep wall of granite called Rooster Rock, making sure you don't get sideways on the hill. This is followed by another steep climb with a narrow slot at the top. You have to turn left as tight boulders wedge against your rocker panels. I found it necessary to winch at this point.

The climb continues to Grouse Lake, marked by a camp spot on the right at 7.9 miles. Bear left at 8.3 miles (06). This is the highest point on the trail, near 9,600 feet. As you descend the other side of the ridge, watch for a mine adit on the left at 8.5. Switchbacks drop steeply down the hill. Bear left at 8.8 miles (07) where a road goes right to Swamp Lake and campsites. The trail levels out somewhat and passes along the southwest side of Swamp Meadow.

At 10.8 miles (08), you climb over a large, difficult boulder field. This marks the beginning of a very nasty descent to Miningtown Meadow. Your vehicle and driving skills will be severely tested. The toughest part ends when you cross Dinkey Creek again at 11.7 miles. A driver's choice at 12.1 is followed by more creek crossings. Stay left where a road joins on the right at 12.4 miles (09) after crossing a corrugated log bridge. The trail ends at a gate at 13.4 miles (10).

Return Trip: Continue past the gate a short distance and stay left on F.S. 9S62. It heads west about 2 miles and connects to F.S. 9S10. Left on 9S10 connects to Rock Creek Road which heads south to Dinkey Creek Road. At Dinkey Creek Road, turn right for Shaver Lake or left for Dinkey Creek (see map of Area 8).

Right on 9S10 goes to Brewer Lake Trail #61. Beyond that, 9S69 runs into 9S09 which connects to Highway 168 at Tamarack Winter Sports Area parking lot. Going this way also takes you past 9S02 which goes south to Bald Mountain Trail # 62.

Services: Dinkey Creek is a small resort with a general store and gas. Many campgrounds dot the area, including places large enough for motorhomes. The Dinkey Creek Ranger Station is also located there. More complete services are available in Shaver Lake.

Maps: Sierra National Forest map, F.S. handout for Swamp OHV Route, USGS 100,000-scale map, Shaver Lake, CA.

Swamp Lake

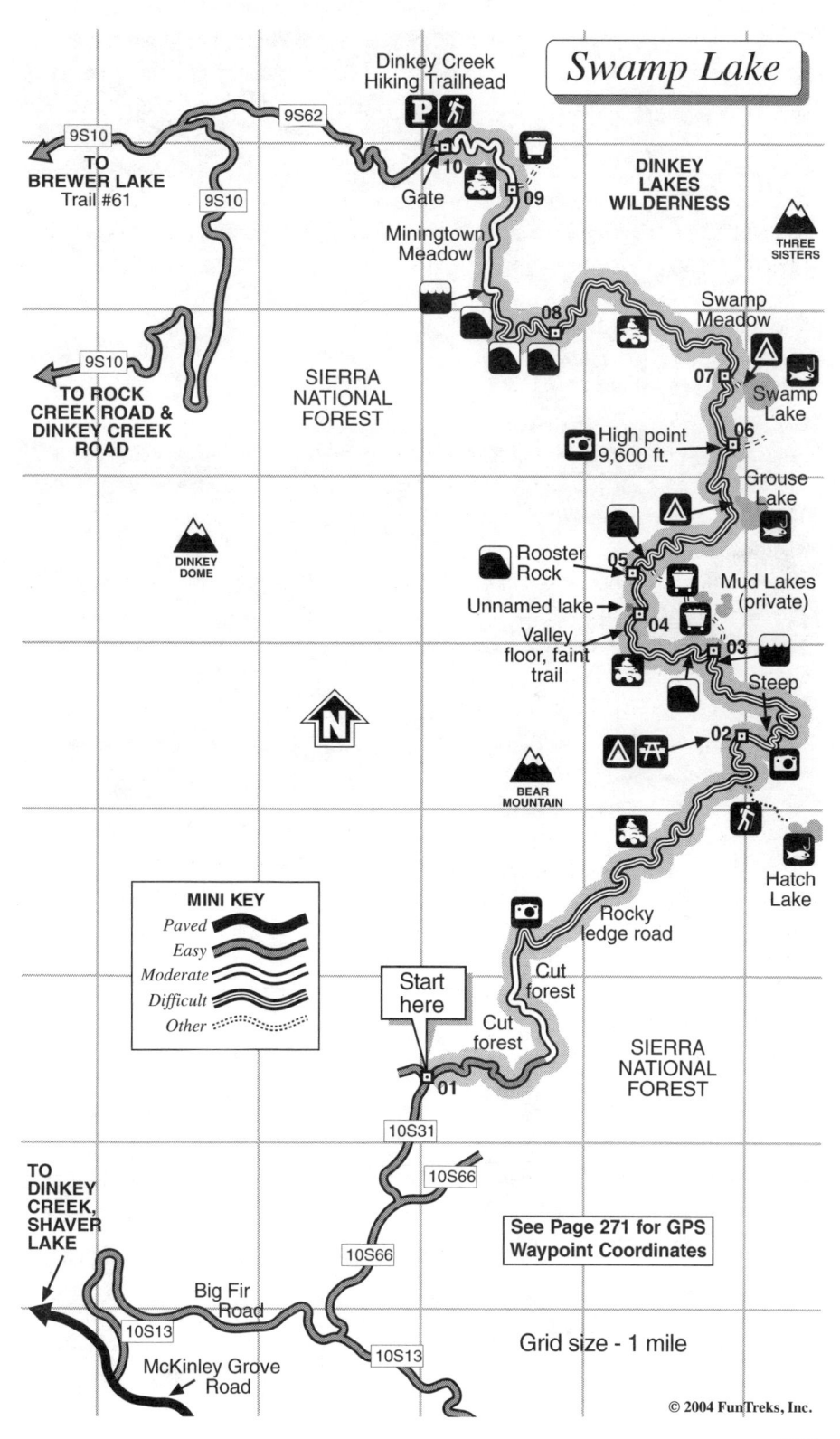

Dinkey Creek Hiking Trailhead

9S10
TO BREWER LAKE
Trail #61

9S62

9S10

Gate

Miningtown Meadow

DINKEY LAKES WILDERNESS

THREE SISTERS

9S10
TO ROCK CREEK ROAD & DINKEY CREEK ROAD

SIERRA NATIONAL FOREST

Swamp Meadow

Swamp Lake

High point 9,600 ft.

Grouse Lake

DINKEY DOME

Rooster Rock

Mud Lakes (private)

Unnamed lake

Valley floor, faint trail

Steep

N

BEAR MOUNTAIN

Hatch Lake

MINI KEY
Paved
Easy
Moderate
Difficult
Other

Start here

Rocky ledge road

Cut forest

Cut forest

SIERRA NATIONAL FOREST

01

10S31

10S66

TO DINKEY CREEK, SHAVER LAKE

10S66

Big Fir Road

10S13

McKinley Grove Road

10S13

See Page 271 for GPS Waypoint Coordinates

Grid size - 1 mile

© 2004 FunTreks, Inc.

209

Looking east to John Muir Wilderness.

A few minor rocky spots along the way.

Boulders (glacial erratics) help define trail.

Beach at Voyager Rock Campground.

Meet at C.G. to run the Dusy/Ershim.

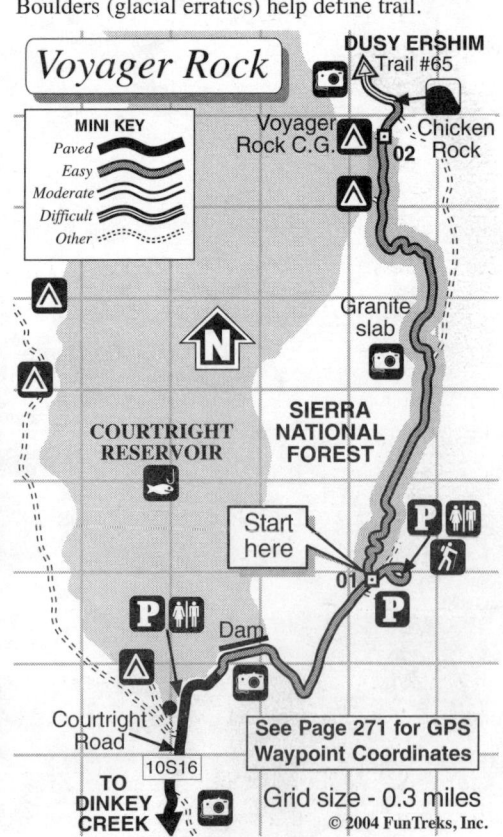

Voyager Rock

MINI KEY
- Paved
- Easy
- Moderate
- Difficult
- Other

DUSY ERSHIM Trail #65
Voyager Rock C.G.
Chicken Rock
02
Granite slab
COURTRIGHT RESERVOIR
SIERRA NATIONAL FOREST
Start here
01
Dam
Courtright Road
10S16
TO DINKEY CREEK

See Page 271 for GPS Waypoint Coordinates

Grid size - 0.3 miles

© 2004 FunTreks, Inc.

210

Voyager Rock 64

Location: East of Shaver Lake and Dinkey Creek.

Difficulty: Easy. Bumpy, single-lane forest road that meanders through trees and over smooth granite slabs. Suitable for any stock, high-clearance SUV.

Features: The drive to trail is very scenic, passing through giant sequoia trees of McKinley Grove and on to stunning granite dome mountains surrounding massive Courtright Reservoir. Trail is in a major recreation area offering power boating, fishing, camping, hiking and mountain biking. Camp along shore of reservoir at Voyager Rock Campground. Backpack into nearby John Muir and Dinkey Lakes Wilderness.

Time & Distance: The trail itself is only 1.9 miles and takes about half an hour. Total trip from Shaver Lake is a half-day adventure. Once you arrive, you'll want to camp overnight and make a weekend out of it.

To Get There: From Highway 168 in Shaver Lake, take paved Dinkey Creek Road east. After about 12 miles, turn right on paved McKinley Grove Road (F.S. 40) just before Dinkey Creek. Go another 14 miles and turn left on paved Courtright Road (F.S. 10S16). Bear right after another 7.6 miles following sign to Maxson Dusy. Go by a parking lot and boat launch on left as road swings right and crosses dam. The road changes to gravel after the dam and curves to the north. In less than a mile, you'll see a small parking lot on the right followed by a gate for the Dusy/Ershim Trail on left. This is where you turn for Voyager Rock (01). Don't worry, the difficult part does not start for another 2 miles. (There is a larger parking lot with modern vault toilet on main road just past the start of trail.)

Trail Description: Reset odometer at start (01). Meander through trees about a mile and cross large granite area. Soon, roads begin to branch left to various camping places along the lake. Voyager Rock Campground is on left at 1.9 miles (02) just before you reach Voyager Rock (A.K.A. Chicken Rock.)

Return Trip: Return the way you came.

Services: Gas, food, camping in Dinkey Creek. Modern vault toilet just past start of trail. Dilapidated, primitive outhouses at Voyager Rock Campground.

Maps: Sierra National Forest map, USGS 7.5-minute map, Courtright Reservoir, CA, DeLorme Atlas and Gazetteer.

Looking south from top of Chicken Rock.

Trail starts here at Chicken Rock. Dusy Creek Bridge built by Fresno 4WD Club.

Log road can be very challenging with wet tires.

ATVs start up lower part of Thompson Hill.  Havoc on Thompson Hill.

You'll need a good spotter.  Thompson Lake. Take insect repellent in warm weather.

Dusy/Ershim Trail 65

Location: Northeast of Shaver Lake between Courtright Reservoir and Kaiser Pass.

Difficulty: Difficult. Over ninety percent of this 30-mile trail is slow-speed rock crawling. The most difficult part of the trail is Thompson Hill (when driven uphill). It starts gradually and gets worse as you climb higher. Also very difficult, is the last two miles of the trail, going south to north, as described here. Many other challenges await. The forest service recommends the trail be driven in a short-wheel-base vehicle with at least 32-inch tires and one locker. The fact is, even better equipped vehicles are seriously tested. Be prepared for breakdowns because help is a long way off. Never drive this trail by yourself. The trail can also be driven from the north starting at White Bark Vista.

Features: A very scenic trail that climbs to 10,000 feet at Thompson Lake, then rarely drops below 9,000 feet after that. You'll pass several excellent lakes offering good camping and fishing. Almost the entire trail passes through wilderness, which is just 300 feet on each side of the trail. Stay on designated routes at all times. Do not camp within 100 feet of lakes and streams. Carry a fire permit and fishing license if applicable. No target shooting anywhere along route. Pack out your trash. Trail is for summer use only and is approved for ATVs and dirt bikes. Make sure you have plenty of mosquito repellent in the warm summer months.

Time & Distance: From Chicken Rock to the gate at White Bark Vista, the trail measures 29.6 miles. It can be driven in a day under ideal circumstances, but it would be an exhaustive experience. Taking two days is still tiring, but many people do it. If you drive the trail in two days, camp at Voyager Rock Campground the night before and start early the next morning. Three days on the trail allows more time to relax and fish.

To Get There: Follow directions to Voyager Rock, Trail #64. At Voyager Rock Campground, continue north a short distance to Chicken Rock. To drive the trail from north to south, see "Reverse Directions."

Trail Description: **Chicken Rock to Thompson Lake:** *Reset odometer at Chicken Rock (officially Voyager Rock) immediately north of Voyager Rock Campground* (01). Chicken Rock follows a hard left turn through an opening in the trees. The climb is steep, but relatively easy, after you get through the boulders at the bottom. Make sure your tires are aired down before starting

Camp spot at Ershim Lake.

Several creek crossings along the route.

Fun to drive.

Great views from high points along trail.

Winch time!

Portion of trail near White Bark Vista.

Years of hard work to keep trail open.

up the hill. Gorgeous views of Courtright Reservoir can be seen to your left as you climb. The obscure trail swings right at the top and heads north along a granite ridge. Watch for boulders that line each side of trail. At 0.4 miles, the trail turns sharply to the left and switchbacks downhill heading southwest through the trees. As you get closer to the reservoir, the trail turns north again and roughly follows the shoreline.

Stay right at 2.4 miles (02) where trails go left to the reservoir. Cross Dusy Creek at 2.5 miles over a stone bridge built by the Fresno 4-Wheel-Drive Club. From here, the trail heads north along Dusy Creek. Notice a large rock projection beyond a meadow at 4.2 miles. If you look closely at the rock, you'll see the face of an old bearded man. Around 6.7 miles, you begin to climb out of a valley towards Thompson Lake. Obstacles become more frequent. A log road through a boggy area at 7.4 miles can be challenging with wet tires. You climb through Thompson Hill with the worst part coming around 8.2 miles. The road eventually levels out but remains very rocky. At 8.9 miles (03), right goes a short distance to camp spots at the wilderness boundary. You must camp here and hike a short distance to the lake. This is a good place to camp on a 3-day trip.

Thompson Lake to Ershim Lake: *Reset odometer at the turnoff for Thompson Lake (03).* Bear left if you are continuing or right if you are coming out of Thompson Lake. The trail remains rocky but major obstacles are few. After 2.5 miles, you'll pass Summit Lake where camping space is very limited. You'll go through Hot Springs Pass soon after Summit Lake. At 6.0 miles (04) look for a wide spot on the left where you can park and camp. This is the approximate halfway point of the trail. From here you can hike south about a quarter mile to East Lake where you'll find beautiful views and good fishing.

The trail meanders west from East Lake then turns north along the eastern slope of Black Peak. A creek crossing at 8.6 miles is one of several tributaries of Big Creek. After passing through a sandy area, you arrive at what appears to be a fork at 9.4 miles. A hiking trail crosses here. Continue north following a sign to Ershim Lake. At 11.3 miles (05), a large sign on the right indicates you've arrived at Ershim Lake at an elevation of 9,080 feet. Right, at the sign, goes to several excellent camping spots next to the lake. You'll find picnic tables and an outhouse. At Ershim Lake, you've covered two thirds of the route. Camp here if you are taking three days for the trip.

Ershim Lake to White Bark Vista: *Reset your odometer at the sign for Ershim Lake (05).* Bear left to continue or right if you are coming out of the campground. Cross a log bridge then climb a nasty boulder field. The trail gets tougher again. Make a sandy creek crossing at 2.1 miles that marks the start of Ershim Meadow, a scenic spot for lunch. Bear left at 4.2 miles (06) where a road goes right to Mallard Lake. Left takes you down a long nasty hill to Lakecamp Lake at 4.7 miles. At 7.2 miles (07), you reach a gorgeous high point with views of Huntington Lake to the south and Edison Lake to the north. A very difficult boulder field follows at 7.5 miles. I had to winch myself, at one point, when all four tires got wedged into the rocks. There's a driver's choice at 7.8 miles. A very tough stretch of rocks follows at 8.9 just before the end of the trail at 9.2 miles (08). Pass through the gate to White Bark Vista, Trail #58.

Return Trip: Drop downhill through White Bark Vista on a graded road about a mile to paved F.S. Road 80 at Kaiser Pass. Bear left on F.S. 80 and follow it downhill 7.4 miles to Highway 168. Right goes to Lakeshore next to Huntington Lake in 0.7 miles. Left goes to Shaver Lake in about 21 miles.

Reverse Directions: Follow directions to White Bark Vista, Trail #58. *Reset odometer at gate to Dusy/Ershim Trail above White Bark Vista* (08). Almost immediately, you encounter a stretch of very difficult rocks as you climb quickly to a scenic high point at 2.0 miles (07). Drop to Lakecamp Lake at 4.5 miles and begin another steep, rocky climb. Stay right at 5.0 miles (06) where a road goes left to Mallard Lake. Pass through Ershim Meadow and cross creek at 7.1 miles.

Reset odometer when you arrive at sign for Ershim Lake at 9.2 miles (05). Left goes to camping; right continues. Continue straight where hiking trail crosses at 1.9. Cross another creek at 2.7. Hiking trail and camping for East Lake on right at 5.3 miles (04). Summit Lake on left at 8.8. At 11.3 miles (03), a fork goes left to Thompson Lake.

Reset odometer (03) and bear right to descend Thompson Hill that follows soon. Cross log road at 1.5 and continue south along Dusy Creek. Cross stone bridge at Dusy Creek at 6.4 then bear left at 6.5 miles (02) where roads go right to north end of Courtright Reservoir. Continue south along east shore of reservoir. Trail turns uphill through tight trees to a granite ridge top at 8.5 miles. Turn south along ridge following trail marked with boulders. Bear left down steep Chicken Rock and pass through an opening in the trees at 8.9 miles (01). Follow road south to a gravel road in another 1.9 miles, using directions and map for Voyager Rock, Trail #64. Use Area 8 Map to return to Shaver Lake.

Services: Vault toilets at start of Voyager Rock Trail #64 and at Kaiser Pass on F.S. 80. Outhouse at Ershim Lake. Closest gas and food at south end of trail is at Dinkey Creek. At north end of trail, stop at Lakeshore. Expect to pay premium prices for gas. You'll find basic services in Shaver Lake.

Maps: Sierra National Forest map, Forest Service handout for Dusy-Ershim OHV Route, USGS 100,000-scale maps, Shaver Lake and Bishop, CA, Sidekick Map Dusy/Ershim Trail, DeLorme Atlas & Gazetteer.

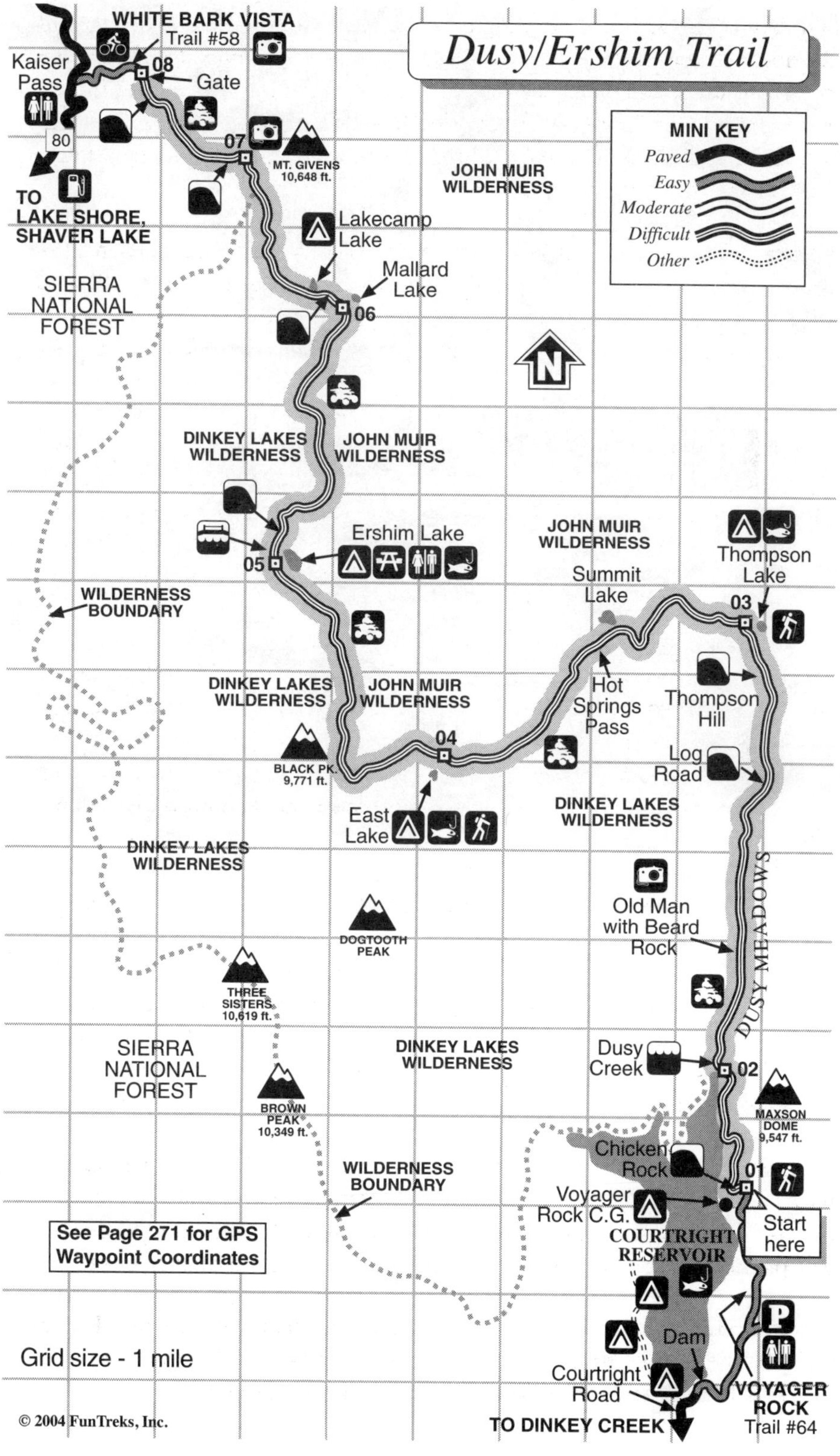

Dusy/Ershim Trail
MINI KEY
Paved
Easy
Moderate
Difficult
Other
WHITE BARK VISTA
Trail #58
Kaiser Pass
08
Gate
80
07
MT. GIVENS 10,648 ft.
TO LAKE SHORE, SHAVER LAKE
JOHN MUIR WILDERNESS
Lakecamp Lake
Mallard Lake
06
SIERRA NATIONAL FOREST
DINKEY LAKES WILDERNESS
JOHN MUIR WILDERNESS
Ershim Lake
05
JOHN MUIR WILDERNESS
Thompson Lake
Summit Lake
03
WILDERNESS BOUNDARY
DINKEY LAKES WILDERNESS
JOHN MUIR WILDERNESS
Hot Springs Pass
Thompson Hill
04
Log Road
BLACK PK. 9,771 ft.
East Lake
DINKEY LAKES WILDERNESS
DINKEY LAKES WILDERNESS
Old Man with Beard Rock
DUSY MEADOWS
DOGTOOTH PEAK
THREE SISTERS 10,619 ft.
SIERRA NATIONAL FOREST
DINKEY LAKES WILDERNESS
Dusy Creek
02
MAXSON DOME 9,547 ft.
BROWN PEAK 10,349 ft.
Chicken Rock
WILDERNESS BOUNDARY
01
Voyager Rock C.G.
Start here
COURTRIGHT RESERVOIR
See Page 271 for GPS Waypoint Coordinates
P
Dam
Grid size - 1 mile
Courtright Road
VOYAGER ROCK
Trail #64
TO DINKEY CREEK
© 2004 FunTreks, Inc.

Wishon Reservoir is popular fishing area.

Steep and rocky in places.

Get out of vehicle and walk short distance for best views

Camp spots at end of trail.

Spanish Route

TO WISHON RESERVOIR
11S07
Start here
01
02
03

JOHN MUIR WILDERNESS BOUNDARY

SIERRA NATIONAL FOREST

SIERRA NATIONAL FOREST

JOHN MUIR WILDERNESS

Spanish Lake

Little Spanish Lake

Closed side road

MINI KEY
Paved
Easy
Moderate
Difficult
Other

See Page 271 for GPS Waypoint Coordinates

Grid size - 1/2 mile

© 2004 FunTreks, Inc.

Spanish Route 66

Location: Southeast of Dinkey Creek, south of Wishon Reservoir.

Difficulty: Difficult. Challenging but doable in an aggressive SUV that already has a few dings and scratches. Tight and brushy. Not suitable for large vehicles. Trail marked with Jeep signs.

Features: An enjoyable trail, quickly accessible from campgrounds near Wishon Reservoir. Long drive from Shaver Lake. Trail ends at John Muir Wilderness boundary. To see Spanish Lakes you must hike steeply downhill on a poorly marked path. Occasional scenic views through gaps in trees.

Time & Distance: 5.3 miles one way. Allow 3-4 hours for round trip.

To Get There: From Highway 168 in Shaver Lake, take paved Dinkey Creek Road east. After about 12 miles, turn right on paved McKinley Grove Road (F.S. 40) just before Dinkey Creek. Stay on this road another 17 miles and cross Wishon Reservoir Dam. After dam, continue about 3 miles and turn right on F.S. Road 11S07 following sign to Spanish Lake. Continue another 1.7 miles to trail on left just after bridge for Rancheria Creek.

Trail Description: Reset odometer at start (01). Pass through gate and zigzag uphill through tight brush. Continue straight when road joins on right at 0.5 and cross small rocky creek. Camp spot on right at 0.7. The trail gets rocky with big tree roots that make it more difficult to squeeze between numerous fallen trees. Trees open briefly with views at granite outcrop at 2.1 miles (02). Stay left through another open granite area at 2.6. Views improve with short walk. After some respite, you begin to climb again with a tough spot at 3.6 miles. Stay left at 4.5 where closed road goes right. Extremely narrow squeeze between trees at 4.6. More rock crawling follows as you near end of trail at 5.3 miles (03) marked by camp spots, fire rings and log picnic tables. Several hiking trails head downhill but fade as you near the lakes. You may need a compass to stay on course.

Return Trip: Return the way you came.

Services: Forest and commercial campground near Wishon Dam with basic supplies. Gas in Dinkey Creek. Camp spots with picnic tables along trail.

Maps: Sierra National Forest map, Forest Service handout for Spanish OHV Route, USGS 7.5-minute map, Rough Spur, CA.

AREA 9

Bakersfield,
Lake Isabella,
Ridgecrest,
Mojave

67. Monache Meadows
68. Sherman Pass 4x4 Trail
69. Rancheria Road
70. Freeway Ridge
71. Jawbone to Lake Isabella
72. Jawbone OHV Area
73. Bonanza Gulch/ EP15
74. Opal Canyon/ Last Chance Canyon
75. Rand Mountain

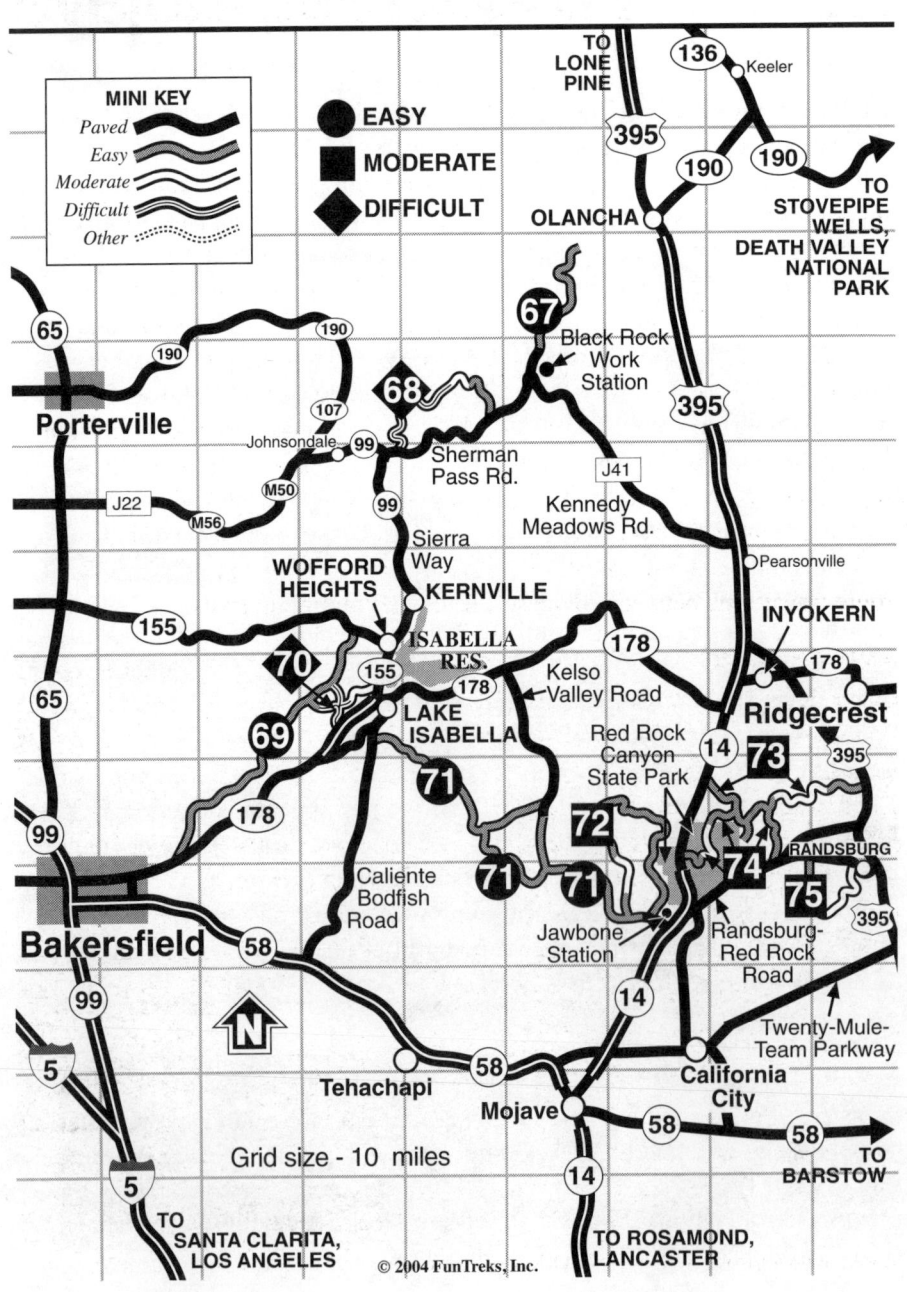

AREA 9
Bakersfield, Lake Isabella, Ridgecrest, Mojave

Highway 178, between Bakersfield and Lake Isabella, is an unforgettable drive along a steep-walled canyon high above the Kern River, one of the most spectacular kayaking and rafting rivers in America. As you climb higher into the mountains, the urge to get off the pavement for a closer look at the area becomes unbearable. Fortunately, you don't have to wait long. Just south of Lake Isabella, difficult *Freeway Ridge* departs directly into the mountains from the north side of 178. There's also a back way to Lake Isabella on easy *Rancheria Road* that avoids most of the paved highway. Great scenery continues north of Kernville on your way to *Sherman Pass* and *Monache Meadows*. In stark contrast to these high mountain trails are the year-around desert trails of *Jawbone OHV Area, Rand Mountain* and Red Rock Canyon State Park. Inside the state park, *Bonanza Gulch/EP15* and *Opal Canyon/Last Chance Canyon* feature famous walk-in mines, historical cabins and old mining equipment. The *Jawbone to Lake Isabella* route transitions between the desert trails and mountain trails.

Looking down from Highway 178 at Kern River on way to *Freeway Ridge, Trail #70*.

Monache Meadows is surrounded by wilderness. Stay on existing routes at all times.

Great camp spot at halfway point.

So. Fork of Kern River often shallow in summer.

Monache Meadows

South Fork Kern River — 04
Sand dune
SOUTH SIERRA WILD.
03
GOLDEN TROUT WILDERNESS
INYO N.F.
MONACHE MTN.
02
Start here
34E38
21S03 34E48 01
INYO N.F.
SEQUOIA N.F.
South Fork Kern River
21S36
SEQUOIA NATIONAL FOREST
21S03
Black Rock Work Station
22S05
22S05
TO KERNVILLE
TO HWY. 395

MINI KEY
Paved
Easy
Moderate
Difficult
Other

See Page 271 for GPS Waypoint Coordinates

Grid size - 2 miles

© 2004 FunTreks, Inc.

Forest portion of route has a few bumps.

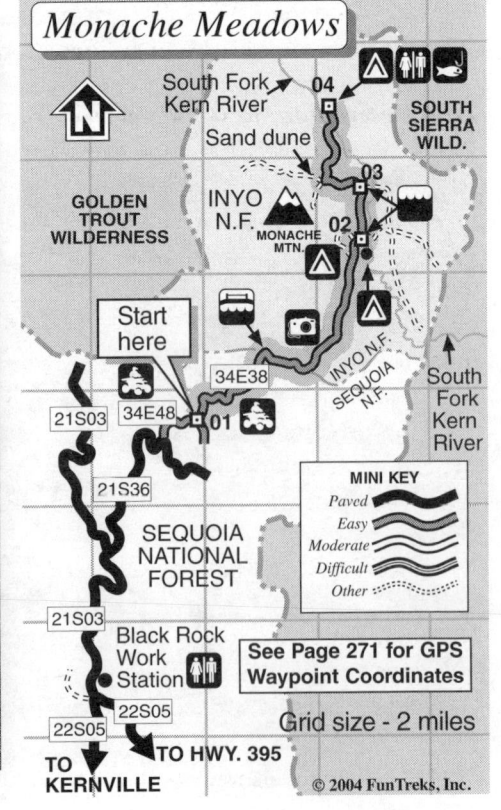

222

Monache Meadows 67

Location: Northeast of Bakersfield and Kernville, northwest of Ridgecrest.

Difficulty: Easy. Gentle, bumpy, single-lane road through forest and meadows. Shallow water crossings except during spring runoff.

Features: Beautiful, scenic valley surrounded by wilderness areas. Remote location keeps traffic down. Explore, camp, fish and relax along river.

Time & Distance: Allow 3 to 4 hours for 18.2-mile round trip.

To Get There: **From Kernville**: Take Sierra Way north 20 miles. Turn right on Sherman Pass Road and go northeast 32 miles following signs to Black Rock Work Station. *Reset odometer.* Continue north on 21S03 and turn right on 21S36 at 3.5 miles. Bear left on dirt road 34E48 at 7.1 miles. Turn right at 7.4 before reaching trailhead 34E38 at 8.1 miles. **From Hwy. 395:** At a point 32 miles south of Olancha on Hwy. 395, head west at Kennedy Meadows turnoff. Stay left on 22S05 before Kennedy Meadows following signs to Black Rock Work Station, a total of 37 miles from 395. *Reset odometer* and follow same directions from work station as stated above.

Trail Description: Reset odometer at start (01). Bear left at trailhead sign and follow narrow road as it weaves through forest. Driver's choice at 1.7 miles. After gate at 2.3 miles, all vehicles must stay on designated roads. Cross tiny bridge over Snake Creek before Monache Meadows comes into view at 2.5. Stay left at 5.2 and right at 5.9. At 6.1 miles (02), ignore first road to left then bear left at camp spot under trees. Cross tributary to fork at 6.2 miles then stay left along west side of river. (Right goes back across river.) At 7.2 miles (03), stay left following sign to Bakeoven Campsites. Turn right before sand dune at 7.8 miles. Turn left at T at 8.4 before reaching campsites at 9.1. Cross river and bear left to more campsites and pit toilet at 9.2 miles (04). Enjoy the campgrounds or explore other side roads in the area. All roads eventually dead end at the wilderness boundary.

Return Trip: Return the way you came.

Services: Water and toilets at Black Rock Work Station (Office closed Tuesdays and Wednesdays.) Roofless pit toilet at camp sites at end of trail. Gas and other basic services in Kernville and Inyokern.

Maps: Sequoia or Inyo N.F., USGS 7.5-min. map, Monache Mountain, CA.

Bakersfield Trailblazers 4WD Club at start.  Club could fix minor damage.

Lucky shot of black bear.  Large tree was cut into smaller pieces and rolled off trail.

Forest Service fixed this later.  View from 33E29 south of Sherman Peak.

Fixing bear-damaged sign.  Fire did not damage camp spots at Bonita Meadows.

Sherman Pass 4x4 Trail 68

Location: Northeast of Bakersfield, north of Kernville and northwest of Ridgecrest.

Difficulty: Difficult. The first half is very steep and susceptible to washouts. The second half is rocky and rutted in places. Aggressive, high clearance SUVs can get through but vehicle damage is possible.

(Author's note: I had a rare opportunity to drive the trail as part of a volunteer work party sent in to see if the trail was passable after the 150,000-acre McNalley Fire the previous summer. Supervised by a ranger from the Sequoia National Forest, the Bakersfield Trailblazers 4-Wheel-Drive Club headed up the mountain to make repairs. In places, the trail was literally obliterated with 6-ft.-deep ruts and giant fallen trees. We repaired small damaged areas, but the worst sections would require major equipment. The club managed to complete the run despite the obstacles. The Forest Service later brought in earth-moving equipment and officially opened the trail.)

Features: Despite the fire damage, this trail is still quite scenic as it climbs to almost 10,000 feet at Sherman Peak. New wildflowers grow in abundance in the fertile soil and wildlife is returning to the area. Because underbrush was burned away, I was able to get a rare picture of a wandering bear (see opposite page). The fire did not reach the east end of the trail where excellent camping was found at Bonita Meadows.

Time & Distance: As described here, the trail measures 16.5 miles and takes 3 to 4 hours depending upon conditions and equipment. You can camp overnight and explore many other roads in the area.

To Get There: Head north on Sierra Way (Mtn. Rd. 99) from Kernville, which is just north of Lake Isabella. The road follows the gorgeous Kern River about 20 miles to Sherman Pass Road. Turn right and go northeast 8.2 miles to the well-marked Sherman Pass 4x4 Trail on the left.

Trail Description: *Reset odometer at start* (01). Head uphill through gate on a steep, narrow road with many tight switchbacks. These switchbacks are prone to washouts and could be rough. Only a chimney remains of a burned cabin at 1.7 miles. At 2.4 a large 5-ft. diameter tree had fallen across the trail during the fire. Thanks to the Bakersfield Trailblazers, this tree was cut into smaller pieces and pushed aside (see photo opposite page). Cross North

Meadow Creek at 2.5. The road, which follows the creek northeast, is partially blocked by fallen trees in places. Some maneuvering around trees may be necessary.

Roads converge at a clearing in an unburned area called North Meadow at 3.4 miles (02). You'll come back to this point later, but for now, turn right and follow North Meadows Pass Road 33E29 towards Sherman Peak. Bear left at 4.3 miles and continue to climb. (North Meadows Pass Road goes right downhill to paved Sherman Pass Road in 2.3 miles.) Sherman Peak is reached at 5.2 miles (03). The peak itself is not that attractive since it is covered with radio towers, but you get a birdseye view of the surrounding mountains and the fire coverage.

Return to North Meadow (02) and *reset your odometer*. Turn right and continue north. As you head through the open trees a short distance, you may see a 4x4 road that goes to the left. Ignore it; it soon dead ends. Stay on the main trail and bear right at about 0.2 miles. (Straight is an alternate route but very confusing.) After turning right, the trail drops down a steep, rocky hill which involves some rock crawling. At the bottom of the hill, at about 0.4 miles (04), the trail swings right. Cross a short boggy area at 0.7, followed by more rock crawling.

Make a hard left by a corral at 3.2 miles (05). A motorcycle trail crosses before reaching a fork at 3.5 miles. Turn left at the fork as the trail winds tightly through the trees with more rock crawling. Bear left at 5.7 miles (06) where a sign indicates the trail is maintained by the Bakersfield Trailblazers and the Ridgecrest Geargrinders. Turn right at 6.4 miles (07) on 22S41, Bonita Meadows Road. Make another right at 7.5 miles (08) as the road gets much easier. Small roads branch off to the right at 8.4 miles to great camp spots under the trees at Bonita Meadows. Paved Sherman Pass Road 22S05 is reached at 9.9 miles (09).

Return Trip: Right on paved 22S05 goes back to start of trail and on to Kernville and Bakersfield. Left goes to the Black Rock Work Station and Monache Meadows, Trail #67. Left eventually connects to Highway 395 about 37 miles southeast of the work station. Take Highway 395 south to Inyokern and Ridgeway.

Services: Closest gas at Kernville and Inyokern. Full services in Bakersfield and Ridgeway. No services along trail, although a portable toilet was located at the start.

Maps: Sequoia National Forest map, Forest Service map of the Kern Plateau Off-Highway Vehicle Routes, USGS 100,000-scale map, Isabella Lake, CA.

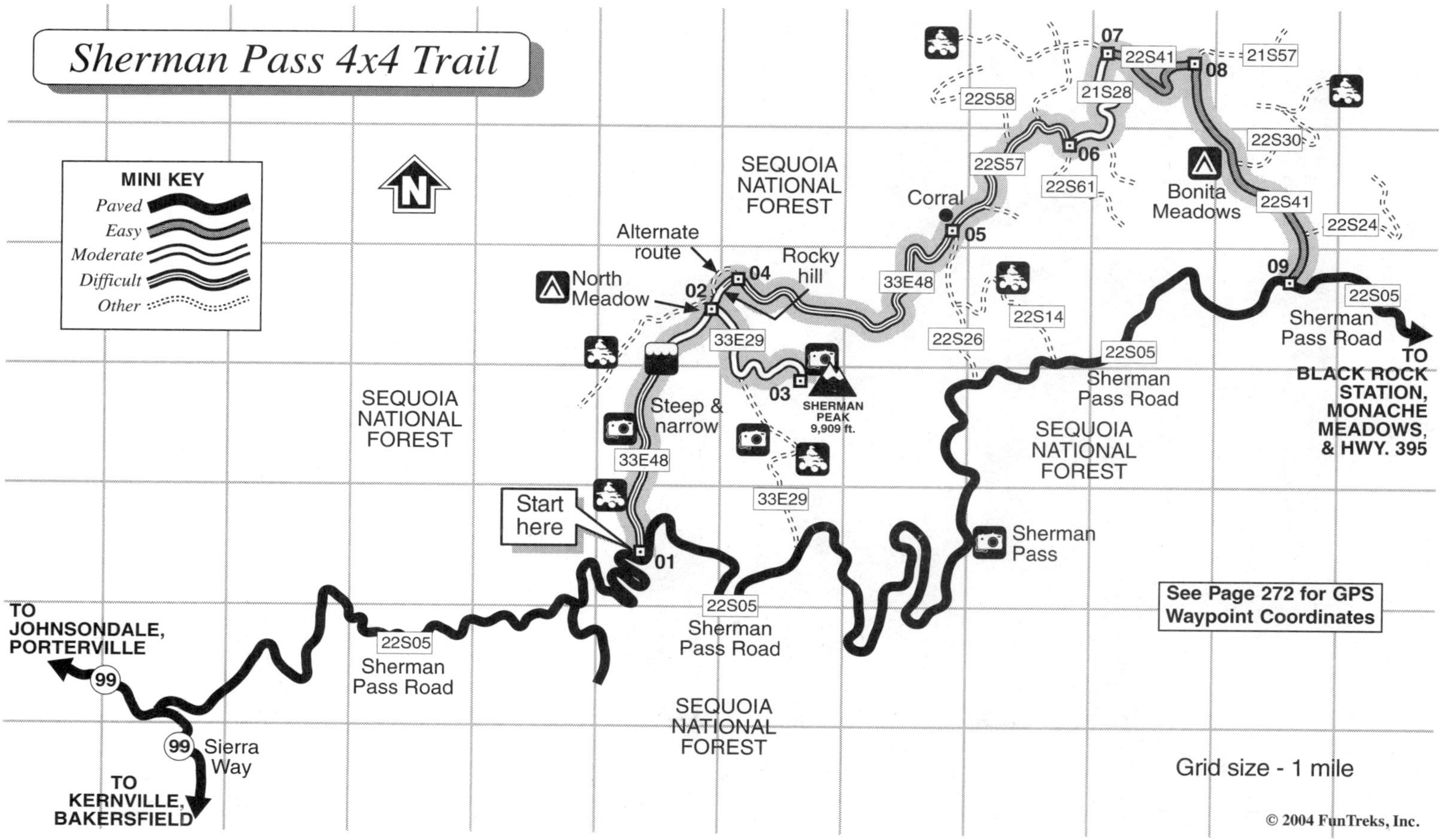
Sherman Pass 4x4 Trail
MINI KEY
Paved
Easy
Moderate
Difficult
Other
N
SEQUOIA NATIONAL FOREST
SEQUOIA NATIONAL FOREST
SEQUOIA NATIONAL FOREST
SEQUOIA NATIONAL FOREST
North Meadow
Alternate route
Rocky hill
Steep & narrow
Start here
Corral
Bonita Meadows
SHERMAN PEAK 9,909 ft.
Sherman Pass
01
02
03
04
05
06
07
08
09
22S05
Sherman Pass Road
33E48
33E29
22S57
22S58
22S61
21S28
22S41
21S57
22S30
22S24
22S14
22S26
TO JOHNSONDALE, PORTERVILLE
99
Sierra Way
TO KERNVILLE, BAKERSFIELD
TO BLACK ROCK STATION, MONACHE MEADOWS, & HWY. 395
See Page 272 for GPS Waypoint Coordinates
Grid size - 1 mile
© 2004 FunTreks, Inc.

Climbing into the Greenhorn Mountains on way to forest.

Oak Flat Lookout.

Great scenery along the route.

Evans Flat Campground has no water.

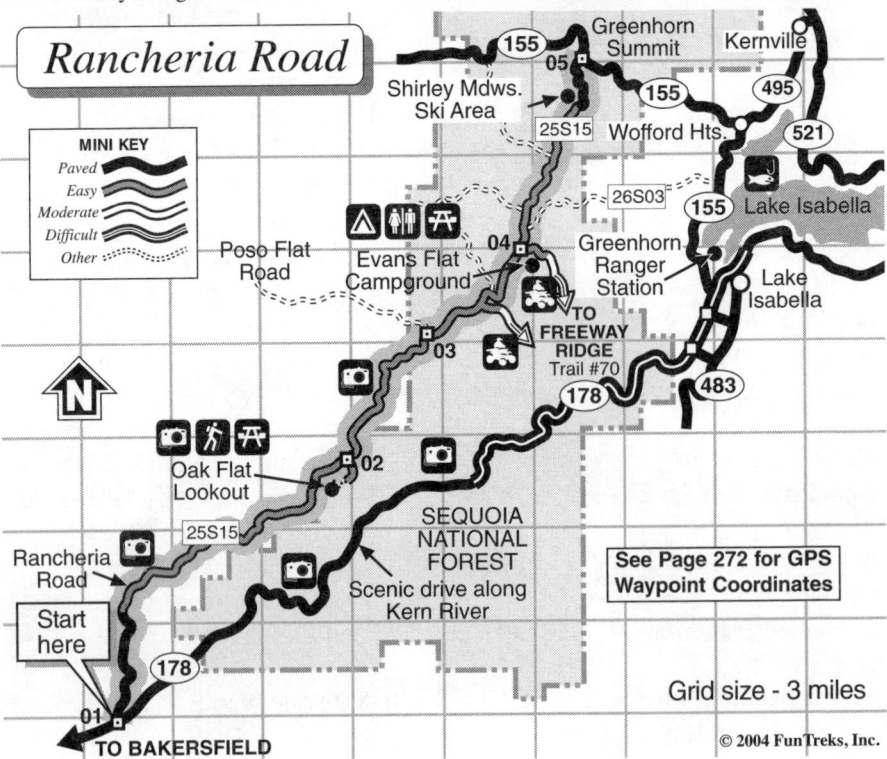

Rancheria Road

MINI KEY
- Paved
- Easy
- Moderate
- Difficult
- Other

See Page 272 for GPS Waypoint Coordinates

Grid size - 3 miles

© 2004 FunTreks, Inc.

228

Rancheria Road 69

Location: Northeast of Bakersfield, southwest of Lake Isabella.

Difficulty: Easy. Smooth graded road suitable for any SUV. If road is wet, 4WD may be needed, especially on steeper side road to Oak Flat Lookout.

Features: Beautiful relaxing drive across open rolling hills of Greenhorn Mountains into Sequoia National Forest. Abundant spring wildflowers. Open range land; watch for cattle. Many side roads to explore in upper forest areas. Return trip through Kern River Valley is outstanding.

Time & Distance: Allow 3 hours for this 37-mile drive. Add for side trip.

To Get There: From northeast side of Bakersfield, take Highway 178 east towards Lake Isabella. Turn left on Rancheria Road three miles east of the intersection of Highways 184 and 178.

Trail Description: Reset odometer at start (01). Head north and continue after pavement ends at 4.2 miles. Continue straight at 8.4 where lesser road goes left. Cattle guard at 14.3 marks first boundary to Sequoia National Forest. At 15.0 miles (02), turn right for a one-mile side trip to Oak Flat Lookout. Drive halfway, then hike. Great views of Kern River from top on clear day. Return to main road, *reset odometer* and continue to right.

Continue climb following signs for 25S15. Pass scenic ranch at 2.3 then bear left at 5.1. Continue straight where Poso Flat Road joins on left at 9.3 miles (03) and reenter forest. Bear right at 10.2 where Basket Pass Road goes left. Bear left at Davis Camp at 10.5 and left again at 12.0. Continue north on main road, passing Rd. 26S27 to Evans Flat Campground on right at 13.7 miles (04). Ignore many side roads until you reach paved parking lot for Shirley Meadows Ski Area at 19.6 miles. Continue on pavement until you reach Greenhorn Summit on Highway 155 at 22.0 miles (05).

Return Trip: Right on Highway 155 takes you downhill to Wofford Heights then south to Highway 178 at Lake Isabella. Take 178 southwest to Bakersfield.

Services: Picnic tables, fire rings and toilets but no water at Evans Flat Campground. Oak Flat Lookout is rentable overnight. (Contact Greenhorn Ranger Station.) Full services in Bakersfield and Lake Isabella area.

Maps: Sequoia National Forest, USGS 250,000-scale map Bakersfield, CA, DeLorme Atlas & Gazetteer.

Starting up *Freeway Ridge*. First part is the toughest.

Trail is fun to drive.

Black Gulch is deeply rutted. Use caution.

Signs help decide which way to go.

Road 32E47 is extremely steep and narrow.

Starting down 32E47.

Freeway Ridge ◆70

Location: Northeast of Bakersfield, west of Lake Isabella.

(Author's note: This loop route is a combination of 3 trails: Freeway Ridge, Black Gulch and 32E47. They connect to Keyesville Road which returns to Highway 155 at Lake Isabella near the main dam.)

Difficulty: Difficult. Very steep and washed out with occasional rock obstacles. Avoid when wet. Drivers should pay close attention to deep ruts on steepest slopes where a misplaced tire can quickly lead to a rollover. The worst stretch is descending 32E47, which has places barely wide enough for a Jeep. Road 32E47 is used mostly by ATVs, dirt bikes and the occasional risk-taking four wheeler. This trail is very prone to washouts. If you can't get through, retrace your route back down Black Gulch Trail.

Features: Start of Freeway Ridge is conveniently located just off Highway 178 southwest of Lake Isabella. The trail climbs rapidly with outstanding views of the lake and surrounding mountains. Lake Isabella is a popular recreation area offering fishing, boating, water skiing, camping and picnicking. Consistent strong afternoon winds make the lake popular for wind surfing. For information, stop at the Greenhorn Ranger Station/Visitor Center off Highway 155 south of the dam.

Time & Distance: Complete route as described here, measures 24.0 miles. Allow 4 to 5 hours for the entire loop.

To Get There: Take Highway 178 from Bakersfield towards Lake Isabella. The 2-lane highway changes to an undivided 4-lane freeway before Lake Isabella. The trail is on the north side of the road near mile marker 37. It is illegal and unsafe to make a left hand turn across the freeway, so continue to the next exit, turn around and come back. The trail is marked 31E73 next to a cattle guard.

    High clearance SUVs can access Black Gulch Trail via Keyesville Road that departs west from Highway 155 just south of Lake Isabella Dam. The trail is challenging but doable if your vehicle has good articulation. SUVs should not attempt Freeway Ridge or 32E47.

Trail Description: Reset odometer at start (01). Head uphill through cattle guard. The rockiest part of the trail is within the first quarter mile. After that the road is mostly dirt but is very steep. The road splits and comes back together a couple of times before reaching a fork at 1.8 miles (02). Bear left

231

uphill on the upper portion of Black Gulch Trail. You'll come back to this point later to finish the lower portion which goes downhill and connects to easier Keyesville Road.

As you continue to climb, the trail splits several times. In some cases, signs identify alternate rougher routes. Just before crossing Bradshaw Creek at 2.7 miles (03), a steep trail comes downhill on the right and joins Black Gulch. This is 32E47, which you may or may not decide to come down later. Stay left at 4.8 miles where a very difficult side road goes uphill to the Mayflower Mine. Stay right over cattle guard at 5.4 and right again on larger road at 5.5 miles (04). The road is easy from this point. Continue straight at 6.9 when a road joins on right. Rancheria Road is reached at 7.0 miles (05) at a point near Davis Camp. Turn right on Rancheria Road 25S15 and head north. Stay right at 9.0 until you reach 26S27 at 10.1 miles (06).

Reset odometer and turn right following signs to Evans Flat Campground. Bear right, immediately, when road forks again. You'll see old-style restrooms on left and camp spots at 0.2. A sign explains the history of the area. Continue east through campground and pass through fence at cattle guard. Bear right at 0.3 and 0.8 miles. Drop down a hill until you see markers for Borderline Trail, which goes east then north. The trail was washed out at 1.2 miles (07). We had to turn right and drop down a steep hill that was only slightly better than the washed-out road. (This spot may be fixed at later date.) Once you drop down this hill, you are committed, so take a close look before proceeding. Bear right at the bottom of hill, heading south on unmarked 32E47. Great views unfold as you descend the trail but it gets much steeper and narrower. The worst part is just before you reconnect with Black Gulch Trail at 4.6 miles (03). Turn left at Black Gulch and return to point where Freeway Ridge joined Black Gulch at 5.6 miles (02).

Reset odometer and turn left, heading downhill on the part of Black Gulch you missed earlier. The road rapidly improves as you descend. A sign at 1.8 miles marks the official start of Black Gulch Trail (going the other way). Stay left at 2.5 and 3.9 miles. Keyesville Road begins at 4.9. Swing right at 5.8 before reaching a marker for Keyesville Townsite on left at 6.4 miles (08). Stay left when the pavement starts at 6.5 miles. You'll go by a popular dirt bike campground before reaching Highway 155 at 8.3 miles (09). The Main Dam Campground is left across the street.

Return Trip: Right takes you back to Highway 178. You'll go by the entrance to the Greenhorn Ranger Station & Visitor Center. Watch for signs.

Services: Pit toilet at Evans Flat C.G., vault toilets at campgrounds along Hwy. 155. Most services in Lake Isabella and full services in Bakersfield.

Maps: Sequoia National Forest map, USGS 100,000-scale map Isabella Lake, CA, DeLorme Atlas & Gazetteer.

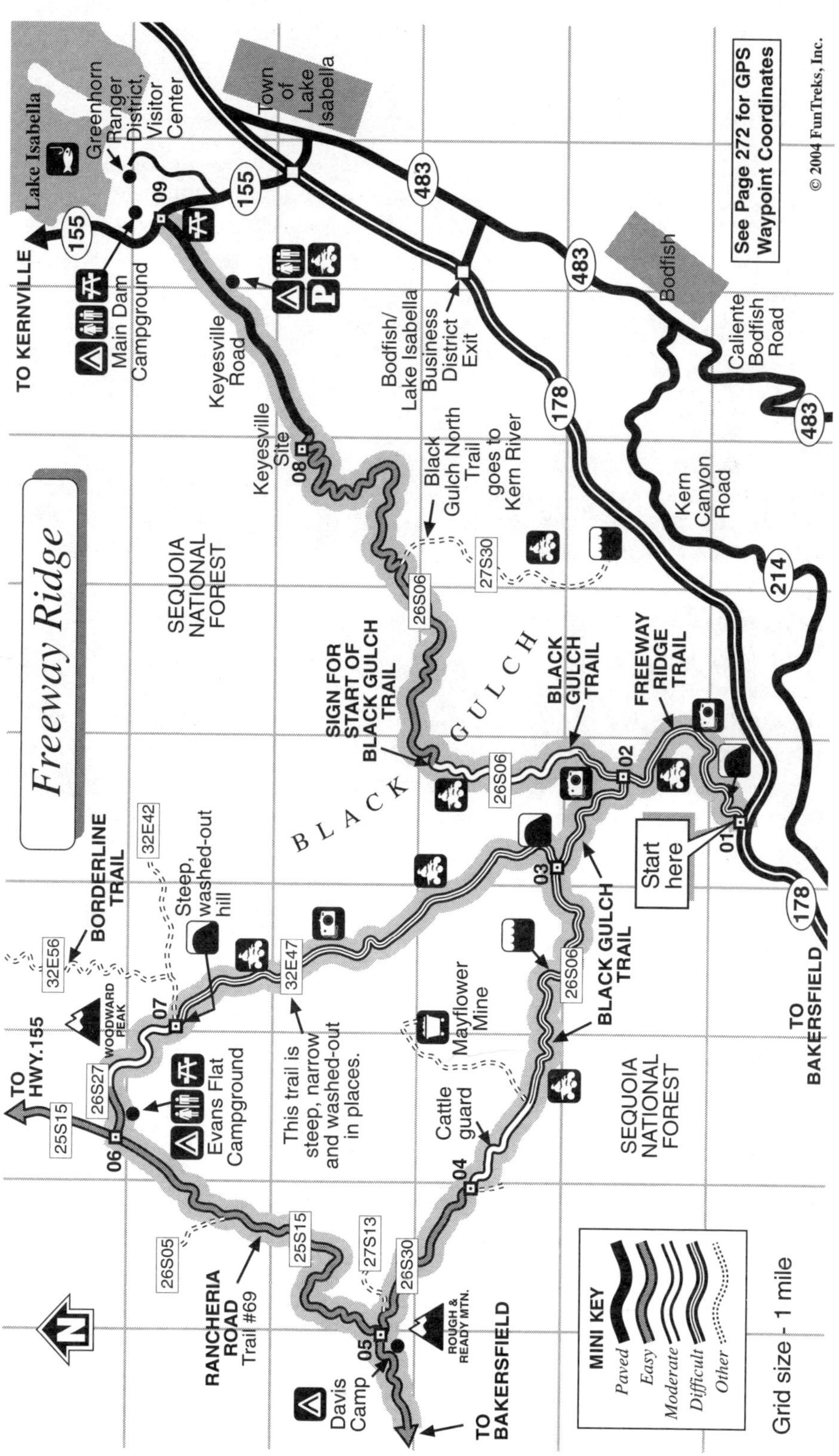

Freeway Ridge
TO KERNVILLE
Lake Isabella
155
Main Dam Campground
Greenhorn Ranger District, Visitor Center
09
155
Town of Lake Isabella
483
483
Keyesville Road
Bodfish/ Lake Isabella Business District Exit
Bodfish
Caliente Bodfish Road
483
178
Keyesville Site
08
Black Gulch North Trail goes to Kern River
27S30
Kern Canyon Road
214
SEQUOIA NATIONAL FOREST
26S06
SIGN FOR START OF BLACK GULCH TRAIL
BLACK GULCH
BLACK GULCH TRAIL
FREEWAY RIDGE TRAIL
26S06
02
Start here
01
178
TO BAKERSFIELD
03
BLACK GULCH TRAIL
26S06
BLACK GULCH TRAIL
BORDERLINE TRAIL
32E42
Steep, washed-out hill
32E56
32E47
This trail is steep, narrow and washed-out in places.
WOODWARD PEAK
07
TO HWY.155
26S27
25S15
06
Evans Flat Campground
Mayflower Mine
Cattle guard
SEQUOIA NATIONAL FOREST
04
26S05
25S15
27S13
26S30
RANCHERIA ROAD Trail #69
ROUGH & READY MTN.
05
Davis Camp
TO BAKERSFIELD
MINI KEY
Paved
Easy
Moderate
Difficult
Other
Grid size - 1 mile
See Page 272 for GPS Waypoint Coordinates
© 2004 FunTreks, Inc.

Stop for information at Jawbone Station.

Staging and camping areas along route.

First half of route crosses open high desert. Road is wide and well maintained.

Cottonwood Creek.

Geringer Grade may be rutted and washed out.

Great views from high points along route in Sequoia National Forest.

High speed biker!

Snow at high points in May.

Dramatic descent into Lake Isabella.

234

Jawbone to Lake Isabella 71

Location: East of Bakersfield between Jawbone Station and Lake Isabella. Jawbone Station is located north of Mojave on Highway 14.

Difficulty: Easy. First half of route is a wide, graded gravel road which crosses high desert terrain. Second half climbs into forest where road is steep, narrow and rutted in places. Higher elevations may not be passable because of snow in the winter. When I drove this trail in mid-May, some snow still remained in the trees above 8,000 feet. Area is extremely remote and a long way from services. Route-finding is complex, so follow directions carefully. Use caution around blind curves where speeding dirt bikes appear instantly. Dirt bike riders should slow down at these points to avoid serious injury.

Features: Trail starts at 2,500 feet and climbs to above 8,000 feet. Depending on time of year, you could start in hot desert and end up in snow covered forest. Trail passes through Jawbone OHV Area, very popular with ATV and dirt bike enthusiasts. Primitive, remote camping along route. Trail ends with spectacular descent to Lake Isabella. Make sure you stop at Jawbone Station and pick up a copy of the *East Kern County "Friends of Jawbone" Off-Highway Vehicle Riding Areas & Trails* map.

Time & Distance: Allow 4 to 6 hours for this 54-mile trip plus commute time. If you have a long drive to start of trail, consider camping overnight along the route. Makes a great weekend adventure.

To Get There: **From Bakersfield**; take Highway 58 east towards Mojave. Before Mojave, take the bypass over to Highway 14 following signs to California City. Head north on Highway 14 about 14 miles and turn left at sign for Jawbone Station near mile marker 35.4. **From Mojave:** Head north on Highway 14 about 18 miles and follow above directions. **From Inyokern:** Head south on Highway 14 past Red Rock Canyon State Park. At the point where Randsburg-Red Rock Road intersects, continue another 1.2 miles south and turn right at sign for Jawbone Station near mile marker 35.4.

Trail Description: Reset odometer as you exit Jawbone Station and head west on paved Jawbone Canyon Road. (01). After a mile, you'll go by two large Los Angeles Aqueduct pipelines. This area is popular for camping and unloading ATVs and dirt bikes. The pavement ends at 4.2 miles. Ignore many side roads as you continue west towards a blue-green colored hill,

235

called Blue Point. At 6.2 miles (02), follow the main road right where a marked, dead-end road goes straight. You'll climb to high views after 7 miles. In the spring, thick wildflowers add bright color to this otherwise barren landscape. Bear left at 11.2 and 11.8 miles where OHV roads intersect. I stopped for lunch at a scenic high point marked by large boulders at 15.0 miles. (The point was high enough to make a cell phone call.) Drop down into Kelso Valley where you'll see ranch houses in the distance. Stay left at a fork at 18.0 miles until you reach a 4-way intersection at 18.4 miles (04). (Right takes you to paved Kelso Valley Road that goes north to Highway 178 at Weldon. Left dead ends.) Continue straight toward Piute Mountain.

Gradually, the terrain begins to change and the road narrows. After crossing Cottonwood Creek at 23.3, you begin the toughest part of the trip as the road begins a steep climb up Geringer Grade into the forest. When I drove this section, a recent storm had washed out parts of the road and 4WD drive was needed to get through. You soon enter Sequoia National Forest. Continue straight where the Pacific Crest Hiking Trail crosses at 26.7 miles. Continue straight at 28.6 miles where 29S02 goes left. Bear left on Piute Mountain Road 27S02 at 31.8 miles (05). (Right goes to paved Kelso Valley Road mentioned earlier.) Stay left again at 32.4 where a private road goes right. Follow sign left on 27S02 towards Walker Basin at 33.7 miles.

Turn right at 37.6 miles (06) where 28S01 goes left. Follow signs to Bodfish and Lake Isabella on what is now Saddle Spring Road 27S02. It becomes narrow and rutted as it climbs above 8,200 feet. Stay right at 39.0 miles where a sign points left to Brown Meadow. Continue straight at 42.5 where an unmarked road goes left. Continue straight at 43.6 past entrance to Saddle Spring Campground. Bear left at 43.7 miles (07) where 28S04 goes right. Dramatic views of the road winding downhill can be seen at 48.6 miles. You exit the forest at 50.8 miles as you descend towards Lake Isabella. Paved Road 483 is reached at 54.0 miles (08).

Return Trip: Turn right on Highway 483 and head downhill 4.4 miles past Bodfish to Elizabeth Norris Road. Turn left for Highway 178. West on Highway 178 goes to Bakersfield, east goes to Inyokern and Ridgecrest.

Services: Water and toilets at Jawbone Station. Premium gas and restaurant at Jawbone Canyon Store just south of Jawbone Station on Highway 14. Gas is also available in Mojave, Tehachapi, California City, Inyokern and Ridgecrest. Most services in Bodfish and Lake Isabella.

Maps: Sequoia National Forest map, East Kern County Off-Highway Vehicle Riding Areas & Trails map, USGS 250,000-scale map, Bakersfield, CA, DeLorme Atlas & Gazetteer.

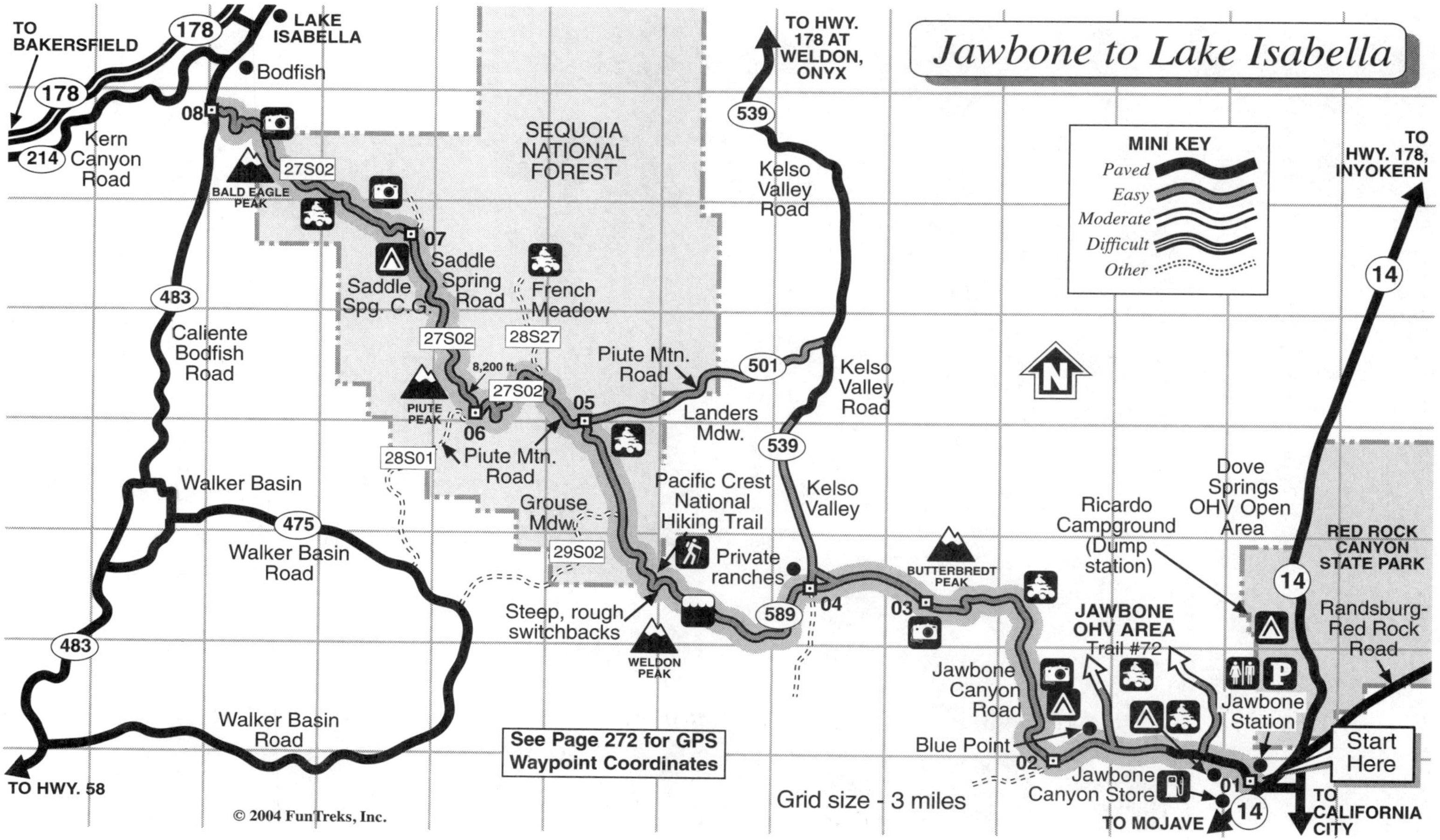
Jawbone to Lake Isabella
MINI KEY
Paved
Easy
Moderate
Difficult
Other
TO BAKERSFIELD
178
214
Kern Canyon Road
LAKE ISABELLA
Bodfish
08
27S02
BALD EAGLE PEAK
07
Saddle Spg. C.G.
Saddle Spring Road
French Meadow
SEQUOIA NATIONAL FOREST
27S02
28S27
8,200 ft.
PIUTE PEAK
06
28S01
Piute Mtn. Road
05
Piute Mtn. Road
Landers Mdw.
501
TO HWY. 178 AT WELDON, ONYX
539
Kelso Valley Road
Kelso Valley Road
539
Kelso Valley
Pacific Crest National Hiking Trail
Private ranches
Grouse Mdw.
29S02
Steep, rough switchbacks
WELDON PEAK
589
04
03
BUTTERBREDT PEAK
483
Caliente Bodfish Road
Walker Basin
475
Walker Basin Road
483
Walker Basin Road
TO HWY. 58
See Page 272 for GPS Waypoint Coordinates
Grid size - 3 miles
Ricardo Campground (Dump station)
Dove Springs OHV Open Area
JAWBONE OHV AREA
Trail #72
Jawbone Canyon Road
Blue Point
02
Jawbone Canyon Store
TO MOJAVE
01
14
Jawbone Station
Start Here
TO CALIFORNIA CITY
RED ROCK CANYON STATE PARK
Randsburg-Red Rock Road
14
TO HWY. 178, INYOKERN

Trail passes Los Angeles Aqueduct pipeline.

Trees provide shade at Dove Spring.

Miles of whoop-ti-dos.

Stay on main roads except in marked open areas.

Joshua trees grow at higher desert elevations.

Turn left out of wash 0.7 miles after this spot.

Mine shaft at San Antonio Mine.

Turn left out of wash at this steep point.

238

Jawbone OHV Area 72

Location: East of Bakersfield, north of Mojave and west of Red Rock Canyon State Park.

Difficulty: Moderate. This trail would be rated easy if it weren't for one steep, rough climb near the end. Stock, high-clearance SUVs can do it, but the last part of the trail may be too much for a novice driver. Soft sand requires tires be aired down. Long-wheel-base vehicles may drag bottom occasionally on undulating terrain. Many crisscrossing roads make route-finding a challenge although main roads are well marked.

Features: Trip provides an inside tour of popular Jawbone OHV Area and Dove Springs Open Area. Fun route is used as Poker Run by local four-wheel-drive clubs. Many challenging side roads to explore. Kids will love miles of roller-coaster whoop-ti-dos and closeup views of Los Angeles Aqueduct. Make sure you stop at Jawbone Station and pick up a copy of the *East Kern County "Friends of Jawbone" Off-Highway Vehicle Riding Areas & Trails* map.

Time & Distance: Allow 4 to 5 hours for this 28.1-mile loop. Add time for side trips.

To Get There: **From Bakersfield**; take Highway 58 east towards Mojave. Before Mojave, take the bypass over to Highway 14 following signs to California City. Head north on Highway 14 about 14 miles and turn left at sign for Jawbone Station near mile marker 35.4. **From Mojave:** Head north on Highway 14 about 18 miles and follow above directions. **From Inyokern:** Head south on Highway 14 past Red Rock Canyon State Park. At the point where Randsburg-Red Rock Road intersects, continue another 1.2 miles south and turn right at sign for Jawbone Station near mile marker 35.4.

Trail Description: Head west from Jawbone Station 1.8 miles on paved Jawbone Canyon Road. Turn right on well marked SC175. *Reset odometer and head north* (01). Bear left at 1.1 as road follows giant aqueduct pipe. Bear left again at 1.6 and 2.8 miles. Make a left on lesser road (still SC175) at 3.9 miles. Bear right at 5.3 (02). (Larger road to left goes to camp spot with lonely tree, picnic table and fire ring. The camp spot services surrounding ATV and dirt bike trails.) Speed must be moderated as whoop-ti-dos get larger. Stay left at 5.7 and right at 6.1. Road runs parallel to another on left. Continue straight where SC99 goes left. Continue straight where SC171 crosses perpendicularly at 7.7 miles (03). Go about 30 feet and bear

239

left downhill. (An arrow appears to point right for SC175, but it is misleading. Right follows a narrow, more difficult ridge route that reconnects with SC175 in a short distance.) SC175 goes downhill and curves right through a narrow ravine. Turn right at 4-way intersection at 8.0 then bear left at 8.4 on a better road. The road follows a concrete aqueduct. Ridges of concrete keep you from driving on it. Stay left below and parallel to what appears to be a dam. At 8.8 miles (04), near the middle of the concrete structure, turn left following obscure sign for SC180.

Reset odometer at start of SC180 and proceed west. Ignore many lesser side roads. Bear left at 0.2. SC180 follows the southern boundary to Dove Springs Open Area. You can go anywhere to the right but not to the left where most trails are marked closed. Continue straight at 1.1 miles where SC173 goes left. Stay left at 3.4 miles (05) when you intersect with SC103. Turn right at 3.6 staying on SC103 (SC99 joins on left). The road is wider but still with whoop-ti-dos. Bear left at 5.7 miles where SC328 goes right. Go by Dove Spring where cattle congregate. Bear left at 5.8 where SC111 goes right.

At 6.8 miles (06), *reset odometer* and turn left on narrower SC124. Joshua trees indicate you are at higher elevation. Since the road runs perpendicular to drainage, whoop-ti-dos are intense. Bear left at 1.2 on SC176. Take center road at 3-way fork at 4.3. Squeeze through distinctive narrow spot at 5.2 (see photo page 238).

A very important spot is reached at 5.9 miles (07). You must turn left and climb steep hill out of sandy wash. (Wash becomes too narrow if you proceed.) This is the only significant challenge on the trail. After hill, bear right at 6.2 where SC171 goes left. At 6.4 miles (08), turn left for short side trip to San Antonio Mine where shafts are enclosed with fencing at several locations. After looking around mine, return to SC176, *reset odometer* and continue south (left). The trail is rough in spots as it gradually descends back down to wash reached at 1.8 miles (09). Turn left and continue south as the wash widens. Jawbone Canyon Road is reached at 6.2 miles (10).

Return Trip: Turn left on Jawbone Canyon Road and return to Jawbone Station in 4.7 miles. After you turn, the road becomes paved in about a half mile.

Services: Water and toilets at Jawbone Station. Premium gas and restaurant at Jawbone Canyon Store just south of Jawbone Station on Highway 14. Gas is also available in Mojave, Tehachapi, California City, Inyokern and Ridgecrest. Primitive camping along route.

Maps: East Kern County Off-Highway Vehicle Riding Areas & Trails map, USGS 100,000-scale map, Tehachapi, CA.

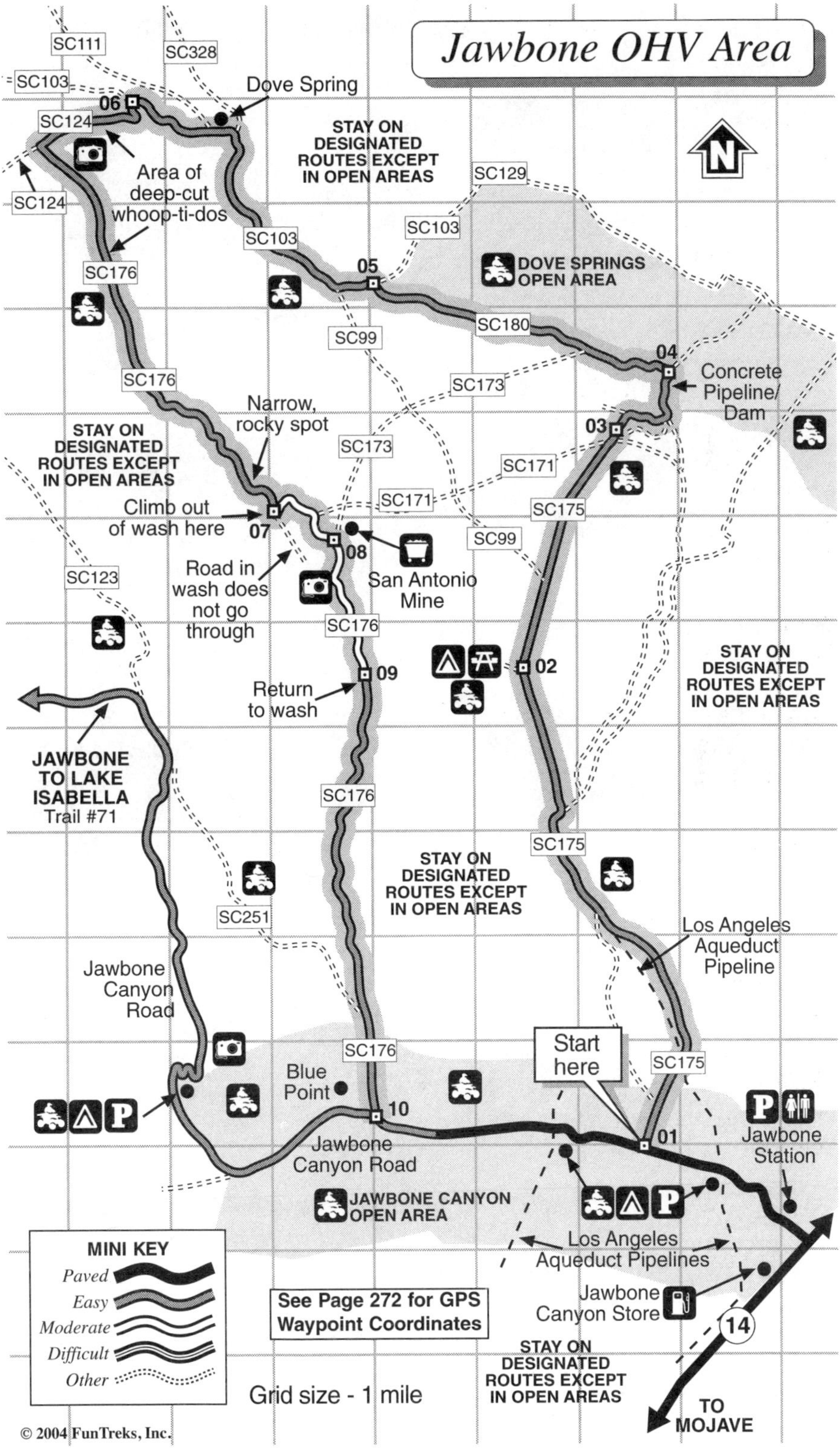

Jawbone OHV Area
SC111
SC328
SC103
Dove Spring
06
SC124
STAY ON DESIGNATED ROUTES EXCEPT IN OPEN AREAS
SC124
Area of deep-cut whoop-ti-dos
SC129
SC103
SC103
DOVE SPRINGS OPEN AREA
05
SC176
SC180
SC99
04
Concrete Pipeline/ Dam
SC176
SC173
Narrow, rocky spot
03
STAY ON DESIGNATED ROUTES EXCEPT IN OPEN AREAS
SC173
SC171
SC171
SC175
Climb out of wash here
07
08
SC99
San Antonio Mine
SC123
Road in wash does not go through
SC176
02
STAY ON DESIGNATED ROUTES EXCEPT IN OPEN AREAS
09
Return to wash
JAWBONE TO LAKE ISABELLA Trail #71
SC176
SC175
STAY ON DESIGNATED ROUTES EXCEPT IN OPEN AREAS
SC251
Los Angeles Aqueduct Pipeline
Jawbone Canyon Road
Start here
SC176
SC175
Blue Point
10
01
Jawbone Station
Jawbone Canyon Road
JAWBONE CANYON OPEN AREA
Los Angeles Aqueduct Pipelines
MINI KEY
Paved
Easy
Moderate
Difficult
Other
See Page 272 for GPS Waypoint Coordinates
Jawbone Canyon Store
14
Grid size - 1 mile
STAY ON DESIGNATED ROUTES EXCEPT IN OPEN AREAS
TO MOJAVE
© 2004 FunTreks, Inc.

This sign is located 1.7 miles southeast of Highway 14 where road is still wide and easy.

Holly Ash Cleanser Mine.

Historic Bonanza Gulch Post Office.

One of several old miners' cabins.

Much to see at Bickel Camp.

Narrow and steep in places.

Pass through rocky canyon on second half of trip.

Bonanza Gulch/EP15 73

Location: South of Inyokern, southwest of Ridgecrest and north of California City. Northeast of Red Rock Canyon State Park.

Difficulty: Moderate. The first half of route through Bonanza Gulch is easy. Second half of route crosses remote, mountainous terrain where trail is narrow and rocky in a few places. Route-finding is complex so pay close attention to directions. Suitable for most stock SUVs with high ground clearance and low-range gearing. Don't go alone.

Features: See giant white caverns of Holly Ash Cleanser Mine, Bonanza Gulch Post Office and old miners' cabins, including the incredible Bickel Cabin with hundreds of pieces of old mining equipment. Trail also goes by famous Burro Schmidt Tunnel described in Trail #74. Last part of trail crosses through the heart of the rugged El Paso Mountains. It is a long, remote and complicated route for those who really want to get deep into the backcountry. You can skip this part of trip by exiting early through Mesquite Canyon.

Time & Distance: Entire route covers 27.6 miles and takes about 5 hours. Shortened route measures 15.7 miles and takes about 3 hours. Add time and mileage for short side trips.

To Get There: From Highway 14, at a point 0.3 miles north of mile post 50 (about 15 miles north of Jawbone Station), turn east on dirt road EP15.

Trail Description: Reset odometer as you turn off Highway 14 (01). Head southeast following sign to Burro Schmidt Tunnel. Bear left at 1.3 miles. Continue straight at 1.7 miles at large sign for Bonanza Trail. Continue straight on EP15 as lesser roads branch off. Stay left at 3.6 where road goes right to Cudahys Old Dutch Cleanser Mine. At 4.6 miles (02), roads go right to the Holly Ash Cleanser Mine. Take a few minutes to explore this area which includes old mining equipment and several large white, caverns where pumice (major incredient in cleanser) was mined. When you're done, come back to this point (02) and *reset your odometer*.

Continue southeast on EP15. Turn left at 0.2 miles on lesser road and head north. The road narrows and turns east. Stay left at 1.3. The small wooden building on the right at 1.4 miles is historic Bonanza Gulch Post Office. Turn right after the building where the road drops into Bonanza Gulch and heads south. You'll go by several old miners' cabins before reaching a 3-way fork at 2.7 miles. Make a soft left turn. Almost immediately, you reach an important intersection at 2.8 miles (03). Hard right goes to Last Chance Canyon, hard left (northeast) goes to Bickel Cabin and left continues on EP15. For now, turn hard left for Bickel Cabin just 0.3 miles north on EP30. After visiting the cabin, return to this intersection (03) and *reset odometer*. Turn left and continue east. At 1.5 miles (04), bear left at rusty barrels to continue on EP15. (Burro Schmidt Tunnel, described in Trail #74, is straight uphill 0.8 miles.) Continue straight at 3.3 miles (05) where EP30 joins on left.

Another important intersection is reached at 4.0 miles (06). Right exits to Randsburg-Red Rock Road via Mesquite Canyon. Follow EP100 south 4.3 miles to end trip early.

To continue on EP15, *reset odometer* and turn left (06). Bear left at 0.1 then left again past Colorado Camp at 1.3 miles. Bear right at 2.1, 2.6 and 2.7 miles. The road gets rougher and narrower with a steep hill at 3.0 miles. Go past tailings of the Apache Mine at 3.2, then bear left at 3.4 and 4.3 miles. Continue straight at 4.6 miles (07) as you cross EP11, then turn right at 5.0 where a sign points left back to EP11. Stay left at 5.5 as you descend into a canyon. Turn right when the trail drops into a wash at 5.9 then climbs left out of the wash at 6.0. The trail gets rough and steep again. Bear left at 6.5 miles (08) and pass through a narrow, rocky canyon. Continue straight at 7.1, 7.5, 7.8 and 8.2. Turn right at 9.0 miles (09) at marker for EP15.

The road begins to improve. Bear left at 10.5 on a better road. Bear right at power lines at 10.8 miles as EP15 joins EP21. Bear right uphill at 10.9. At 12.2 miles (10), turn left on lesser road then immediately turn right. Continue straight at 13.3 miles. At 13.5 miles, bear left on EP15 as EP21 continues straight. Make a right at 13.8 and another right at 14.1 miles (11) where EP33 goes left. Bear left at 14.4 miles on a very narrow but easy road. One last right turn at 16.1 miles takes you to paved Highway 395 at 16.2 miles (12).

Return Trip: Left on Highway 395 goes to Ridgecrest and Inyokern. Right goes to Randsburg where you can take Randsburg-Red Rock Road back to Jawbone Station, Mojave and Bakersfield.

Services: Nothing along trail. Closest gas at end of trail is south to Johannesburg. Premium gas available at Jawbone Canyon Store on Highway 14. Popular general store in Randsburg. Gas and food in California City.

Maps: East Kern County Off-Highway Vehicle Riding Areas & Trails Map. For best detail, use USGS 7.5-minute maps Saltdale NW, Garlock and El Paso Peaks, CA. The use of GPS is highly recommended on this trail.

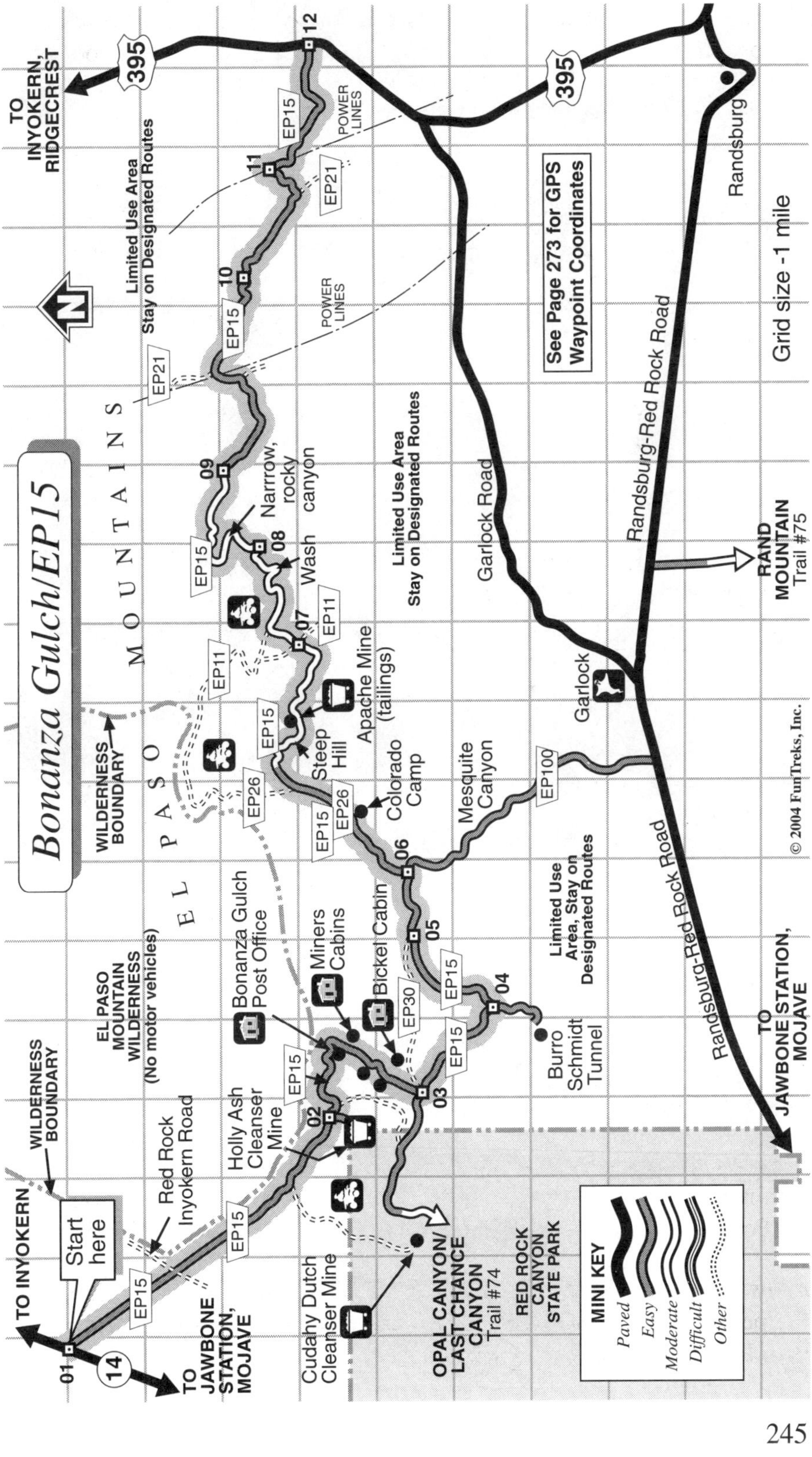

Bonanza Gulch/EP15
TO INYOKERN, RIDGECREST
395
TO INYOKERN
TO JAWBONE STATION, MOJAVE
14
01
Start here
EP15
WILDERNESS BOUNDARY
Red Rock Inyokern Road
Holly Ash Cleanser Mine
02
Cudahy Dutch Cleanser Mine
OPAL CANYON/ LAST CHANCE CANYON Trail #74
RED ROCK CANYON STATE PARK
EL PASO MOUNTAIN WILDERNESS (No motor vehicles)
Bonanza Gulch Post Office
Miners Cabins
Bickel Cabin
EP30
03
04
Burro Schmidt Tunnel
05
06
EP26
Colorado Camp
Mesquite Canyon
EP100
Steep Hill
Apache Mine (tailings)
EP11
07
Wash
08
Narrow, rocky canyon
09
EL PASO MOUNTAINS
EP21
10
11
12
POWER LINES
Limited Use Area Stay on Designated Routes
Limited Use Area, Stay on Designated Routes
Garlock
Garlock Road
Randsburg-Red Rock Road
RAND MOUNTAIN Trail #75
TO JAWBONE STATION, MOJAVE
Randsburg
See Page 273 for GPS Waypoint Coordinates
Grid size -1 mile
MINI KEY
Paved
Easy
Moderate
Difficult
Other
© 2004 FunTreks, Inc.

Highest point of trail looking down on multicolored bluffs of El Paso Mountains.

Narrow and rough.  Last Chance Canyon with Cudahys Camp in foreground.

All kinds of old mining equipment to see at Bickel Camp. Leave everything as you find it.

Burro Schmidt's tool shack. Look, but don't touch.  Burro Schmidt Tunnel.

246

Opal Cyn./ Last Chance Cyn. 74

Location: North of Mojave and California City, southwest of Ridgecrest. Western half of trail is inside Red Rocks Canyon State Park.

Difficulty: Moderate. One section of Opal Canyon is very narrow, steep and rocky. Part of Last Chance Canyon follows a sandy wash where you'll need to air down your tires to avoid getting stuck. Trail is suitable for stock, high-clearance four-wheel-drive SUVs. Remote location; don't go alone. Travel is restricted to designated routes only. No vehicles in wilderness.

Features: Rugged Opal Canyon drops into Last Chance Canyon providing striking high views of unusual red and pink buttes. See historic Bickel Mining Camp and famous Burro Schmidt Tunnel.

Time & Distance: Allow about 4 hours driving time for this 20-mile trip.

To Get There: Take Highway 14 to mile marker 44 across from the entrance to Dove Springs OHV Area. This point is about 29 miles north of Mojave and 3.5 miles north of the entrance to Red Rock Canyon State Park's Ricardo Campground and Visitor Center.

Trail Description: Reset odometer as you turn east off Highway 14 (01). Cross cattle guard and swing left (north) following a graded dirt road that parallels Hwy. 14. Turn right at 0.6 miles on Opal Canyon Road. Head south and turn left at 2.2 miles (02) (look for small "Opal" sign). After another mile, stay right as roads branch left to Opal Canyon. Continue straight uphill at 3.8 miles (03) where a tiny, hard-to-read sign points left to private Barnett Opal Mine. Stay left at next fork and climb to top of rocky ridge with views of multicolored bluffs below. The road going down is very rocky, narrow and loose. Important: Stay left at 4.6 miles (04) heading northeast. (Note: If you miss this turn and go right, you could end up on a dangerous trail that also descends to Last Chance Canyon.) The correct route drops downhill and enters a wash which connects to Last Chance Canyon at 5.7 miles (05). The trails meet near Cudahys Mining Camp.

 Reset odometer and follow wash to left. The trail goes left up a steep rocky hill at 0.2 miles. (Note: At time of this writing, plans were underway to reroute trail to avoid this hill. You may have to make adjustments depending upon how the trail is changed.) After the hill, bear right where a road goes left and drop back down into a sandy wash. At 0.7 miles, go by a dilapidated house trailer at a mine on the right. Stay on the main road, ignoring side roads as the wash widens. Several major roads converge at 3.2 miles (06).

Stay right in a wide wash. Bear slightly right at 3.6 out of the wash then right again at 4.1 miles (07). EP30 goes left here to Bickel Mining Camp, a worthwhile side trip described in Trail #73. At 4.2, bear left where Pleasant Valley Road goes right.

Bear right at 5.6 miles (08). You'll come back to this spot. Bear left at 6.3 until you reach Burro Schmidt's cabin at 6.4. The property is privately owned and was occupied at the time of this writing. Register and proceed uphill at no charge, although donations may be suggested. The tunnel is reached at 6.5 miles (09). Return the way you came and turn right at 7.4 miles (08). Continue straight at 9.0 miles then again at 9.2 miles (10) where EP30 joins on left. Bear right at 9.9 miles (11) on EP100. (EP15/EP26 goes left as described in Trail #73.) Follow EP100 as it descends through Mesquite Canyon. Continue straight at 10.2 and 10.7. Randsburg-Red Rock Road is reached at 14.2 miles (12).

Return Trip: Right takes you back to Highway 14, Jawbone Station and Mojave. Left goes to Highway 395, Randsburg and Ridgecrest.

Services: Nothing on trail. Gas is available in Johannesburg to the east, Inyokern and Ridgecrest north, California City and Mojave south. Premium gas is available at the Jawbone Canyon Store on Highway 14 just south of Jawbone Station. Randsburg has a popular, old fashioned general store that has been in business over 100 years. Red Rock Canyon State Park Visitor Center is located west of Highway 14 at the Ricardo Campgrounds. This beautiful campground is large enough for motor homes and has water and a dump station at the visitor center.

Historical Highlights: William Henry (Burro) Schmidt started digging his tunnel the same year as the Great San Francisco Earthquake in 1906. His plan was to charge a toll to shortcut passage through the area. Long before he finished, a good road was built around Copper Mountain, rendering his tunnel obsolete. No one knows why he continued to dig, mostly by hand, a total of 38 years. He was dubbed the "Human Mole" when he was featured in "Ripley's Believe It or Not" and Time Magazine in the 1940s. The tunnel is almost 2,000 feet long with a great view on the other side. You can hike through it with a flashlight. Some say the tunnel will outlast the pyramids of Egypt. Schmidt operated the tunnel as a tourist attraction until his death at the age of 83 in 1954.

Maps: East Kern County Off-Highway Vehicle Riding Areas & Trails Map, Hileman's Gem, Mineral and 4-Wheel-Drive Map of Last Chance Canyon #1. For best detail, use USGS 7.5-minute maps Saltdale NW and Garlock, CA. The use of GPS is highly recommended on this trail.

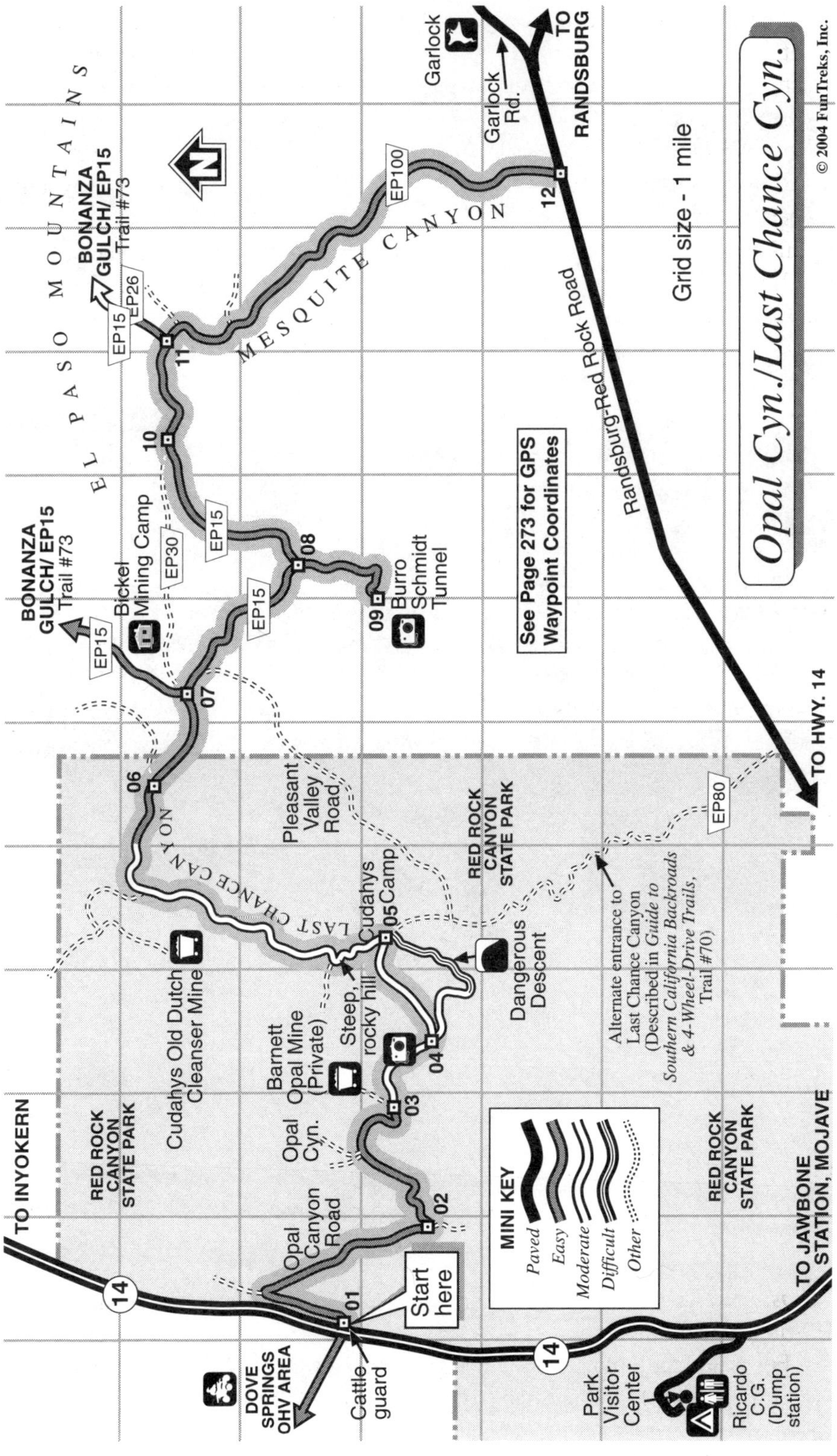
Opal Cyn./Last Chance Cyn.
© 2004 FunTreks, Inc.
Grid size - 1 mile
TO INYOKERN
TO JAWBONE STATION, MOJAVE
TO HWY. 14
TO RANDSBURG
DOVE SPRINGS OHV AREA
Cattle guard
Start here
Park Visitor Center
Ricardo C.G. (Dump station)
RED ROCK CANYON STATE PARK
Opal Canyon Road
Opal Cyn.
Barnett Opal Mine (Private)
Steep, rocky hill
Cudahys Old Dutch Cleanser Mine
Cudahys Camp
Dangerous Descent
Pleasant Valley Road
LAST CHANCE CANYON
BONANZA GULCH/ EP15 Trail #73
Bickel Mining Camp
Burro Schmidt Tunnel
See Page 273 for GPS Waypoint Coordinates
EL PASO MOUNTAINS
MESQUITE CANYON
Randsburg-Red Rock Road
Garlock
Garlock Rd.
Alternate entrance to Last Chance Canyon (Described in Guide to Southern California Backroads & 4-Wheel-Drive Trails, Trail #70)
EP15
EP26
EP30
EP80
EP100
14
01
02
03
04
05
06
07
08
09
10
11
12
MINI KEY
Paved
Easy
Moderate
Difficult
Other

Start of trail on north side.    Trail begins easy as it heads into the mountains.

Main roads are not wide enough for oversized vehicles.    A few tippy spots.

Ore bin seen along route.    Starting down from Government Peak on shelf road.

General Store, Mercantile Shop and Post Office in Randsburg.

250

Rand Mountain 75

Location: North of California City, south of Randsburg and Ridgecrest.

Difficulty: Moderate. Lower portion of trail is easy, but as you climb higher into the mountains, the trail becomes narrrow, steep and rocky in places. Suitable for aggressive stock, high-clearance, 4WD SUVs. Not for wide, oversized or long-wheel-based vehicles. Light brush may touch vehicle. Use caution; many open mine shafts are located throughout the area. Route-finding is complex with many crisscrossing roads at top of mountain.

Features: Many ATV and dirt bike riders know this mountain as the "California City Riding Area." The area includes roads wide enough for SUVs and Jeeps. There are many marked routes in the area, which you must stay on at all times. This is a sensitive desert tortoise area. It is against the law to pick up a desert tortoise unless it is in grave danger. (See page 21 for more information.) All roads west of R43 were closed in 2002 to help protect the desert tortoise. More roads could be closed if rules are not followed. You are expected to know and follow all rules.

Time & Distance: Allow about 4 hours for this 17.2-mile loop.

To Get There: I entered from the north side on R43 starting from Randsburg-Red Rock Road 1.5 miles east of Garlock Road. If you are coming from California City, you can enter from various points on the south side from Randsburg-Mojave Road. R43 is the southernmost entry point and is located about 15 miles northeast of California City.

Trail Description: Reset odometer at start (01). Head south on well marked R43. Continue straight at 4.0 miles where R50 crosses (it is closed to the right). Continue straight at 4.3 and 4.8 miles as you enter low foothills. Bear right on R43 at 6.2 miles where R49 goes straight. Stay left at 7.3 where closed R48 goes right. At 8.0 miles (02), R43 goes right to Randsburg-Mojave Road. *(Note: Anyone coming from California City would probably come in this way.)*

Reset odometer and continue northeast from this point (02) on R20. Shady rock outcrop at 0.2 is a good spot for lunch. Continue straight at 0.4 miles where R47 comes in on right from Randsburg-Mojave Road. Stay right at 0.6 where R30 goes left. Stay left on R20 at 1.8 miles where R69 comes in on right from Randsburg-Mojave Road. The road gets rougher and steeper. At 2.8 miles (03), bear left through a narrow section with mines and a dry well. Turn right at 3.0 and climb steeply towards Sidney Peak. This is

251

the toughest part of trail. A scenic high point is reached at 3.1 miles. As you start down the other side, avoid the difficult trail that goes right to the top of Sidney Peak. At 3.2 miles (04), stay right downhill on R20. Bear left at 3.5 where R73 goes right. Continue straight on R20 at 3.9 where R75 crosses. Within 100 feet (05), R20 goes right and exits the area.

Reset odometer (05) and continue straight on R77. Continue straight at 0.7. Bear right at 1.0 and left at 1.2 on R30. Continue straight at 1.4 where R24 goes right. Go straight again at 1.8 where R83 crosses. At 1.9 miles (06), another fork is reached.

Reset odometer and turn left on R85 (06). (Road to right is closed.) Continue straight at 0.1 on R85/R30. (Road to right goes to Government Peak with high views of Randsburg and surrounding area.) A narrowing shelf road winds steeply downhill. It is not difficult, but shift into low range to minumize use of brakes. Pass through a heavily mined area and bear left past an ore bin at 0.9 miles. Turn right at 1.0 miles staying on R30. Continue downhill through area of mine tailings avoiding uphill side roads. Road follows fenced area with "No Trespassing" signs. Bear right along fence at 1.7 miles where R34 goes left. Stay right at 2.2, then turn left away from fence at 2.3 miles. Continue straight at 2.6 as the terrain flattens out. Turn right at 2.9 miles on R44. Paved Randsburg-Red Rock Road is reached at 3.4 miles (07).

Return Trip: Randsburg is 1.5 miles to the right. Beyond Randsburg is Highway 395 which goes to Ridgecrest, Johannesburg and Red Mountain. Highway 395 also connects to California City via Randsburg-Mojave Road and paved Twenty-Mule-Team Parkway. Left on Randsburg-Red Rock Road goes to Red Rock Canyon State Park and intersects with Highway 14, which goes south to Jawbone Station, California City and Mojave.

Services: The 100-year-old general store in Randsburg is a popular tourist attraction but also sells a variety of useful merchandise. Randsburg does not have gas but gas is available in nearby Johannesburg on Highway 395. Otherwise, most services are available in Ridgecrest, Inyokern and California City. Premium gas is available at the Jawbone Canyon Store on Highway 14 south of Jawbone Station.

Maps: East Kern County Off-Highway Vehicle Riding Areas & Trails Map, Hileman's Gem, Mineral and 4-Wheel-Drive Map of California City #5, USGS 100,000-scale map Cuddeback Lake, CA. The use of GPS is highly recommended on this trail.

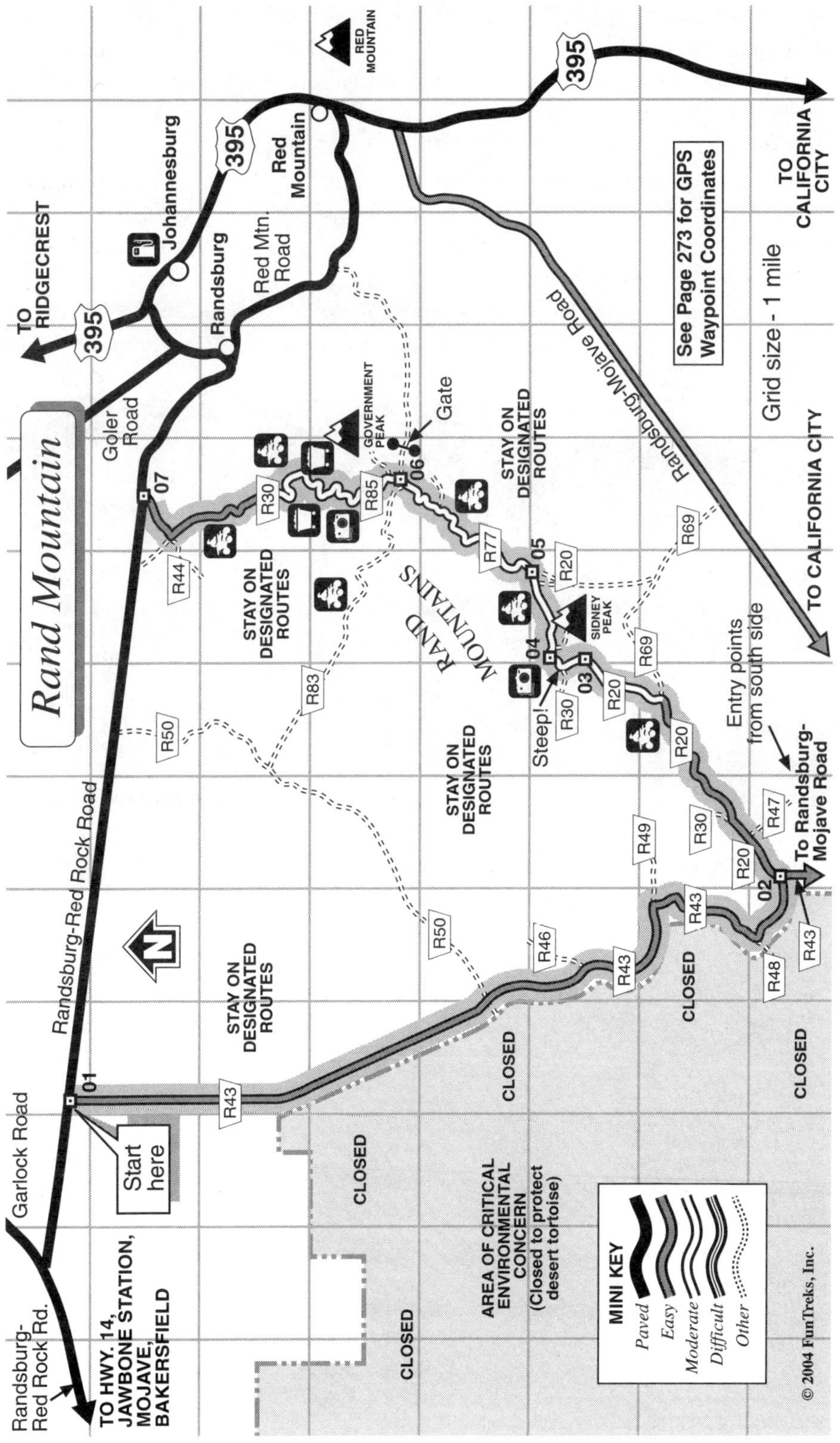
Rand Mountain
TO RIDGECREST
395
Johannesburg
Randsburg
Red Mtn. Road
Red Mountain
RED MOUNTAIN
Goler Road
Randsburg-Red Rock Road
Garlock Road
Randsburg-Red Rock Rd.
TO HWY. 14, JAWBONE STATION, MOJAVE, BAKERSFIELD
Start here
GOVERNMENT PEAK
Gate
SIDNEY PEAK
RAND MOUNTAINS
Steep!
STAY ON DESIGNATED ROUTES
CLOSED
AREA OF CRITICAL ENVIRONMENTAL CONCERN (Closed to protect desert tortoise)
Randsburg-Mojave Road
TO CALIFORNIA CITY
Entry points from south side
To Randsburg-Mojave Road
See Page 273 for GPS Waypoint Coordinates
Grid size - 1 mile
R20
R30
R43
R44
R46
R47
R48
R49
R50
R69
R77
R83
R85
01
02
03
04
05
06
07
MINI KEY
Paved
Easy
Moderate
Difficult
Other
© 2004 FunTreks, Inc.

Buttermilk Country, Trail #41, rated easy.

APPENDIX

Upper part of the *Rock Pile* on Niagara Rim, Trail #29, rated difficult.

GPS Basics

Frequently asked Questions:

What is GPS? GPS stands for Global Positioning System. Satellites circle the earth and broadcast signals to receiving units below. These signals allow you to determine your position on the earth. Five to 12 satellites can be picked up at any one time. A GPS unit with 12-satellite capability has the best chance of determining your position quickly.

Is GPS necessary? No. Some people prefer to rely on instinct, orienteering and map-reading skills. In many areas, roads are well defined and easy to follow. You may travel with people who are familiar with the trail or you may prefer hiring a guide. Most of the trails in this book can be driven without the use of GPS.

Then why should I buy a GPS unit? It's the fastest and easiest way to determine your position. Like any new device, you'll wonder how you got along without it.

What kind of GPS unit do I need? There are many brands and models in all price ranges. It depends on your needs. Don't get one with less than 12 parallel satellite channels. It's handy to be able to download and upload data to a computer, but this is not required. Some GPS units allow you to upload maps into the unit. The amount of space available for the maps is usually a function of price.

How complicated is it to use a GPS unit? My GPS unit came with a small 100-page user's manual. It took a little time to read but it was simple and easy to understand. After a little practice, using the unit becomes second nature. Basic units are much simpler.

What are waypoints and trackpoints? Waypoints are important locations you choose to mark along your route, like where you start, key intersections along the way, and your final destination. Waypoints are recorded when you consciously hit a button. Trackpoints are automatically recorded as you move along. They're often referred to as a breadcrumb trail.

How accurate is GPS? It's gotten much better since the government reduced the *Selective Availability* error. Prior to that, they scrambled the signal, allowing a worst-case error of about a 300-ft. radius. Clinton's announcement on May 1, 2000, says that error is now down to 20 meters or about 60 ft. Subsequent tests of the new system are showing even better accuracy. There's been talk of rescrambling the signals since the 9-11 disaster, but so far that hasn't happened. If it does, you will see greater errors in your GPS coordinates.

Do I need a computer to use a GPS unit? No, but if you have a computer, you'll be able to do a lot more. You can download waypoints and trackpoints to your home computer onto digital maps and see exactly where you went. You can print maps showing your exact route. You can save a large number of routes to upload to your GPS unit anytime you want. You can exchange routes and maps with friends. You can store many detailed maps in the computer at a very low cost per map. You can see a much bigger picture of a map than what you see on your tiny GPS screen. You can use maps with more detail. If you use a laptop, you can take it with you and follow your progress on the screen. You can download hundreds of waypoints and trackpoints instantly into your GPS unit and avoid the tedious task of entering them by hand. Most GPS units don't have a keypad, so entering numerical data takes a long time without a computer.

Is a laptop easy to use in the field? No. It's hard to find a good place to set it up. The screen is hard to see in the sun. It's exposed to damage from dust and vibration. I keep mine in its case much of the time and pull it out when I need it. Despite these drawbacks, it has been indispensable at times and saved me many hours of wandering around aimlessly. I know I'll never get lost when I have it with me.

I already have paper maps. Will a GPS unit help me? Yes. You can plot your GPS location on any map that has tick marks along the edge for latitude/longitude or UTM coordinates. You can get a general idea where you are by sighting across the map. To determine your exact position, you'll need to draw lines. (A template is needed with UTM.) Large fold-out maps can be awkward in the car. I like the handy booklet-style format of an atlas like the DeLorme *Atlas & Gazetteer* or Benchmark's *Road & Recreation Atlas*.

What settings do I use on my GPS unit? For latitude/longitude coordinates, this book uses hours/minutes/seconds, so set your display to read this way. Many people display in hour/minutes/tenths of minutes, which looks similar, but the readings will appear in error. In the continental United States, set your Datum on NAD27CONUS.

What's UTM (Universal Transverse Mercator)? It's an alternative to using Latitude/Longitude coordinates. Many people prefer it because it's easier to plot on a map. Most topo maps have ruled UTM grid lines. Others argue that UTM is not as accurate as Lat./Long. Some maps may have only one set of coordinates. Most GPS units give coordinates both ways. Both are given in this book.

What maps do I need? Again it depends on your needs. The greatest amount of detail is shown on USGS 7.5 minute maps, but many maps are needed to cover a large area. Forest Service maps are practical when you're on forest land but don't help in other areas. The BLM also has maps but they vary in quality. Your best buy is an atlas-style map that covers an entire state. If you're using a computer, several companies now offer statewide map packages with the same detail as 7.5 minute maps. A state the size of California requires about 12 CDs for these rasterized maps. The packages also include the software to manipulate the data. Vector quality maps have less detail but cover more area.

What's the difference between rasterized and vector maps? A rasterized image looks like a photograph of the original map. It takes a lot of computer space. When you zoom out you lose detail. Up close, however, it has the best detail. A vector map is a line conversion and looks more like a drawing in flat color. It lacks detail, but looks the same as you zoom in and out. It doesn't require as much computer space and can be downloaded directly into some new GPS units.

What's mapping software do? Among other things, it allows you to manipulate maps on the screen, download and upload your waypoints and trackpoints, save map images and print them out. It finds the next map as you run off the page and switches automatically to the next map when you're moving in your vehicle with your GPS on.

What specific equipment and maps do you use, Mr. Wells? I use a Garmin II Plus GPS receiver. I bought two additional accessories— a dash mount and a computer cord. The computer cord is split with one part that goes to my cigarette lighter which powers the GPS unit. I've never needed an outside antenna.

I have a Dell Inspiron 7000 laptop with a 14.5″ screen, 4 gig HD, 64 MB ram, and 300 MHz. It has two 4-hour batteries, but since I don't leave the computer on all the time, I've never needed the second battery.

I've been using this equipment for over four years, which means it is not state-of-the-art; however, for my needs it works perfectly. Make sure you compare brands and check out the latest equipment before you buy.

I use a CD map package called All Topo Maps by iGage. The California set includes 2,850 USGS 7.5 minute maps, 121 USGS 1:100,000-scale maps and 38 USGS 1:250,000-scale maps. Because of what I do, I have special needs that the average person doesn't. The maps are complete with collars and are as close as you can get to using a real USGS map. The software has an excellent search tool with a large data base. When I have questions, I have no problem getting through on their toll-free tech support number.

What other mapping software is available?
Some of the top brands include National Geographic, Garmin, DeLorme and Maptech. Some offer rasterized maps, others offer vector maps and some offer both. They are all excellent packages with a variety of high-tech features. Each has advantages and disadvantages depending upon your specific needs. Before you buy, shop around and compare all brands. Go to a store that has them installed on a computer so you can try them out. Not all stores carry all brands.

How much did you spend on your GPS equipment? My equipment is about four years old now, so take that into consideration. The Garmin II Plus was about $250 plus a little more for the accessories. My Dell laptop was about $3,000. I recently checked the cost of the iGage mapping package; it still sells for about $120. I also carry many folding maps that would be expensive to replace.

I don't want to spend that much but would still like to have a GPS unit. What can I do? The most important thing a GPS unit does is tell you where you are. A simple unit will do that. You can buy a quality GPS unit with basic features for about $100. If you don't have any maps, invest in a DeLorme *California Atlas and Gazetteer,* which costs about $20. With this you can plot your general position quickly and easily. Simply look along the edge of the map for longitude and latitude. I use this method about 95% of the time.

If you have a home PC, I'd definitely spend a little more for a GPS unit that can download and upload data to your computer. The first time you try to key waypoints into your GPS unit, you'll know why a computer is important.

How can I learn more about GPS?
A great deal of free information is available online. I like Garmin's Web site (www.garmin.com). They have an excellent 24-page *GPS Guide for Beginners* (www.garmin.com/aboutGPS/manual.html) that you can download as a PDF file. Also, check out www.GPSNOW.com, which sells GPS equipment and mapping products. They show and compare most GPS products and have the latest information on new products. You can also contact the manufacturers directly. (See addresses and phone number section that follows.)

If you don't have access to the Web, go to your local bookstore or library. I bought a copy of *GPS Made Easy* by Lawrence Letham (see references and reading section). It explains GPS in easy-to-understand terms.

GPS Waypoint Coordinates

The following table lists waypoints for each trail. Waypoints are shown in Latitude/Longitude (degrees/minutes/seconds) and UTM coordinates. No coordinate should be in error by more than a radius of 20 meters or approximately 60 feet. All coordinates were compiled using All Topo Maps (iGage) software (Datum=NAD27). You should set your GPS unit on Datum NAD27CONUS.

Wpt.	Mile	Latitude North	Longitude West	UTM Easting	UTM Northing	Zone
1. MT. SHASTA LOOP
1	0.0	41 18 19.0	122 18 30.2	557898	4572666	10
2	6.2	41 18 39.1	122 12 31.4	566236	4573357	10
3	11.7	41 21 47.4	122 5 8.6	576471	4579263	10
4	15.2	41 24 11.3	122 4 46.4	576939	4583707	10
5	17.9	41 25 50.2	122 4 23.9	577430	4586763	10
6	3.8	41 28 36.7	122 5 7.0	576376	4591887	10
7	7.0	41 29 34.2	122 8 24.3	571781	4593612	10
8	14.1	41 33 32.8	122 12 28.8	566044	4600915	10
2. BOWERMAN RIDGE
1	0.0	40 56 41.5	122 44 44.4	521409	4532457	10
2	6.4	40 52 48.8	122 44 34.6	521658	4525280	10
3	10.5	40 49 51.2	122 46 0.0	519673	4519799	10
4	4.7	40 53 13.6	122 45 53.1	519819	4526042	10
5	7.9	40 54 53.9	122 46 15.6	519285	4529132	10
3. SHASTA BALLY PEAK
1	0.0	40 36 54.2	122 31 8.8	540679	4495926	10
2	4.6	40 36 46.5	122 34 24.9	536072	4495666	10
3	6.0	40 36 5.3	122 34 50.8	535470	4494392	10
4	7.0	40 35 46.1	122 35 26.1	534643	4493795	10
5	12.9	40 36 3.4	122 39 4.0	529519	4494307	10
4. LOST COAST, REDWOODS
1	0.0	39 46 50.0	123 49 49.2	428895	4403522	10
2	6.0	39 50 5.4	123 50 33.0	427909	4409555	10
3	19.3	39 58 24.5	123 57 54.0	417593	4425048	10
4	7.0	40 2 19.9	124 1 52.8	412013	4432371	10
5	42.7	40 21 19.7	123 55 23.8	421597	4467412	10

Wpt.	Mile	Latitude North			Longitude West			UTM Easting	UTM Northing	Zone
5. COW MOUNTAIN OHV AREA										
1	0.0	39	5	52.2	123	5	0.3	492785	4327428	10
2	2.3	39	4	49.9	123	5	17.0	492385	4325510	10
3	7.6	39	2	48.9	123	1	59.7	497123	4321775	10
4	8.0	39	2	34.6	123	2	13.8	496784	4321334	10
5	2.8	39	1	28.6	123	0	36.3	499128	4319298	10
6	5.5	39	2	51.0	123	1	13.9	498224	4321841	10
6. PELIGREEN JEEPWAY										
1	0	40	17	52.1	121	48	1.6	601952	4461291	10
2	12.6	40	14	5.1	121	46	29.1	604231	4454323	10
3	1.4	40	13	18.6	121	46	13.5	604620	4452893	10
4	2.9	40	12	31.5	121	46	45.9	603875	4451432	10
5	0.4	40	12	35.0	121	47	13.4	603224	4451529	10
6	4.7	40	11	25.3	121	50	47.5	598190	4449315	10
7	4.4	40	13	20.6	121	53	48.5	593864	4452814	10
8	11.2	40	16	11.2	121	52	30.1	595651	4458096	10
9	13.1	40	16	37.4	121	50	39.9	598245	4458940	10
10	15.8	40	18	2.4	121	51	21.9	597218	4461548	10
7. HIGH LAKES										
1	0.0	40	4	51.9	121	33	1.9	623586	4437553	10
2	6.0	40	1	57.2	121	31	37.5	625673	4432201	10
3	7.8	40	2	39.2	121	30	12.1	627676	4433529	10
4	17.3	40	1	21.3	121	24	15.1	636178	4431272	10
5	1.0	40	0	47.9	121	23	27.4	637328	4430264	10
6	3.9	40	0	1.6	121	21	44.8	639786	4428881	10
7	0.7	40	0	32.4	121	21	26.9	640195	4429837	10
8	0.3	39	59	7.9	121	21	23.8	640316	4427235	10
9	2.5	40	0	22.4	121	19	46.0	642593	4429575	10
8. STAG POINT										
1	0	39	41	57.9	120	57	53.4	674493	4396166	10
2	6.1	39	43	49.9	121	0	40.7	670431	4399531	10
3	8.3	39	44	21.2	121	1	31.6	669197	4400469	10
4	13.5	39	45	29.6	121	4	27.6	664962	4402488	10
5	15.1	39	46	32.8	121	4	1.1	665550	4404449	10
6	17.8	39	47	33.1	121	4	46.9	664422	4406283	10
9. CLEGHORN BAR										
1	0.0	39	47	54.8	120	52	52.5	681399	4407337	10
2	5.5	39	48	50.1	120	56	50.1	675707	4408910	10
3	8.6	39	48	10.9	120	59	0.5	672634	4407630	10
4	3.0	39	49	4.5	121	0	45.5	670102	4409229	10
5	3.3	39	49	10.9	121	0	49.0	670014	4409422	10

Wpt.	Mile	Latitude North	Longitude West	UTM Easting	UTM Northing	Zone
10. POKER FLAT						
1	0.0	39 33 13.2	120 49 55.6	686263	4380257	10
2	7.8	39 37 49.1	120 51 44.4	683464	4388701	10
3	1.3	39 38 35.3	120 51 38.1	683580	4390128	10
4	4.2	39 40 27.5	120 51 22.6	683867	4393595	10
5	2.1	39 41 40.2	120 50 33.6	684979	4395867	10
6	3.5	39 42 57.1	120 52 52.8	681608	4398159	10
7	8.4	39 41 42.1	120 55 47.6	677499	4395748	10
8	13.7	39 41 29.1	120 58 28.8	673669	4395258	10
11. GOLD VALLEY						
1	0.0	39 37 10.7	120 39 59.0	700312	4387936	10
2	1.5	39 37 58.3	120 40 41.8	699253	4389376	10
3	3.7	39 39 1.7	120 41 7.8	698584	4391314	10
4	5.3	39 39 11.5	120 42 25.3	696729	4391569	10
5	7.6	39 40 38.1	120 41 56.6	697345	4394259	10
6	10.7	39 42 23.4	120 42 58.4	695791	4397466	10
7	13.1	39 42 55.8	120 44 38.5	693379	4398406	10
8	12.9	39 46 18.0	120 37 9.2	703914	4404916	10
12. SNAKE LAKE						
1	0	39 40 38.8	120 38 44.1	701931	4394397	10
2	2.8	39 39 42.5	120 40 28.1	699499	4392599	10
3	3.5	39 40 5.2	120 40 57.9	698770	4393279	10
4	5.1	39 40 43.3	120 41 34.9	697857	4394432	10
3	6.8	39 40 5.2	120 40 57.9	698770	4393279	10
13. DEER LAKE						
1	0.0	39 37 10.7	120 39 59.0	700312	4387936	10
2	2.1	39 38 50.6	120 40 14.0	699874	4391005	10
3	1.2	39 39 39.2	120 40 30.7	699439	4392493	10
14. SIERRA BUTTES						
1	0.0	39 33 56.6	120 38 4.7	703196	4382022	10
2	2.5	39 34 33.8	120 39 36.7	700971	4383111	10
3	4.8	39 35 3.6	120 40 23.7	699825	4384002	10
4	5.2	39 35 16.6	120 40 1.4	700346	4384416	10
5	1.2	39 35 43.0	120 39 11.2	701523	4385260	10
6	2.7	39 36 51.8	120 39 56.2	700396	4387355	10
7	3.1	39 37 10.7	120 39 59.0	700312	4387936	10
15. TYLER-FOOTE CROSSING						
1	0.0	39 16 10.5	121 1 12.4	670800	4348353	10
2	8.9	39 20 29.8	120 58 29.9	674515	4356433	10
3	6.4	39 24 21.9	120 58 8.9	674857	4363599	10

Wpt.	Mile	Latitude North	Longitude West	UTM Easting	UTM Northing	Zone
4	13.2	39 27 50.9	120 50 50.4	685192	4370288	10
5	3.4	39 27 17.2	120 50 10.9	686162	4369272	10
6	4.4	39 26 23.8	120 48 45.7	688238	4367675	10
7	6.5	39 25 33.2	120 48 53.1	688098	4366110	10
8	9.5	39 24 6.7	120 49 31.3	687250	4363422	10
9	5.5	39 22 5.4	120 53 56.3	680998	4359531	10

16. BEAR VALLEY LOOP

1	0.0	39 33 25.0	120 14 8.2	737508	4382025	10
2	2.1	39 32 31.4	120 13 7.3	739014	4380417	10
3	4.0	39 31 35.1	120 13 44.6	738177	4378655	10
4	5.6	39 31 23.4	120 14 36.7	736944	4378256	10
5	6.6	39 31 35.8	120 15 17.8	735951	4378609	10
6	7.3	39 31 34.6	120 15 59.9	734946	4378539	10
7	8.0	39 31 13.9	120 16 32.8	734180	4377878	10

17. FORDYCE CREEK

1	0.0	39 19 53.8	120 34 17.7	709313	4356180	10
2	1.9	39 20 58.9	120 34 17.4	709266	4358188	10
3	3.5	39 21 19.1	120 33 0.2	711097	4358860	10
4	3.8	39 21 22.8	120 32 47.9	711389	4358984	10
5	7.0	39 21 40.2	120 30 42.2	714383	4359601	10
6	8.0	39 22 9.5	120 30 29.2	714669	4360512	10
7	8.3	39 22 22.0	120 30 31.4	714605	4360899	10
8	8.9	39 22 38.6	120 30 6.1	715199	4361425	10
9	9.5	39 22 56.4	120 30 17.2	714918	4361967	10
10	10.0	39 23 17.5	120 30 10.6	715058	4362623	10
11	10.5	39 23 27.9	120 30 29.4	714599	4362930	10
12	10.9	39 23 36.6	120 30 22.5	714756	4363203	10
13	12.3	39 24 32.0	120 30 11.4	714973	4364920	10

18. SIGNAL PEAK

1	0.0	39 19 53.8	120 34 17.7	709313	4356180	10
2	1.5	39 19 49.8	120 33 16.2	710789	4356098	10
3	5.7	39 20 16.9	120 32 8.7	712384	4356975	10
4	1.7	39 20 40.8	120 30 20.3	714957	4357786	10
5	7.0	39 18 43.7	120 32 35.6	711817	4354085	10

19. SHIRTTAIL CANYON

1	0.0	39 5 20.7	120 57 0.8	677283	4328455	10
2	9.4	39 6 32.5	120 51 27.4	685242	4330852	10
3	11.9	39 5 35.0	120 51 24.3	685358	4329083	10
4	18.0	39 2 26.1	120 53 6.3	683044	4323202	10
5	19.4	39 2 26.1	120 54 3.2	681675	4323169	10
6	6.6	39 4 7.7	120 57 17.0	676944	4326193	10

Wpt.	Mile	Latitude North			Longitude West			UTM Easting	UTM Northing	Zone

20. MT. WATSON
1	0.0	39	10	22.1	120	8	49.0	746477	4339623	10
2	6.0	39	13	18.4	120	9	20.8	745542	4345035	10
3	7.5	39	13	8.7	120	8	21.5	746974	4344782	10
4	6.0	39	15	39.1	120	4	13.6	752770	4349609	10

21. BLACKWOOD CANYON, ELLIS PEAK
1	0.0	39	6	9.8	120	12	14.8	741776	4331689	10
2	3.3	39	4	36.3	120	14	3.9	739244	4328725	10
3	8.1	39	2	45.3	120	13	34.3	740060	4325327	10
4	11.1	39	3	57.3	120	11	47.4	742560	4327625	10
5	7.3	39	4	12.8	120	8	21.5	747495	4328258	10

22. HELL HOLE
1	0.0	39	4	16.5	120	25	8.0	723300	4327648	10
2	4.0	39	5	22.7	120	21	55.0	727881	4329822	10

23. RUBICON
1	0	39	0	15.0	120	18	42.0	732798	4320469	10
2	0.3	39	0	19.7	120	18	26.8	733159	4320626	10
3	0.6	39	0	43.4	120	18	23.0	733229	4321359	10
4	0.7	39	0	48.5	120	18	23.9	733204	4321515	10
5	0.5	39	1	8.8	120	18	26.9	733113	4322141	10
6	2.8	39	1	15.2	120	16	29.3	735936	4322419	10
7	3.0	39	1	11.0	120	16	17.2	736229	4322299	10
8	4.3	39	0	25.8	120	15	38.4	737205	4320934	10
9	4.7	39	0	19.8	120	15	22.0	737606	4320760	10
10	5.6	39	0	15.0	120	14	36.1	738713	4320646	10
11	6.6	39	0	59.5	120	14	38.2	738623	4322017	10
12	6.8	39	1	6.1	120	14	39.9	738576	4322219	10
13	1.1	39	1	51.1	120	15	6.6	737890	4323587	10
14	4.8	39	2	14.2	120	13	17.2	740499	4324379	10
15	8.3	39	2	45.6	120	10	2.0	745163	4325494	10
16	10.8	39	4	13.8	120	8	21.3	747501	4328290	10

24. BARRETT LAKE
1	0	38	51	9.3	120	14	24.2	739509	4303830	10
2	3.3	38	53	36.2	120	14	22.5	739414	4308361	10
3	4.3	38	54	20.5	120	13	49.7	740163	4309751	10

25. STRAWBERRY PASS
1	0.0	38	47	27.6	120	9	4.6	747427	4297232	10
2	0.6	38	47	6.6	120	8	50.7	747785	4296593	10
3	3.2	38	46	7.0	120	6	35.5	751105	4294858	10
4	6.2	38	45	11.1	120	5	9.4	753238	4293202	10

Wpt.	Mile	Latitude North			Longitude West			UTM Easting	UTM Northing	Zone
5	9.1	38	43	42.3	120	4	14.1	754661	4290508	10
6	12.5	38	42	16.5	120	2	15.2	757619	4287955	10

26. DEER VALLEY

1	0.0	38	36	28.5	119	55	28.3	245338	4277119	11
2	2.8	38	34	18.2	119	54	49.1	246158	4273069	11
3	6.6	38	32	22.0	119	53	44.4	247611	4269439	11

27. CORRAL HOLLOW

1	0.0	38	27	25.9	120	3	7.8	757229	4260455	10
2	2.3	38	28	46.3	120	3	45.8	756228	4262904	10
3	6.3	38	28	18.6	120	5	26.1	753825	4261973	10
4	6.7	38	25	24.0	120	7	38.4	750786	4256488	10
5	7.6	38	24	47.9	120	8	9.9	750057	4255352	10

28. SLICKROCK TRAIL

1	0	38	28	8.0	120	0	36.9	760845	4261870	10
2	2.1	38	26	44.4	120	0	43.0	760781	4259287	10
3	2.9	38	26	27.0	120	0	25.2	761231	4258767	10
4	5.2	38	25	6.6	120	0	24.0	761341	4256287	10

29. NIAGARA RIM

1	2.8	38	18	38.7	119	53	21.8	247362	4244038	11
2	0.0	38	17	46.5	119	50	59.3	250773	4242323	11
3	1.5	38	18	51.4	119	51	16.8	250411	4244336	11
4	2.3	38	19	18.4	119	51	6.5	250688	4245161	11
5	3.0	38	19	30.1	119	51	26.7	250207	4245536	11
6	0.4	38	19	42.2	119	51	18.2	250425	4245903	11
7	0.7	38	19	55.7	119	51	48.7	249696	4246342	11
8	2.6	38	20	14.8	119	52	50.5	248215	4246979	11
9	5.7	38	19	21.5	119	54	40.4	245495	4245417	11

30. EAGLE PEAK

1	0.0	38	16	4.2	119	54	51.9	245023	4239345	11
2	2.5	38	17	7.0	119	52	59.6	247813	4241194	11
3	3.1	38	16	48.0	119	52	43.1	248197	4240596	11
4	5.1	38	16	41.9	119	50	52.9	250869	4240326	11
5	0.4	38	16	37.2	119	53	2.8	247708	4240279	11

31. DODGE RIDGE

1	0.0	38	10	24.0	119	57	23.7	240998	4228974	11
2	2.0	38	9	55.4	119	58	56.1	238722	4228165	11
3	8.9	38	6	31.4	120	3	57.2	231184	4222114	11
4	12.6	38	4	43.8	120	5	49.9	228328	4218887	11

Wpt.	Mile	Latitude North			Longitude West			UTM Easting	UTM Northing	Zone

32. BODIE GHOST TOWN
1	0.0	38	18	33.5	119	12	46.5	306514	4242246	11
2	5.0	38	20	51.7	119	9	3.9	312022	4246377	11
3	7.3	38	21	22.1	119	7	35.2	314197	4247263	11
4	0.8	38	21	16.9	119	7	1.5	315010	4247087	11
5	6.7	38	16	47.0	119	5	54.6	316446	4238727	11
6	15.5	38	12	49.9	119	0	52.7	323621	4231255	11

33. KAVANAUGH RIDGE
1	0.0	38	3	41.5	119	14	25.4	303448	4214804	11
2	1.6	38	4	55.1	119	14	15.2	303751	4217069	11
3	3.1	38	4	41.3	119	15	33.5	301833	4216690	11
4	1.9	38	6	13.7	119	14	59.9	302721	4219516	11
5	3.7	38	5	8.0	119	15	21.7	302139	4217504	11
6	1.1	38	6	49.4	119	14	14.7	303846	4220591	11
7	8.6	38	11	48.4	119	13	4.5	305779	4229766	11

34. COPPER MOUNTAIN
1	0.0	38	5	16.8	119	11	19.2	308055	4217636	11
2	3.2	38	3	25.7	119	13	31.8	304742	4214288	11
3	5.5	38	2	44.6	119	11	53.3	307114	4212962	11
4	6.0	38	2	33.2	119	11	35.5	307539	4212601	11
5	0.4	38	3	3.7	119	11	43.8	307358	4213547	11
6	2.1	38	4	3.2	119	12	25.8	306379	4215404	11

35. HORSE MEADOWS
1	0.0	37	57	33.2	119	7	16.1	313653	4203208	11
2	2.2	37	55	18.7	119	8	25.5	311863	4199101	11
3	3.4	37	55	11.6	119	9	6.6	310854	4198904	11
4	1.6	37	54	23.6	119	7	49.1	312713	4197380	11
5	3.9	37	55	3.8	119	5	47.2	315717	4198552	11

36. DEADMAN PASS
1	0.0	37	39	25.5	119	3	39.3	318204	4169561	11
2	1.9	37	40	38.0	119	3	31.9	318433	4171793	11
3	2.6	37	41	5.4	119	3	52.2	317954	4172648	11

37. BACKWAY TO INYO CRATERS
1	0.0	37	38	48.6	118	57	46.0	326838	4168240	11
2	1.1	37	39	19.0	118	56	52.8	328161	4169148	11
3	2.2	37	39	5.5	118	55	55.3	329561	4168705	11
4	3.1	37	39	36.0	118	56	3.7	329375	4169647	11
5	4.5	37	39	27.0	118	56	52.9	328163	4169395	11
6	4.7	37	39	36.2	118	56	51.2	328210	4169678	11
7	0.1	37	39	33.7	118	56	58.6	328028	4169606	11

Wpt.	Mile	Latitude North			Longitude West			UTM Easting	UTM Northing	Zone
8	1.0	37	39	12.6	118	57	30.8	327226	4168971	11
9	3.2	37	40	21.1	118	58	2.8	326486	4171100	11
10	3.4	37	40	11.5	118	58	15.5	326169	4170809	11
11	5.0	37	40	28.6	118	59	20.9	324578	4171369	11
12	1.2	37	40	54.4	118	59	36.9	324202	4172174	11
13	1.3	37	41	18.4	119	0	17.1	323233	4172933	11

38. LAUREL LAKES

Wpt.	Mile	Latitude North			Longitude West			UTM Easting	UTM Northing	Zone
1	0	37	37	25.5	118	54	21.0	331810	4165574	11
2	2.1	37	36	8.1	118	54	58.3	330847	4163207	11
3	4.8	37	34	30.1	118	54	38.1	331262	4160198	11

39. SAND CANYON

Wpt.	Mile	Latitude North			Longitude West			UTM Easting	UTM Northing	Zone
1	0	37	30	53.7	118	38	14.9	355284	4153050	11
2	0.7	37	31	23.1	118	38	34.4	354821	4153967	11
3	7.5	37	29	15.9	118	42	31.1	348939	4150149	11
4	9.4	37	27	40.3	118	42	42.7	348600	4147207	11

40. WHEELER RIDGE

Wpt.	Mile	Latitude North			Longitude West			UTM Easting	UTM Northing	Zone
1	0.0	37	29	15.9	118	42	31.1	348939	4150149	11
2	3.1	37	29	3.9	118	40	19.6	352162	4149722	11
3	3.2	37	26	50.9	118	40	29.0	351859	4145625	11

41. BUTTERMILK COUNTRY

Wpt.	Mile	Latitude North			Longitude West			UTM Easting	UTM Northing	Zone
1	0.0	37	20	6.9	118	30	57.7	365696	4132936	11
2	5.9	37	18	32.0	118	36	27.5	357530	4130148	11
3	8.3	37	17	1.9	118	36	34.6	357308	4127372	11
4	10.5	37	16	37.1	118	37	36.3	355777	4126634	11
5	2.3	37	16	45.1	118	34	44.9	360001	4126810	11
6	6.4	37	18	37.6	118	31	23.9	365007	4130195	11

42. COYOTE FLAT

Wpt.	Mile	Latitude North			Longitude West			UTM Easting	UTM Northing	Zone
1	0.0	37	20	48.1	118	26	16.2	372643	4134099	11
2	3.9	37	18	51.7	118	29	16.5	368152	4130580	11
3	12.3	37	14	38.2	118	29	32.7	367628	4122776	11
4	3.0	37	13	13.3	118	31	27.8	364751	4120203	11
5	7.5	37	14	24.4	118	32	38.8	363037	4122423	11
6	3.0	37	12	37.0	118	28	37.8	368924	4119017	11
7	6.7	37	10	32.1	118	26	50.7	371504	4115128	11
8	9.0	37	10	5.8	118	28	46.7	368631	4114361	11

Wpt.	Mile	Latitude North			Longitude West			UTM Easting	UTM Northing	Zone

43. SILVER/WYMAN CANYONS

1	0.0	37	23	59.5	118	21	4.9	380389	4139885	11
2	11.8	37	25	9.3	118	11	17.7	394853	4141842	11
3	0.0	37	26	25.0	118	11	7.9	395124	4144172	11
4	15.8	37	24	25.9	117	58	22.2	413902	4140286	11

44. MAZOURKA CANYON

1	0.0	36	47	49.9	118	11	43.0	393360	4072840	11
2	12.4	36	54	0.9	118	5	4.2	403376	4084154	11
3	6.9	36	58	46.1	118	6	13.4	401764	4092962	11
4	6.4	37	0	55.8	118	7	12.9	400340	4096976	11
5	16.9	37	7	22.3	118	4	35.9	404357	4108841	11

45. ARMSTRONG CANYON 1

0.0	36	56	4.7	118	15	21.8	388140	4088154	11	
2	8.1	36	56	42.1	118	20	29.8	380538	4089413	11
3	9.1	36	56	47.0	118	21	10.3	379537	4089578	11

46. MOVIE ROAD/ALABAMA HILLS

1	0.0	36	35	44.5	118	6	28.7	400893	4050392	11
2	5.7	36	38	54.1	118	8	29.7	397956	4056268	11
3	6.0	36	35	50.0	118	12	10.3	392406	4050665	11

47. SWANSEA-CERRO GORDO ROAD

1	0	36	31	28.1	117	54	14.7	419057	4042301	11
2	12.9	36	37	31.8	117	54	41.4	418499	4053514	11
3	4.2	36	36	28.0	117	51	10.7	423716	4051499	11
4	10.1	36	32	43.3	117	48	26.5	427737	4044540	11
5	11.2	36	32	22.8	117	47	38.2	428931	4043898	11
6	7.8	36	29	11.4	117	51	56.6	422453	4038059	11

48. RACETRACK VIA HUNTER MOUNTAIN

1	0.0	36	21	51.2	117	37	29.9	443930	4024327	11
2	8.3	36	27	54.4	117	37	32.8	443931	4035518	11
3	15.8	36	31	36.1	117	32	45.8	451114	4042304	11
4	5.5	36	33	26.9	117	29	0.3	456737	4045691	11
5	5.0	36	35	55.9	117	27	45.9	458610	4050271	11
6	16.2	36	43	46.6	117	30	15.3	454975	4064794	11
7	21.6	36	45	36.2	117	32	29.0	451678	4068190	11
8	7.8	36	39	56.6	117	34	2.2	449304	4057737	11
9	9.6	36	38	29.5	117	34	25.2	448718	4055058	11
10	7.1	36	37	12.0	117	38	52.6	442061	4052712	11

Wpt.	Mile	Latitude North	Longitude West	UTM Easting	UTM Northing	Zone
49. HOLLISTER HILLS SVRA						
1	----	36 45 30.2	121 23 47.0	643143	4069066	10
2	----	36 45 30.5	121 24 23.6	642233	4069059	10
50. OLD COAST ROAD						
1	0.0	36 22 21.3	121 54 5.5	598539	4025632	10
2	10.4	36 17 19.1	121 50 35.9	603873	4016383	10
51. PREWITT RIDGE						
1	0.0	36 0 35.1	121 27 4.6	639574	3985940	10
2	6.7	36 3 14.7	121 29 21.1	636082	3990803	10
3	4.5	35 58 18.1	121 26 24.4	640648	3981734	10
4	5.1	35 58 17.9	121 27 3.0	639681	3981712	10
5	7.3	35 59 4.1	121 28 1.1	638204	3983113	10
52. SOUTH COAST RIDGE						
1	0	36 0 35.1	121 27 4.6	639574	3985940	10
2	4.5	35 58 18.1	121 26 24.4	640648	3981734	10
3	10.4	35 53 31.0	121 22 25.5	646779	3972985	10
4	12.1	35 53 7.1	121 23 46.7	644756	3972215	10
5	18.1	35 53 9.2	121 27 27.4	639221	3972189	10
53. PICHACHO PEAK						
1	0.0	36 21 40.8	120 45 33.1	701054	4026158	10
2	1.4	36 21 40.9	120 44 45.0	702253	4026188	10
3	3.0	36 21 9.1	120 44 5.3	703265	4025231	10
4	4.6	36 21 21.2	120 42 50.6	705119	4025647	10
5	4.7	36 21 18.4	120 42 50.0	705135	4025562	10
6	0.7	36 20 44.4	120 42 47.1	705233	4024515	10
7	2.9	36 20 50.1	120 41 43.0	706827	4024730	10
8	3.7	36 20 52.8	120 41 17.3	707466	4024829	10
9	5.3	36 21 9.2	120 40 25.2	708752	4025365	10
10	8.1	36 22 40.0	120 41 32.4	707010	4028122	10
54. OCEANO DUNES SVRA						
1	0.0	35 6 20.4	120 37 46.3	716056	3887133	10
2	2.1	35 4 30.1	120 37 43.0	716221	3883739	10
3	5.5	35 2 6.1	120 37 8.8	717195	3879320	10
55. PINE MOUNTAIN						
1	0	35 21 18.5	120 15 3.1	749813	3915698	10
2	2.3	35 20 11.5	120 13 32.6	752156	3913697	10
3	6.6	35 19 48.8	120 16 9.4	748215	3912887	10
4	7.7	35 19 55.6	120 16 54.6	747066	3913067	10
5	9.2	35 20 50.4	120 17 40.6	745860	3914722	10

Wpt.	Mile	Latitude North			Longitude West			UTM Easting	UTM Northing	Zone
56. GARCIA RIDGE										
1	0.0	35	15	58.5	120	24	24.7	735891	3905455	10
2	3.5	35	15	57.6	120	21	37.3	740124	3905538	10
3	4.9	35	15	50.6	120	20	36.3	741670	3905365	10
57. TWIN ROCKS										
1	0.0	35	6	39.1	120	5	40.7	764806	3889003	10
2	1.5	35	7	27.7	120	6	39.1	763284	3890459	10
3	4.7	35	9	10.2	120	5	12.0	765397	3893682	10
4	8.5	35	8	5.3	120	6	59.5	762734	3891602	10
5	9.5	35	7	40.2	120	6	59.2	762763	3890827	10
6	2.8	35	6	54.9	120	9	7.3	759561	3889338	10
7	5.7	35	7	41.6	120	11	25.7	756014	3890679	10
58. WHITE BARK VISTA										1
0.0	37	17	29.2	119	6	4.1313749		4129069	11	
2	1.1	37	17	28.3	119	5	13.3	314999	4129013	11
59. MIRROR/STRAWBERRY LAKES										
1	0.0	37	12	2.3	119	8	12.6	310356	4119066	11
2	0.6	37	12	22.3	119	7	49.1	310950	4119670	11
3	0.5	37	12	35.4	119	7	41.0	311159	4120067	11
4	1.4	37	12	56.1	119	7	24.0	311592	4120697	11
5	0.3	37	12	9.7	119	7	49.8	310924	4119281	11
6	1.7	37	12	19.4	119	6	45.9	312506	4119545	11
60. COYOTE LAKE										
1	0	37	12	2.4	119	8	12.4	310362	4119068	11
2	2.2	37	11	29.7	119	6	40.8	312598	4118009	11
3	3.8	37	11	11.6	119	5	33.0	314257	4117416	11
61. BREWER LAKE										
1	0	37	8	52.9	119	9	21.2	308533	4113265	11
2	2.4	37	9	51.6	119	7	41.6	311031	4115021	11
3	3.1	37	9	58.7	119	7	25.9	311423	4115229	11
62. BALD MOUNTAIN										
1	0	37	6	4.7	119	10	7.8	307264	4108108	11
2	0.3	37	5	55.0	119	10	23.9	306861	4107820	11
3	0.9	37	5	44.8	119	10	54.5	306098	4107523	11
4	1.1	37	5	49.9	119	11	3.1	305890	4107684	11
5	0.5	37	6	12.1	119	10	51.2	306198	4108359	11
6	1.7	37	6	40.7	119	11	25.2	305380	4109263	11
7	3.3	37	6	51.5	119	11	56.8	304607	4109614	11
8	6.3	37	8	48.6	119	11	5.9	305947	4113193	11

Wpt.	Mile	Latitude North			Longitude West			UTM Easting	UTM Northing	Zone
9	1.1	37	6	13.0	119	12	18.4	304047	4108438	11
10	1.1	37	5	57.0	119	11	34.2	305126	4107920	11
11	1.7	37	5	31.5	119	11	30.9	305189	4107133	11
12	2.1	37	5	35.2	119	11	3.4	305871	4107231	11

63. SWAMP LAKE

Wpt.	Mile	Latitude North			Longitude West			UTM Easting	UTM Northing	Zone
1	0.0	37	4	24.0	119	6	3.3	313233	4104868	11
2	4.2	37	6	0.7	119	4	15.5	315960	4107791	11
3	5.6	37	6	26.3	119	4	25.0	315743	4108586	11
4	6.5	37	6	39.6	119	4	54.2	315031	4109011	11
5	6.8	37	6	47.6	119	4	55.2	315010	4109259	11
6	8.3	37	7	28.6	119	4	22.1	315856	4110504	11
7	8.8	37	7	46.0	119	4	21.0	315893	4111038	11
8	10.8	37	8	1.7	119	5	29.5	314215	4111560	11
9	12.4	37	8	43.6	119	5	44.5	313873	4112859	11
10	13.4	37	8	55.1	119	6	16.3	313097	4113230	11

64. VOYAGER ROCK

Wpt.	Mile	Latitude North			Longitude West			UTM Easting	UTM Northing	Zone
1	0.0	37	4	57.5	118	57	42.7	325618	4105637	11
2	1.9	37	6	13.2	118	57	40.9	325709	4107968	11

65. DUSY/ERSHIM TRAIL

Wpt.	Mile	Latitude North			Longitude West			UTM Easting	UTM Northing	Zone
1	0.0	37	6	20.1	118	57	37.8	325789	4108181	11
2	2.4	37	7	44.9	118	57	53.7	325452	4110801	11
3	8.9	37	12	5.9	118	57	35.9	326058	4118837	11
4	6.0	37	10	52.7	119	1	28.8	320266	4116700	11
5	11.3	37	12	51.4	119	3	31.7	317316	4120425	11
6	4.2	37	15	11.1	119	2	41.7	318640	4124705	11
7	7.2	37	16	39.2	119	3	52.6	316953	4127457	11
8	9.2	37	17	25.4	119	5	12.6	315015	4128925	11

66. SPANISH ROUTE

Wpt.	Mile	Latitude North			Longitude West			UTM Easting	UTM Northing	Zone
1	0.0	36	57	3.3	118	58	0.0	324886	4091033	11
2	2.1	36	56	45.2	118	56	30.1	327100	4090428	11
3	5.3	36	55	22.1	118	55	4.9	329156	4087826	11

67. MONACHE MEADOWS

Wpt.	Mile	Latitude North			Longitude West			UTM Easting	UTM Northing	Zone
1	0.0	36	9	44.4	118	13	54.3	389209	4002456	11
2	6.1	36	12	27.8	118	10	32.1	394320	4007426	11
3	7.2	36	13	16.5	118	10	38.1	394190	4008929	11
4	9.2	36	14	18.8	118	11	9.6	393427	4010858	11

		Latitude			Longitude			UTM	UTM	
Wpt.	Mile	North			West			Easting	Northing	Zone

68. SHERMAN PASS 4X4 TRAIL

Wpt	Mile	Lat N			Long W			Easting	Northing	Zone
1	0.0	35	59	15.0	118	24	47.4	372607	3983286	11
2	3.4	36	1	9.0	118	24	7.3	373662	3986784	11
3	5.2	36	0	36.8	118	23	22.3	374775	3985775	11
4	0.4	36	1	22.1	118	23	53.8	374006	3987183	11
5	3.2	36	1	46.3	118	22	1.8	376820	3987887	11
6	5.7	36	2	38.5	118	20	48.9	378667	3989472	11
7	6.4	36	3	3.2	118	20	44.3	378791	3990229	11
8	7.5	36	2	57.6	118	19	59.4	379913	3990043	11
9	9.9	36	1	22.5	118	19	7.2	381179	3987092	11

69. RANCHERIA ROAD

Wpt	Mile	Lat N			Long W			Easting	Northing	Zone
1	0.0	35	25	0.8	118	49	50.1	333796	3920617	11
2	15.0	35	32	22.7	118	42	1.0	345862	3934019	11
3	9.3	35	36	41.9	118	37	49.1	352338	3941900	11
4	13.7	35	38	38.1	118	35	28.0	355945	3945421	11
5	22.0	35	44	19.0	118	33	19.6	359342	3955874	11

70. FREEWAY RIDGE

Wpt	Mile	Lat N			Long W			Easting	Northing	Zone
1	0.0	35	34	54.6	118	33	13.9	359209	3938482	11
2	1.8	35	35	34.3	118	32	52.5	359767	3939695	11
3	2.7	35	36	0.5	118	33	30.8	358816	3940517	11
4	5.5	35	36	27.0	118	35	46.2	355421	3941389	11
5	7.0	35	37	0.2	118	36	56.6	353669	3942440	11
6	10.1	35	38	38.4	118	35	28.7	355929	3945432	11
7	1.2	35	38	16.0	118	34	37.9	357194	3944721	11
8	6.4	35	37	34.7	118	30	35.6	363269	3943351	11
9	8.3	35	38	28.4	118	28	58.6	365736	3944970	11

71. JAWBONE TO LAKE ISABELLA

Wpt	Mile	Lat N			Long W			Easting	Northing	Zone
1	0.0	35	18	2.3	118	0	2.6	409014	3906645	11
2	6.2	35	18	32.7	118	5	52.5	400187	3907674	11
3	15.0	35	22	23.6	118	9	46.1	394372	3914857	11
4	18.4	35	22	40.2	118	12	58.1	389534	3915425	11
5	31.8	35	26	38.3	118	19	30.8	379723	3922888	11
6	37.6	35	26	53.1	118	22	38.7	374990	3923409	11
7	43.7	35	31	20.5	118	24	43.4	371964	3931691	11
8	54.0	35	34	9.1	118	30	21.6	363524	3937012	11

72. JAWBONE OHV AREA

Wpt	Mile	Lat N			Long W			Easting	Northing	Zone
1	0.0	35	18	45.8	118	1	42.2	406512	3908010	11
2	5.3	35	22	45.1	118	2	58.2	404672	3915404	11
3	7.7	35	24	36.9	118	2	4.1	406073	3918832	11
4	8.8	35	25	12.2	118	1	29.1	406966	3919910	11
5	3.4	35	25	53.8	118	4	41.8	402121	3921243	11

6	6.8	35	27	25.3	118	7	0.3	398660	3924103	11
7	5.9	35	24	1.9	118	5	32.4	400805	3917811	11
8	6.4	35	24	0.2	118	5	8.0	401421	3917751	11
9	1.8	35	22	40.8	118	4	35.9	402206	3915296	11
10	6.2	35	19	0.8	118	4	29.8	402286	3908516	11

73. BONANZA GULCH/EP15

1	0.0	35	30	2.6	117	56	52.6	414025	3928786	11
2	4.6	35	27	3.4	117	53	45.5	418689	3923223	11
3	2.8	35	25	59.5	117	53	23.1	419236	3921248	11
4	1.5	35	25	13.6	117	52	18.2	420859	3919820	11
5	3.3	35	26	7.6	117	51	12.2	422540	3921471	11
6	4.0	35	26	11.2	117	50	30.4	423595	3921571	11
7	4.6	35	27	24.6	117	47	21.1	428386	3923792	11
8	6.5	35	27	54.4	117	46	2.0	430385	3924695	11
9	9.0	35	28	18.7	117	44	56.5	432043	3925431	11
10	12.2	35	28	3.5	117	42	24.3	435874	3924936	11
11	14.1	35	27	48.3	117	40	53.3	438166	3924451	11
12	16.2	35	27	19.8	117	39	13.2	440682	3923555	11

74. OPAL CANYON/LAST CHANCE CANYON

1	0.0	35	24	50.3	117	58	46.0	411073	3919193	11
2	2.2	35	24	12.3	117	57	55.8	412328	3918012	11
3	3.8	35	24	28.6	117	56	58.1	413787	3918500	11
4	4.6	35	24	14.1	117	56	23.3	414662	3918045	11
5	5.7	35	24	39.2	117	55	34.4	415902	3918805	11
6	3.2	35	26	13.4	117	54	10.6	418043	3921688	11
7	4.1	35	25	60.0	117	53	24.8	419194	3921254	11
8	5.6	35	25	13.8	117	52	18.5	420852	3919828	11
9	6.5	35	24	38.2	117	52	30.9	420530	3918732	11
10	9.2	35	26	7.7	117	51	12.4	422533	3921472	11
11	9.9	35	26	11.7	117	50	31.9	423557	3921587	11
12	14.2	35	23	19.1	117	48	57.7	425888	3916249	11

75. RAND MOUNTAIN

1	0.0	35	23	23.3	117	46	18.4	429907	3916347	11
2	8.0	35	17	46.9	117	44	12.3	433012	3905960	11
3	2.8	35	19	18.5	117	42	9.4	436136	3908758	11
4	3.2	35	19	34.9	117	42	8.4	436164	3909265	11
5	3.9	35	19	43.4	117	41	24.2	437281	3909519	11
6	1.9	35	20	47.8	117	40	28.3	438708	3911491	11
7	3.4	35	22	49.4	117	40	36.0	438540	3915238	11

Glossary

A.C.E.C. Area of Critical Environmental Concern
Adventure Pass - A special permit required if you stop to recreate along a route in Angeles, Los Padres, Cleveland and San Bernardino National Forests. No permit required if you are just passing through.
Airing down - Letting air out of your tires to improve traction.
Articulation - Flexibility of your suspension system. Greater articulation keeps your wheels on the ground on undulating terrain. Also referred to as *wheel-travel*.
ATV - All-terrain vehicle. Also called a *quad*.
BLM - Bureau of Land Management.
Cairn - A stack of rocks that marks an obscure trail.
Clevis - A U-shaped device with a pin at one end that is used to connect tow straps.
Come-along - A hand-operated ratchet that functions as a winch.
Dispersed camping - Free camping on public lands away from developed recreation facilities. Usually limited to 14 days or less depending upon area. Camp near existing roads and use existing sites whenever possible. Pack out your trash.
Dry camping -Camping where no water is provided.
Dual-purpose motorcycle - A street-legal dirt bike.
Glacial erratic -A boulder transported from its original resting place by a glacier. Final resting place is usually somewhere it doesn't seem to belong.
Green Sticker - A special license for vehicles not equipped for highway use. Includes ATVs, dirt bikes, sand rails, dune buggies and snowmobiles.
High centered - When your undercarriage gets stuck on a rock, mound, log, or ridge. Usually requires you to jack up your vehicle to get free.
High-lift jack - A tool that allows you to quickly lift your vehicle high off the ground. Considered a necessity on hard-core trails. Also substitutes for a winch.
Lift - A vehicle modification that raises the suspension or body of a vehicle to provide greater ground clearance.
Locker - Optional gearing installed inside your differential that equalizes power to wheels on both sides of an axle. Eliminates loss of power when climbing steep undulating hills. Not the same as locking-in your hubs.
Low range - A second range of gears that increases the power of your vehicle. Used for climbing steep grades, especially at higher altitude.
Mortero - Indian grinding hole. Depressions in rock formed by pounding grain or seeds with an elongated rock or pestle.
Red Sticker - Same as Green Sticker except riding days are limited. Check with each specific OHV area for specific dates when riding is not permitted.
Skid plates - Plates that protect vulnerable parts of your undercarriage.
Snatch block - A pulley that opens so it can be slipped over your winch cable.
Street legal vehicle - Any vehicle equipped and licensed to drive on the highway.
SVRA - State Vehicular Recreation Area.
Switchback - A tight turn on a zigzag road that climbs a steep grade.
Tow point, tow hook - A point on your vehicle that enables you to quickly and safely attach a tow strap. Considered a basic necessity for four-wheeling.

References & Reading

4 Wheeler's Guide, Trails of the Tahoe National Forest, by William C. Teie, Deer Valley Press, Rescue, CA. Includes color maps, photos and illustrations of 20 four-wheel-drive trails in the Tahoe National Forest. (ISBN 0-9640709-7-9, 2001)

4 Wheeler's Guide to the Rubicon Trail, by William C. Teie, Deer Valley Press, Rescue, CA. Includes color maps and photos of the Rubicon Trail. (ISBN 0-9640709-5-2, 1998)

Backcountry Adventures Northern California, By Peter Massey and Jeanne Wilson, Swagman Publishing,Inc., Castle Rock, CO. Covers 152 SUV backroads in northern California. Includes history, color photos, maps and GPS coordinates. (ISBN 1-930193-08-4, 2002)

Backcountry Adventures Southern California, By Peter Massey and Jeanne Wilson, Swagman Publishing,Inc., Castle Rock, CO. Covers 153 SUV backroads in southern California. Includes history, color photos, maps and GPS coordinates. (ISBN 1-930193-04-1, 2002)

California Coastal Byways, By Tony Huegel, Wilderness Press, Berkeley, CA. Covers 50 SUV backroads along California's coast. Guidebook includes maps and photos. (ISBN 0-89997-282-9)

California Desert Byways, By Tony Huegel, Wilderness Press, Berkeley, CA. Covers 60 SUV backroads in California desert regions. Guidebook includes maps and photos. (ISBN 0-89997-304-3, revised 2002)

California Road & Recreation Atlas, Benchmark Maps, Medford, OR. Tabloid size map book covering all of California. (ISBN 0-929591-43-7)

Death Valley SUV Trails, by Roger Mitchell, Track & Trail Publications, Oakhurst, CA. Covers 46 SUV backroads in Death Valley. Guidebook includes maps, photos, history and geology. (ISBN 0-9707115-0-6, 2001)

GPS Made Easy by Lawrence Letham, published by the Mountaineers, Seattle, WA. Hundred-page handbook covers the basics of GPS. (1998)

(A) Guide to California Off-Road Adventures, California State Parks, Sacramento, CA. Full-color, fold-out map of all OHV areas in California. (Revised annually)

High Sierra SUV Trails, Volume I, The East Side, by Roger Mitchell, Track & Trail Publications, Oakhurst, CA. Covers 35 four-wheeling excursions along the east side of the Sierra Nevada Mountains. Guidebook includes maps, photos, history and geology. (ISBN 0-9707115-1-4, 2002)

High Sierra SUV Trails, Volume II, The Western Slope, by Roger Mitchell, Track & Trail Publications, Oakhurst, CA. Covers 40 four-wheeling excursions along the west side of the Sierra Nevada Mountains. Guidebook includes maps, photos, history and geology. (ISBN 0-9707115-2-2, 2002)

Inyo-Mono SUV Trails, by Roger Mitchell, Track & Trail Publications, Oakhurst, CA. Covers 40 four-wheeling excursions in Inyo & Mono Counties. Guidebook includes maps, photos, history and geology. (ISBN 0-9707115-3-0, 2003)

Northern California Atlas & Gazetteer, DeLorme, Yarmouth, ME. Tabloid size map book covering Oregon border to San Jose. (ISBN 0-89933-287-0)

On Location in Lone Pine, by Dave Holland, The Holland House, Granada Hills, CA. Photos, stories & detailed maps of movie locations in Lone Pine's Alabama Hills. (ISBN 0-929413-01-9, 1990)

Sidekick Off-Road Maps, by Rick Russell, Sidekick, Chino, CA. Individual folded maps include directions, maps and photos of specific trails. Northern trails include the Rubicon (ISBN 1-8880824-17-5) and Dusy/Ershim Trail (ISBN 1-8880824-20-5).

Sierra Nevada Byways, By Tony Huegel, Wilderness Press, Berkeley, CA. Covers 50 SUV backroads in California's Sierra Nevada Mountains. Guidebook includes maps and photos. (ISBN 0-89997-273-X, revised 2002)

Southern & Central California Atlas & Gazetteer, DeLorme, Yarmouth, ME. Tabloid size map book covering San Jose to Mexico border. (ISBN 0-89933-285-4)

Addresses & Phone Numbers

(Note: All information correct as of Mar. 1, 2004.)

Bureau of Land Management
Web site: www.blm.gov

California State Office
2800 Cottage Way, Suite W-1834
Sacramento, CA 95825-1886
(916) 978-4400

Arcata Field Office
1695 Heindon Road
Arcata, CA 95521
(707) 825-2300

Bakersfield Field Office
3801 Pegasus Drive
Bakersfield, CA 93308
(661) 391-6000

Bishop Field Office
351 Pacu Lane, Suite 100
Bishop, CA 93514
(760) 872-5000

Eagle Lake Field Office
2950 Riverside Drive
Susanville, CA 96130
(530) 257-0456

Folsom Field Office
63 Natoma Street
Folsom, CA 95630
(916) 985-4474

Hollister Field Office
20 Hamilton Court
Hollister, CA 95023
(831) 630-5000

Ridgecrest Field Office
300 South Richmond Road
Ridgecrest, CA 93555
(760) 384-5400

Redding Field Office
355 Hemsted Drive
Redding, CA 96002
(530) 224-2100

Ukiah Field Office
2550 North State Street
Ukiah, CA 95482
(707) 468-4000

Chambers of Commerce

Angels Camp/Calaveras Cnty. - (209) 736-2580
Auburn - (530) 885-5616
Bakersfield - (661) 327-4421
Bishop - (760) 873-8405
Chico - (530) 891-5556
Coalinga - (559) 935-2948
Eureka - (707) 442-3738
Fort Bragg/Mendocino Coast - (707) 961-6300
Fresno - (559) 495-4800
Grass Valley - (530) 273-4667
Hollister/San Benita County (831) 637-5315
Lone Pine - (760) 876-4444
Mammoth Lakes - (760) 934-3068
Markleeville/Alpine County - (530) 694-2475
Merced - (209) 722-3864
Modesto - (209) 577-5757
Monterey - (831) 648-5360
Mt. Shasta - (530) 926-3696
Oroville - (530) 538-2542
Paradise - (530) 877-9356
Pasa Robles - (805) 238-0506
Pismo Beach - (805) 773-4382
Placerville - (530) 621-5885
Porterville - (559) 784-7502
Red Bluff - (530) 527-6220
Redding - (530) 225-4433
Reno, NV - (775) 337-3030
Ridgecrest - (760) 375-8331
Sacramento Metro - (916) 552-6800
San Francisco - (415) 392-4520
San Jose - (408) 291-5250
San Luis Obispo - (805) 781-2777
Santa Maria - (805) 925-2403
Santa Rosa - (707) 545-1414
Sonora/Tuolumne County -(209) 532-4212
South Lake Tahoe - (530) 541-5255
Stockton - (209) 547-2770
Susanville/Lassen County - (530) 257-4323
Tahoe City/North Lake Tahoe - (530) 581-6900
Tehachapi - (661) 822-4180
Truckee - (530) 587-2757
Ukiah - (707) 462-4705
Weaverville - (530) 623-6101
Weed - (530) 938-4624
Willits - (707) 459-7910
Yuba/Sutter Counties - (530) 743-6501

Maps, Books & GPS Sources

4X4*BOOKS*.com
(308) 381-4410
Fax: (877) 787-2993

All Topo Maps (iGage Map Corp.)
P.O. Box 58596
Salt Lake City, UT 84158
(888) 450-4922, www.igage.com

DeLorme Mapping
P. O. Box 298
Yarmouth, ME 04096
(207) 846-7000, www.delorme.com

Garmin International
1200 E. 151st Street
Olathe, KS 66062
(800) 800-1020, www.garmin.com

Lowrance Electronics, Inc.
12000 E. Skelly Drive
Tulsa, OK 74128-1703
(800) 324-1356, www.lowrance.com

Magellan Corporation
960 Overland Court
San Dimas, CA 91773
(909) 394-5000, www.magellangps.com

Maptech
10 Industrial Way.
Amesbury, MA 01913
(888) 839-5551, www.maptech.com

National Geographic Maps
P.O. 4357
Evergreen, CO 80437 1-800-962-1643
www.nationalgeographic.com/maps

National Parks/Rec. Areas
Web site: www.nps.gov

Death Valley National Park
P.O. Box 579
Death Valley, CA 92328-0579
(760) 786-2331

Lassen Volcanic National Park
P.O Box 100
Mineral, CA 96063
(530) 595-4444

Redwood National & State Parks
1111 Second Street
Crescent City, CA 95531
(707) 464-6101

Whiskeytown -Shasta-Trinity National Recreation Area
P.O. Box 188
Whiskeytown, CA 96095
(530) 242-3400

Yosemite National Park
P.O. Box 577
Yosemite National Park, CA 95389-0577
(209) 372-0200

Off-Highway Vehicle Areas

Clear Creek Management Area
BLM Hollister Field Office
(831) 630-5000

Cow Mountain OHV Area
BLM Ukiah Field Office
(707) 468-4000

Jawbone Canyon & Dove Springs OHV Areas
BLM Ridgecrest Field Office
(760) 384-5400

Pozo LaPanza OHV Area
Los Padres National Forest
Santa Lucia Ranger District
(805) 925-9538

State Parks/ SVRAs
State Parks Web site: www.parks.ca.gov

Andrew Molera State Park
Big Sur Station #1
Big Sur, CA 93920
(831)667-2315

Bodie State Historic Park
P.O. Box 515
Bridgeport, CA 93517
(760) 647-6445

California Department of Parks & Recreation
Off-Highway Motor Vehicle Recreation Division (OHMVR)
P.O. Box 942896
Sacramento, CA 94296-0001
(916) 324-4442

Hollister Hills SVRA
7800 Cienega Road
Hollister, CA 95023
(831) 637-3874

Humboldt Redwoods State Park
P.O. Box 100
Weott, CA 95571
707-946-2409

Malakoff Diggins State Historic Park
23579 North Bloomfield Road
Nevada City, CA 95959
(530) 265-2740

Oceano Dunes SVRA
928 Pacific Boulevard
Oceano, CA 93445
(805) 473-7220

Plumas-Eureka State Park
310 Johnsville Road
Blairsden, CA 96103
(530) 836-2380

Red Rock Canyon State Park
(Mojave Desert Information Center)
43779 15th Street West
Lancaster, CA 93534
(661) 942-0662 (Menu selection #3)

Sinkyone Wilderness State Park
P.O. Box 245
Whitethorn, CA 95489
(707) 986-7711

U.S. Forest Service
Web site: www.fs.fed.us

Eldorado National Forest Supervisor's Office
100 Forni Road
Placerville, CA 95667
(530) 622-5061

> **Amador Ranger District**
> 26820 Silver Drive
> Pioneer, CA 95666
> (209) 295-4251
>
> **Georgetown Ranger District**
> 7600 Wentworth Springs Road
> Georgetown, CA 95634
> (530) 333-4312
>
> **Pacific Ranger District**
> 7887 Highway 50
> Pollock Pines, CA 95726
> (530) 644-2349
>
> **Placerville Ranger District**
> 4260 Eight Mile Road
> Camino, CA 95709
> (530) 644-2324

Inyo National Forest Supervisor's Office
351 Pacu Lane, Suite 200
Bishop, CA 93514
(760) 873-2400

Ancient Bristlecone Pine Visitor Center
Schulman Grove
(760) 873-2500 (Open Summer Only)

Interagency Visitor Center
P.O. Box R (At Highways 395 and 136)
Lone Pine, CA 93545
(760) 876-6222

Mammoth Ranger Station & Visitor Center
P.O. Box 148
Mammoth Lakes, CA 93546
(760) 924-5500

Mono Lake/Lee Vining Visitor Center
P.O. Box 429
Lee Vining, CA 93541
(760) 647-3044

Mt. Whitney Ranger Station
P.O. Box 8
Lone Pine, CA 93545
(760) 876-6200

White Mountain Ranger Station
798 North Main
Bishop, CA 93514
(760) 873-2500

Lassen National Forest Supervisor's Office
2550 Riverside Drive
Susanville, CA 96130
(530) 257-2151

> **Almanor Ranger District**
> P.O. Box 767
> Chester, CA 96020
> (530) 258-2141
>
> **Eagle Lake Ranger District**
> 477-050 Eagle Lake Road
> Susanville, CA 96130
> (530) 257-4188
>
> **Hat Creek Ranger District**
> P.O. Box 220
> Fall River Mills, CA 96028
> (530) 336-5521

Los Padres National Forest Supervisor's Office
6750 Hollister Avenue, Suite 150
Goleta, CA 93117
(805) 968-6640 (Adventure Pass same number)

> **Monterey Ranger District**
> 406 S. Mildred
> King City, CA 93930
> (831) 385-5434

Santa Lucia Ranger District
1616 N. Carlotti Road
Santa Maria, CA 93454
(805) 925-9538

Plumas National Forest Supervisor's Office
159 Lawrence Street
Quincy, CA 95971
(530) 283-2050

Beckwourth Ranger District
Mohawk Road, P.O. Box 7
Blairsden, CA 96103
(530) 836-2575

Challenge Visitor Center
18050 Mulock Road
Challenge, CA 95925
(530) 675-1146

Feather River Ranger District
875 Mitchell Avenue
Oroville, CA 95965
(530) 534-6500

Mt. Hough Ranger District
39696 State Highway 70 (NW of Quincy)
Quincy, CA 95971
(530) 283-0555

Sequoia National Forest Supervisor's Office
900 W. Grand Avenue
Porterville, CA 93257
(559) 784-1500

Cannell Meadow Ranger District
105 Whitney Road
Kernville, CA 93238
(760) 376-3781

Greenhorn Ranger District
4875 Ponderosa Drive
Lake Isabella, CA 93240
(760) 379-5646

Shasta-Trinity National Forest USDA Service Center
3644 Avtech Parkway
Redding, CA 96002
(530) 226-2500

Mt. Shasta Ranger District
204 West Alma
Mt. Shasta, CA 96067
(530) 926-4511

Weaverville Ranger District
210 Main Street, Highway 299
Weaverville, CA 96093
(530) 623-2121

Sierra National Forest Supervisor's Office
1600 Tollhouse Road
Clovis, CA 93611
(559) 297-0706

High Sierra Ranger District
29688 Auberry Road
Prather, CA 93651
(559) 855-5355

Stanislaus National Forest Supervisor's Office
19777 Greenley Road
Sonora, CA 95370
(209) 532-3671

Mi-Wok Ranger District
P.O. 100
Mi-Wuk Village, CA 95346
(209) 586-3234

Summit Ranger District
#1 Pinecrest Lake Road
Pinecrest, CA 95364
(209) 965-3434

Tahoe National Forest Supervisor's Office
631 Coyote Street
Nevada City, CA 95959
(530) 265-4531

Big Bend Visitor Information Center
49685 Hampshire Rocks Road
(Big Bend exit off I-80)
Soda Springs, CA 95631
(530) 426-3609 (Open May-Oct.)

Foresthill Ranger District
22830 Foresthill Road
Foresthill, CA 95631
(530) 367-2224

North Yuba Ranger Station
15924 Highway 49
Camptonville, CA 95922
(530) 288-3231

Sierraville Ranger District
317 So. Lincoln Street
P.O. Box 95
Sierraville, CA 96126
(530) 994-3401

Truckee Ranger Station
9646 Donner Pass Road
Truckee, CA 96161
(530) 587-3558

Toiyabe National Forest Supervisors Office
1200 Franklin Way
Sparks, NV 89431
(775) 331-6444

Bridgeport Ranger District
HCR 1 Box 1000
Bridgeport, CA 93517
(760) 932-7070

4-Wheel-Drive Associations

Blue Ribbon Coalition
www.sharetrails.org
(208) 237-1008

California Association of 4-Wheel Drive Clubs
(Note: Web site includes complete listing of over 140 four-wheel-drive clubs in the state.)
www.cal4wheel.com
(800) 494-3866

California Off-Road Vehicle Association
(CORVA)
www.corva.org

National Off-Highway Vehicle Conservation Council
www.nohvcc.org
(800) 348-6487

Tread Lightly
www.treadlightly.org
(800) 966-9900

4-Wheel-Drive Guide Services

Ecological 4-Wheeling Adventures
P.O. Box 12137
Costa Mesa, CA 92627
(949) 645-7733
www.ECO4WD.com

Offroad Outfitters Backcountry Guide Service
(Same number as J&S Trucking)
117 Otto Circle
Sacramento, CA 95822
(916) 424-1250 (Ask for Jim Bramham, ext. 2)
E-Mail: offroadoutfitter@earthlink.net

The Driving Company
540 N. Santa Cruz Avenue, Suite 140
Los Gatos, CA 95030
(408) 370-9321
www.thedrivingcompany.com

Western Adventures
4x4 Driving School and Guide Service
P.O. Box 2451
Ramona, CA 92065
(760) 789-1563
www.4westernadventures.com

Other contacts

Cerro Gordo Mines & Ghost Town
P.O. Box 125
Keeler, CA 93530
(760) 876-1860

Tehama State Wildlife Area
30490 Plum Creek Road
Paynes Creek, CA 96075
(530) 597-2201

Fordyce Creek Stream Flow Rates

Go to: www.dreamflows.com/realtime.html
Fordyce Creek is listed under California Sierra-West Slope Rivers. During the Sierra Trek, flow rates are controlled between 25 and 50 cfs (cubic feet per second). Anything higher is considered too deep to safely cross. Your best chance of a low flow rate, other than during the Sierra Trek, is in late September until the first snowfall.
Warning: At any time, flow rates can dramatically increase without notice stranding vehicles between stream crossings for many months. Owners have been forced to hire helicopters to retrieve their vehicles. Other vehicles have been left all winter to be crushed by heavy snows.

Index

A

Adventure Pass 14, 16, 175, 177, 185, 189, 274
Airing down 27, 274
Alabama Hills Arch 153, 158, 159
Alleghany 77-79
Altitude sickness 19
Andrew Molera State Park 172, 173
Angels Camp 106, 277
Ansel Adams Wilderness 132, 133, 134
Armstrong Canyon, 6, 9, 10, 152,153, 156, 157, 268
Arnold 5-7, 106, 107, 111, 113, 115
Artist's Point 122, 123
ATVs 13, 14, 15, 76, 104, 112, 142, 169, 182, 183, 200, 212, 274
Auburn 5-7, 80, 81, 277
Auburn State Recreation Area 90, 91
Avenue of the Giants 33, 41-43

B

Backway to Inyo Craters 6, 8, 10, 124, 136, 137, 266
Baker Creek 146-149
Bakersfield 5-7, 220, 221, 277
Bald Mountain 6, 9, 10, 190, 191, 202-205, 270
Ball Peen Hill 82, 83
Barker Meadow OHV Trail 95
Barnett Opal Mine 247, 249
Barrett Lake 6, 9, 10, 80, 81, 104, 105, 264
Bassetts 46, 65, 67
Bear Harbor 33, 40, 41, 43
Bear Lake 94, 95
Bear Trap Cabin 112, 113
Bear Valley 5, 6, 106, 107, 111, 113, 115
Bear Valley Loop 6, 9, 10, 80, 82, 83, 263
Bear Valley Ski Area 107, 112, 113
Ben Lomond Mountain 52, 54, 55
Benmore Creek Loop 44, 45
Bickel Camp 242-249
Big Pine 5-7, 151-153, 155, 157
Big Rocks 188, 189
Big Sluice 98, 101-103
Bishop 5-7, 124, 125, 147-149, 150, 151, 277
Bixby Bridge 172, 173
Black Gulch 230-233
Blackrock Work Station 222, 223
Blackwood Cyn., Ellis Peak 6, 9, 10, 80, 81, 94, 95, 264
Blairsden 67
BLM (Bureau of Land Management) 14, 15, 179
Blue Lake Road 110, 111
Bodfish 220, 233, 236, 237
Bodie Ghost Town 6, 8, 10, 124-127, 266
Bonanza Gulch Post Office 242-245
Bonanza Gulch Road at Hollister 170, 171

Bonanza Gulch/EP15 6, 9, 10, 220, 221, 242-245, 273
Bonita Meadow 224-227
Bowerman Barn 36, 37
Bowerman Ridge 6, 8, 10, 32, 33, 36, 37, 260
Brewer Lake 6, 9, 10, 190, 191, 200, 201, 270
Bridgeport 5-7, 118, 124-127, 129, 131, 279, 280
Buck Island Lake 31, 98, 100-103
Burro Schmidt Tunnel 242-249
Buttermilk Country 6, 8, 10, 124, 144, 145, 254, 267

C

Cabrillo Highway 172
Cadillac Hill 99, 100, 102, 103
California Association of 4-Wheel Drive Clubs 3, 81, 85, 281
California City 220, 239, 240
California City Riding Area 251
Campbell Lake 54, 55
Campfires 22
Caples Lake 108, 109
Cerro Gordo Ghost Town 152, 153, 160, 161, 281
Challenge 46, 280
Chemung Mine 126, 127
Chicken Rock 190, 210-213, 217
Chico 7, 46, 53, 277
Cienega Road 166, 170, 171
Cisco 80, 85-87
Clear Creek Management Area 16, 178-181, 278
Cleghorn Bar 6, 9, 10, 46, 47, 58, 59, 261
Coalinga 5-7, 166, 167, 179, 277
Cold Springs 106, 123
Colfax 90, 91
Colfax-Foresthill Bridge 90, 91
Committee Trail 86, 87, 89
Cone Peak 174, 175
Conway Summit 128-131
Copper Mountain 6, 8, 10, 11, 124, 130, 131, 266
Corral Hollow 6, 9, 10, 106, 107, 112, 113, 265
Courtright Reservoir 190, 216, 217
Cow Mountain OHV Area 6, 9, 10, 32, 33, 44, 45, 261, 278
Coyote Flat 6, 9, 10, 124, 146-149, 267
Coyote Lake (in Bishop area) 148, 149
Coyote Lake (in Shaver Lake area) 6, 9, 10, 190, 191, 198, 199, 270
Crooked Tree 122, 123
Crowley Lake 124
Cudahy Camp 246, 249
Cudahys Old Dutch Cleanser Mine 243-245, 249

D

Deadman Pass 6, 8, 10, 124, 125, 134, 135, 266
Death Valley National Park 16, 152, 153, 162-165, 278

282

Deer Lake 6, 9, 10, 46, 47, 70, 71, 262
Deer Valley 6, 9, 10, 106, 107, 110, 111, 265
Desert Tortoise 21, 251
Dinkey Creek 190, 206, 219
Dirt bikes 5, 13, 14, 15, 150, 169
Dodge Ridge 6, 8, 10, 106, 107, 122, 123, 265
Dove Springs 238-241
Downieville 5, 6, 46, 47, 60-63
Dual-purpose motorcycles 14, 15, 274
Dunderberg Road 128, 129
Dusy/Ershim Trail 6, 9, 10, 190, 191, 193, 210-217, 271, 276
Dye Creek Jeepway 48, 50, 51

E
Eagle Lakes Road 85-89
Eagle Peak 6, 9, 10, 106, 107, 120, 121, 265
East Lake 215-217
Edwards Crossing 76, 79
El Paso Mountains 243, 245, 246, 249
Ellis Lake 94, 95
Ellis Peak 94, 95
Ershim Lake 214-217
Eureka 5-7, 32, 33, 41-43, 277
Evans Flat Campground 228, 229, 232, 233
Everitt Memorial Highway 34

F
Feather River 47, 56-59
Fir Cap OHV Trail 61, 63
Fordyce Creek 6, 9, 10, 80, 81, 84-87, 263
Foresthill 80, 91, 97
Fort Bragg 32, 41, 277
Fort Hunter Liggett Military Reservation 174, 176
Foster Ridge 200
Founders Tree 33, 40, 43
Four Corners 41-43
Four Hills Mine 64, 65-67
Freeway Ridge 6, 9, 10, 220, 221, 230-233, 272
Fresno 5-7, 190, 191, 277

G
Garberville 43
Garcia Ridge 6, 9, 10, 15, 166, 167, 186, 187, 270
Gargoyle Nature Trail 120, 121
Garlock 245, 249
Gatekeeper 98, 101, 103
Gene Autry Rock 158
Georgetown 80, 99
Gibbs Lake 132, 133
Gilroy 166
Glacial Erratic 122, 210, 274
Gold Lake 5, 6, 46, 47, 68-71
Gold Lake Highway 70, 71, 74
Gold Valley 6, 9, 10, 46, 47, 64-67, 262
Gorda 166, 172, 176, 177
Government Peak 250, 252, 253
GPS 17, 20, 256-260, 275, 278
GPS Coordinates 260-273
Graeagle 46, 65-67
Granite Bowl 98, 99, 101, 103
Graniteville Road 79
Grapevine Jeepway 48, 50, 51

Grass Valley 5-7, 46, 47, 277
Green-sticker vehicles 6, 14, 274
Grouse Lake 208, 209

H
Harkless Flat 154, 155
Hartley, H.W. 84, 86
Heartbreak Hill 116-119
Hell Hole 6, 9, 10, 80, 81, 96, 97, 264
Hermit Valley Campground 110, 111
High Lakes 6, 9, 10, 46, 52-55, 261
High centered 24, 274
High-lift jack 21, 28, 274
Hollister Hills 6, 9, 10, 13, 166-171, 269, 278
Holly Ash Cleanser Mine 242-245
Horse Meadows 6, 8, 10, 124, 132, 133, 266
Howland Flat 60-63
Humboldt Redwoods State Park 32, 33, 40-43, 278
Humboldt Road 53-55
Hunter Mountain 162-165
Huntington Lake 192, 193, 216
Hydraulic Mining 62, 76, 77, 90
Hyperthermia 19
Hypothermia 20

I
Ice House Road 80, 97, 101-103
Idria 178, 180, 181
Inskip 46, 53-55
Inyo Craters 136, 137
Iowa Hill 90, 91
Ishi Wilderness 48, 50, 51

J
Jawbone OHV Area 6, 9, 10, 220, 221, 238-241, 272
Jawbone Station 220, 234-237, 239-241, 243, 244
Jawbone to Lake Isabella 6, 8, 10, 220, 221, 234-237, 272
John Muir Wilderness 140-143, 147-149, 210, 211, 218, 219
June Lake Loop 124, 133

K
Kaiser Pass 190, 192, 193, 213, 216, 217
Kavanaugh Ridge 6, 9, 10, 124, 128, 129, 266
Kelso Valley Road 220, 236, 237
Kennedy Meadows Road 220, 223
Kern River 221, 222
Kernville 220-221, 223, 225, 226
Keyesville Road 231-233
King Range National Conservation Area 42
Kings Beach 80, 93
Kirk Creek Campground 174, 175
Kyburz 80, 105, 109

L
La Porte 7, 46, 47
Lake Alpine 106, 111, 113, 115
Lake Isabella 5-8, 220, 221, 228, 229, 233, 234
Lake Tahoe 80, 81, 92-95, 99, 106, 107
Lakes Basin Recreation Area 47, 65, 67, 69, 71, 74
Lakeshore 192, 193, 216

283

Lassen Volcanic National Park 49-50, 278
Launna's Hill 86, 87
Laurel Lakes 4, 6, 9, 10, 124, 125, 138, 139, 267
Laws Railroad Museum 150, 151
Lee Vining 5-7, 11, 16, 124-133
Leggett 7, 41, 43
Lion's Butt 116-119
Lippincott Road 162, 164, 165
Little Deer Lake 68, 69
Little Grass Valley Reservoir 46, 47, 56, 57
Little Sluice 98, 101, 103
Lone Pine 5-7, 152, 153, 158, 159, 276, 277
Long Barn 106, 122, 123
Long Lake 52, 54, 55
Longley Meadow 144, 145
Loon Lake 80, 98, 101-103
Los Angeles Aqueduct 238-241
Lost Burro Mine 162-165
Lost Coast, Redwoods 6, 8, 10, 40-43, 260
Lundy Lake 130, 131

M

Malakoff Diggins State Historic Park 77-79, 279
Mammoth Lakes 5-7, 124, 125, 134, 135, 136, 277
Mammoth Mountain 134-143
Manzanar National Historic Site 152
Markleeville 106, 110, 111, 277
Masonic 126, 127
Mazourka Canyon 6, 9, 10, 152-155, 268
McKinley Grove 207, 209, 211, 219
McNalley Fire 224, 225
Meadow Lake 80, 84-87
Mendo Lake Road 44, 45
Military Pass 33-35
Mirror/Strawberry Lakes 6, 9, 10, 190, 191, 194-197, 270
Mojave 5-7, 220, 221, 237, 241, 245
Mokelumne Wilderness 110, 111
Molina Ghost Run 167, 179, 180
Monache Meadows 6, 8, 10, 220-223, 271
Mono Basin Scenic Area Visitor Center 133, 279
Mono Lake 11, 126, 127, 130, 131
Morris Lake 52-55
Movie Road/Alabama Hills 6, 8, 10, 152, 153, 158, 159, 268, 276
Moving Rocks 162-165
Mt. Shasta 5-8, 32-35, 277, 280
Mt. Shasta Loop 6, 8, 10, 32, 33, 34, 35, 260
Mt. Watson 6, 8, 10, 80, 81, 92, 93, 264
Mt. Whitney 12, 152, 153, 158, 159

N

Nacimiento-Fergusson Road 166, 174-177
National Forests 16
Nevada City 46, 77-79
Niagara Rim 6, 9, 10, 106, 107, 116-119, 255, 265
North Bloomfield 77-79

O

Oak Flat Lookout 228, 229
Oakland Pond 68, 69

Oceano Dunes SVRA 6, 9, 10, 166, 167, 182, 183, 269, 279
OHV areas 13-16, 45, 169, 179, 183, 185, 239
Olancha 7, 152, 220
Old Coast Road 6, 8, 10, 166, 167, 172, 173, 269, 286
Opal Cyn./Last Chance Cyn. 6, 9, 10, 220, 221, 246-249, 273
Oroville 7, 46
Owens Valley 147, 153, 155, 156, 161

P

Pacific Crest National Scenic Trail 64-66, 70, 71, 95, 236
Packer Saddle 65, 67, 70, 71, 74, 75
Panamint Springs 152, 161, 163-165
Papoose Flat 154, 155
Paradise 7, 46, 53
Patriarch Tree 150, 151
Paynes Creek 46, 49
Peligreen Jeepway 6, 9, 10, 46, 48, 49, 261
Philbrook Lake 53, 55
Pichacho Peak 6, 9, 10, 166, 167, 178-181, 269
Pine Mountain 6, 9, 10, 15, 166, 167, 184, 185, 269
Pinecrest 106, 107, 117, 120-123
Piute Mountain Road 236, 237
Placerville 7, 80, 99, 101, 102, 105, 109, 277
Plum Creek Road 49-51
Plumas-Eureka State Park 47, 65-67, 279
Plumbago Mine 78, 79
Poker Flat 6, 9, 10, 46, 47, 60-63, 262
Ponderosa Way 49, 51
Pozo La Panza OHV Area 13, 184-187
Prewitt Ridge 6, 8, 10, 15, 166, 167, 174, 175, 269

Q

Quincy 46, 58, 62, 67

R

Racetrack via Hunter Mountain 6, 9, 10, 152, 153, 162-165, 268
Rancheria Road 6, 8, 10, 220, 221, 228, 229, 272
Rand Mountain 6, 9, 10, 220, 221, 250-253, 273
Randsburg 7, 220, 245, 248-253
Randsburg Red Rock Road 220, 237, 244, 245, 248, 249, 251-253
Rasterized maps 258
Red Bluff 5-7, 46, 47, 45, 49-51, 277
Red Lake 198, 199
Red Mountain Area (near Shaver Lake) 194, 195, 198, 199
Red Rock Canyon State Park, 220, 221, 235, 237, 239, 243, 245, 247-249
Redcrest 32, 33, 42, 43
Redding 5-7, 32, 33, 39, 277
Red-sticker vehicles 14, 274
Ricardo Campground 237, 248, 249
Ridgecrest 5-7, 220, 221, 236, 240, 277
Roberts Ranch 150, 151
Rock Creek Road 140, 141
Rock Pile 116-119

Rubicon 6, 9, 10, 13, 31, 80, 81, 98-103, 264, 275, 276
Rubicon Bridge 100, 102, 103
Rubicon Springs 102, 103
Run-A-Muck Event 83

S

Saddleback Mountain Lookout 60, 61, 63
Saline Valley 16, 152, 163-165
Saline Valley Salt Tram 160, 161
San Antonio Mine 238, 240, 241
San Jose 5-7, 16, 166, 167, 169, 170, 277
San Luis Obispo 5-7, 166, 167, 183, 277
Sand Canyon 6, 9, 10, 124, 140-143, 267
Santa Rita Flat 154, 155
Santa Rosa 5-7, 16, 32, 33, 45, 277
Schober Mine 146-149
Schulman Grove 150, 151
Shasta Bally Peak 6, 8, 10, 32, 33, 38, 39, 260
Shaver Lake 5-7, 190, 191, 202
Sheep Camp 38, 39
Shelter Cove 42, 43
Sherman Pass 4x4 Trail 6, 9, 10, 220, 221, 224-227, 272
Sherman Peak 224-227
Shirley Meadows Ski Area 228, 229
Shirttail Canyon 6, 8, 10, 80, 81, 90, 91, 263
Sidewall Suicide 116-119
Sidney Peak 252, 253
Sierra Buttes 6, 8, 10, 46, 47, 70, 72-75, 262
Sierra Buttes Lookout 65, 72-75
Sierra City 46, 73-75, 277
Sierra Grandstand Tour 122, 123
Sierra Nevada Mountains 13, 16, 125, 130, 131, 140, 141, 144-147, 154, 275, 276
Sierra Trek 3, 81, 84-87
Sierraville 7, 46, 83
Signal Peak 6, 9, 10, 80, 81, 88, 89, 263
Silver/Wyman Canyons 6, 8, 10, 124, 150, 151, 268
Sinkyone Wilderness State Park 41, 43, 279
Sixteen-to-One Mine 79
Skyway (Highway) 46, 53-55
Slickrock Trail 6, 9, 10, 106, 107, 114, 115, 265
Smith Lake 66, 67
Snake Lake 6, 9, 10, 46, 47, 68, 69, 262
Sonora 5-7, 106, 117, 118, 121, 123, 277
South Coast Ridge 6, 8, 10, 15, 166, 167, 176, 177, 269
Spanish Lakes 218, 219
Spanish Route 6, 9, 10, 190, 218, 219, 271
Spider Lake 81, 101, 103
Stag Point 6, 9, 10, 46, 47, 56, 57, 261
Stairsteps 184, 185
Stirling City 46,53, 54
Strawberry Pass 6, 9, 10, 106, 107, 108, 109, 264
Stream flow rates 281
Street-legal vehicles 14-16, 39, 61, 115, 274
Summit City 84, 86, 87
SVRA (State Vehicular Recreation Areas) 5, 13, 15, 169, 182, 274, 278

Swamp Lake 6, 9, 10, 190,191, 206-209, 271
Swansea 160, 161
Swansea-Cerro Gordo Road 6, 9, 10, 152, 153, 160, 161, 268
Swimming spots 76, 77, 81, 90, 91, 183

T

Tahoe City 7, 80, 93, 95, 102, 277
Tahoma 80, 94, 103
Tank Traps 168-171
Teakettle Junction 16, 162-164
Tehama State Wildlife Area 49-51, 281
Thompson Hill 212, 213, 215, 217
Thompson Lake 212, 213, 215-217
Thousand-Dollar Hill 101
Tioga Pass 16, 124, 132, 133
Tippy situations 25, 89, 99, 100, 102, 109, 117, 157, 203, 204, 250
Toms Place 124, 140, 141
Trail Etiquette 22
Tread Lightly 21, 281
Trinity Lake 36, 37
Truck Hill 168-171
True Big Sluice 101, 103
Twin Rocks 6, 9, 10, 15, 166, 167, 188, 189, 270
Tyler-Foote Crossing 6, 8, 10, 46, 76-79, 262

U

U.S. Geological Survey maps 17
Usal Beach 33, 40-43
Utica Reservoir 114, 115
UTM (Universal Transverse Mercator) 257

V

Vector Maps 258
Virginia Lakes Road 128-131
Voyager Rock 6, 8, 10, 190, 191, 210, 211, 213, 217, 271

W

Weaverville 37, 277, 280
Weed 34,35
Wentworth Springs 101-103
West Lake 195-197
Wheeler Ridge 6, 9, 10, 124, 142, 143, 267
Whiskeytown Lake 32, 33, 38, 39
Whiskeytown-Shasta-Trinity National Rec. Area 36-38
White Bark Vista 6, 8, 10, 190-193, 213, 215, 270
Wilderness Areas 22, 125, 223
Willow Creek Road 176, 177
Winch 9, 21, 28, 29
Winching 28, 194, 206
Wishon Reservoir 190, 218, 219
Wofford Heights 220, 228, 229
Wrights Lake 80, 104, 105

Y

Yankee Jim's Road 90, 91
Yosemite National Park 16, 106, 125, 133, 278
Yuba City 7, 46

285

The Author & His Vehicles

Charles A. Wells graduated from Ohio State University in 1969 with a degree in graphic design. After practicing design in Ohio, he moved to Colorado Springs, CO, in 1980 and worked 18 years in the printing business. Over the years, he and his family enjoyed a wide array of recreational activities including hiking, biking, rafting, and skiing. He bought his first SUV in 1994 and immediately got hooked exploring Colorado's remote backcountry. He later joined a four-wheel-drive club, did more traveling and learned about hard-core four-wheeling. This book follows five successful backroad guidebooks—two on Colorado and one each on Arizona, Moab, UT, and southern California.

The author drives all the trails himself, writes the directions from detailed notes, shoots the photos and creates the maps using computer software and GPS track logs. As a result, his guidebooks include meaningful detail and are extraordinarily accurate. The vehicles he used to drive the trails, over the years, are shown below.

Author with 1994 Jeep Grand Cherokee, Engineer's Pass, CO. Factory equipped with automatic transmission, skid plates and tow points. Author added CB radio and LT235-75R15 BFG all-terrain tires.(Author's note: I replaced this vehicle in 2002 with a new Grand Cherokee.)

1995 Jeep Cherokee at Spider Lake on the Rubicon. Equipped with Tomken rocker skids, bumpers, tire carrier, brush guard and 5″ lift; 8,000 lb. Warn winch; Dana 44 rear axle; 410 gears; ARBs front & rear; Tera Low 4/1 transfer case; skid plates; stock 4-liter engine; K&N air filter; interior roll cage; 33 x 10.50 BFG A/T tires; tow points; fold-in mirrors; and CB radio.

2001 Jeep Wrangler (under tow) at start of Old Coast Road. Equipped with TeraFlex 3″ lift with long-arm kit, 9,000 lb. Warn winch, Dana 44 rear axle; 410 gears, Tera Low 4/1 transfer case, ARB lockers front and rear, York on-board air system, Predator transmission skid plate, High-Country rocker panel guards, Curry bumpers, Alumiflex tie rod, Xenon extended flairs, stock 4-liter engine, 33 x 12.50 BFG A/T tires and CB radio. (Author's note: I finally wore out my much-loved Cherokee at left and replaced it with the smaller Wrangler for easier towing behind my motorhome.)

Order Form

Phone orders: **Call toll-free 1-877-222-7623**.
We accept VISA, MasterCard, Discover and American Express.

On line: Order from our secure Web site at:
www.funtreks.com

Postal orders: Send check, name, address, and telephone number to: FunTreks, Inc. P.O. Box 49187, Colorado Springs, CO 80949-9187. If paying by credit card, include your card number and expiration date.

Fax orders: Fax this order form to 1-719-277-7411. Include your credit card number and expiration date.

Please send me the following book(s):
I understand that if I am not completely satisfied, I may return the book(s) for a full refund, no questions asked.

Qty.

❏ Guide to Northern California Backroads & 4-Wheel Drive Trails, _____
   ISBN 0-9664976-5-1, 286 pages, Price $19.95

❏ Guide to Southern California Backroads & 4-Wheel Drive Trails, _____
   ISBN 0-9664976-4-3, 286 pages, Price $19.95

❏ Guide to Arizona Backroads & 4-Wheel Drive Trails, _____
   ISBN 0-9664976-3-5, 286 pages, Price $19.95

❏ Guide to Moab, UT Backroads & 4-Wheel Drive Trails, _____
   ISBN 0-9664976-2-7, 268 pages, Price $19.95

❏ Guide to Colorado Backroads & 4-Wheel Drive Trails, (Original) _____
   ISBN 0-9664976-0-0, 248 pages, Price $18.95

❏ Guide to Colorado Backroads & 4-Wheel Drive Trails Vol. 2 _____
   ISBN 0-9664976-1-9, 176 pages, Price $15.95

Name: (Please print)_____
Address: _____
City: _____ State: _____ Zip: _____
Telephone: (_____) _____

Sales Tax: Colorado residents add 2.9%. (Subject to change without notice.)

Shipping: $5.00 for the first book and $2.00 for each additional book.
(Subject to change without notice.)

Payment: ❏ Check   ❏ VISA   ❏ MasterCard   ❏ Discover   ❏ Am. Express
Card number:_____ Exp. date:_____
Name on card:_____

Call toll-free 1-877-222-7623 -Thanks for your order